CONTEMPORARY PAGAN AND NATIVE FAITH MOVEMENTS IN EUROPE

EASA Series

Published in Association with the European Association of Social Anthropologists (EASA)
Series Editor: Eeva Berglund, Helsinki University

Social anthropology in Europe is growing, and the variety of work being done is expanding. This series is intended to present the best of the work produced by members of the EASA, both in monographs and in edited collections. The studies in this series describe societies, processes, and institutions around the world and are intended for both scholarly and student readerships.

CONTEMPORARY PAGAN AND NATIVE FAITH MOVEMENTS IN EUROPE

Colonialist and Nationalist Impulses

Edited by Kathryn Rountree

berghahn
NEW YORK • OXFORD
www.berghahnbooks.com

Published in 2015 by
Berghahn Books
www.berghahnbooks.com

©2015, 2018 Kathryn Rountree
First paperback edition published in 2018

Library of Congress Cataloging-in-Publication Data
A C.I.P. cataloging record is available from the Library of Congress.
LCCN: 2015006168
https://lccn.loc.gov/2015006168

British Library Cataloguing in Publication Data
A catalogue record for this book is available from the British Library

ISBN 978-1-78238-646-9 (hardback)
ISBN 978-1-78533-823-6 (paperback)
ISBN 978-1-78238-647-6 (ebook)

Contents

Figures

Acknowledgements

My sincere thanks to the volume's contributors for their rich and diverse contributions. It has been a privilege and a fascination to engage with your work. I am indebted to Jim Lewis, Sabina Magliocco, Graham Harvey and Liselotte Frisk who helped by recommending authors to round out the collection. I gratefully acknowledge the financial support of Massey University, the School of Social and Cultural Studies and the School of People, Environment and Planning for supporting my fieldwork in Malta over the years. My thanks, also, to Massey's wonderful librarians and my anthropological colleagues. I am very grateful to James Carrier, the EASA book series editor, whose solicitous and gracious shepherding of the project has eased the work, and to Adam Capitanio, Molly Mosher and Charlotte Mosedale at Berghahn Books for their attentive and encouraging assistance along the road to publication. Special thanks to the project's three reviewers whose careful reading and perceptive comments were greatly appreciated.

Introduction

Context Is Everything

Plurality and Paradox in Contemporary European Paganisms

Kathryn Rountree

Modern Pagan and Native Faith groups and movements have sprung up across Europe – as in the rest of the world – in recent decades, yet comparatively little has been published about them compared with the extensive literature on British and American Pagans and Pagan traditions.[1] This is beginning to change, especially in relation to Central and Eastern Europe.[2] All such movements, wherever they are, share some important characteristics – especially the valorization of human relationships with the rest of nature and polytheistic cosmologies – and could be said to belong to a global new religious phenomenon, albeit one that frequently invokes ancient religions.[3] But local expressions are extremely diverse – even within a single country – in terms of their beliefs, practices, values and politics. The relative importance of ecology, magic, ethnic politics and indigenous tradition varies enormously. Amidst this variety, large numbers of Pagans and Native Faith followers participate in global communities and communication networks via the Internet, bypassing cultural and geographical boundaries.[4] Thus they have it both ways, asserting the primacy of the local while enjoying connections with, and often borrowing from, their counterparts in other places.

This volume examines a variety of such groups and movements across the European region, many of whose goals involve the construction of authentic, indigenous, personal and group identities in the face of hegemonic, pan-regional and globalizing forces during a challenging period in Europe. Often side by side, there are revival or reconstructionist groups with intensely local concerns informed by nationalistic impulses – particularly in post-Soviet Europe, but elsewhere too – and numerous other groups which take their cue from British and American-derived traditions such as initiatory Wicca, Druidry, Goddess Spirituality or Michael Harner's Core Shamanism, albeit with creative local inflections and inventions. In their discussions of various groups the volume's contributors explore what might be seen as two broad impulses under the contemporary Pagan and Native Faith umbrella, one colonialist and one nationalistic.[5] They show how these two impulses – by no means mutually exclusive – play out, intersect and collide, morph and transform. Tensions in the relationships between universalism and particularism, indigeneity and nationalism, politics and religion, tradition and innovation, left- and right-wing, modernity and anti-modernity, pre-modern and postmodern are explored.

The idea for this book, particularly the theme of its subtitle, was conceived in two moments – one in a teahouse in Budapest in September 2011 and the other in a café on the Sliema waterfront in Malta in June 2012. In the first, I found myself with twenty-or-so mostly strangers, crowded around some pushed-together tables: half were Hungarian Pagans attending their regular Moot and the rest were delegates at a conference who shared a research interest in modern Paganisms. (Some of the scholars were also Pagans of one stripe or another.) The evening gathering had been organized by the coordinator of the Pagan Federation International, the overseas wing of the U.K.-based Pagan Federation,[6] who was attending the conference and thought it would be interesting and pleasant for us all to get together. During the convivial evening I got talking with a Wiccan man of about thirty, who began telling me, darkly, about some trends in Hungarian Paganism he found disconcerting. One was a burgeoning interest in Wicca among people who played Live Action Role-Playing games and their consequent misconceptions about Wiccan magic. His more troubling concern, though, was the growth of a local ethnic Pagan group based on the *táltos* (traditional Hungarian shaman-like healers), a group he described as politically right-wing who 'use táltos' as a rallying point in attempts to reclaim land alienated during the Second World War and to 'get rid of gypsies and Jews'. He, on the other hand, was a follower of British-originated Wicca and disapproved strongly of mixing religion and politics, especially right-wing nationalistic politics. He seemed very concerned that his form of modern Paganism could, and would, be mistaken for the other kind.

The second moment was when I was chatting with a long-time friend and research participant in Malta where I have been doing research among modern Witches and Pagans since 2005. The coven she belonged to had for some time been working towards getting its 'proper lineage' in Alexandrian Wicca, a British-based Witchcraft tradition which emphasizes training and initiation. My friend said that the group members had been taking lessons via Skype from an Alexandrian High Priestess living in Cornwall, England, tuning in to classes through their computers along with fellow students living in various parts of the world. The ninety-year-old Priestess had travelled to Malta twice to initiate members to the 'first degree' of the tradition. The group's rituals were also being conducted remotely via Skype: members gathered around a computer and the officiating High Priestess and Priest were located physically in the U.K. Previously the coven's rituals had been run by their own Maltese High Priestess and High Priest in the beautiful Goddess temple they had created or outdoors in a natural setting, but the coven had been informed that such priestly roles could only be held by 'third-degree' (the highest level of) initiates of the tradition, and that initiation must be given by a third-degree Alexandrian. The British Priestess was, however, happy for them to weave their own creative and locally distinctive elements into their religious practice. My friend said the new system was good, because they were now learning to 'do things properly' and becoming 'more knowledgeable', but that the rituals around the computer felt 'dead' and the 'energy wasn't the same' as when they went to the beach and conducted the rituals themselves. (I should note that some others in the Maltese Pagan community disagreed with the direction this group was taking, claiming that the Maltese Neolithic Goddess was 'much older than Stonehenge and the Wiccan Holly King' and that they did not need to learn everything from British Witches.)

I was surprised that after creating and running their own rituals for several years, guided by a very organized, dedicated and knowledgeable Priest and Priestess, this coven would now choose to defer to, and become dependent upon, 'authorities' in the U.K. Listening to my friend's account, it occurred to me that this group was participating willingly in what sounded like a form of religious colonialism, particularly in the context of Malta's past colonial relationship to Britain. I have written before (Rountree 2010, 2011) about a tendency in Malta to value the foreign over the local, and something of a cultural cringe with respect to things British in particular, related to Malta's long period as a British colony (1800–1964). While there is a defensive pride about things Maltese, it is also the case that many Maltese rank foreign products, foreign media and a British university education, for example, more highly than the local varieties. Maltese Pagans have embraced participation in the global Pagan movement and sources of inspiration outside their own culture, especially British ones. The story my friend told me about the Skype lessons and rituals seemed to recapitulate this tendency. Wicca has, of course, been imported into many other societies where it may take on a local character or be consciously indigenized as contributors to this volume discuss (see Jenny Butler's chapter on Celtic Wicca in Ireland and Léon van Gulik's on Greencraft Wicca in Belgium).

Both the anecdotes I have related above speak to tensions between the local, foreign and global within modern Paganism and Native Faith movements. In both these instances the foreign is more highly valued and trusted, but for different reasons. The Hungarian Wiccan in the Budapest teahouse objected to what he saw as the misuse of Hungarian religious tradition for contemporary nationalist political goals and preferred to follow an apolitical religious tradition, even if its source was foreign and from the West. The Maltese coven wanted to fully understand and embrace initiation into Alexandrian Wicca in order to be 'truly', 'properly' Wiccan – a religious identity apparently very different from that of the Catholic majority in Malta. To do so the group members felt they had to go to, and accept the authority of, the tradition's British source. The concerns in both cases were about the authenticity and integrity of their chosen (new) religious path. Because Wicca is probably the best-known and most written-about tradition within contemporary Paganism globally, it has accrued considerable legitimacy and authenticity as a coherent new religious tradition.

However, other varieties of Paganism and Native Faith – those reviving or reconstructing ancient, indigenous religious traditions embedded in local cultures and places – configure authenticity and legitimacy differently. In such cases, more so in Central and Eastern Europe, religious authenticity derives from the perceived connection with the indigenous, cultural or ethnic roots of the faith, where, as Adrian Ivakhiv (2009: 214) has explained in the light of his work in Ukraine, 'blood' and 'tradition' – and ultimately nationality and nation-state – are rooted in a specific territory, an idea with precursors in European and Soviet thought. The nature–society relation is not structured in the way it is by most Anglo-Americans: humans are not seen as 'distinct from nature, but as culturally or ethnically "rooted" within the natural world'. Thus, Ivakhiv (2009: 221) claims, religion and ethnic politics cannot be separated: identity is 'based on a primordialist and territorialized notion of ethnicity'.

Ethnic Paganisms have been widely described as responses to concerns about foreign colonizing ideologies, internationalization, globalization, cosmopolitanism, crises in ethnic identity and anxieties about cultural erosion (Aitamurto 2007; Ališauskienė and Schröder 2012; Bourdeaux 2000; Ferlat 2003; Gardell 2003; Ivakhiv 2009; Miller 2007; Shnirelman 2002; Strmiska 2005). Since the disintegration of the Soviet Union, 'ethnic nationalism, neo-traditionalism, anti-Westernism and a revived Eurasianism (in Russia) have surfaced in … the popular and intellectual culture of Eastern Europe' (Ivakhiv 2009: 222–23). Different religions have 'come out from under the surface', writes Lindquist (2011: 72), 'to be reconstructed and reinvented, and to assume the role of moral and spiritual guidance, ecological compass, and sometimes public national ideology in various designs of ethnonationalism'. 'Traditional', 'ancient' or 'indigenous' religions are being used to provide the symbolic capital for new nationalisms. Since the end of the 1980s, Neo-Pagans in post-Soviet lands have been 'searching for both a primordial past and a pure ethnic culture, which they view as invaluable resources to overcome the hardship and ideological vacuum of the transitional period' (Shnirelman 2002: 197). Ethnic nationalists in these societies have advocated a return to the 'genuine' spirituality of the pre-Christian period to assist the rebuilding of nation states, presenting an 'anti-colonial message' which 'emphasized the necessity to mobilize local cultural resources in order to struggle against the destructive external forces that were aiming, or were thought to be aiming, to enslave the people and destroy their culture' (Shnirelman 2002: 203).

Thus authenticity is a prevailing preoccupation for participants in and scholars of Paganisms and Native Faiths. As Strmiska (2012: 27) says, 'the question of authenticity' is one that 'goes to the heart of a recurring dilemma for Pagans and Pagan movements everywhere'. The key attraction and emotional charge of a particular movement may be that its authenticity is claimed to be founded on the revival or reconstruction of an ancient religion connected to a local cultural heritage, landscape and ethnic identity. However, it is not, of course, only in Central and Eastern Europe where the ancient and indigenous are valorized and this valorization did not begin with modern Pagans. Since the seventeenth century there has been a 'romanticist idealization of Indigenous cultures as a model for utopian ideas, rituals and symbolic configurations … in Western culture', with indigenous people portrayed as living noble, happy, spiritual lives in harmony with nature in contrast with the losses and damage wrought by industrialization and the colonial encounter (Waldron and Newton 2012: 68). Much of modern Western Paganism can be traced to the late eighteenth- and nineteenth-century Romanticism (Hutton 1999), which flourished alongside the development of various modern nationalisms across Europe.

A number of chapters in this book show that modern Pagans not only are interested in connecting with their own indigenous roots, but also draw connections between themselves and other indigenous peoples, some of whom are immigrants living in their societies (see chapters by Kraft, Butler, Gregorius and Hegner). Moreover, personhood and nationhood, ethnicity and connection to place may be configured in diverse and unconventional ways – so, for example, followers of Germanic Paganism and the Norse deities are found throughout the world, not only in the countries with which they were originally associated. Cultural belonging may be configured according to the place one inhabits and with whom one lives – irrespective of place of birth and ethnicity – amidst processes of migration and reterritorialization. Transnational and transcultural kinships are forged among followers of different indigenous religions, particularly among followers of shamanisms.

It seems there are broadly two ways in which modern Pagans and followers of Native Faiths conceptualize relationships between people (ancient and modern), religion and landscape. Some Pagans (see chapters by Butler, Kraft, Hegner, Gregorius, Amster and Velkoborská) stress the importance of (1) the sacred relationship between themselves and the particular tract of land in/on/with which they live, and (2) the sacred relationship between ancient people and that same tract of land. But these Pagans do not believe that they need to be blood-related or ethnically connected to those ancient people in order for their (contemporary Pagan) religious ideas, sentiments and practices to be 'authentic'. It is enough for the land to serve as the common denominator. Common habitation – albeit diachronically – connects ancient people to modern people, and all people to the spirit or divine realm, inspiring various, perhaps quite different, forms of sacred relationship and religious practice. A lived relationship with the same land is enough to confer authenticity on their contemporary Paganism. Other groups, particularly followers of Native Faiths in Central and Eastern Europe (see chapters by Peers, Szilágyi and Västrik), emphasize points (1) and (2) above, and also a third point: the importance of an ethnic connection and continuity between the ancient inhabitants and themselves. In such places, however, there may also be other groups who are not concerned with ethnicity, instead prioritizing their relationship to the land and/or participating in a global tradition such as Goddess Spirituality or Wicca (see chapters by Velkoborská and Hegner).

In the context of living in a globalized, hyperconnected world, as all Pagans and Native Faith followers inevitably do, tensions between the local and global are constant despite the unavoidable – often sought-after and embraced – cross-fertilization of ideas, beliefs, values, products, preoccupations, practices and so on. The case studies in this book show that this is as true in contemporary Paganism and Native Faith movements as it is in a great many other areas of contemporary social and cultural life globally. All the groups discussed here, irrespective of the importance they attach to an ancient religion or which country they inhabit, draw to some extent, consciously or unconsciously, on elements derived from (often) culturally and geographically distant and disparate sources made available through the Internet, a large Pagan (and growing academic) literature, and people moving about sharing knowledge, a common feature of religious 'travelling carriers' in the globalized world (Handelman and Lindquist 2011: 41). The sources practitioners use are numerous and eclectic: the resources of other contemporary and ancient Pagan traditions along with elements from diverse religious and non-religious sources, including New Age phenomena, various forms of Christianity, Buddhism, Hinduism, Vodou, Western Esotericism, indigenous people's shamanic traditions, Zoroastrianism, archaeology and sacred sites, folklore, history, literature, linguistics, the environmental movement, feminism and other liberatory social movements, right- and left-wing political movements, historical reenactment groups, popular culture and the media, and many other sources. The imagination and creative invention also play an important role – sometimes unacknowledged, at other times vigorously celebrated (Magliocco 2009).

Looking across all these groups and movements, it appears that some Pagans and Pagan groups in some places choose to participate in global and globalizing religious processes, while other Pagans and Native Faith groups aim precisely to counter such processes, downplay them, or adapt imported global traditions to give them a local character and relevance. In many instances, the two processes – globalizing and localizing – are bound up with each other, as a number of chapters show (see those by Fedele, Howell, van Gulik, Kraft, Peers, Gregorius, Hegner and Rountree). Undoubtedly some Pagans' involvement in ethnic politics causes discomfort and conflict within the wider Pagan community, as well as outside it. In some groups the term 'Pagan' is regarded as problematic because it is seen as Christian-derived and the religion of the foreigner, colonizer or invader. Preferred terms are 'Native Faith', 'traditional religion', 'indigenous faith', 'nativist', 'reconstructionist' or the specific name of a local group or tradition such as Rodnoverie[7] (in Russia), Forn Siðr (in Denmark), Maausk (in Estonia), Dievturi (in Latvia), Romuva (in Lithuania) or Brothrjus Wulfe (in the Czech Republic). Scott Simpson and Mariusz Filip (2013) provide a detailed discussion of the language used in Central and Eastern European groups and revisit the long-standing debate about whether scholars should use 'Pagan' (often preceded by 'modern' or 'contemporary') or some version of 'Neo-Pagan' (Neopagan, neo-Pagan, neopagan) to refer to the followers of contemporary traditions. I will not revisit the debate here, except to say that virtually all people who are part of this religious phenomenon do not include the prefix 'Neo'; they simply call themselves 'Pagans' or by the name of the particular tradition (for example, Wiccan, Heathen or Druid). Scholars tend to use both 'Neo-Pagan' (to make it clear they are talking about a new religious movement rather than a pre-Christian religion) and 'Pagan' (in keeping with practitioners' preferred appellation), and both terms appear in this volume. It is now conventional to spell 'Pagan' with a capital *P* to refer to the contemporary religious phenomenon and with a small *p* to refer to pre-Christian religions.

While on the subject of controversial terms, I would note that 'indigenous' and 'indigeneity' are also problematic terms which have occasioned rigorous debate among anthropologists and others (e.g. Saugestad 2001; Kuper 2003; Kenrick and Lewis 2004; Barnard 2006; Wolfe 2006; Grixti 2011). Saugestad (2001: 43) has proposed four criteria for 'indigenous people': first-come (descended from people who were there before others), non-dominance (living under alien state structures), cultural difference (from the majority population) and self-ascription ('indigenous people' self-identify as such and claim indigenous status). Such attempts to define, however, incite debate over ethnographic cases which do not fulfil all four criteria. Kuper (2003: 395) has argued that the very idea of an 'indigenous people' is essentialist, founded 'on obsolete anthropological notions and on a romantic and false ethnographic vision'. Hence 'indigenous' could be seen simply as a new word for 'primitive' (Barnard 2006: 2). As Barnard (2006: 7) points out, though, while anthropologists hotly debate 'the indigenous' as an anthropological concept, the concept is 'defined intuitively by ordinary people – indigenous and non-indigenous alike – around the world, it does have meaning'. In the following chapters 'indigeneity' is variously conceptualized and discursively employed; context provides the clue to intended meaning. 'Indigenous' is yoked with 'people', 'culture', 'ethnicity', 'identity', 'rights' and 'religion'. It is used fairly loosely to refer to 'local', 'ancient' or 'rooted in' (place, ethnic or cultural group, nation, religion) or it may furnish the symbolic capital for ethnonationalism.

While a strong connection exists between indigeneity, ethnicity, attachment to place and nationalism in many Central and East European Paganisms, in other groups in Central and Eastern Europe and elsewhere the first three of these are less likely to be yoked with nationalism – at least, a politicized form of nationalism. Moreover, even where indigeneity and ethnicity are strongly connected with local nationalisms, a form of transnationalism may also be identified involving these groups and individuals, whereby they may come together at festivals, conferences and other gatherings to share ideas, knowledge and rituals. This has been particularly notable with transnational groups of modern shamans. Any resulting eclecticism does not imply a lack of concern for ethnicity or indigenous tradition. Lindquist (2011: 76) describes how, in 1993, Michael Harner of the Center for Shamanic Studies in California and some associates joined with Mongush Barakhovich Kenin-Lopsan, a Tyvan poet and playwright, and other Tyvan shamans to organise the First International Conference on Shamanism in Tyva (an autonomous republic in the Russian Federation). For a couple of weeks Harner and fellow shamans from the U.S., Austria, Germany and Switzerland (some of whom were anthropologists) worked together with Tyvan shamans. In 1997 a ten-day gathering of shamans and other indigenous religious specialists was held at a Tibetan Buddhist retreat centre in Savoy in the French Alps to learn from one another's practices.[8] Another example is the Sami shamanic festival, *Isogaisa*, held annually in Norway since 2010, which brings together shamans from all over the world (see the chapter by Kraft in this volume). Each of these cases reveals both attachment to a specific indigenous ethnic tradition and a desire to share transnationally.

This volume's contributing authors come from several disciplinary backgrounds – Socio-cultural Anthropology, Folklore Studies, Religious Studies and Cultural Psychology – and to a degree these influence their research preoccupations, theoretical perspectives and positioning as researchers in relation to the topics and communities they discuss. Scholars' particular research interests also play a part in their choice of focus and analysis and the discourses they invoke:

for example, gender and religion (Fedele) or politics and religion (Szilágyi). The research methods they have used – for example, participant observation or content analysis of media sources and online archives – also bring variety and blur disciplinary differences, as does the scope of focus (for example, country overview or intimate ethnography of a small group). Together these studies enrich our understanding of this diverse, growing and changing religious phenomenon in a region hitherto under-represented in scholarly literature on contemporary Paganism and Native Faith movements.

I have resisted dividing the book's chapters into sections based on geography within Europe. While it is true that groups in a particular region may share some broadly similar characteristics – influenced, for example, by the Roman Catholic context of southern Europe or by the post-Soviet context of eastern Europe – it would be a mistake to suggest that expressions of Paganism can be categorized straightforwardly according to region. There are broad patterns and tendencies, but the overall picture is complex and changing. Within any national context it is likely that there exists a plurality of traditions, coexisting peaceably or with varying degrees of mutual disapproval and occasional conflict. As Aitamurto and Simpson (2013) emphasize, post-Soviet societies all have different political histories and their experiences of communism were diverse. While the centrality of nation, ethnic group or tribe may be common to many groups' ideals, these groups are highly diverse and nationalism is given different levels of importance and takes a variety of forms. Stereotypes can be misleading.

While Native Faith movements are frequently associated with the politics of nationalism, cultural reclamation and nation-building, it is not the case that the transnational Pagan traditions are apolitical. The focus and forms of political engagement are different. Many eclectic Pagans, Druids and modern shamans have for decades been deeply involved in environmental politics and activism. Gender politics are at the heart of Goddess Spirituality and some of its best-known leaders have been feminist and environmental activists for close to half a century. Thus contemporary Paganisms and Native Faiths have commonly been harnessed to sanction, sacralize and endorse a variety of 'big ideas', ranging on the political spectrum from ethnonationalism to environmentalism to feminism and a variety of other movements for social equity.

In the following review of the book's chapters I try to indicate the overlapping themes as well as the idiosyncrasies of individual case studies. In the chapter after this introduction, Siv Ellen Kraft describes how the revival of Sami shamanism in Norway beginning in the late 1970s was linked with a broader cultural revival among the (Christianized) Sami people in connection with environmental protests, and resulted in changes to the legal and political status of Sami as an indigenous people. Amidst a period of consciousness-raising among a new generation of Sami, the founder of Sami neo-shamanism made a journey 'home' in search of his Sami roots, where he met a Chilean shaman with an African *djembe*-drum who became his guide. He also made journeys to California where he was trained by one-time anthropologist Michael Harner in the universalist practice of 'Core Shamanism'. Thus, until the early twenty-first century, it is debatable whether the shamanism prac-tised by this Sami man and others in Oslo could be called specifi-cally *Sami* shamanism – it undoubtedly drew on eclectic sources, some of which came from geographically and culturally distant places and times.

Kraft outlines a process whereby a distinctive Sami neo-shamanism was pieced together in which indigenous ethnic identity became important. She argues that contemporary Sami shamans confound Michael Strmiska's oft-quoted model linking 'Reconstructionist' forms of modern Paganism with 'people for whom ethnic identity is very important', and 'Eclectic' forms with a tendency to select ideas, practices and deities from a variety of sources while emphasising 'a spirituality of nature' (Strmiska 2005: 20–22). Sami neo-shamans con-sciously draw upon eclectic cultural resources in constructing their contemporary practice while being deeply concerned with issues of ethnicity, cultural continuity and heritage. By embracing 'a spiritual-ity of nature' they forge connections with indigenous peoples more widely, thereby integrating the local and universal.

By the time Asatro (contemporary Nordic Paganism) began flour-ishing in Denmark in the mid 1990s, practitioners were, on the whole, opposed to the mixing of religion and ethnic politics, both because they knew the trouble this had caused in some other Pagan commu-nities and wanted to avoid similar conflicts, and because they were influenced by the strong Danish cultural aversion to mixing religion and politics. Most Danish followers of Asatro in Matthew Amster's research rejected the idea that their faith was somehow genetic or ethnically based, but stressed the importance of the local landscape and the 'logic' that the Norse gods will be felt most vividly in Nordic countries. However, Amster also gives examples of individuals who held distinctly left- and right-wing political views which influenced them respectively towards eclecticism and universalism on one hand, or towards the view that Asatro is exclusively for Danes and xeno-phobic attitudes towards immigrants on the other.

As Kraft claims in the case of the Sami, Amster contends that the reconstructionist/eclectic model is disrupted in the Danish setting. He describes how concerns about ethnic political ideas and intoler-ance in portions of the largest Danish Asatro organization led some members to form a splinter group, Nordisk Tingsfællig. This group dedicated itself to practising apolitical Asatro and ritual innovation, because they felt Asatro rituals had become too influenced by Wicca. Thus they wanted to move away both from the politics of ethnicity and nationalism usually associated with reconstructionist Paganism and from the influence of foreign traditions normally associated with eclectic Paganism. Instead they sought a greater local authenticity and historical accuracy in constructing their rituals but eschewed an ethnic agenda.

Modern Heathenism in Sweden, like some other movements dis-cussed here, is a series of paradoxes. Fredrik Gregorius shows that on one hand Heathens present their religion as the reinvigoration of an organic, authentic Nordic culture, while on the other they use non-local sources such as Wicca and neo-shamanism to transform Heathenism from a theoretical and emotionally charged ideal into a living religion. While Heathen identity draws on the idea of an essen-tial, deeply rooted Nordic culture, most Heathen groups welcome members with non-Scandinavian backgrounds and are not concerned about Sweden's increasingly multicultural society. It is Heathens in the United States who are more likely to embrace ideas about eth-nicity and Nordic genetic connections. Although Swedish Heathens are influenced by American authors and ideas, they are sceptical of American Heathens' ability to follow the faith while living so far from the cultural and natural environments fundamental to what Gregorius terms this 'organic religion'.

In their quest for religious legitimacy in the local religious market and society, Swedish Heathens use two apparently con-tradictory forms of leverage. On one hand they emphasize a con-gruence between Heathen ideals and the important ideals of the wider Swedish society – democracy, ecology and equality – which they claim have a cultural foundation in pre-Christian Norse reli-gion. On the other, they align themselves with, and draw inspira-tion from, immigrant religious minorities within Sweden, primarily practitioners of indigenous religions such as Hinduism and Afro-Caribbean religions such as Vodou. By positioning themselves as another minority faith, they obtain leverage from a public debate about multiculturalism and immigrant religions. Thus, as in the case of Sami neo-shamans, Swedish Heathenism reveals a dynamic interplay between reconstructionism and eclecticism, local and non-local indigenous religions, local Pagans and local non-Pagans, and national and transnational relationships in modern Paganism.

The Czech Pagan scene is highly diverse, incorporating ethnic Pagan reconstructionists and eclectic Witches, Wiccans, Druids and others. Like the Danish splinter group Nordisk Tingsfællig, the Brotherhood of Wolves (*Brothrjus Wulfe*) described by Kamila Velkoborská split off from the Czech Ásatrú scene following disagreements and power struggles. The Wolves also eschew an ethnic or political agenda (despite some members' earlier involvement in White Power groups) and seek authenticity by creatively combining elements of Germanic religious heritage with an intimate connection with the immediate landscape. Uniquely, though, their faith centres on the Great Wolf Fenris of the Eddas and is embodied in a lifestyle revolving around Czechoslovakian Wolfdogs (which most members breed) and an attempt to live as modern pseudo hunter-gatherers. The group traces a correlation between the tragic demise of *Canis lupus* in Eurasia and North America, the fate of Fenris in Old Norse mythology and the demise of human intimacy with nature. Drawing a parallel between their lives with their Wolfdogs and the lives of ancient tribes who lived in harmony with nature and other beings, including wolves, members of the Brotherhood see the Wolfdog – once wild, now domesticated – as representing their compromised life as Pagans in the modern world.

Just as the development of Sami neo-shamanism belonged to a more general project of Sami nation-building, with, for example, its annual festival receiving financial support from the Sami Parliament and other municipal and national sources, Eleanor Peers shows how a revival of shamanism in the Sakha (Yakutia) Republic, northeastern Siberia, is related to a wider post-Soviet nationalist revival of cultural and religious traditions, beginning in the 1980s, in which shamanic specialists became nationalist activists. As a result, shamanic ability is now highly valued and shamans are coopted to collaborate with politicians, cultural workers and academics in the design and production of public events. One example is the important annual *Yhyakh* cultural festivals in which elaborate rituals are funded by the Sakha (Yakutia) Republic's governing body. Peers argues that despite what it shares with neo-shamanic and other new religious developments in other societies and despite drawing on some of those trends, the revival of Sakha shamanism has been shaped by a distinctive local heritage. This includes the pre-Soviet Sakha shamanic tradition, which survived both Christian missionization and Soviet-era repression, and, secondly, the Republic's experience of Soviet modernization and, subsequently, the post-Soviet national revival. She demonstrates how the meshing of local and global elements produced a social transformation unique to Sakha (Yakutia), but which has parallels in other national contexts.

Like a number of other Native Faith movements which emerged in post-Soviet societies at the end of the 1980s and in the early 1990s, the Estonian Maausk movement (whose followers are called Maausulised), discussed by Ergo-Hart Västrik, stresses continuity between itself and indigenous ethnic traditions, is anti-West and hostile to Christianity (seeing it as a subjugation tool of the foreigner) and is closely tied with a developing nationalist discourse. Maausk, however, has links with an earlier ethnic religion, *Taara usk*, established in the 1920s by intellectuals influenced by Romanticism and Estonian nationalism.[9] Banned by the Soviets in 1940, Taara usk's ideas reemerged following the Soviet collapse in the form of Maausk, 'the faith of the earth', again driven by intellectuals involved in conservative politics. The Maausulised currently enjoy considerable local popularity and positive local media coverage, are involved in lobbying for heritage protection and wilderness preservation, are active in debates about religious freedom and indigenous rights, and have joined with the University of Tartu in a research project aimed at registering and studying sacred natural sites. In terms of their integration into a wider nationalist revival of cultural and religious traditions, there are echoes of Peers' discussion of the revival of shamanism in the Sakha (Yakutia) Republic and Szilágyi's account of a 'Pagan metaculture' in Hungary. And outside the post-Soviet context, there are similarities with the way that Sami neo-shamans are being drawn into a wider project of nation-building in Norway.

In the introduction to their book *Religion, Politics and Globalization: Anthropological Approaches*, Handelman and Lindquist (2011: 42) write that: 'In late modernity the pluralization of religious options became a focus of theorizing.... The argument is that the disestablishment of the official churches engenders the pluralistic setting in which religions of all kinds thrive, as world-views and practices, in public spheres and in popular imagination'. This is the scene Tamás Szilágyi portrays in Hungary at the end of socialism in the context of the Christian churches' failure to rebuild their religious and sociopolitical base. As I indicated at the beginning of this chapter when describing my teahouse encounter in Budapest, those

Hungarian Pagans who follow a Western-originated and now global tradition such as Wicca or Goddess Spirituality may have some quite different priorities and views from those involved in an ethnic religious tradition. Szilágyi's focus is on groups of the latter kind. As well as the numerous small, explicitly religious Pagan communities which operate on the periphery of Hungarian religious life, Szilágyi identifies a 'Pagan metaculture' which has spilled out of the field of religion into the wider culture, particularly into popular culture and right-wing politics. This metaculture offers a 'non-institutionalized transcendent worldview' and emphasizes Hungarian cultural and religious heritage and practices, nature-centred thinking and alternative healing modalities. As Ališauskienė and Schröder (2012: 3) write in *Religious Diversity in Post-Soviet Society*, 'While Neopagan religious communities have remained numerically small, the power of the idea of cultural heritage advocated by them easily transcends the boundaries of the religious field in societies where discourses of a deep-rooted national cultural identity are thriving'.

The relationship between Native Faith and nationalism is highly charged in the German context, where the historical association between nationalism and the National Socialist regime, with its interest in Teutonism and 'blood and soil' ideology, means Neo-Pagans fear – and risk – being branded neo-Nazis and therefore engage in a wary, secretive dance with the indigenous and local. Concentrating on the unique geopolitical urban context of Berlin, Victoria Hegner charts the reconstructionist beginnings of Neo-Paganism in West Berlin during the early 1980s, then goes on to discuss a group with whom she has done fieldwork, the Moon-Women, who manage to disrupt the connection between Native Faith and nationalism by reconfiguring notions of 'ethnicity' and 'belonging' within the contemporary cosmopolitan Berlin context.

From the earliest days, reconstructionism and eclecticism, nationalism and a form of religious colonialism, were part of the growth of Paganism in West Berlin. Hegner describes how shortly after a nascent Neo-Pagan community developed in the city during the early 1980s – one emphasizing the triad of blood, tradition and territory and intent upon rehabilitating the old Germanic mythology and festivals – ambassadors of Anglo-American forms of Paganism visited the city. In 1986 Starhawk, whose *The Spiral Dance* had been translated into German in 1983, came from California spreading news of the revival of Goddess religion. In 1988 the well-known Wiccan author Vivianne Crowley visited from Britain and began initiating people into Wicca. Hegner describes how some of the early reconstructionist German Pagans were critical of, and disappointed by, the ways in which these high-profile Anglo-American visitors constructed Paganism, questioning their historical sources and eclectic approaches. Other German Pagans, however, especially women, were inspired by the feminist and socialist politics of Starhawk's new Witchcraft and Goddess religion. Like the reconstructionist Pagans of the 1980s, today's Moon-Women cautiously seek to rehabilitate the Germanic pantheon and mythology and celebrate their connection to the local landscape. But unlike those early reconstructionists, they are eclectic, explicitly creative and inclusive in their approach. Hegner attributes the changes in Neo-Paganism to changes in Berlin as a hot, new sociocultural space.

Nationalism within Paganism and Native Faith groups has come to be associated with reconstructionist groups who emphasize ethnic connections with a particular place and people and are often feared by other Pagans, rightly or wrongly, to be politically right-wing. Jenny Butler shows that there are other ways to conceive of the relationship between Paganism and nationalism. In Ireland Paganism is not a medium through which nationalism develops or is expressed. Rather, Irish nationalism and Irish Paganism have both drawn on a common reservoir of cultural resources, namely Ireland's land, ancient monuments, language, myth and folk culture. Instead of aligning with a politically oriented nationalism, Irish Pagans gravitate towards Romantic Nationalism with its emphasis on shared culture, morality and spiritual values. National identity is less important to them than an emplaced Pagan identity and a more broadly shared 'Celtic' identity, which has the advantage of circumventing further battles over what constitutes 'Irishness'. Unlike groups who use ethnic connections with the ancient past and territory to legitimize their exclusivity, Irish Pagans see the ancient past as supporting a discourse of greater inclusivity. Butler shows how they also adapt not-so-ancient traditions – some of which are part of the prevailing Catholic religion, such as devotions at holy wells – because these are seen as evidence of the continuity of pre-Christian pagan practices within Irish Christianity. Although Wicca has been imported to Ireland, a local Celtic Wicca has emerged, with practitioners worshipping only Celtic deities and favouring practices believed to have an Irish precedent.

Wicca has also been customized on the European continent. Once British Traditional Wicca had expanded beyond Britain, in some places it morphed into derivative traditions as a result of fusions and transformations, becoming eclectic in practice and theology. Léon van Gulik explores the tensions between eclecticism and tradition-alism among Flemish followers of Greencraft Wicca, for whom, like the Irish Pagans, Celticity is important. Greencrafters are part of the British-derived Alexandrian lineage and follow its practices, but have steered clear of 'Wiccan imperialism' by also developing a systematic body of additional ideas, principles and practices in an effort to uncover what they believe to be the universal roots of ancient European nature religions and to reconcile these with Celtic ethnicity. Van Gulik discusses two aspects of the Greencraft system: the Celtic Tree Calendar they have constructed based on that of the British poet and writer Robert Graves in *The White Goddess* (1966), and their experiences and experiments in relation to the stone circles they visit in various parts of Europe and also create in their own back yards. While Greencrafters' activities involve an eclectic bricolage of cultural material, van Gulik argues that they nonetheless aim to make their system 'ethnically commensurate' and cosmologically consis-tent by combining elements that are allegedly Celtic in origin or at least indigenous to northern Europe. He argues there is no longer such a thing as an 'authentic Celt'; all contemporary Celticities are constructions.

Another tradition which has spread – or been spread – from its British base to Germany, Spain, Hungary, Sweden, The Netherlands, Australia and Argentina is the Goddess Conference, which originated in Glastonbury in 1996. Drawing on fieldwork with Iberian follow-ers of Goddess Spirituality, Anna Fedele analyses the transplantation of the 'Goddess Conference package' (see Bowman 2009) to Spain in 2010 and concludes, in the wake of the event's failure in 2012, that to be accepted such Anglo-traditions need to be adapted to a local context through a process of cultural and religious translation medi-ated by local leaders familiar with the local milieu. In the case of Spain and Portugal, this milieu is traditionally Catholic. Although they may criticize aspects of Christianity, these Catholic-raised Goddess followers incorporate many Christian, especially Catholic, elements (see Fedele 2013). For them the Virgin Mary is a Christian version of the ancient Goddess and Mother Earth; the saints are Christianized Pagan gods and goddesses. Fedele argues that this study reveals the ways in which Pagans negotiate tensions between local, cultural or national identities on one hand, and wider, increasingly globalized influences on the other. Indigenizing imported forms of Paganism provides them with a vital sense of authenticity; nevertheless Iberian Pagans are also keen to be part of the international Pagan movement. Thus they are caught up in two fields of tension: between their own spirituality and Goddess traditions from the U.K. and U.S., with whose spiritual ideas and practices they share a strong affinity, and between themselves and the local Catholic society, with whom they share a strong cultural affinity and Catholic heritage.

The Italian Pagan community, situated in another predominantly Roman Catholic society and also the host to a string of high-profile Pagan teachers and authors from Britain and the U.S., has indigenized and reappropriated the various modern Pagan traditions which have come to Italy rather later than elsewhere, with apparently fewer tensions than those experienced by Iberian followers of Goddess Spirituality. Francesca Ciancimino Howell argues that although Wicca, Druidry, Goddess Spirituality and other traditions have been introduced and 'taught' by British and American visitors, Italian sources can be shown to have played an influential role in the birth of Wicca in Britain, and imported traditions can be related to enduring vernacular religious complexes and magical lore within Italy. Howell charts the diverse and deeply entwined local and global strands and connections within contemporary Italian Paganism.

As I said at the beginning of this introduction, it was while talking with a Maltese Pagan friend about how her coven had recently handed over the running of its rituals to a High Priestess in Cornwall, having accepted that they needed to be trained and initiated by this British expert, that the idea came to me of considering a colonialist impulse in contemporary Paganism. While it is reasonably commonplace for scholars to point to a nationalist impulse, particularly in Native Faith movements, the colonizing aspects of some forms of modern Paganism have not hitherto been acknowledged or addressed, perhaps because until recently much of the research, at least that published in English, has focussed on the countries which are the source of the colonizing. From the contributions to this book, it is clear that since the late 1980s British and American literature and the visits of bestselling authors and high-profile teachers from the U.K. and U.S. have had a considerable role in spreading the gospel of the Goddess in Europe, meeting with a variety of local responses ranging from enthusiasm to disapproval. Most noticeably, though, globally available, Anglo-American ideas and materials have been adapted by local people to local contexts. In the case of the Maltese coven mentioned above and discussed in the final chapter, what might be seen as a colonizing and indeed overtly controlling process can be viewed more profitably in the light of the country's historical relationship with colonization and local processes of indigenization. The contributions to this book demonstrate that as Paganism spreads and morphs in

the postmodern, globalized world, where identities, affinities, align-
ments and collectivities are configured and made over in numerous
novel ways, the concept of colonialism itself becomes problematized
and subject to revision.

I sincerely thank the volume's contributors for their engagement with its theme and sharing the rich and diverse results of their
research. While there was unfortunately only space for thirteen case
studies in the volume, both the variety and some common trends
across the region are abundantly apparent. So is the fact that the
Pagan and Native Faith scene is dynamic, complex and constantly
changing. Generalizations about, for example, groups in post-Soviet
societies or in a particular geographical subregion (such as northern
or southern Europe) may be confounded by the diversity of groups
present in a single national context. Although thirteen countries are
represented, the chapters should not be regarded as 'country studies',
but rather as studies of particular groups in particular countries.
A study of Goddess Spirituality in Hungary or Sweden, Wicca in
Spain or Hungary, Slavic Paganism in the Czech Republic or neo-
shamanism in Malta would have yielded different perspectives of
what is happening in these countries, let alone what is happening in
the countries not represented here. Above all, these studies emphasize the importance of local sociocultural, historical, political, religious and environmental contexts in determining the diverse shapes
that Paganisms and Native Faith movements take in the current
sociopolitical-religious space of Europe. Moreover, they show that a
particular local context may inspire quite different responses.

Notes

1 It is common in Pagan scholarship and among Pagans to give an initial
capital letter to 'Witch', 'Pagan', 'Witchcraft' and 'Paganism' when referring to these modern religions and their adherents following the common
practice when referring to religions and their followers (e.g. Christian,
Christianity).

2 A key source is *The Pomegranate: The International Journal of Pagan
Studies* and the recent anthology *Modern Pagan and Native Faith
Movements in Central and Eastern Europe* (Aitamurto and Simpson 2013).
See also Gardell (2003), Ivakhiv (2005, 2009), Shnirelman (2000, 2002,
2007), Simpson (2000), Strmiska (2005, 2012), Szilárdi (2009), Pilkington
and Popov (2009) and York (1995).

3 There are exceptions to polytheism; for example, in advocating the return of Ukrainians to their pre-Christian faith, Lev Sylenko advocated the monotheistic worship of the god Dazhbog (Shnirelman 2002: 204).

4 Over the years there have been attempts to put local and global figures on numbers of Pagans. After a rapid expansion from the last two decades of the twentieth century through till the first decade of the twenty-first century, growth slowed by the end of that decade, in part due to the end of the Teen Witch fad (Lewis 2012: 128). The 2011 census figure for total Pagans in England and Wales was 78,566 (Lewis 2012: 132). In 2008 an American Religious Identification Survey was carried out by the Graduate Center of the City University of New York; the number of total Pagans was 711,000 (rounded to the nearest thousand). The figure represents a statistical extrapolation based on a survey of 50,000 people in the United States (Lewis 2012: 133). The Canadian census in 2011 recorded a total of 26,495 Pagans (e-mail from Shai Feraro to New Religious Movements Scholars group, 28 September 2013). In the 2013 New Zealand census the total was 7,572 (http://www.stats.govt.nz/Census/2013-census/data-tables/total-by-topic.aspx?gclid=CLXRobb6wr0CFQccpQodtjkAQQ) and in the 2011 Australian census the figure was 32,083 (Lewis 2012: 134–35). The above total figures of Pagans are broken down into the various traditions (Pagan, Wicca, Druidism, Witchcraft, Heathen, Pantheism and so on).

5 For example, see the 'Return of the Hellenes' movement in Greece (Miller 2007). See also Snook's (2013) discussion of American Heathens. Heathenry is a reconstructionist religious movement whose practitioners align themselves with ancient Germanic and Norse cosmology.

6 The Pagan Federation International has thirty-five member countries or regions. http://www.paganfederation.org. Accessed 3 April 2014.

7 Modern Slavic Paganism or Native Faith is known by various terms including Rodnovery and Ridnoviry. In Russia the term is Rodnoverie.

8 A documentary film entitled *Fire on the Mountain: A Gathering of Shamans* was made about this event by the Canadian director David Cherniack. http://www.youtube.com/watch?v=awEfLq7W5Tc. Accessed 21 October 2014.

9 Dievturība was a parallel ethnoreligious movement established in Latvia in the 1920s (Shnirelman 2002: 200).

References

Aitamurto, K. 2007. 'Russian Paganism and the Issue of Nationalism: A Case Study of the Circle of Pagan Tradition', *The Pomegranate: The International Journal of Pagan Studies* 8(2): 184–210.

Aitamurto, K. and S. Simpson (eds). 2013. *Modern Pagan and Native Faith Movements in Central and Eastern Europe*. Durham: Acumen.

Ališauskienė, M. and I. Schröder (eds). 2012. *Religious Diversity in Post-Soviet Society: Ethnographies of Catholic Hegemony and the New Pluralism in Lithuania*. Farnham: Ashgate.

Barnard, A. 2006. 'Kalahari Revisionism, Vienna and the "Indigenous Peoples" Debate', *Social Anthropology* 14(1): 1–16.

Bourdeaux, M. 2000. 'Religion Revives in All its Variety: Russia's Regions Today', *Religion, State and Society* 28(1): 9–21.

Bowman, M. 2009. 'From Glastonbury to Hungary: Contemporary Integrative Spirituality and Vernacular Religion in Context', in G. Vargyas (ed.), *Passageways: From Hungarian Ethnography to European Ethnology and Sociocultural Anthropology*. Department of European Ethnology and Cultural Anthropology, Budapest: The University of Pécs, L'Harmattan Publishing House, pp. 195–221.

Fedele, A. 2013. 'The Metamorphoses of Neopaganism in Traditionally Catholic Countries in Southern Europe', in R. Blanes and J. Mapril (eds), *Sites and Politics of Religious Diversity in Southern Europe: The Best of All Gods*. Leiden and Boston: Brill, pp. 51–72.

Ferlat, A. 2003. 'Neopaganism and New Age in Russia', *Folklore* 23: 40–48.

Gardell, M. 2003. *Gods of the Blood: The Pagan Revival and White Separatism*. Durham, NC: Duke University Press.

Grixti, J. 2011. 'Indigenous Media Boundaries: Reconsidering the Binary of Indigeneity and Settler State', *Proceedings of the Australian and New Zealand Communication Association Conference: Communication on the Edge*, Waikato University, New Zealand, pp. 1–13. http://www.anzca.net/component/docman/cat_view/47-anzca-11/48-refereed-proceedings.html?start=25/. Accessed 3 April 2014.

Handelman, D. and G. Lindquist. 2011. 'Religion, Politics and Globalization: The Long Past Foregrounding the Short Present – Prologue and Introduction', in G. Lindquist and D. Handelman (eds), *Religion, Politics and Globalization: Anthropological Approaches*. New York and Oxford: Berghahn, pp. 1–66.

Hutton, R.H. 1999. *The Triumph of the Moon: A History of Modern Pagan Witchcraft*. Oxford: Oxford University Press.

Ivakhiv, A. 2005. 'In Search of Deeper Identities: Neopaganism and Native Faith in Contemporary Ukraine', *Nova Religio: The Journal of Alternative and Emergent Religions* 8(3): 7–38.

———. 2009. 'Nature and Ethnicity in East European Paganism: An Environmental Ethic of the Religious Right?', in B. Davy (ed.), *Paganism: Critical Concepts in Religious Studies*, vol. 2: *Ecology*. London: Routledge, pp. 213–42.

Kenrick, J. and J. Lewis. 2004. 'Indigenous Peoples' Rights and the Politics of the Term "Indigenous"', *Anthropology Today* 20: 4–9.

Kuper, A. 2003. 'The Return of the Native', *Current Anthropology* 44: 389–402.

Lewis, J.R. 2012. 'The Pagan Explosion Revisited: A Statistical Postmortem on the Teen Witch Fad', *The Pomegranate: The International Journal of Pagan Studies* 14(1): 128–39.

Lindquist, G. 2011. 'Ethnic Identity and Religious Competition: Buddhism and Shamanism in Southern Siberia', in G. Lindquist and D. Handelman (eds), *Religion, Politics and Globalization: Anthropological Approaches*. New York and Oxford: Berghahn, pp. 69–90.

Magliocco, S. 2009. 'Reclamation, Appropriation and the Ecstatic Imagination in Modern Pagan Ritual', in M. Pizza and J. Lewis (eds), *Handbook of Contemporary Paganism*. Leiden: Brill, pp. 223–40.

Miller, J. 2007. 'The Return of the Hellenes', story for 'Worlds of Difference: Local Culture in a Global Age, a Radio Documentary Project of Homelands Productions'. Retrieved 6 October 2013 from http://www.homelands.org/worlds/hellenes.html.

Pilkington, H. and A. Popov. 2009. 'Understanding Neo-Paganism in Russia: Religion? Ideology? Philosophy? Fantasy?', in G. McKay, *Subcultures and New Religious Movements in Russia and East-Central Europe*. Oxford: Peter Lang, pp. 253–304.

Rountree, K. 2010. *Crafting Contemporary Pagan Identities in a Catholic Society*. London: Ashgate.

———. 2011. 'Localising Neo-Paganism: Integrating Global and Indigenous Traditions in a Mediterranean Catholic Society', *Journal of the Royal Anthropological Institute* 17(4): 846–72.

Saugestad, S. 2001. *The Inconvenient Indigenous: Remote Area Development in Botswana, Donor Assistance and the First People of the Kalahari*. Uppsala: Nordiska Afrikainstitutet.

Shnirelman, V. 2000. 'Perun, Svarog and Others: Russian Neo-Paganism in Search of Itself', *Cambridge Anthropology* 21(3): 18–36.

———. 2002. '"Christians! Go Home": A Revival of Neo-Paganism between the Baltic Sea and Transcaucasia (An Overview)', *Journal of Contemporary Religion* 17(2): 197–211.

———. 2007. 'Ancestral Wisdom and Ethnic Nationalism: A View from Eastern Europe', *The Pomegranate: The International Journal of Pagan Studies* 9(1): 41–61.

Simpson, S. 2000. *Native Faith: Polish Neo-Paganism at the Brink of the Twenty-First Century*. Krakow: Nomos.

Simpson, S. and M. Filip. 2013. 'Selected Words for Modern Pagan and Native Faith Movements in Central and Eastern Europe', in K. Aitamurto and S. Simpson (eds), *Modern Pagan and Native Faith Movements in Central and Eastern Europe*. Durham: Acumen, pp. 27–43.

Snook, J. 2013. 'Reconsidering Heathenry: The Construction of an Ethnic Folkway as Religio-Ethnic Identity', *Nova Religio: The Journal of Alternative and Emergent Religions* 16(3): 52–76.

Strmiska, M. (ed.). 2005. *Modern Paganism in World Cultures: Comparative Perspectives*. Santa Barbara: ABC-CLIO.

Strmiska, M. 2012. 'Modern Latvian Paganism: Some Introductory Remarks', *The Pomegranate: The International Journal of Pagan Studies* 14(1): 22–30.

Szilárdi, R. 2009. 'Ancient Gods – New Ages: Lessons from Hungarian Paganism', *The Pomegranate: The International Journal of Pagan Studies* 11(1): 44–57.

Waldron, D. and J. Newton. 2012. 'Rethinking Appropriation of the Indigenous: A Critique of the Romanticist Approach', *Nova Religio: The Journal of Alternative and Emergent Religions* 16(2): 64–85.

Wolfe, P. 2006. 'The Concept of Indigeneity', *Social Anthropology* 14(1): 25–27.

York, M. 1995. 'Pan-Baltic Identity and Religio-Cultural Expression in Contemporary Lithuania', in R. Towler (ed.), *New Religions and the New Europe*. Aarhus: Aarhus University Press, pp. 72–86.

1

Sami Neo-shamanism in Norway

Colonial Grounds, Ethnic Revival and Pagan Pathways

Siv Ellen Kraft

Introduction

Sami neo-shamanism is a recent movement connected to nation-building and a broader field of Sami revivalism, shaped by the global New Age scene, 'Core Shamanism' from the United States and indigenous spiritualities more widely. This chapter explores the various local and global impulses involved and discusses these in relation to established perspectives in contemporary Pagan studies. Michael Strmiska's (2005) influential model incorporating an 'eclectic' and a 'reconstructionist' version of neo-Paganism constitutes a main point of departure for the approach here. Unlike the religionist approaches which to some extent have dominated the field,[1] Strmiska offers a prosaic attempt to distinguish between different Pagan pathways based on practitioners' views on the past and their perceived relationship to issues of ethnicity. At one end of Strmiska's continuum are movements which seek to reconstruct an ancient religious tradition associated with a particular ethnic group or region, striving to come as close as possible to the 'original' version. At the other end of the continuum are eclectic movements that mix old and new elements freely, and emphasize the relationship between nature and humanity over ethnic identity (Strmiska 2005: 18–22).

Although useful in regard to parts of the field, these distinctions indicate some stereotypes that have been common in neo-Pagan and indigenous studies, including notions of tradition-bound indigenous people, serious Pagans and superficial New Agers. More importantly,

Strmiska's model fails – at least in the case of the Sami – to make sense of the complex mixtures of the postcolonial era, including the intersections between neo-Paganism and New Age, between colonizing and nationalist impulses, and between reconstructionism and eclecticism.

The Norwegian Sami: A Historical Sketch

Commonly referred to as the homeland of the Sami, Sápmi covers an area extending from northern Scandinavia to northwestern Russia, including parts of Norway, Sweden, Finland and Russia. Among the estimated eighty thousand self-defined Sami currently living in these areas, approximately fifty thousand live in Norway (Sami Instituhtta 2013), who are the empirical focus here. They regard themselves as one people across national borders and are recognized by international law as an indigenous people.

The pre-Christian Sami religion (*Noaidevuohta*) is usually described as a combination of animism, shamanism and polytheism. Precisely when Christianity was introduced to these landscapes is unclear, but grave excavations reveal that the cross was associated with Sami burial practices from the thirteenth century. From the sixteenth century the building of churches was part of a more conscious colonizing effort, and by the seventeenth century a systematic and active mission was established. From this period cultic drums were confiscated, holy places were desecrated and the demonizing and persecution of Sami religious concepts and practices became the norm. The result, to quote a classical study of the Lule Sami by the historian of religion Håkan Rydving, was *The End of Drum-Time* (Rydving 1993).

During the mid to late nineteenth century a conservative Lutheran revival movement, later to become known as Laestadianism, spread among Sami communities.[2] Laestadianism may to some extent have protected Sami cultural traditions as a place of refuge, 'a sanctuary for the minority populations, at a time – from 1870 down to World War II – when the authorities were tightening the screw of Norwegianization in the name of Social Darwinism and Nationalism' (Minde 2008: 9; see also Paine 1965). Laestadianism was, at the same time, from the start hostile to pre-Christian practices of the past, which members learnt to see as pertaining to a heathen if not demonic religion. It has also, due partly to the fact that it was never exclusively a Sami movement but rather one that crossed ethnic boundaries,

more or less consistently opposed initiatives taken by the ethnopolitical movement.

Demonstrations against the damming of the Alta Kautokeino
River in the late 1970s are usually regarded as a turning point in the
history of the Sami. The protesters failed to protect the river, but
huge mass demonstrations and hunger strikes laid the foundations for
what has been referred to as the '78-generation' – a Sami version of
the protests of the 1968 generation (Aspevoll 2006) – along with state
reforms of the legal and political status of the Sami. Having started
out as an issue involving Norwegian environmental organizations
and local people in Alta, the saving of the river soon became a Sami
issue – and, in addition, the first Sami issue to be framed in terms of
indigenous rights. It was followed by important changes regarding
the situation of the Norwegian Sami, including the establishment of a
Sami parliament in 1989,[3] and led – perhaps most importantly – to
consciousness raising among a new generation of Sami. Many of the
Sami youngsters involved had grown up with little knowledge of
Sami culture and language. Their parents, in order to secure for their
children a better future, had 'shielded' them from a culture they had
learnt to consider shameful and backward, and an identity that had
become a social stigma (Eidheim 1998).[4]

The Birth of Sami Neo-shamanism

Today known as the founder of Sami neo-shamanism and the first
professional Sami neo-shaman, Ailo Gaup participated in demonstrations against the damming of the Alta Kautokeino River and
describes this as a political and spiritual awakening (Gaup 2005).
Gaup was born in Finnmark, a Sami area in northern Norway, but
was sent to a foster family in south Norway as an orphan and was
thus brought up away from the homeland of his ancestors – both
culturally and geographically.

In his semi-autobiographical book, *The Shamanic Zone* (2005),
Gaup describes the demonstrations as one of three major steps in his
spiritual development. The second step took the form of a journey
back to the core Sami area of Finnmark in search of his Sami roots, of
traces of shamanism and of a *noaide* (shaman) who could teach him
the art of trance journeys. Gaup had at this point studied scholarly
accounts of the pre-Christian Sami religion but lacked knowledge of
the methods for performing the trance journey. In Kautokeino he met
a Chilean refugee with practical knowledge about how to proceed.

What started, to use Strmiska's vocabulary, as a 'reconstructionist' journey to the homeland of his ancestors, thus – within this very homeland – turned into an eclectic project in the form of a trance journey guided by Chilean traditions and an African *djembe*-drum (Gaup 2005: 86–98).

The third and most decisive step in Gaup's training took place in the 1990s during several extended stays at the Esalen Institute in Big Sur, California, where Michael Harner conducted courses in shamanic training. Having been trained in the 'universal' or 'near-universal' practices of Core Shamanism,[5] as Harner terms it, Gaup settled in Oslo and established himself among other professional shamans on the Norwegian alternative scene. Norwegian neo-shamanism at this point differed little from its Core Shamanism counterpart in the United States. A study of the leading New Age magazine *Alternativt Nettverk* (Alternative Network) found, for instance, that in the 1990s there were abundant references to indigenous people around the world, but references to the pre-Christian Sami religion had not yet been introduced (Christensen 2005). A fieldwork study in Tromsø (northern Norway) in the early 2000s similarly found few references to the pre-Christian Sami religion or to place-specific elements (Andreassen and Fonneland 2002/2003).

Approximately five years into the new millennium, this scenario changed. A sequel to the previous study of *Alternativt Nettverk* argued that interest in the Sami had increased, that a new generation of professional Sami neo-shamans had been established,[6] and that ancient Sami gods and practices had been added to the repertoire of Norwegian neo-shamanism (Christensen 2007). By the end of the first decade of the twenty-first century, a broad variety of offers was available, including courses on Sami shamanism, guided vision quests in Sápmi, healing sessions inspired by Sami shamanism, and courses in the making of ritual drums (*runebomme*). Adding to these products, a Sami shamanistic festival and a new religious organization have been established. The festival *Isogaisa* was initiated in 2010 as an annual event and receives financial support from the Sami Parliament and various other municipal and national sources. Shamans gather from 'every corner of the world' for a week-long combination of musical festival, seminars, courses and entertainment (Isogaisa 2014).

Three years later a local shamanic association called *Sjamanistisk Forbund* applied for and was granted the status of religious community by the county governor of Troms. As a registered religious community it qualifies for financial support relative to membership and has a licence to perform baptisms, weddings and funerals. Not

exclusively a Sami movement, the shamanic association is concerned
with the preservation of both Sami and Norse shamanic traditions.
There is a focus on both Sami and Norwegian ethnic identity, and –
as will be discussed below in more detail – attempts to merge the two
through evoking an ancient past in which they (presumably) were
not yet divided.[7]

Nature, Ethnicity and Links to the Past

European Pagans, Strmiska (2005: 16) notes, tend to emphasize 'cultural and spiritual traditions preserving ethnic identity', in contrast
with an emphasis on nature and a downplaying or dismissal of the
relevance of ethnic identity among Canadian and U.S. American
Pagans. The explanation, he suggests, can be found in differences
regarding ethnic issues, in the 'sheer complexity of ethnic identity
in modern Canada and the United States' (2005: 17) and the more
straightforward cultural setting of Europeans Pagans, in which
understanding and articulation of one's ethnic identity is 'often a far
more simple matter'.

While Sami neo-shamanism constitutes an example of the emphasis on ethnic identity among many European Pagans, it departs from
all the other tendencies referred to in this category. Issues related to
ethnic identity are, as already indicated, far from simple. The Sami
context includes communities who never 'lost' their ethnic identity
(particularly among the core Sami areas of Finnmark), individuals
who only as adults became aware of the Sami background of – in
some cases – their parents and grandparents, and individuals who
deny any connection with the Sami, whether due to continued feelings of shame and stigma or to lack of interest. Ethnic identity is nevertheless central to Sami neo-shamanism along with a strong emphasis
on nature. In fact, the complexities of ethnicity can – together with
the historical gap between the traditions of the past and the current
revival – to some extent explain the importance of nature. Time may
have passed, but the landscapes are still there offering points of connection between then–now and them–us. Ancestral landscapes are
generally favoured as sites of vision quests and trance journeys.
Shamans operating in southern parts of Norway offer tours to these
northern landscapes, usually to places known to have been sacred in
the past. The sacred geography of Sápmi is, moreover, evolving as
a result of both legal conditions and broader Sami interests in preserving it. Sacred places are perceived as important parts of the Sami

cultural heritage and are, in addition, singled out in both Norwegian legislation and in international laws as particularly worthy of protection (Kraft 2010).

Adding to this spatial dimension, the importance placed on nature can also be connected to the search for historical continuity and to notions of a timeless essence in Sami identity. Descriptions of the Sami's relationship to nature as 'spiritual' have been common during the last two decades, not only in religious circles and popular culture, but to some extent also in legal documents, public school educational programmes and statements by the Sami Parliament (Kraft 2009a). To Sami, neo-shamanism allows for notions of continuity with what is commonly referred to as the 'nature religion' of the past, in spite of obvious differences in settings, context, ideas and practices.

The concept of a spiritual relationship to nature can, due to the same logic, serve to distinguish Sami neo-shamanism from 'Norwegianness' (in which nature is also an important symbol, but without the spiritual dimension (Gullestad 1990)) and provide a mark of commonality with other indigenous peoples for whom the spiritual dimension is similarly pronounced. It is thus an identity-marker which distinguishes Sami neo-shamans from Norwegians (and Westerners in general), while at the same time linking them to indigenous peoples past and present.

Perhaps most surprising among links made to the pre-Christian past is the view of Laestadianism. Neo-Paganism is commonly perceived as opposed and hostile to Christianity of all sorts.[8] In the Sami case, Laestadianism has emerged as a connection to the pre-Christian path: as a bridge between then and now. What Minde (2008) has referred to as a radical and romantic version of the 'preservation thesis' in scholarly studies of Laestadianism appears to have been important to this construct. Laestadianism, this theory claims, provided room and shelter for ancient Sami religious ideas and practices, allowing their 'essentials' to remain intact. The old religion never really disappeared. Rather, the noaide found shelter under the cloak of the Laestadian healer (*leser*); the trance journey of the noaide lived on as *rørelse* (ecstatic outbursts known to occur during Laestadian ceremonies); and *joik* – the musical expressions of the noaide – lived on as folk-religious practices outside of the church.

Although marginal in scholarly circles (where it has been heavily criticized – see Kraft 2007 and Minde 2008), the preservation thesis has fared well outside of academia, where a few scholars with public profiles have added authoritative weight to it, and it appears to be taken for granted in Sami neo-shaman circles. Today the most influential voice of the radical version of the preservation thesis is Professor of Pedagogics at the University of Tromsø, Jens Ivar Nergård. Nergård is the author of several articles and books on Sami culture and religiosity (e.g., Nergård 2006). He is frequently cited in northern Norwegian media and has been involved in important governmental committees and actions (Kraft 2009a, 2009b). Synonymization of the noaide and the Laestadian healer is the most common expression of such perspectives. Ailo Gaup, for instance, in his books and on his Internet home pages, describes his first meeting with a noaide (the late Mikkel Gaup) during the above-mentioned demonstrations against the damming of the Alta Kautokeino River (Gaup 2005). Mikkel Gaup was at that time a well-known Laestadian leser and healer. However, during the last decade, he and others like him have been regularly referred to as shamans and, accordingly, as carriers of ancient traditions and links to the past.

Various other phenomena have, through the same logic, appeared as bridges to the past. The famous Sami world musician Mari Boine, to provide one publicly visible example, in her authorized biography describes how poems by Ailo Gaup opened for her a door to powers that she had been aware of during childhood, but had never understood or dared to take seriously (Tonstad 2012). Further developed through participation in Gaup's neo-shamanic courses, these interests have also shaped her views on music. Sami shamanism is to Boine an 'almost invisible thread' which runs through the 'shaking at the (Laestadian) houses of worship' and the Laestadian healers of her upbringing (Tonstad 2012: 109). She seeks during her concerts to invite people into this world of ancient powers – 'a dimension in which the audience opens the doors to their innermost being and becomes susceptible to spirit and journeys' (ibid., my translation).

A relative lack of hostility towards Laestadianism, at least in the public sphere, can be connected to its position as a preserver of the ancient past and of the inner essence of Sami spirituality. In addition, and equally important, Laestadianism is integral to the recent history of the Sami. This is not a missionary movement that invaded the Sami from outside. It was initiated and shaped from within, and its (Sami) members were victims of the same processes of colonization as the Sami in general. One important task of the noaide, according to Ailo Gaup, is to heal the wounds left by forced assimilation (Gaup 1992). Mari Boine, similarly, has been publicly open about the strictness of her Laestadian upbringing and her parents' continued hostility towards her choice of career, but has placed these stories in the context of the traumas inflicted upon the Sami from outside.

The position of mainstream Christianity and the Norwegian Lutheran national church is more ambiguous. The Norwegian state church has historically been an important contributor to the forced assimilation of the Sami and is, as such, more objectively to blame. However, the church leadership has apologized officially for these sins of the past and has, through initiatives such as a Sami Church Council (*Samisk Kirkeråd*, founded in 1992), made efforts to improve relations and facilitate Sami representation.[9] Meanwhile, parts of the mainstream Sami Christian communities are developing new and more pro-Sami theologies, many based upon a view of the pre-Christian Sami religion as 'the old testament of the Sami',[10] and at least some of them have been influenced by the previously mentioned preservation thesis (Kraft 2009a). Neo-shamans are not included among present forms of continuing influence. Mainstream Christians agree on a view of Sami neo-shamanism as basically a part of the New Age movement with few, if any, connections to the past.

Shamanism as World Heritage

Reconstructionism and eclecticism can be understood as different identity discourses, Strmiska (2005) suggests. Among these, Sami neo-shamans are on one level an example of the reconstructionist version, 'concerned with claiming an identity for themselves as faithful links in a long chain of spiritual but also ethnic and cultural traditions grounded in a particular place and among a particular people' (Strmiska 2005: 21). The discourse of eclectic Pagans 'flows in a different direction', with different traditions considered as gateways 'into deeper spiritual experience' and 'a general source of spiritual inspiration' (2005: 21–22). Again, Sami neo-shamanism is an example. The reconstructionist agenda of Sami neo-shamanism is set within a perennialist vision, which in practice ends up at the 'eclectic' end of Strmiska's continuum. Leading Sami neo-shamans like Ailo Gaup describe shamanism as having a universally common source consisting of many indigenous traditions. Shamanism is not a 'religion', because it was 'never founded, nor did it arise' (Sjamansonen 2013). It 'has been there all the time as an opportunity placed in us, as a learning experience pathway, and it constitutes today a "spiritual world heritage"' (ibid.). The 'us' in this statement refers to humanity writ large. Unlike the rest of humanity, however, indigenous peoples have kept alive these traditions from the past and are therefore in a privileged position to understand and transmit them. The preference of a strict Sami or more eclectic approach varies among established Sami neo-shamans, but the idea of such traditions as globally connected appears to be widespread, along with the notion of universal access combined with the privileged position of indigenous people.

The relationship between Sami neo-shamanism and a broader version of northern shamanism further complicates a distinction between eclectic and reconstructionist identity discourses. Indicative in this regard, *Sjamanistisk Forbund* was initiated by the Norwegian neo-shaman Kyrre Gram Franck, also known as White Cougar, in response to a vision from his ancestors (Fonneland 2015). White Cougar initially termed the movement the 'Norwegian Shaman Association', but upon a request from a Sami neo-shaman, Ronald Kvernmo, and after consultation with the spirits, he dropped 'Norwegian' to avoid provoking Sami participants. The main goal of the organization, initially presented in White Cougar's vision and included in its mission statement, is to further northern shamanic traditions and to reconstruct the primordial roots of Nordic shamanism – preferably five to ten thousand years back in time (Fonneland 2015). At this time, White Cougar believes, boundaries between the nature-related religious practices of different local tribes had not yet been clearly established.[11] Nordic shamanism is thus included in the perennialist notion of a 'spiritual world heritage' described by Ailo Gaup. Like Gaup, White Cougar is engaged in a reconstructionist favouring of a particular ethnic tradition (Nordic shamanism), and, like Gaup, he considers different shamanistic traditions as sources for the recovery of this particular path. Information and inspiration from other cultures may, he claims, 'to some extent contribute to the development of northern shamanic practice' (ibid.). Debates on the web pages of *Sjamanistisk Forbund* (http://sjamanforbundet.no/) reveal concerns in regard to the very idea of an organization, but little if any tension between Sami and Norwegian members or difficulties with the choice between a distinctive Sami or Norse/Sami approach (ibid.).

The distinction between reconstructionism and eclecticism, and between an ethnicity-based faith movement and 'New Age Paganism', is also confused by the relationship between professional neo-shamans and their clients. Both Norwegian and Sami neo-shamans operate in the New Age marketplace and offer their spiritual products for a price. Their customers range from those focusing particularly on Sami shamanism along reconstructionist lines to those who pick and choose more freely among whatever is available, including different shamanic traditions and other New Age products.

Discussions on the web pages of Ailo Gaup indicate, for instance, that many of his followers combine various approaches, even if they hold on to Gaup as their main teacher.

The combination of perennialism and a favouring of indigenous teachers and pathways constitutes a professional asset, distinguishing Sami neo-shamans from their non-Sami colleagues, while at the same time providing access for all. The Norwegian media and popular culture add further weight to this logic. Both local (northern Norwegian) and national news media have during the past decade given quite extensive attention to Sami neo-shamanism. In addition, journalists tend to place all Sami spiritual entrepreneurs within a shamanistic discourse more or less regardless of their beliefs and activities. An example of this is Ester Utsi – the founder and head of a guest house and spiritual retreat in Finnmark – who offers a wide selection of what from a religio-historical perspective classify as familiar New Age products, including crystal therapy, healing sessions and a pilgrimage in the tracks of her reindeer-herding ancestors, with planned stops along the route connected to the chakras, starting with the root chakra and ending at the crown. However, she is frequently referred to as a 'Sami shaman', and her offers are consistently framed as 'local' and 'traditional' – based on the traditions of her family and the ancient pathways of the Sami. In sharp contrast with media representations of New Age entrepreneurs, moreover, she is represented as a creative, sincere and positive contributor to both the Sami revival and local business. 'New Age' is normally a stigmatizing term in the Norwegian newsroom, connected to fake, superficial and money-making projects, whose actors are both naive and cynical (Kraft 2011). Sami shamanism, in contrast, is more or less consistently represented as belonging to an ancient tradition, as well as to the Sami revival and other indigenous cultures, and is usually treated respectfully and sympathetically. The colonial legacy can to some extent explain this situation, but the above tendencies also indicate the strength of what may be referred to as 'indigenous spirituality', with shamanism perceived as somehow typical of indigenous peoples, including the Sami.

Sami Neo-shamanism and Indigenous Spirituality

The coupling of shamanism and indigenous people is not unique to the Norwegian mediascape. It belongs, rather, to a more or less globally recognizable discourse on 'indigenous religion' as not only an umbrella category for the highly diverse traditions and practices of 'indigenous people', but also a specific formation equipped with a worldview and particular vocabulary of ideas and practices. I have in studies of Sami nation-building suggested the term 'indigenous spirituality' to denote this discourse (Kraft 2004, 2010). By indigenous spirituality I mean a more or less global discourse concerning the identity of indigenous people, based on centuries of primitivist discourse as well as the political agenda of the international indigenous movement, and constructed in contrast with 'Western' people, religions and traditions. A spiritual relationship to nature is perhaps the central concept of this discourse, along with references to a holistic worldview and environmentally friendly traditions and practices, frequently summarized in the notion of indigenous people as children of Mother Earth. A particular relation to time and space constitutes other central denominators. The category 'indigenous', Peter Beyer (2007: 103) has noted, is local by definition: it is what was 'here from the origins' as opposed to that which came here 'from somewhere else', relatively recently, and it is glocal in a 'rather particular sense' – as 'local variations on a globalized theme' (Beyer 2007: 103, 104).[12] Last, but not least, a sense of mission is frequently expressed. In the words of Gro Harlem Brundtland, former Norwegian Prime Minister and Director General of the World Health Organization:

> Indigenous peoples teach us about the values that have permitted humankind to live on this planet for many thousands of years without desecrating it. They teach us about holistic approaches to health that seek to strengthen the social networks of individual and communities, while connecting them to the environment in which they live. And they teach us about the importance of a spiritual dimension to the healing process.... Indigenous peoples teach us how to live more correctly. (Cited in Niezen 2009: 19)

The decision to dam the Alta Kautokeino River was made during Brundtland's era as Norwegian prime minister, two decades before her move to the international arena of the indigenous movement.[13] At that time, neither politicians nor protesters – Sami and Norwegians alike – used the spiritual vocabulary that was later to develop. The ethnopolitical leaders chose secular symbols: the *lavvu* (Sami traditional turf hut), *kofte* (Sami clothing) and the reindeer. Religious symbols, scholars have claimed, were taboo (Flemmen and Kramvig 2008: 114–17). Due primarily to their stigmatized past, one may assume, little serious research had at that time emerged, thus leaving the missionaries' accounts of the past unchallenged. The past, moreover, was no longer there – in terms of live traditions or memories – and the indigenous search for it had yet to happen.

During the last decade, (unspoken) restrictions on the use of Sami-Christian symbols have gradually weakened, alongside a turn to the vocabulary of indigenous spirituality. At Sápmi Theme Park, established around the turn of the century and situated near the Sami parliament buildings in Karasjok, information signs are shaped in the form of drums (Viken 2006). The drum has been included on the official map of Sápmi, drawn by the Sami artist Hans Ragnar Mathisen, and also appears on postcards (Conrad 2004). It was the main symbol on the web portal Sami Tour, a joint marketing agency for Sami tourism on the Internet that was launched in 2001[14] and was financed partly by the Sami Parliament (Fonneland 2013b). Sami-run schools offer courses in drum making (Fonneland and Kraft 2013). Sápmi Theme Park also provides tourists with a digital noaide as a guide to the products offered.

Outside of Sápmi, Sami art, music, film and popular culture have served to spread and popularize similar images for Sami audiences as well as for Norwegians. Nils Gaup's 1987 film *Pathfinder* (*Veiviseren* in Norwegian), featuring a prehistoric Sami society centred around a noaide, was a commercial success, was nominated for an Oscar, and is commonly regarded as important to identity-building among the Sami (Christensen 2013). The above-mentioned Mari Boine has throughout her career drawn inspiration from Sami traditions and the pre-Christian religion,[15] and her music may – as the foremost representative of indigenous and world music in Norway – more than any other single factor have helped normalize links to the pre-Christian past and indigenous cultures.

The Sami Parliament has supported many of these projects financially and through public awards and positive statements, but has, apart from references to 'a spiritual relationship to nature' and efforts towards the preservation of sacred places of the past, contributed little to the promotion of religious symbols and spiritual discourses. What today could be termed a spiritual or civil religious dimension of Sami nation-building belongs primarily to the less official fields of tourism, festivals, fiction, music and film, all of which are connected to both global trends and indigenous discourses. The result is not a faith movement in the ordinary sense of the term, but overlapping discourses that allow for both secular and religious interpretations and experiences.

A particularly suggestive example of such intersections is the staging of rituals or ritual-like performances in secular settings. The virtual noaide at Sápmi Theme Park and the Sami Tour web portal have already been mentioned. Rituals offered at the *Riddu Riddu* festival in Manndalen indicate both blurred boundaries between the secular and the spiritual, and the space provided for Sami neo-shamanism. Initiated by a group of youngsters in 1991, *Riddu Riddu* is an annual indigenous peoples' festival, gathering some 3,500 participants from all over the world.[16] Although mainly a music festival, it also facilitates an exchange of knowledge across indigenous cultures and, as a part of this project, 'traditional' rituals have regularly been organized. In 2003 the local media reported on what they described as the shamanic sacrifice of a goat performed by three Tuvan shamans. The incident was met with anger from local Christians, who feared that such performances could 'bring back shamanism' (Enoksen 2003a). The town council also discussed the possible revival of shamanism and for this reason considered withdrawing its economic support of the festival. However, the then bishop, Per Oscar Kjølaas, was supportive of the event. He argued that it was both understandable and positive that different aspects of Sami culture and history were now being brought to light, and, in addition, that the fact that historical references to Sami shamanism are limited makes it 'natural to gather information from people with a religion that may have much in common with Sami pre-Christian beliefs' (Enoksen 2003b, my translation).

At the 2007 *Riddu Riddu* festival, the play *Matki* was offered as an outdoor experience in which actors and audiences travelled to the world of the shaman. The play started with the purification of the participants, followed by a drum-guided journey in search of power animals. The audience and actors then had to solve a labyrinth task accompanied all the while by a joik-singing shaman and a dancer portraying the pre-Christian Sami goddess *Sáráhkká*. In the *Riddu Riddu* programme ritual participants were invited to a 'personal journey':

> The shaman lets part of you die and part of you wake up. The actor gives you a role, yourself. The healer helps you with your past and present. … Along the way you will meet Stallo, oracles, angels, crystal elves, the Mystic and many others. You can rest on a reindeer skin, in a *lavvu*. Become purified. You can die and be born again. Move on in life. As a newborn infant with all the experiences that the journey gives you … there is nothing new under the Sun. Wake up to the Old Time, revisited now. (*Riddu Riddu* programme, my translation, 27 July 2008)

Adding to this, celebrity shamans were given leading roles as actors; the chief shaman was played by Mikkel Gaup, who is today the best-known Sami actor in Norway, and whose interest in Sami neo-shamanism and healing is well known. Regional newspapers also noted that the director of *Matki* had attended courses by Ailo Gaup, who was one of the leading actors. This, in other words, was offered as both entertainment and ritual, and it was left for the participants to decide what to make of it – and what to experience through it. Indicative of broader tendencies in regard to the use of symbols and rituals from the pre-Christian Sami past, such initiatives tend to be positioned ambiguously between religion and a broader category of cultural heritage. In the context of Sami nation-building, symbols and practices from the pre-Christian past are usually classified as 'Sami cultural heritage'. Through this mild version of religiously-based nationalism, a discourse which has spread amongst European nation states during the two last decades, Sami nation-building can be placed on a par with Norwegian nation-building, without provoking Christians.[17]

Sami Religion: Cultural Heritage and Pagan Pathway

Sami neo-shamanism differs from many of the trends that have been depicted in Pagan studies and fits poorly with many of the established distinctions, patterns and categories. It does not, first, make sense to situate this movement at either end of Strimska's scale as reconstructionist or eclectic. Rather, I have argued in this chapter, these together constitute its theological profile. This combination, moreover, has been shaped by the complex mixtures of a postcolonial landscape, including the need for pragmatic manoeuvres on sensitive sites and the needs of professional businesses. The combination of reconstructionism and eclecticism allows for the open access demanded by the New Age market, while maintaining the main asset of Sami shamanism – its status as traditional and indigenous. In contrast with outward-looking shamans among Native Americans, the Sami neo-shamans are not accused of selling the secrets of the Sami or commercializing ancestral traditions. Rather, they are treated by Christian Sami as something else – as a part of the New Age movement. Meanwhile, discourses connected to Sami nation-building contain few, if any, references to Laestadianism, but draw increasingly on the religious symbols and rituals of the pre-Christian past. Although usually couched in the language of cultural inheritance, this recently established resource of Sami nation-building overlaps with the symbolic and ritual vocabulary of Sami neo-shamanism.

Christianity in this context carries colonial connotations and in addition lacks potential as a boundary marker between the Sami and Norwegians. The pre-Christian past, in contrast, allows for notions of independent origins, for boundary markers between Sami and Norwegian landscapes and for links to the broader community of indigenous peoples.

Notes

1 For a critical review of Pagan studies, see Davidson (2012).
2 The revival was led by a Sami theologian and Dean called Lars Levi Laestadius. See Kristiansen (2005) for an introduction to Laestadianism.
3 The Sami Parliament has only a consultative and advisory function to central government. It does not have legislative power.
4 Identity as Sami was in certain areas more or less wiped out. Ivar Bjørklund (1985) found in a study of the coastal area Kvænangen, based on censuses, that 1,200 were registered as Sami or Kven (descendants of Finnish people) in 1930. In 1950 the number had reduced to five.
5 Core Shamanism is defined on the web pages of Michael Harner's Foundation for Shamanic Studies as a system 'designed for Westerners to apply shamanism and shamanic healing successfully to their daily lives. This system is based upon the underlying universal, near-universal, and common features of shamanism – together with journeys to other worlds – rather than upon culture-specific variations and elaborations' (http://www.shamanism.org, accessed 21 June 2013).
6 Most profiled among these are Ailo Gaup, Eirik Myrhaug, Anita Biong and Ronald Kvernmo.
7 See Fonneland (2013a) for a more detailed account of the process leading up to the shamanic association and current attempts to develop a ritual repertoire and leadership structure.
8 Rountree (2011), in a study of Wicca and Paganism in Malta, provides another exception to this broader tendency.
9 The council consists of seven members with representatives from the three Sami groups in Norway – the North Sami, the Lule Sami and the South Sami – and has as its mission to further, protect and coordinate Sami church life.
10 The Sami priest Bierna Bientie and the leader of the Sami Church Council Tore Johnsen are perhaps the most radical and best-known voices of such attempts at reconciliation with the past. See, for instance, Bientie (2008) and Johnsen (2007). See Kraft (2009b) for a further discussion.

11 This is reflected in the programme of the organization and was confirmed in interviews with the religious historian Trude Fonneland (Fonneland 2013a).

12 For references to the spiritual dimensions of indigenous people and indigeneity, see Brosius (1997), Christensen (2013), Niezen (2009, 2012) and Tafjord (2015).

13 Brundtland was elected general director of the World Health Organization in 1998 and held this position until 2003.

14 The home page of the website (www.samitour.no, accessed 20 November 2013) featured a drum, and a drum-skin texture formed a background for the pages on the site. In addition, drumming was heard while browsing the site. The site was shut down in the spring of 2014.

15 Boine has received several awards, including the Nordic Council Music Prize. She was appointed knight in the Royal Norwegian Order of St Olav in 2009 and has, since 2012, held a position as an artist with national funding (*statsstipendiat*), the highest honour that can be bestowed on an artist in Norway.

16 *Riddu Riddu* is supported financially by the Sami Parliament and is commonly regarded as an important forum for the exhibition and exploration of Sami indigenous identity.

17 See Døving and Kraft (2013) for a study of the Norwegian discourse on cultural inheritance, which is based exclusively on Christianity.

References

Andreassen, B.O. and T. Fonneland. 2002/2003. 'Mellom Healing og Blå Energi: Nyreligiøsitet i Tromsø', *Din: Tidsskrift for Religion og Kultur* 4: 30–36.

Aspevoll, T.F. 2006. 'Sjamanen', *Klassekampen*, 11 March.

Beyer, P. 2007. 'Globalization and Glocalization', in J.A. Beckford and N.J. Demerath (eds), *The Sage Handbook of the Sociology of Religion*. Los Angeles: Sage, pp. 98–117.

Bientie, B. 2001. 'Det er Landet som eier Folket: Et Sørsamisk Økoteologisk Perspektiv', in H.J. Schorre and T.S. Tomren (eds), *Grønn Postill: Økoteologi og Kirkehverdag*. Oslo: Verbum forlag, pp. 134–41.

Bjørklund, I. 1985. 'Fjordfolket i Kvænangen: Etnisk Mangfold i ei Nordnorsk Bygdebok', in E. Niemi (ed.), *Minoritetsforskning og Kulturpolitikk*, NAVF 1985 – Forskningsnytt fra Norges Almenvitenskapelige Forskningsråd, 30(6–7).

Brosius, J.P. 1997. 'Endangered Forest, Endangered People: Environmentalist Representations of Indigenous Knowledge', *Human Ecology* 25(1): 47–69.

Christensen, C. 2005. 'Urfolk på det Nyreligiøse Markedet: En Analyse av Alternativt Nettverk'. Master's thesis, University of Tromsø.

———. 2007. 'Urfolksspiritualitet på det Nyreligiøse Markedet: En Analyse av Tidsskriftet Visjon/Alternativt Nettverk', *Din: Tidsskrift for Religion og Kultur* 1: 63–78.

———. 2013. 'Religion som Samisk Identitetsmarkør: Fire Studier av Film'. Ph.D. dissertation, University of Tromsø.

Conrad, J. 2004. 'Mapping Space, Claiming Place: The (Ethno-)Politics of Everyday Geography in Northern Norway', in A. Siikala, B. Klein and S. Mathisen (eds), *Creating Diversities: Folklore, Religion and the Politics of Heritage*. Helsinki: The Finnish Literature Society, pp. 165–89.

Davidson, M.A. 2012. 'What Is Wrong with Pagan Studies', *Method and Theory in the Study of Religion* 24(2): 183–99.

Døving, C.A. and S.E. Kraft. 2013. *Religion i Pressen*. Oslo: Universitetsforlaget.

Eidheim, H. 1998. 'Ethno-Political Development among the Sami after World War II: The Invention of Selfhood', in H. Gaski (ed.), *Sami Culture in a New Era: The Norwegian Sami Experience*. Karasjok: Davvi Girji, pp. 29–61.

Enoksen, R. 2003a. 'Frykter Sjamanisme på Riddu Riddu', *Nordlys*, 22 May.

———. 2003b. 'Sjamanisme på Riddu Kirka', *Nordlys*, 22 May.

Flemmen, A.B. and B. Kramvig. 2008. 'Møter: Sammenstøt av Verdier i Samisk-Norske Hverdagsliv', in O. Leirvik and Å. Røthing (eds), *Verdier*. Oslo: Universitetsforlaget, pp. 101–20.

Fonneland, T. 2013a. 'Isogaisa: Samisk Sjamanisme i festivaldrakt', *Aura* 5: 102–31.

———. 2013b. 'Sami Tourism and the Signposting of Spirituality: The Case of Sami Tour – a Spiritual Entrepreneur in the Contemporary Experience Economy', *Acta Borealia* 30(2): 190–208.

———. 2015. (In press). 'Approval of the Shamanistic Association: A Local Northern Norwegian Construct with Trans-local Dynamics', in J. Lewis and I.T. Bårdsen (eds), *Nordic New Religions*. Leiden: Brill.

Fonneland, T. and S.E. Kraft. 2013. 'Sami Shamanism and Indigenous Spirituality', in I.S. Gilhus and S. Sutcliff (eds), *New Age Spirituality: Rethinking Religion*. Durham: Acumen Publishing, pp. 132–45.

Gaup, A. 1992. *Natten Mellom Dagene*. Oslo: Gyldendal.

———. 2005. *The Shamanic Zone*. Oslo: Three Bears Company.

Gullestad, M. 1991. 'Naturen i Norsk Kultur: Foreløpige Refleksjoner', in T. Deichman-Sørensen and I. Frønes (eds), *Kulturanalyse*. Oslo: Gyldendal, pp. 81–96.

Isogaisa. 2014. http://www.isogaisa.org/. Accessed 5 May 2014.

Johnsen, T. 2007. *Jordens Barn, Solens Barn, Vindens Barn: Kristen tro i et Samisk Landskap*. Oslo: Verbum Forlag.

Kraft, S.E. 2004. 'Et hellig fjell blir til. Om Samer, OL og arktisk magi', *Nytt Norsk Tidsskrift* 3/4: 237–49.

———. 2007. 'Natur, Spiritualitet og Tradisjon: Om Akademisk Romantisering og Feilslåtte Primitivismeoppgjør' (Review-artikkel om Jens Ivar Nergårds, *Den levende erfaring: En studie i samisk kunnskapsproduksjon*), *Din: Tidsskrift for Religion og Kultur* 1–2: 53–62.

———. 2009a. 'Sami Indigenous Spirituality: Religion and Nation Building in Norwegian Sápmi', *Temenos: Nordic Journal of Comparative Religion* 4: 179–206.

———. 2009b. 'Kristendom, Sjamanisme og Urfolksspiritualitet i Norsk Sápmi', *Chaos* 51: 29–52.

———. 2010. 'The Making of a Sacred Mountain: Meanings of "Nature" and "Sacredness" in Sápmi and Northern Norway', *Religion: An International Journal* 40: 53–61.

———. 2011. *Hva er nyreligiøsitet*. Oslo: Universitetsforlaget.

Kristiansen, R. 2005. *Samisk Religion og Læstadianisme*. Oslo: Fagbokforlaget.

Minde, H. 2008. 'Constructing "Læstadianism": A Case for Sami Survival?', *Acta Borealia: A Nordic Journal of Circumpolar Societies* 15(1): 5–25.

Nergård, J.I. 2006. *Den Levende Erfaring: En Studie i Samisk Kunnskapsproduksjon*. Oslo: Cappelen.

Niezen, R. 2009. *The Rediscovered Self: Indigenous Identity and Cultural Justice*. London: McGill-Queen's University Press.

———. 2012. 'Indigenous Religion and Human Rights', in J. Witte and M.C. Green (eds), *Religion and Human Rights: An Introduction*. Oxford: Oxford University Press, pp. 119–34.

Paine, R. 1965. 'Læstadianismen og Samfunnet', *Tidsskrift for Samfunnsforskning* 6: 60–73.

Rountree, K. 2011. 'Localizing Neo-Paganism: Integrating Global and Indigenous Traditions in a Mediterranean Catholic Society', *Journal of the Royal Anthropological Institute* 17: 846–72.

Rydving, H. 1993. *The End of Drum-Time: Religious Change among the Lule Saami, 1670s–1740s*. Uppsala: Acta Universitatis Upsaliensis.

Sami Instituhtta. 2013. 'Prosjekt om samisk statistikk'. Last updated 24 June 2008. http://www.sami-statistics.info. Accessed 1 June 2013.

Sjamansonen. 2013. http://www.sjaman.com/. Accessed 21 June 2013.

Strmiska, M.F. 2005. 'Modern Paganism in World Cultures: Comparative Perspectives', in M. Strmiska (ed.), *Modern Paganism in World Cultures: Comparative Perspectives*. Santa Barbara: ABC-CLIO, pp. 1–53.

Tafjord, B.O. 2015. In press. 'How Talking about an Indigenous Religion May Change Things: An Example from Talamanca'. *Numen*.

Tonstad, P.L. 2012. *Fly Med Meg*. Oslo: Kagge Forlag.

Viken, A. 2006. 'Tourism and Sami Identity: An Analysis of the Tourism–Identity Nexus in Sami Community', *Scandinavian Journal of Hospitality and Tourism* 6(1): 6–24.

2

It's Not Easy Being Apolitical

Reconstruction and Eclecticism in Danish Asatro

Matthew H. Amster

Introduction

This chapter considers the marginal position of ethnic politics in the context of contemporary Danish Asatro[1] (Nordic neo-Paganism) and recent efforts of ritual innovation.[2] It begins by sketching the general context of Danish Asatro, where one observes a common concern regarding the mixing of religion and politics, offering examples of individuals at the extremes of the political spectrum in the movement. It then turns to a discussion of the emergence of a new Asatro group, Nordisk Tingsfællig (NTF), which was formed in 2010 out of a concern for practising religion in an environment free of politics.

Forn Siðr is the largest Asatro organization in Denmark, claiming approximately seven hundred members nationwide (Forn Siðr: Asa- og vanetrosamfundet i Danmark 2013). Since 2003 Forn Siðr has been recognized by the government as an official religious organization (*trossamfund*), a situation that legitimizes the Asatro movement. Forn Siðr functions as an umbrella organization for individuals in the numerous, smaller, local groups in Denmark, where most religious ritual activity actually takes place. In breaking away from Forn Siðr and forming NTF, the founders of this latter group, many of whom had been active in founding Forn Siðr, sought to create an organization that would be more definitively apolitical, as well as to move away from some of the increasingly standardized ritual practices of Danish Asatro. Members of NTF, as is discussed below, are in the process of innovatively seeking to create new forms of ritual

more closely linked to historical sources – a kind of hybrid of reconstructionist and eclectic forms of Paganism – yet do so in a way that
unambiguously rejects the possibility of their practices being linked
in any way to ethnically tinged or nationalistic political views.

The discussion offered here thus provides a counter example to
other neo-Pagan movements in Europe, particularly those in Russia
and Ukraine, which have been characterized as linking reconstructionist forms of religious expression to nationalistic impulses or
racially motivated and exclusionary expressions of ethnicity (Ivakhiv
2005; Shnirelman 2007). As Strmiska (2005) has noted, one can
see this trend among modern Pagan groups who seek to recreate a
more 'authentic' or primordial form of religion, with a tendency for
such 'Reconstructionist' forms of religious expression to be linked
to politically controversial ethnic or nationalistic projects. At the
other end of the spectrum, Strmiska (2005: 20) identifies 'Eclectic'
neo-Paganisms,[3] referring to those whose practices are universalistic
in style and whose adherents generally oppose a tendency to associate religion with ethnic politics. Such a dichotomy or spectrum of
'Eclectic' and 'Reconstructionist' forms of neo-Paganism is not so
clear in Denmark. As this chapter shows, Danish Asatro is marked by
heterogeneous and individualistic forms of spiritual expression and,
in most cases, people in the movement want to foster an environment
free of politics. The case of NTF's formation offers an example of a
reconstructionist-type group that, unlike those Strmiska describes,
firmly rejects even the slightest taint of a political agenda, representing a kind of unique hybrid that is well suited to the Danish context.

Asatro (or Ásatrú) is a polytheistic religious movement focused on
the Norse gods and beings historically rooted in northern Europe.
It is also today a complex and multifaceted global movement that
exists in many forms, including far right- and left-wing manifestations. People who identify as Asatro tend to draw inspiration from a
range of Icelandic texts: central among them are the Eddas, the richest
source of information on Norse mythology. This corpus of texts
includes the *Hávamál*, a poem attributed to the god Odin, which
offers detailed guidance on ethics and conduct and is thus used by
people in shaping their contemporary religious practice. The Eddas
inscribe stories about two classes of gods and mythical figures, most
notably the Æsir and Vanir, formerly warring gods who eventually
joined forces. Most Asatro groups today worship both the Æsir and
Vanir, though the term 'Asatro' ('belief in the Æsir') only implies the
first pantheon – one reason why groups prefer names like Forn Siðr
(essentially meaning the 'old ways'), and then refer to the fact that

they worship both Æsir and Vanir in their statement of beliefs. Some of the better-known Æsir gods are Odin, Thor, Frigg and Balder, while Vanir include the famous siblings Freya and Freyr.

The roots of modern Danish Asatro can be traced to a similar movement that emerged in the 1970s in Iceland (Strmiska 2000) and which has been followed by similar groups forming in Sweden and Norway in the 1980s and 1990s (Gregorius 2008; Skott 2000). A wide variety of Asatro and related, often far right-wing Odinist groups exist around the world, including White separatist groups (Gardell 2003) and left-oriented Heathen and Pagan groups aligned with Wicca and New Age movements (Strmiska 2007). A notable theme in the literature on Asatro is the tendency for groups to factionalize or split based on differences of political orientation, leading to break-ups and reorganizations (Kaplan 1996).

To date, little has been written about Asatro from a scholarly per-spective in Denmark (Bøgelund 2008; Warmind 2007), though the movement has been heavily covered in the Danish popular press. Despite the country's central location in the former Viking world, only since the mid 1990s has there been a florescence of Asatro activ-ity. People interviewed in the course of this research universally acknowledged this florescence as one linked to the spread of infor-mation on the Internet, which gave people access to ideas and inspi-ration from other movements around the world (c.f. Rountree 2010: 58). From the very beginning, people in the movement in Denmark were largely aware of conflicts over politics that occurred in other countries and were eager to avoid repeating such conflicts; hence a concerted effort to articulate tolerant views was part of Forn Siðr's ideological principles when it was established in the late 1990s.

Ritual and Belief in Danish Asatro

The research upon which this chapter is based was conducted between January and August 2012.[4] I conducted sixteen in-depth interviews, was present at seven rituals and was permitted to film four of these rituals in their entirety (two group *blót* rituals – see discussion below – and two private ones). There is considerable diversity in how people conceptualize their spiritual beliefs in Danish Asatro and wide acceptance of the fact that people do not adhere to a consistent set of beliefs. As a result of this heterogeneity in the move-ment, people are essentially free to invent the religion for themselves, though the typical rituals held by most groups have become fairly

standardized. This was a source of concern for many people I interviewed, who resisted the idea of having a fixed set of ritual expecta-
tions. Contemporary Danish neo-Paganism, or Heathenry (this term
is closer to the Danish terms *Hedenskab* and *Hedensk*), is also very
influenced by Danish values that include a strong aversion to mixing
religion and politics.

The main framework for ritual practice is to hold blóts, a term
which implies giving sacrifice, having its etymological root in the
practice of giving blood sacrifice (Strmiska 2007: 165).[5] Blóts today
are generally held four times a year around the time of the solstices
and equinoxes, a fact that suggests influence from the global neo-
Pagan scene, as well as having some basis in Norse paganism. The
basic template for a blót is for people to gather in a circle in a special
location in nature (such as a forest, bog or meadow) at sundown, led
by one or more person/s acting as a ritual leader of the ceremony,
referred to as a *gode* or *gydje* (for men and women respectively).
Remote locations may be chosen, but ancient or historically important sites may also be used. All present will usually stand for the
entire ceremony, which begins with the circle being formally closed
by the gode or gydje, who simply announces that the ceremony is to
begin (see Figure 2.1). The enclosed space is then used to make toasts
to the gods as a horn of mead is passed around the circle. During
the blót, people can freely offer their thoughts and words into the
circle, with many offering objects, including food and drink, as a sacrifice. Most blóts include three rounds of toasts, sometimes focused

Fig. 2.1 *Aarhus Blótlaug's midsummer ritual, held at Lindholm Høje, June 2012. Author's photograph.*

on a particular deity or theme, and will always include the opportunity for personal reflection. Typically the first round of toasts is for a specific god or gods, the second is for the ancestors and the third reserved for personal toasts and reflection.

As the horn is passed, people can choose to speak to the gods and hail them or can remain silent, either drinking from the horn or pouring out mead as an offering, before passing it to the next person. There is generally no set script for a blót, although the gode or gydje usually has an overall plan or outline in mind expressing the general aims of the blót, which will often be influenced by the season in which the ceremony is being held. An important component of most blót rituals is the feast which is held afterwards, considered an integral part of the ritual. In most instances, people will ideally gather for the entire weekend, often at a rented camp or retreat (Scout camps are a favourite), where they can spend an entire night eating, drinking and socializing. The consumption of alcohol is a significant part of the overall proceedings, and blóts are festive events and a time to meet up with good friends.

A common theme echoed by the majority of Asatro interlocutors was that Christianity, as it exists today in Denmark, has little to offer them personally. This perspective is one shared by many secular Danes, who have been described as one of the least religious peoples in the world and even, perhaps in somewhat overstated terms, as 'a society without God' (Zuckerman 2008).[6] Many Asatro emphasized their view that pre-Christian values also have something important to offer as a critical part of their identity as modern Danes, noting values such as the importance of deeds over thoughts and action over belief, which was often contrasted with Christianity's focus on thought and intention. Virtually everyone described in individualistic terms how Asatro fitted their own notions of freedom and self-sufficiency, which they believed all people should have in determining their choice of spirituality (or lack of it), and this included a disdain for proselytizing. This expression of the importance of individual autonomy helps contextualize why many Asatro are also resistant to being part of large, formal organizations such as Forn Siðr. Many people who self-identified as Asatro eschewed involvement in formal groups, and among those active in Forn Siðr, many asserted that their main affinity was to smaller, local groups who make up the component-member blóts that constitute Forn Siðr. A number of individuals encountered at Viking markets also claimed to be Asatro, but often did not participate in any formal blót groups or organization. It is impossible to estimate the number of such solo worshippers. One woman in her late twenties, a devoted Viking martial artist, considered herself to be Asatro, but told me that she had never been to a formal blót, nor did she have the desire to do so. For her, being Asatro was deeply connected to her own sense of spirituality, though she rarely performed rituals at home either. Being a Viking martial artist and attending Viking events and markets was a better expression of her beliefs than being part of a blót group. Comparing herself to mainstream Christians in Denmark who go to church infrequently, she asked: 'Why can't I be Asatro that way too?'

Many people asserted that Asatro was not really a new religion, but rather that they were rediscovering something that had always been there and just fallen out of common practice. Thus, as Gregorius has noted in Sweden, 'Modern Asatro does not create a new ethnic identity, but rather gives an already existing ethnic identity new content' (Gregorius 2008: 43).[7] When asked whether one needs to have Danish blood to feel these gods, most (but not all) of the people I spoke to overwhelmingly rejected the idea that it was somehow genetic, though many stressed that the geography and physical landscape, including the presence of the sea, were important components of their special relationship to the gods and their nature-oriented spirituality. It was seen as 'logical' that the Norse gods would be felt and experienced most vividly in the Nordic countries, but this would not preclude non-Nordic people from experiencing them. As Signe, a woman in her forties, explained:

> What really matters is what you feel deep within yourself, and in your heart, that you can connect to some of the values that are in Asatro. It doesn't depend on what background you actually come from. If you can really deeply believe that you want to live the way that the *Hávamál* says, that you want to live a life in honour, honour your word, respect other people, fight for what you believe in, bring sacrifices for things that you want, then you can call yourself an Asatro, no matter what colour your hair, or what background you have.

Each person interviewed offered a slightly different take on what the gods and the religion (or religion in general) meant to them. Martin, a man in his early sixties, who defines himself as a devout Asatro practitioner and is active in many groups, explained that he also considers himself to be an 'atheist', since he does not believe gods exist in a literal sense. Martin uses Asatro 'as a tool in the modern world to get in touch with things in nature that are not easy to grasp', and for him the gods are highly symbolic aspects of nature and humanity that are themselves fundamentally 'true and real'. For Martin, as for many others within the movement, being Asatro has been a kind of 'coming home' to something 'familiar' after feeling disappointed with the Christian Church. Others asserted that they believed the gods were real, but not necessarily resembling anthropomorphic entities as depicted in mythology. One person spoke about the gods in physiological terms, as a type of chemical process in the brain, while another said that the gods were a kind of linguistically formed thought process. Quite commonly, the gods were described in terms of their attributes or the aspects of humanity each represents (for example, Thor as powerful, Odin as wise, Freya as loving).[8] One person suggested that they are 'archetypes' that represent 'forces in the universe that we can't control one way or another'. Only a few people said that they thought of the gods as literal beings whom they could actually see and hear speak, and even for these people the focus was mainly on what the gods symbolized and represented.

A number of people suggested that if they travelled elsewhere they might feel the presence of other local gods, just as a person coming from another country to Denmark might be attuned to the power of the Norse gods. However, there were others who expressed a different view on this, raising the possibility that being Asatro was somehow a genetically rooted predisposition. The people who expressed such beliefs were also aware of the controversial nature of such views, and felt that they could not be vocal about expressing them in Forn Siðr. A man in his fifties who has held leadership roles in Forn Siðr said that in his view all Danish people have a 'predisposition for Asatro' and 'some of that collective memory is in the genes', but this does not make a person a racist or neo-Nazi: 'that is not racism in my world; that is almost logical'.

Expressed in less controversial terms, many people described how they felt a connection to the Norse gods that had deep personal roots, as part of their family upbringing and even education, often claiming it to be something they had felt since childhood and citing stories they had heard in school and from parents and grandparents, which had fed a natural curiosity and interest in developing a sense of connection to these particular gods. Describing their initial 'discovery' that they were Asatro, people often presented the realization as something they came to entirely on their own, often before they knew of any organizations they could join to worship these gods collectively. Clearly there are no firm rules guiding what it means to be Asatro in Denmark today in terms of either belief or ritual practice, and virtually everyone I spoke with asserted that this is part of what makes being Asatro interesting. Not surprisingly, the very act of creating standardized rituals, as has been necessary to do as part of Forn Siðr's recognition as an official religion by the government, has been a source of tension since people in the community hold such heterogeneous beliefs and resist adhering to fixed rules about how rituals should be performed.[9]

The Issue of Politics in Danish Asatro: Three Examples

There now follow examples of three individuals, the first and second representing views from right- and left-wing perspectives respectively and the third a more typical, middle-of-the-road or mainstream orientation. The purpose of presenting these three viewpoints is to show a range of political views among modern Asatro and illustrate how the very act of having a political orientation in the movement puts individuals in a kind of marginal position, which I believe reflects the common aversion to mixing religion and politics in Danish society.

I arrived in Denmark in the dead of winter, assuming that this would be a good time to begin research and meet people willing to have in-depth conversations about their personal involvement in Asatro, given it was a cold and dark time of year, when people were often at home and welcomed visitors. I contacted the public representative for the Aarhus Blótlaug, asking to be put in touch with people who would be willing to be interviewed and requesting permission to attend any upcoming events. My request for contacts was forwarded to the entire group membership and I rapidly received calls and emails from people eager to meet. What was notable about the people who initially contacted me was how atypical they were in light of the majority of people I eventually talked to who were involved in Danish Asatro. Among these interviews were both extreme right- and left-wing members of the Aarhus Blótlaug, each eager to have their highly idiosyncratic views heard, in no small measure because such views were not widely accepted in mainstream Asatro.

One of these interviews was with a sincere, young, working-class man in his early twenties. Not long ago, as a teenager, Rasmus (a pseudonym) had violently clashed with rival Muslim youth gangs and he had recently served time in prison for an assault with a weapon. This conflict-ridden upbringing clearly shaped his xenophobic views toward Muslim immigrants, and Rasmus felt that Asatro was a religion exclusively for Danes, something that he saw as clearly having a genetic foundation in his blood. He was proud of the numerous tattoos that adorned his body emphasizing Norse mythological images and runic sayings and providing an indelible link to his ances-tors. Despite his extreme views on immigration and the primordial aspects of the Asatro religion, Rasmus acknowledged the importance of members of the Danish Asatro movement distancing themselves from the neo-Nazi groups, with whom he does not share political sympathies, being explicitly opposed to fascism. In speaking with Rasmus for many hours, it was clear that his views were nuanced and complex and that Asatro had become a positive outlet for him, pro-viding a community of support and rich symbolic resources to affirm his identity. However, Rasmus felt his particular views could not be openly expressed in the Danish Asatro scene and explained that he was normally very careful to express them only 'in subtle ways'.

At the other end of the political spectrum is Ole Nielsby, a man in his sixties and one of the original founders of Forn Siðr. Ole embraces a kind of universalistic polytheism and personally acknowledges the existence of deities not just in the Nordic tradition, but in fact, in all traditions. Ole thinks it is possible that all gods are real, whether they are Norse, Greek, Inuit or even the monotheistic Christian God. For Ole, the world is a highly spirited place. While he sees no inherent connection between ethnicity and religion, he does see his spiritual-ity as being fundamentally political in that it shapes a worldview that demands political action against monolithic structures of the military-industrial complex which he fears is too much in control of people's lives. For Ole, political and spiritual views are inherently entangled and, like Rasmus with whom he regularly interacts, he acknowledged this has also placed him in a marginal position in Danish Asatro. Ole traces his particular marginality to an interview he did in 2002 for a primetime television show in which he and some members of Forn Siðr performed a ritual to show the Danish general public that what Forn Siðr (newly formed at the time) was doing was not some sort of Satanic ritual or animal sacrifice as some believed. At the festive meal that followed, Ole made a toast to a Greek god and asked the journalist hosting the show to use that toast in the television pro-gramme. When it was broadcast, he said, it 'caused a great stir in the Asatro movement', particularly since Forn Siðr was in the process of seeking government recognition. Ole's toast was seen as a kind of Norse Pagan blasphemy, because, as he explained, 'it is forbidden in an official blót to call on other deities outside the Nordic tradition, which I think is ridiculous' and clearly 'a concept of religious purity that comes from Christianity'.

Christina is a teacher and mother in her early forties. When we met she was new to the Asatro movement, having only been involved for about a year. Her husband is an atheist and not involved, though she shares her interest in Asatro with her twelve-year-old son who has had a longstanding interest in the Norse gods. Christina explained that it was her son's interest that drew her into the movement, and that getting involved has provided a source of common activity and interest for them. Christina began our conversation talking about Christianity and how, despite trying to find meaning in going to church, she considers the Danish Church to be sterile and boring, with no real room for people to express themselves or come together as a community. In contrast, she described being in a blót as a kind of big 'group therapy session' and a place of peacefulness and calm. Before coming to Asatro, Christina had dabbled in Buddhism and alternative spirituality, including training as a Reiki healer, which she has tried without success to combine with Asatro beliefs. For Christina, Asatro is about people coming together and sharing as a community, offering a needed break from a modern society, which she believes is on the wrong track.

Christina adhered to her own personal version of Asatro and stressed that it is well suited to Danish society, where individualistic approaches to spirituality and belief are permissible. For instance, she pointed out that while she personally believed in reincarnation, this is not something that was common among fellow Asatro. 'I am a very modern person in that I take a bit from here and there, from all the religions, and then just bake a cookie of my own and eat it, and that's my religion'. Christina expressed her feeling that Danes are not very friendly to one another and that this has left a 'hole in society that needs filling in some way'.[10] In Asatro, she has found an alternative to the secular mainstream.

> We talk about all sorts of things when we help each other in preparing the dinner we eat after the blót. I think we need that here in Denmark, I think we need to find communities again. But nobody seems to have the time. It's all about job and family, and we run around, and our kids go to soccer and handball, and we drive them around and there's no peace, there's no calmness any more. I think we are all stressed out, and it is not good for our nation to be so stressed.

Christina was decidedly uninterested in the topic of links between ethnic politics and Asatro, and essentially unaware of past or present tensions in Forn Siðr regarding such issues. This was simply not something that had been apparent to her from the three blóts she had attended, and questions about politics seemed to take her by surprise. In terms of her own views, she was opposed to the anti-immigrant policies of the populist, right-oriented Danish People's Party (Dansk Folkeparti). She was personally committed to tolerance and multi-culturalism and disturbed by the idea that discriminatory or racist views might be present in Forn Siðr, an organization in which she was enthusiastic to become more involved. However, she asserted that if such views existed, she had not witnessed them, speculating that one might perhaps find such views expressed in online forums, rather than in face-to-face at settings – an insight I found quite plau-sible given that online forums seem to allow people to feel less shy about expressing controversial positions. Christina, like most Asatro, was drawn to the religion for reasons of spirituality and community, and did not perceive it as a place for political expression.

The examples of Rasmus, Ole and Christina illustrate the tenuous place of politics in Danish Asatro. As members of the same blót group, they also show how quite diverse views can coexist in this movement, where open expressions of politics are generally not a very visible part of the ritual activities that periodically bring people together.

The Birth of Nordisk Tingsfællig (2010–Present)

Nordisk Tingsfællig (NTF) was conceived as a response to discon-tent among a small group of longstanding members of Forn Siðr, including the then-current chair of the board and other former board members. During the annual Forn Siðr *Alting* (the annual member-ship meeting) in spring of 2010, Danny Johansen, a career soldier and outgoing chair of the board, introduced a motion together with another member to make it unacceptable for members of Forn Siðr to express anti-monotheistic (that is, anti-Christian, anti-Islamic, anti-Semitic etc.) views. When I spoke with Danny at an NTF midwinter gathering in February 2012, he explained that they had introduced the motion as a symbolic gesture to spark debate, and with the hope of exposing what they saw as complacence toward intolerant views inside Forn Siðr. While they had expected it to fail, they were nonetheless surprised by how forcefully the motion was opposed. The way the vote went led Danny, along with ten others, to resolve to leave Forn Siðr and start a new organization – just six years after Forn Siðr had gained recognition as an official organiza-tion, something many of them had personally worked very hard to obtain. Today, NTF is still a very small group with about twenty members.

One explanation for the controversy at the 2010 Forn Siðr Alting was that members of another new group, called Hefjendur, were vocally opposed to the motion. Hefjendur had been started in 2007 and, like NTF, consists of about twenty to thirty members, with about ten core members. Hefjendur joined Forn Siðr as an affiliated group in 2009 and was perceived as having right-wing views, based on the online postings of its members. In particular, controversy was sparked over the fact that members of Hefjendur and the organization's website have used the term 'ethnopluralism', a term used by the European Right when advocating ethnic separatism.[11] Hefjendur's website asserts that they 'take pride in being Nordic' and states clearly that they are opposed to oppressing others and are anti-totalitarian (*Fælles ideologiske principper* 2013). Unfortunately, I did not interview members of Hefjendur to get their perspective.

The idea behind the formation of NTF was that it would be apolitical, leaving no room for any question about rejecting intolerance in any form. As Mathias Nordvig, one of the founders and the main ritual organizer, pointed out: 'The problem is that politics – this constant either fear of or love for the radical Right – plays such a big role in this environment'. Mathias feels that one cannot be naive and take an ambiguous stance on such issues, which he thinks has started to happen inside Forn Siðr as people with right-wing views join the organization. In contrast, NTF has been careful in crafting its founding in such a way that its position on intolerance cannot be altered or overturned by a future board. The organization's foundational documents assert they 'will not in any way or on any level be associated with either groups or individuals who equate religion and race, blood, genes [or] ethnicity or who assume that one of these factors is a prerequisite for the other' (Nordisk Tingsfælligs formål 2013). The motivation for NTF forming was thus propelled by wanting to disassociate from Forn Siðr out of concern for what its founders perceived to be a growing acceptance of intolerant views in the organization.

It is important to note, however, that some people in Forn Siðr saw the departure of these members and the creation of NTF as an overreaction, and one that also had to do with personal disagreements. A number of people active in Forn Siðr, including in leadership roles, assured me that intolerance in any form is not openly accepted in the organization and things have been calm at subsequent Altings since 2010. Unquestionably, there are more people with left-leaning political views in Forn Siðr than people with right-wing views, and I was told that people with such diverse views coexist mainly by avoiding discussing politics.

Since forming, NTF has not only been trying to decisively remove politics, or even the hint of politics, from religious practice, but its members have also pursued a creative religious agenda. Through the framework of NTF, members have sought to create an alternative to what some in the group see as a rather weak expression of spirituality in modern Asatro; NTF is trying to connect more explicitly to Old Norse sources for modern aims. This is in no small measure due to the influence of Mathias Nordvig, who is in the final stages of a Ph.D. and doing some teaching in the Nordic Language and Literature division of the Department of Aesthetics and Communication at Aarhus University, and is a scholar of old Nordic literature.

Mathias grew up in Greenland, raised by his Danish Asatro mother who regularly held family feasts to honour the gods. He refers to himself as an '*Asadyrker*' (or Asa-practitioner) rather than Asatro (or Asa-believer), since this places emphasis on actions and deeds rather than belief and creed, the latter being aspects of religion he claims are more important to Christianity. Through his work in NTF, he has actively been using his knowledge of old sources to creatively craft new religious practices, as evidenced by the ritual at the Gudenå spring, described below. Mathias and others in NTF want to try to move away from what have become fairly standard ritual practices in modern Asatro – the holding of blót circles – and invent something new. In Mathias's view, standard Asatro blóts are inappropriate to the Danish context, having been more or less adapted from the Wicca movement, and, as he sees it, having diverse ways to worship is 'really what being polytheistic should be about'.

The Ritual at the Gudenå Spring

Mathias's goal was to design something that both had contemporary significance and resonated more concretely with what can be gleaned from old sources. He is acutely aware that he and his fellow NTF members are not trying to reenact what was done in the Viking era, nor making claims to be doing truly authentic rituals, which they know is not possible. At the same time, he personally rejects what he calls the 'Wicca-esque' format of mainstream blóts and is eager to experiment with creating something different that may eventually be adapted by NTF. With this in mind Mathias (under the auspices of a ritual group he created called Hiort Godeord) crafted an annual ritual cycle that begins the New Year with a spring fertility ritual, the first one of which was held on 17 May 2012 at the springs in the

Fig. 2.2 *Mathias (left) leading the procession with the statue of Freya to the Gudenå spring. Author's photograph.*

centre of Jutland, which are the sources of the two major rivers in western Denmark.[12]

The ritual centred around a goddess figure, who, Mathias notes, has historically gone by many names, but most commonly Freya, represented at the ritual by a carved wooden statue. A number of ceremonies were performed as part of this afternoon-long event, starting with a gathering by a burial mound near the springs, where the ancestors and gods were consulted to take part in the proceedings. This was followed by a procession, with singing, carrying the statue of Freya ceremoniously to the spring where the Gudenå (the Gods' River) has its ultimate source (Figure 2.2). Once at the spring, each member took part in a ritual of cleansing (Figure 2.3), as well as having a private moment alone with the statue of Freya, where they could make their own requests and then hammer a Danish two-kroner coin, which has a hole in the centre, onto the figure – a ritual copied from Celtic sources but which Mathias speculates had Norse parallels (Figure 2.4). A number of offerings were made, mostly consisting of food and alcoholic drinks. This was then followed by a picnic lunch, itself a part of the ritual, since eating with the gods is viewed as a ritual undertaking.

After the event, the statue of Freya was given an itinerary around Denmark, being transported to various locations where she could gather strength and stay in members' homes before returning to the mouth of the river in mid-October of 2012 for a final ceremony near Randers. Mathias described this culminating ceremony (at which I

Fig. 2.3 *Participants wash with water from the Gudenå spring as part of the cleansing ritual. Author's photograph.*

Fig. 2.4 *Hammering a Danish two-kroner coin onto the statue of Freya. Author's photograph.*

was not present) as taking place near a small dock, with all present standing on land, toasting the goddess, as each member went out on the dock and prayed to Freya individually, placing home-baked bread on a small raft which was floated out into the river. Once again offerings of two-kroner coins were made, this time to the river. Mathias said that next time they plan to make a small Viking ship to float their offerings out to sea. For Mathias, the key architect of these rituals, the cycle was designed to promote a connection to the landscape and the fertility and power that emerges from nature, using the Gudenå spring as a literal location, a source of this local power, and spreading its power into the wider world:

> What is important in relation to this ritual is to bring the goddess of fertility out, to make sure she gets the power that she needs from the spring of Gudenå, which is a power centre in the country, and then make sure she is taken to other places around the country to spread the power to other places, so everybody can gain something from this religious action. (Mathias Nordvig, 17 May 2012)

A key motivation for designing new rituals was linked to Mathias's desire to put a more concerted focus on actions, rather than words. 'I was thinking regarding this ritual, that it is important that we actually do something, that we show what we are doing rather than say it'. He acknowledged that there is no point in trying to reconstruct rituals that are no longer viable in modern Danish society, such as animal sacrifice, even if the historical sources point to it having been done. Nonetheless, the idea of creating rituals focused on actions and deeds, and which actively engage with the gods, is at the core of his mission to improve Danish Asatro, and Mathias calls himself a 'fundamentalist' practitioner of this religion.

Not surprisingly, Mathias is also knowledgeable about the Asatro movement worldwide and fully aware of the political views that have been linked to Nordic-inspired and Germanic forms of Paganism. He is personally disappointed by the extremes one finds in the movement, and thinks that people in the Danish movement take too lightly the racist implication of certain views. He also finds the movement as a whole, not just in Denmark, too 'New Age' in orientation, noting that people are focused more on their own personal satisfaction than actively worshiping the gods. He jokingly called blóts 'therapy sessions' rather than religious rituals, and personally does not want to stand in a circle passing a horn with mead. While other NTF members expressed similar views, many still participate in standard blót ceremonies. It is clear, however, that people in NTF are trying to experiment with ritual innovation, and this is entirely permissible as part of the range of expressions in Danish Asatro. Whether NTF will grow and flourish like Forn Siðr or fade away, as has happened with many other groups, remains to be seen.

Conclusion

As mentioned at the outset of this chapter, Strmiska (2005) has suggested that one can identify two different general types in terms of the orientations of modern Pagan groups. On one end of this spectrum are what he calls 'Reconstructionists', who attempt to do things as authentically as possible and who tend to also see ethnic identity, race and nationalistic agendas as linked to, and in some instances the basis or motivation for, neo-Pagan revivals. At the other extreme are 'Eclectics', who Strmiska suggests are more accepting of innovation and reinterpretation, prone to borrow from other Pagan groups, and generally not concerned about ethnicity or heritage as a basis for participation. 'Not surprisingly, people for whom ethnic identity is very important tend to prefer the Reconstructionist form of modern Paganism, and people with little interest or even a positive distain for issues of ethnic identity tend to prefer the Eclectic type' (Strmiska 2005: 20). Strmiska is careful to note that this pattern is not always straightforward and it is possible to find variations. Indeed, NTF essentially reverses this correlation, providing an example of a group for whom authenticity and historical accuracy are explicitly linked to a vehemently non-political agenda, fiercely opposing the linking of religion to ethnic politics. In this sense, NTF are eclectic-reconstructionists, who reject and embrace elements of both predispositions.

As Blain (2005: 181) has pointed out in the case of Britain, people involved in contemporary Heathenry are 'attempting to "reindigenize" their perceptions and worldview, to develop a spirituality that works in today's cultures but connects with history and prehistory'. As I have observed in Denmark, one of the biggest challenges for such groups is how 'to link spirituality with the land in ways that avoid the clichés of nationalist discourse' (Blain 2005: 206). As part of trying to find this balance, members of NTF are exploring new rituals that, they hope, are a bit more authentic and true to the spirit of ancient sources, aware of the limits of doing this and forcefully rejecting even a hint of ethnic politics. It is not surprising that such a movement would emerge and be led by people who are cognizant of the controversial ethnic claims that have been made in the name of Norse gods elsewhere and want to use their knowledge of Nordic culture and religion to worship and affirm something positive. As eclectic-reconstructionists, members of NTF want to create rituals that link them to the local landscape, but which do so in a fashion that does not support an ethnic agenda, or imply the exclusion of others. In this sense, their project is consistent with mainstream Danish values, which embrace freedom of expression and multiculturalism.

Notes

1 There are variations in spelling of this term, mostly due to the language one uses, but even within a country there is some variation. I use 'Asatro', as this is what most people say and write in Denmark (Bøgelund 2008; Gotved 2001; Warmind 2007), as well as in Sweden on the websites of Asatro groups. The typical Anglicized version is 'Asatru', and there is even one Danish book on *Moderne Asetro* – which is probably better phonetically for Danish (Kamp 2008). Many groups use the Icelandic spelling, 'Ásatrú'.

2 The fieldwork upon which this chapter is based took place from January to August 2012, while I was a Visiting Associate Professor in the Department of Culture and Society at Aarhus University. I am grateful to the department for their generous support in making this research possible, particularly Mads Daugbjerg, who was responsible for bringing me to Aarhus and frequently worked alongside me, and Rane Willerslev who sponsored my grant. I am also deeply indebted to Vinni Bøgelund, who collaborated on much of this research and provided invaluable insight into the Danish Asatro movement, including comments on an earlier draft of this chapter. Finally, I thank members of the Aarhus Blótlaug, Nordisk Tingsfællig and Forn Siðr, who gave generously of their time, inviting me into their homes, and afforded me access to their rituals. Any misunderstandings or misrepresentations that may remain in this work are solely my own.

3 Strmiska (2005: 19–22) capitalizes 'Reconstructionist' and 'Eclectic', describing them as two poles on a continuum of modern Pagan religious movements.

4 The initial purpose of my 'visiting researcher' grant at Aarhus University was to document and film Viking reenactors, which quickly expanded to also looking at Danish Asatro. This research remains part of a larger research project looking at multiple facets of contemporary interest in the Viking age.

5 In Denmark, actual blood sacrifice is not included in the blót, though such practices have been revived in Asatro blóts in the United States (Strmiska 2007).

6 While it is true that secularism is widespread in Danish society, it is also important to acknowledge that Christianity still plays an important part in the foundations of Danish values (Rubow 2011: 98).

7 My translation from the original Swedish: 'Modern asatro skapar inte en ny etnisk identitet utan ger en redan existerande etnisk identitet ett nytt innehåll'.

8 Skott (2000: 45) notes a similar pattern in Swedish Asatro where people have highly individualistic beliefs and will typically choose from among the gods those that they wish to worship, often seeing different gods as representative of different symbols or principles.

9 The process of codifying Forn Siðr, including creating well-defined rituals and the roles of religious specialists, was a necessary part of being recognized as an official religion. Forn Siðr's original application for recognition was rejected in 1999, at which time they were given instructions on what they needed to do to gain recognition. Government recognition was ultimately obtained on 6 November 2003. When I spoke with founders and past and former board members of Forn Siðr, some expressed the view that government recognition has been mostly positive, as it allows them to perform weddings and funerals and provides broader legitimacy. Others expressed concern that setting standards for rituals is fundamentally at odds with what the religion means to them, and too much of a compromise.

10 Gregorius points out that in Sweden Asatro helps create feelings of togetherness for people who are otherwise reserved and disconnected, citing one Asatro member who told him that 'before blóts people are reserved, but afterwards they become more open-hearted with one another' (2008: 222, translated from the original Swedish).

11 It is important to note that ethnopluralism is not the same as multiculturalism. It is right-wing terminology – a code for 'everyone should be able to have their own place', suggesting that immigrants remain in ethnic enclaves.

12 In an effort to remain non-dogmatic and non-prescriptive, NTF is currently set up as having only one official 'ritual', their annual general assembly (Alting). Any other rituals are organized by individual members and made open by invitation. This structure was designed to avoid having a fixed set of ritual practices, with the hope that these can develop over time. As a result, the ritual at the Gudenå spring was, technically, not an official NTF event, but rather Mathias's own 'private initiative', performed under the auspices of a ritual group he created called Hiort Godeord ('The Deer Parish'). However, it was well attended by the NTF membership, much of the planning for the event took place in the context of NTF and it is listed as an NTF event on their website's main page for spring 2013 (Nordisk Tingsfællig 2013). Indeed, my invitation to film the ritual was formally approved at the NTF Alting.

References

Blain, J. 2005. 'Heathenry, the Past, and Sacred Sites in Today's Britain', in M. Strmiska (ed.), *Modern Paganism in World Cultures: Comparative Perspectives*. Santa Barbara: ABC-CLIO, pp. 181–208.

Bøgelund, V. 2008. 'Asatro: Harreskovens Blótgilde', in B. Andersen, H. Bertelsen, V. Bøgelund, A. Christoffersen and R.D. Pedersen, *Senmoderne Religiøsitet i Danmark*. Aarhus: Systime, pp. 16–51.

Fælles ideologiske principper. 2013. Retrieved 18 June 2013 from http://www.hefjendur.dk/faelles-ideologiske-principper.

Forn Siðr: Asa- og vanetrosamfundet i Danmark. 2013. http://www.fornsidr.dk. Accessed 18 June 2013.

Gardell, M. 2003. *Gods of the Blood: The Pagan Revival and White Separatism*. Durham, NC: Duke University Press.

Gotved, G.V. 2001. *Asatro: De Gamle Guder i Moderne Tid*. Copenhagen: Aschehoug.

Gregorius, F. 2008. 'Modern Asatro: Att Konstruera Kulturell och Etnisk Identitet'. Ph.D. dissertation, Lund University, Centrum for Teologi och Religionsvetenskap.

Ivakhiv, A. 2005. 'The Revival of Ukrainian Native Faith', in M. Strmiska (ed.), *Modern Paganism in World Cultures: Comparative Perspectives*. Santa Barbara: ABC-CLIO, pp. 209–39.

Kamp, M. 2008. *Moderne Asetro: Et Undervisningsmateriale til Folkeskolens Overbygning og Andra Intresserede*. Copenhagen: Books on Demand GmbH.

Kaplan, J. 1996. 'The Reconstruction of the Ásatrú and Odinist Traditions', in J. Lewis (ed.), *Magical Religion and Modern Witchcraft*. Albany: State University of New York Press, pp. 193–236.

Nordisk Tingsfællig. 2013. http://www.nordisktingsfaellig.dk/9295/Forside. Accessed 18 June 2013.

Nordisk Tingsfælligs formål. 2013. http://www.nordisktingsfaellig.dk/9355/Formål. Accessed 18 June 2013.

Rountree, K. 2010. *Crafting Contemporary Pagan Identities in a Catholic Society*. Farnham: Ashgate.

Rubow, C. 2011. 'Religion and Integration: Three Danish Models for the Relationship between Religion and Society', in K. Fog Olwig and K. Paerregaard (eds), *The Question of Integration: Immigration, Exclusion and the Danish Welfare State*. Newcastle upon Tyne: Cambridge Scholars Publishing, pp. 94–111.

Shnirelman, V. 2007. 'Ancestral Wisdom and Ethnic Nationalism: A View from Eastern Europe', *The Pomegranate: The International Journal of Pagan Studies* 9(1): 41–61.

Skott, F. 2000. *Asatro i Tiden*. Göteborg: Språk Och Folkminnesinstitutet.

Strmiska, M. 2000. 'Ásatrú in Iceland: The Rebirth of Nordic Paganism?' *Novo Religio* 4(1): 106–132.

——. 2005. 'Modern Paganism in World Cultures: Comparative Perspectives', in M. Strmiska (ed.), *Modern Paganism in World Cultures: Comparative Perspectives*. Santa Barbara: ABC-CLIO, pp. 1–53.

——. 2007. 'Putting the Blood Back into Blót: The Revival of Animal Sacrifice in Modern Nordic Paganism', *The Pomegranate: The International Journal of Pagan Studies* 9(2): 154–89.

Warmind, M. 2007. 'Asatro i Danmark: Spredning og Vækst af en "Ny Religion"', in M. Warburg and B. Jacobsen (eds), *Tørre tal om Troen: Religionsdemografi i det 21 Århundrede*. Højbjerg: Forlaget Univers, pp. 216–29.

Zuckerman, P. 2008. *Society without God: What the Least Religious Nations Can Tell us about Contentment*. New York: New York University Press.

3

Modern Heathenism in Sweden

A Case Study in the Creation of a Traditional Religion

Fredrik Gregorius

Introduction

Claiming ancient roots is a common way of seeking legitimacy for religious practices. While some new religions embrace their novelty, others are less eager to do so, seeking instead to prove continuity between their faith and older practices and strong cultural roots. 'Tradition' as a source of legitimacy has been a recurring theme in the Pagan community and has led to several controversies and, at times, clashes with the academic community, as Pagans often tend to present ideas about their history which are in conflict with what academics believe about their history (Hutton 1999). The aim of this chapter is to explore the means by which members of one part of the Pagan community, practitioners of Heathenism in Sweden, seek to present their faith as a 'traditional faith' rather than a modern invention. This is done despite the knowledge within the movement that no real continuity exists between their modern practice and the older practice of Old Norse paganism.

Modern Heathenism in Sweden is an umbrella term comprising different groups that seek to recreate the religion of pre-Christian Scandinavia. Although Heathenism is a new religious movement which is part of the much larger Pagan milieu, many followers of Heathenism are uncomfortable with being labelled as members of a 'new religion' and an ideological substratum presents modern Heathenism as the essence of Scandinavian culture which has been lying dormant within the culture. These followers of Heathenism do not perceive themselves as new actors in the Swedish religious marketplace, but rather as practitioners of a tradition with more authentic roots than other imported Pagan religions in Sweden, such as Wicca. Their sense of being part of an authentic form of Paganism which is more integrated in Swedish culture is illustrated by their rejection of the term *Asatru* and adoption of the term *Forn Sed* (ancient custom) as the preferred designation for their religious practice. The term *Asatru* means 'faith in the Æsir', one of the major divine families of gods in Old Norse religion, and was constructed in the nineteenth century. Because of this relatively recent construction, it is regarded as an inauthentic term for their faith.

Nonetheless, practitioners have been forced to use Wicca, Shamanism and Western magical traditions as well as academic sources to transform Heathenism from a theoretical and emotional idea into a living religion with an actual practice. Thus there is a dissonance between the tradition's self-image and its actual history. Despite being inspired by modern Pagan literature, practitioners of Heathenism have, at the same time, distanced themselves from other Pagan traditions in order to maintain a sense of authenticity. This chapter discusses the ways in which this rejection has become part of the construction of a modern Heathen identity which seeks to find a position in the Swedish religious market.

Terminology

Finding a term for the different groups and individuals that embrace and base their practice on Old Norse paganism is far from easy. 'Asatru' was for a long time the most commonly used term by both practitioners and scholars, but fewer and fewer now use it; instead practitioners prefer the term 'Forn Sed' (*Om Forn Sed* 2013). This term points to a belief in a custom based on older forms of practice rather than to a new religious movement, and is clearly a more satisfactory emic term. The problem with 'Forn Sed' is that it fails to encompass the whole spectrum of different groups that use Old Norse religious concepts and the term has for obvious reasons gained little use outside Sweden and Scandinavia. It is still very new among Pagans, although becoming increasingly common. Another problem is that use of the term creates a picture of the Swedish milieu as being more distinct from its international Pagan counterparts than it is.

Apart from 'Asatru', the most commonly used term is 'Heathenism' (or 'Heathenry') and it has been typically used in academic studies on the phenomenon (Harvey 2000; Blain 2005; Blain and Wallis 2006, 2009). 'Heathenism' is used in this chapter to refer to the modern practices and religious beliefs based on interpretations of Old Norse religion. The term 'Old Norse religion' refers to pre-Christian Scandinavia and is thus distinct from Heathenism, which refers to present-day practices and beliefs. The term 'Paganism' is used as an umbrella term for all forms of modern religions which base their practices on interpretations of pre-Christian religions. Practitioners of Heathenism differ on the issues of race and ethnicity and Heathenism can be divided into several subcategories. All three forms described below can be defined as 'ethnic', especially the last two.

- *Racial Heathenism.* Ideas and concerns about race are the most significant factor determining why a person turns to this form of Heathenism. The most prominent form is Wotanism. Rooted in racial ideology, it tends to be cross-cultural as the primary motivation is the preservation of the 'White race' and not a single culture. In Sweden, this form of Heathenism has not played a significant role.
- *Genealogical Heathenism.* This form emphasizes kinship with other people of the same ethnic group. The key is a relationship between today's Heathens and practitioners of older forms of paganism based on genetic kinship. In Sweden, the most famous example of this was the now defunct Norröna Samfundet (the Nordic Assembly).
- *Cultural Heathenism.* Here cultural identity is most significant and genetic factors are not relevant. This form of Heathenism is the most common in Sweden.

Old Norse Heritage in Sweden

Modern Heathens in Sweden face a situation that could be felt as a form of cultural paradox. The Viking is one of the central symbols of Swedish identity.[1] The fact that a nation state of Vikings as such did not exist matters little for most people. In most cities you can find T-shirts that say: 'Sweden: Land of the Vikings', expressing the kinship felt with the era. The impact of the Vikings, though at times controversial, is found everywhere in Sweden, as in other Scandinavian countries. Streets are named after gods and places from Nordic mythology, Viking-style jewellery can be found in most stores, companies are named after Viking gods, Viking villages are built that attract large numbers of tourists every year and the old Nordic myths are taught in schools. Old Norse religion has left traces in language, folk traditions and folklore, even if the degree to which this is true is debated in academic circles (Gregorius 2009: 141). It is still possible to find people in the Swedish countryside who maintain practices based on folk traditions, such as putting out porridge for the *Tomte*, a gnome-like creature considered to live around barns and houses that can be both helpful and chaotic. While somewhat historically doubtful, the popular Swedish midsummer celebration is commonly regarded as a festival with Heathen origins. References to folklore and myths and their use can be found increasingly in Scandinavian literature and films. Recent years have seen a rise of this both in more serious works like the Swedish novel *Stallo* (2012) by Stefan Spjut and more humorous ones like the Norwegian film *Troll Hunters* (2010). In music it is found particularly in Scandinavian metal music where Old Norse and Viking themes are prominent. Often a band which started out using Satanic images later abandoned these for Nordic symbols. While somewhat controversial because of their use by far-Right groups, and the Left's fear that embracing ethnic markers like the Viking will lead to a more segregated society, the Vikings and their religion are central markers of Swedish identity. Even the anti-racism movement in Sweden often portrays the Vikings as early multiculturalists, giving further evidence that the Viking age is given almost a normative function.[2] It is against this background that modern Heathens, and their at times complex relationship to the rest of Sweden, must be understood.

Taking the cultural context into consideration, one can understand why Heathenism finds such a fertile place in the Swedish religious market and a strong undercurrent of surviving pre-Christian practices can be found. Non-Heathen Pagans in Sweden, such as local Wicca covens, also use Old Norse symbols and often include references to the old religion. Esoteric groups like the Swedish Dragon Rouge and international orders like the Temple of Set and Ordo Templi Orientis have all integrated Old Norse symbols in their practices and often use Old Norse names for their local chapters (Gregorius 2009: 220). It is thus fairly easy to imagine a strong, living interest in Old Norse religion in Sweden and using this as a means of legitimization. As will be shown, however, the situation is complex and the immediacy of the symbols can actually be a problem for future growth.

Heathenism in Sweden

Heathenism did not begin as the revival of a rural folk religion but as a mainly urban movement, part of the New Age and the wider Pagan community in Sweden. Many Heathens had a background in Viking and medieval reconstructionist societies like the Society for Creative Anachronism. The first Heathen and Heathen-inspired groups began to appear in the 1970s, but none ever had more than a few hundred members. From early on the Swedish Heathen community displayed two basic trends: a more free and liberal, shamanistic-based *sejdr*[3] environment that often developed out of the New Age movement, and a more reconstructionist environment, called *sed* in Swedish. These two trends often existed simultaneously, at times causing internal friction because they touched upon the critical question of what defines Heathenism and how wide the definition should be.

One of the earliest attempts to create an association for Heathens was Breidablikk-Gildet (Guild of Breidablikk), founded in 1975. Breidablikk-Gildet advocated a nationalistic, romantically inspired view of life where Heathenism was seen as the Swedish people's spiritual origins. It peaked in the mid 1980s with about 130 members and ceased to exist in the late 1980s (Gregorius 2009: 80). Another early group was Telge Fylking (the name refers to a fortification outside of Stockholm, *fylking* meaning castle), founded in 1987 outside Stockholm. From the beginning it aligned closely with Breidablikk-Gildet, but over time they moved apart. For Telge Fylking Heathenism was both a folk religion and a nature religion. Telge Fylking identified Heathens with other so-called 'nature people', a view that also formed the basis of their stand against Christianity. Telge Fylking would become the first Heathen group in Sweden to take a clear stand against racial interpretations of Old Norse religion, emphasizing instead values of hospitality and generosity towards immigrants and the socially disadvantaged. Members of the group also appeared in the Swedish media quite often and were generally regarded positively. This trend of positive representation by the media has, with some exceptions, continued in Sweden. In the mid 1990s Telge Fylking stopped making public appearances (such as giving lectures, appearing in the media and conducting open rituals), but has continued as a private group of around ten people. Many of the ideas formulated by them subsequently found their way into later Swedish Heathen organizations and the group has been a major source of inspiration, particularly for the so-called 'sed' interpretation of Heathenism (Gregorius 2009: 81).

Yet another early group was Yggdrasil ('Yggdrasil' is the name of the World-Tree that unites the different worlds in Old Norse religion), which represented the shamanistic or sejdr element. Shamanism in Sweden developed mainly from the New Age movement and the practice is somewhat controversial in Pagan circles as many consider it to have no foundation in historical records and to be based on the cultural exploitation of indigenous people. Shamanism became popular through the work of writers like Carlos Castaneda, Michael Harner and Mircea Eliade, the last two giving some form of academic authority to the idea of Shamanism as a universal phenomenon, one of the basic tenets of modern Shamanism (Znamenski 2007).[4] In 1976 a small group formed in Stockholm which later became Yggdrasil, though Yggdrasil was not officially founded until 1982. The central figure was Jörgen Eriksson I, who became interested in Shamanism when he attended a ceremony in the United States led by representatives of the Hopi people, which resulted in a kind of mystical experience. When he sought out those who led the ceremony to find out more, they replied that he should look for the answer in his own roots (Lindquist 1997: 29).

Eriksson's story reflects a structural narrative that recurs among esoteric and Pagan groups in various forms, especially in connection with the founding of a new organization. It aims to create a form of legitimacy for the new organization, or to legitimize its leaders' actions and right to teach. Eriksson thus received a form of recognition and encouragement to follow the path he had chosen from people considered authorities (the Hopi). In 1997 Yggdrasil became part of the Stockholm-based Merlin Orden (today Svenska Misraimförbundet – the Swedish Misraim Assembly) (Lindquist 1997: 47). Jörgen Eriksson has become probably the most widely read Heathen writer in Sweden. Besides books on Shamanism, he has, under the pseudonym Atrid Grimsson, published books on Swedish folk magic and rune magic.

Apart from Telge Fylking and Yggdrasil there were some other smaller organizations. One was Svitjods Asa Gille,[5] founded in 1990 by Frömund Ansheille. He called himself *Allsherjargode* (High Priest) of Svitjod (a pre-Christian name for what later became Sweden) and claimed to be heir to an over 7,000-year-old unbroken line of *Frej*-priests (meaning his genealogical line was devoted to the Vanir god, Frej) (Gardell 2003: 385; von Schnurbein 1993: 188). Svitjods Asa Gille was one of the few examples of Swedish Heathenism that claimed a form of family succession as its authority. These smaller groups quickly disappeared in the middle of the 1990s.

Samfundet Forn Sed/Sveriges Asatrosamfund

Samfundet Forn Sed/Sveriges Asatrosamfund (Swedish Forn Sed Assembly/Swedish Asatru Assembly) is the largest Swedish Heathen organization. Samfundet Forn Sed was founded in 1994 as Sveriges Asatrosamfund. In 1996 it began to publish the magazine *Mimers Källa* (Mimir's Well. Mimir was a figure in Old Norse religion connected to wisdom who had his head cut off after a war between the gods. Odin sacrificed one of his eyes to Mimir's well to gain wisdom and the ability to see into the future). The plan was to become a recognized religious organization and achieve the three thousand members needed to gain the right to perform marriages and funerals. In their early writings Samfundet members did not consider this would be very difficult, as interest in Heathenism was believed to be huge. This idea has persisted in the organization despite the fact that at most it has had only around four hundred members (Gregorius 2009: 89). On Easter Monday in 2000 Samfundet members held a public ceremony during which they called upon the old gods and sacrificed vegetables and corn at Uppsala Mounds. Representatives from the media were invited. The *blót* (Heathen ritual) was relatively high profile and reports of it were generally positive. These blóts have continued as an annual tradition, at most attracting one hundred participants (Gregorius 2009: 91). In 2000 Samfundet claimed the highest numbers ever for the association – 450 members – however, according to a former chairman, the real number was around 350 (Gregorius 2009: 89).

From 2001 to 2005 Samfundet experienced several internal problems and conflicts that reached a peak in 2004. There were a number of reasons for the conflicts, mostly problems with the board of directors, but the conflicts were also related to members' concepts of what Heathenism was all about – for example, how open they should be to innovations and experimental forms of spirituality. After a period of extreme chaos, where for a while there were two boards which did not recognize each other, in 2005 Samfundet entered a more stable period of development. At that time it had only around ten members. It soon began to grow and a year later had around fifty members. Since then there has been a slow but steady increase (Gregorius 2009: 92), and today Samfundet claims to have three to four hundred members (Erik, personal correspondence, 15 September 2011).

In 2007 Samfundet was finally registered as a religious organization, but without the legal right to perform weddings and funerals. It has become more stable and the changing of boards and chairpersons is done without controversy. There is a problem, however, in getting members to become actively involved; the majority are inactive (Erik, personal correspondence, 15 September 2011).

Samfundet members are against racial interpretations of Heathenism. While embracing a form of cultural essentialism, where Swedish culture is considered to be essentially unchanging, they welcome people from all backgrounds as members. It is also an open, democratic organization, where outsiders can easily read protocols and internal debates. It has rarely made any theological statements and tries to keep a balance between reconstructionism and the more eclectic shamanistic scene.

Other Groups

Around the same time that Samfundet was formed other organizations also appeared, but most have since disbanded. One still active is Samfälligheten för Nordisk Sed (the Community for Nordic Custom), founded in 1997 with the aim of being an organization of local groups of practitioners of 'Nordic custom'. It is somewhat controversial and the members do not see themselves as part of the Pagan or Heathen community. Instead they view themselves as followers of a more authentic form of Heathenism found in Swedish folk practices, though such assertions are rather doubtful (Gregorius 2009: 97). Although they claim to be the largest Heathen organization in Sweden, evidence suggests there may only be a handful of members. Their Facebook group had twenty-six members on 5 May 2014, and while it is impossible to draw firm conclusions from that, it indicates the level of interest that the group generates.[6] Another organization that gained some prominence during the mid 2000s was Norröna Samfundet. It disbanded around 2006 after internal conflicts and a decline of interest. It never seems to have had more than one hundred members (Gregorius 2009: 100). In contrast with other Heathens they believed that only people of Scandinavian descent should practise Heathenism and became for that reason a controversial section of Swedish Heathenism.

The Current Situation in Swedish Heathenism

There are no absolute numbers on how many people in Sweden today consider themselves Heathens. However, it is possible to calculate approximate figures based on the number of members of various organizations. No other Heathen group is as large as Samfundet, which today claims around four hundred members. The smaller, independent blót-groups rarely have more than a dozen members. Thus it seems likely that there are currently only a few hundred people in Sweden who belong to some form of Heathen organization. It is impossible to determine how many Heathens there are outside the organizations, but hypothetical assumptions can be made. From book sales, presence on social forums and so forth, there is little indication that there is a massive interest in Heathenism and taking different calculations into consideration, the conclusion seems to be that Heathens should be counted in the hundreds or at most at around one thousand (Gregorius 2009: 105). It is unlikely that there is a large group of Heathens who for various reasons have chosen not to join any organization, register on any Internet site or make contact with other Heathens. No figures are available on the relative numbers of men and women in Swedish Heathenism. According to former chairman Henrik Hallgren, one third of the members in Samfundet are women (personal correspondence). There are several reasons for the gender imbalance, but one has to do with the way that both Norse religion and the cultural construction of the Viking are often presented as very masculine.

Heathens' Perception of their Numbers

Heathens estimate the number of believers in the thousands. However, one very rarely encounters specific examples of organizations faking their own numbers, although there have been some instances. Rather, estimates are based on an optimistic calculation of the number of adherents outside the organizations. The idea behind this is perhaps easy to understand: they see themselves as part of a rapidly growing movement or part of an older religion that recently came to the surface, but one where most devotees still choose to remain anonymous. While few Heathens claim any connection themselves to older traditions, they are often open to the idea that older forms might still exist in the countryside. An exception is the members of Samfälligheten för Nordisk Sed, who claim that they derive from this older, rural Heathenism. They do not, however, claim that most traditional Heathens are members of their organization. Their website claims that probably around half a million people in Sweden today are Heathens (*Vanliga frågor* 2013). No account of how they arrived at these numbers exists.

The idea of a large number of people who are Heathens, but for a variety of reasons have chosen not to be public or become members of an organization, seems to play an important role in creating a sense of justification that Heathenism is more integrated in Swedish culture than other new religions and Pagan traditions. I call this 'the myth of the silent majority': the idea that unknown practitioners numerically exceed those who are active in the movement (Gregorius 2009: 107). The basis for ambitious estimates often emerges from anecdotal evidence, as in the case of one member who met someone at a bar who was 'into Heathenism' but not a member of an organization; the member subsequently argued that there must be 'tons of those people'. Another member claimed as a result of similar social encounters that there were most likely over three thousand Heathens in most Swedish cities (personal correspondence). Sometimes there is a perception that there are older practitioners who keep their faith secret. It is not difficult to understand how impressions of large numbers of Heathens exist. As stated above, Sweden is filled with images from the Viking era and it constitutes one of the central – and by far most popular – cultural tropes for national identity. The gods of the Old Norse religion are well known by most Swedes, but such knowledge and interest do not equal a religious interest. Indeed such familiarity may even create an obstacle to people seeing elements that are already an important part of the cultural narrative as contemporary religious symbols. The Edda is not primarily encountered as a religious text, but as a representation of something one's ancestors believed in; it is therefore placed in the category of myth or fairy tale.

Culture and Heathenism

As stated above, the claim of legitimization among Swedish Heathens is based on the idea that they are continuing a tradition – while their religion is in a sense new, it is not completely novel but based on an undercurrent within the culture they inhabit. It is possible to crystallize a number of basic concepts about Swedish and Nordic culture that are more or less recurrent and strongly held among Heathens. These are:

1. The notion of an organic culture: beneath the blanket of Christianity is a more genuine and authentic Nordic culture which is really more suitable for Swedes.
2. A strong identification between culture and nature.
3. The identification of pre-Christian Nordic culture with the cultures of indigenous peoples, who they believe live in greater harmony with nature and have a more authentic experience of the world.
4. In order to reconnect with their true identity, people should seek in the past – the period before Christianity separated us from our roots. (Gregorius 2009: 116)

These aspects should not be seen as separate from each other, but as connected and highlighted in various degrees depending on the underlying ideologies of different groups and individuals. The Heathen concept of 'culture' in Sweden is often very open and Heathens mostly have no problem accepting people from a non-Scandinavian background. This is not necessarily the situation in all countries and in the United States ideas about genetics have been more prominent (Gardell 2003: 261; Kaplan 1996: 214). While the openness in Sweden in a sense can seem to contradict the idea of an organic cultural identity, Heathens themselves see no conflict between these two positions, and most are well aware that cultures are changing and see no threat in the development of a Swedish multicultural society. Still, Heathenism is based on an organic concept of culture founded on the idea that it is possible to find something essential and unaltered behind the contemporary manifestations of existing cultures. For example, an introduction to Samfundet states: 'Traditionally, ancient custom was an integral part of folk culture; it was developed in an organic way, not regulated by any formal institution they chose to go into' (Sveriges Asatrosamfund 2008: 3). Contemporary society is often considered to have lost touch with the original culture it emerged from and one of Heathenism's goals is to re-establish this connection. The concept of an organic culture views the Christianization of Sweden negatively. Christianity becomes a representation of 'the Other', serving also as a symbol for other areas of modernity that Heathenism is critical of, such as industrialization, urbanization, pollution and materialism. Despite this, Heathens are often very open to cooperation with Christian Churches and like to see themselves as actors in the same religious market as more established religious institutions, rather than as part of the 'new religions' or Pagan market (Gregorius 2009: 121).

The organic concept of culture also forms the basis for identification with other indigenous religions. Among these it seems that more and more the primary kinship is with Hinduism and there is also a growing interest in Afro-Caribbean religions like Vodou (Erik, personal correspondence, 15 September 2011). In both of these cases the interest is not only a theoretical, spiritual kinship; Heathens also draw practical inspiration from these traditions. Some Swedish Heathens have created *veve*-inspired symbols for the Æsir and Vanir (the two major divine families in Old Norse religion), for example. (Veve symbols are used in Vodou to represent different spirits.) However, this does not mean that there is any interest in eclectically mixing the gods and spirits from these traditions in Heathen practice.

Forn Sed

A way that Heathens display the organic connection between religion and Swedish culture is in their use of the term *forn sed*, ancient custom, which gained popularity in the middle of the 2000s (Gregorius 2009: 129). The term comes from the Old Norse *forn Sidr*. References to it can be found in 'Olav the Holy's tale' in *Heimskringla*, Sturluson's history of the kings of Norway, where it was used as a derogatory term for people who had not yet converted to Christianity (Sturluson 1993: 88). There is no evidence that the term was used by followers of Old Norse religion, but is it perceived as more authentic than 'Asatru' and expresses Heathens' self-image that theirs is a way of life rather than merely a religion based on beliefs in a certain set of gods. This 'custom' is seen as being integrated in Swedish cultural identity.

What this sed is – apart from religion – is often rather vague, and seems to be based mainly on a feeling that there is something deeper. The idea is to a degree a paradox as sed is thought to be found in old Nordic rural customs, but as yet undogmatic and open to change. Still there is a clear line between what can and cannot be included in Heathen practice and there is a reluctance to mix elements from other faiths.

Folklore and Heathenism

Few Heathens believe that much is preserved from the period before Christianity or that it is possible to see themselves as part of a surviving pagan religion, but many believe that some remains from pre-Christian times exist in Swedish folk customs. Heathens differ in their views of folklore. Some see it as almost completely Heathen, while others believe that only some elements survived and these became integrated with Christianity. Thus it is possible to speak of two poles in Heathens' views of folklore. An additional scale would rate from high to low the importance of folklore for the modern faith and practice. Rather than seeing these as fixed positions, most Heathens are somewhere between these poles (Gregorius 2009: 137). Integrating aspects from folklore into one's practice can enhance a feeling of being part of something larger as folklore and customs are still alive in Sweden, primarily in parts of the countryside. For example, some Heathens embrace the rural custom of putting out porridge for the Tomte. But for most Swedes this is seldom taken seriously and the inclusion of such elements in the faith makes Heathens seem peculiar to non-Pagan Swedes (Daun 1998: 174; Gregorius 2009: 139).

The relationship between pagan and Christian elements in folklore is complex and the early ideological interpretations of folk customs as the remains of older cultures makes it difficult to determine which are recent innovations and which could be actual remains. To draw clear boundaries is often difficult, if not impossible. Is the popular image of the Devil, for example, based on the demonization of older pagan gods, or did later folklorists in the nineteenth century see in the popular image of Satan various pagan gods? Names like 'Go Far' are used by the ethnologist Hyltén-Cavallius as evidence of how Thor survived in Christian culture. However 'Go Far' is also a name of the Devil and it could just as easily be assumed that it was through the writings of Hyltén-Cavallius that the identification between Go Far and Thor became established and that it did not exist before (Hyltén-Cavallius 1921: 172; Wall 1992).

Heathenism in the Religious Market

Heathenism's development in Sweden must be understood as a consequence of Heathens' behaviour in the different social fields in which they strive to find legitimization. Primarily Heathens are trying to obtain recognition and acceptance from other major actors in the religious market, such as established denominations, but they also seek recognition from other religions internationally with which they see more spiritual connections.

The importance of religion in Sweden is generally considered to be small. Sweden is often described as one of the world's most secular countries; according to the *Eurobarometer* report of 2010 only 18 per cent of Swedes believe in a God. A larger portion, 45 per cent, says that they believe in some sort of spiritual power and 35 per cent state they do not believe in God (*Eurobarometer Report for the European Commission* 2010: 381). In contrast with these figures, a large number of Swedes believe in supernatural phenomena such as reincarnation and astrology (Hammar 1997: 24), suggesting a general interest in spiritual matters despite a low interest in organized religion. While only a small minority can be considered believing Christians or attend any Church services (around 5 per cent), the majority of Swedes, around 67 per cent at the end of 2012, are members of the Church of Sweden – though it should be noted that there has been a substantial decline in membership of over 1 per cent each year (Svenska Kyrkan 2014). The situation Heathens have to confront is a culture where religion is regarded as a private matter, most people are uninterested in organized religion, many have only a vague spiritual belief and most citizens are members of the Church of Sweden. Religion also has a very limited impact on Swedish public life. In the *World Values Survey* of 2005–2008 Swedes can be seen as exceptional in their embrace of both secular-rational values and self-expression values to a greater degree than any other country (*World Values Survey* 2013). In recent years religion has again become a part of a public discussion due mainly to an increase of Muslim immigrants. This has led to an increased awareness about the role religion can play, but has not made Sweden any less secular.

Secular Values and Religion

As religion increasingly becomes a private matter, religious institutions no longer serve as a primary mediator of ethical values. Rather, societal values are justified without religion. Religious organizations may nonetheless – with more or less sound arguments – claim that their religion is the foundation from which these values are taken. Heathenism is one such actor and constructing a form of Heathen identity based on secular values has been one way of legitimizing

Heathens' role as caretakers of Swedish culture. Within Heathenism in Sweden three such values – democracy, ecology and equality – today are being interpreted as having their cultural foundation in pre-Christian Norse religion. This can be used as a means of making the religion meaningful today and creating legitimization for the faith, but it also affects the direction that interpretations of Old Norse religion take within Heathenism. For example, ideas like the 'Nine Noble Virtues',[7] popular among Heathens in the U.S., are rarely found as a central tenet in Sweden; instead the above-mentioned values of democracy, ecology and equality, important in Swedish culture more generally, are embraced. In practice this can be seen in the way Samfundet is organized and how one rarely finds charismatic leaders or dogmatic statements made by the organization. It is also open to public discussion regarding belief and practices and has adapted its expression of faith to fit the standards of contemporary society. Samfundet's statement on the principles of its organization exemplifies this:

- Have a democratic ethos.
- Have a basic precept of religious tolerance and religious freedom.
- Oppose racism.
- Practice the religion in accordance with Swedish law and regulations.
- Do not slaughter animals as part of a ceremony.
- Keeps festivals free from illegal drugs. (Samfundet Forn Sed Sverige 2013)

In a similar fashion Heathenism in Sweden is presented as an ecological religion rather than a purely ethnic one. This is based on embracing secular values and adopting a form of reasoning more easily understood than cultural arguments. This is not primarily concerned with Green political positions, but with justifying the religion in terms of many Swedes' ideas about nature as a source of spirituality. Heathenism as a nature religion thus connects with a larger, secular, nature spirituality found in the country. Most Swedes, however, have only a vague, non-articulated view of it. The trend that sees nature as the basis for spirituality has also influenced Christianity in Sweden and the Church of Sweden is also trying to translate its religion into an ecological one (Bergmann 1998: 243).

Heathens present their faith as based on equality and absence of gender divisions. Samfundet has a priest and a priestess, but in contrast with Wicca, there is no gender-based ritual aspect to this where some parts are only for the male and others for the female. Some members have expressed the idea that Old Norse religion had queer values and certain myths about Thor and Odin are presented as examples of cross-dressing; in their view this provides evidence that Old Norse society was open to queer and LGBT people (Svd Nyheter 2009). Despite being open to queer theories, however, there are still ideas that femininity is primarily related to the Earth and motherhood.

In their views on democracy, ecology and equality, Heathens have consistently embraced secular values but interpret them as being found in Old Norse religion. Instead of breaking with secular values, they see themselves as representing these more strongly than many others in society. Ironically, the Church of Sweden is probably the religious actor whose embrace of similar values most closely resembles Heathenism in that it has also internalized the values of democracy, ecology and equality as Christian values. The differences between Heathenism and the Church of Sweden are thus not as great as Heathens often want to claim. Rather, the difference between them is whether such values should be seen as fundamentally Christian or Heathen (Gregorius 2009: 244).

Heathenism – an Ethnic Religion?

As mentioned above, ideas about culture in Heathenism are based on an open approach where people from different backgrounds are welcome and Heathens rarely have a negative view on immigration and multiculturalism. Multiculturalism has created a structure for Heathens to seek legitimization from the rest of society by employing a rhetoric influenced by the debate about multiculturalism and presenting themselves as a minority faith, similar to the position held by immigrant religions. This creates a somewhat complex and paradoxical situation as their religious identity is based upon being representative of the cultural 'essence' of the majority. The reason for this strategy is that as more voices are raised for minority rights a narrative can be created where Heathens can present themselves as one of the groups excluded from society, and therefore demand as much respect as other minority religions (Gregorius 2009: 250). This contrasts, however, with the fact that Heathens primarily base their values on the surrounding community. Thus Heathens only partially constitute a minority; their identity as Heathen does not affect the whole of their social existence, which makes it difficult to fully compare a Swedish Heathen with a Muslim immigrant from Iraq who lacks the same opportunities to otherwise be an integral part of society. What is important here is the self-image developed within Heathenism and how it leads to the establishment of various rhetorical forms to create the means to act within various social and religious fields. There is a positive correlation between the emergence of a multicultural society in Sweden and Heathens' employment of rhetoric regarding the need for tolerance towards alternative faiths.

Heathenism and Other Pagans

Heathenism is part of global Paganism and it is primarily in relation to other Pagan groups that Heathens make their voices heard and position themselves. However, this is something Heathens do not always want to admit: they would rather see themselves as part of the larger religious field and interact with major religions such as Christianity or Islam. Some Heathens see other Pagan traditions, especially Wicca or Thelema,[8] as less authentic than their tradition. Especially negative is their attitude to Pagan or esoteric societies who embrace Nordic symbolism in a way that is not consistent with Heathen opinion. This is sometimes seen as a form of spiritual theft. Criticism also occurs internally, with claims that other forms of Heathenism are less authentic than their own ideological framework. This is a kind of legitimizing strategy which aims to forge a relation to a more established social field by distancing itself from religions and groups considered less accepted.

Swedish and Foreign Heathenism

Although Swedish Heathens have a relatively critical image of American Heathenism, the Swedish environment is clearly influenced by it. American writers like Stephen Flowers (under his pseudonym Edred Thorson) have had a substantial influence on Swedish Heathens (Gregorius 2009: 256). Some of those interviewed for this study had a perception that American Heathenism was more racist than Swedish. Still the most common criticism of U.S. Heathenism is that the country lacks a cultural and geographical basis for the faith. If Heathenism is an organic religion that emerges in relation to the natural environment of Scandinavia, it is argued, it would be difficult for people who live in California or Texas to engage in Heathenism. In contrast with their perceptions of America, Heathens' image of Iceland is based on an almost romantic, and at times rather unrealistic, veneration. Iceland is regarded as an essentially Heathen country. There has, nonetheless, been some critique of what is perceived as an ethnocentric view among Heathens in Iceland. Icelandic Heathenism has not, however, had the same ideological impact as American Heathenism and serves mainly as symbolic inspiration. Relationships between Swedish Heathens and people from other Scandinavian and European countries, particularly Denmark, have expanded in recent years. These relationships have not always been free of problems, sometimes due to differences of opinion about the importance of ethnicity, but relations seem to be mainly friendly.

Heathenism and 'Traditional Religions'

Recognition from what Heathens consider 'traditional religions' is more important than recognition from other Pagan or Heathen groups, because such recognition confirms the identity of Heathenism as a traditional religion. In connection with Samfundet's participation at the World Congress of Ethnic Religions (WCER) in India in 2006, the former chairman, Henrik Hallgren, wrote:

> There were 75 different traditions from different ethnic nature-based religions meeting, a major step towards global cooperation. There was also recognition that Asatru is actually part of a worldwide movement for traditional religions' preservation and enhancement. And this is important for us to realize: we are not alone. We are not an obscure little sect based on nostalgia and fake dreams. We are a living spiritual force in society. The tradition we practise is an earthy religion with a close affinity to other communities and traditions worldwide. (Hallgren 2006)

Being given legitimacy from, for example, Hindu groups strengthens the feeling among Heathens that they are followers of a religion with deep roots. The WCER can be seen as a manifestation of a development whereby increased contact between European Pagans and followers of traditional religions from other parts of the world is being established. The consequences for Swedish Heathenism of becoming a player in this environment could lead to an increased focus on the preservation of cultural identity.

Conclusions

Heathens have embraced contemporary values and integrated them as part of their religious identity. These are regarded as essential conditions for achieving some form of social acceptance. There are no required lifestyle changes within Heathenism and the degree of socialization into the Heathen environment is low; there is no requirement that Heathens accept specific religious beliefs, and it is not a religious identity that affects all aspects of life, rather mainly the religious sphere in terms of rituals and choice of literature. This can lead to a degree of social acceptance by the wider society; but does it motivate people to join or get involved? Heathenism has reached a situation where pressure from the surrounding community is minor and for a religious movement this can be problematic. A religion that places low demands on members also tends to be a religion that does not offer much. According to sociologists Roger Finke and Rodney Stark, those religious groups that have higher demands also offer the most:

> Humans want their religion to be sufficiently potent, vivid and compelling so that it can offer them rewards of great magnitude. People seek a religion that is capable of miracles and that imparts order and sanity to the human condition. The religious organizations that maximize these aspects of religion, however, also demand the highest price in terms of what the individual must do to qualify for these rewards. (Finke and Stark 1992: 275)

Heathenism does not offer its followers any sense of exclusive salvation or an understanding of 'truth'. The closest to something resembling a gain from joining Heathenism is a vague idea of living in harmony with one's surroundings and that the gods will be favourable to those who make offerings to them. Heathenism could, however, attract people by offering an experience of a sense of mystery and through its existing emotional appeal to the symbols of Heathenism. One can see this in the case of Wicca, which has successfully embraced the image of the Witch. The problem for Heathens, however, becomes something of a paradox. It is by highlighting their relationship to Nordic culture that Heathens claim and justify their religious identity. Most Swedes know the names of the Norse gods like Odin, Thor and Freyr. The problem is that although many Swedes feel a kinship with ancient Nordic culture, they have compartmentalized the old gods within the category of fairy tales and sagas and not in the realm of spirituality.

Although there is little to indicate a rapid growth of Heathenism, this does not mean that Heathenism could not establish itself as a permanent feature in the Swedish religious field as a minority religion. Developments in Heathenism towards a professional priesthood and the establishment of rituals like baptisms, weddings and seasonal blóts give a sense of greater continuity and professionalism. There are currently Heathens who have held their faith for over twenty years and thus contribute a sense of stability. Through increased international contacts and relations with other Pagans in Sweden they could create a small – but not necessarily less effective or plausible – structure that confirms their beliefs. In such an environment Heathenism could be accepted as representative of Swedish culture and so reinforce its self-image.

Notes

1 I have chosen consciously to use the term 'Viking' here, well aware that it is generally not an accepted term for the era among scholars of Old Norse religion. The reason is to emphasize that it is the semi-mythical Viking who has come to play the role of signifier for national identity.

2 An example of this was *Tor, Kristus och Allah* (Thor, Christ and Allah), an exhibition in 2004 at the Viking village of Birka that aimed to portray the place as a centre for multicultural meetings.

3 *Sejdr* is a term used for magical practices in Iron Age Scandinavia that some have interpreted as a Nordic form of shamanism.

4 On the controversy regarding modern Shamanism, see Znamenski (2007).

5 This name roughly translates as 'Svitjod's [one of the old names of Sweden] Guild for the Æsir', but the meaning is more: 'Guild for the followers of the Æsir'.

6 https://www.facebook.com/groups/127463393941239/?fref=ts. Accessed 5 May 2014.

7 The Nine Noble Virtues are: courage, truth, honour, fidelity, discipline, hospitality, self-reliance, industriousness and perseverance. They were developed in the 1970s by the Odinic Rite in England.

8 Thelema is an esoteric religion with strong Pagan components which was founded by the British writer Aleister Crowley (1875–1947) early in the twentieth century. It is based on the idea of humankind entering a new aeon, called the Aeon of Horus, where the primary spiritual law is to find one's will.

References

Bergmann, S. 1998. 'Jord, Kultur och Ande: Komposten i Humanekologisk och Teologisk Belysning', in S. Bergman and C.R. Bråkenhielm (eds), *Vardagskulturens Teologi*. Nora: Nya Doxa, pp. 224–50.
Blain, J. 2005. 'Heathenry, the Past, and Sacred Sites in Today's Britain', in M.F. Strmiska (ed.), *Modern Paganism in World Cultures: Comparative Perspectives*. Santa Barbara: ABC-CLIO, pp. 181–208.
Blain, J. and R. Wallis. 2006. 'Re-presenting Spirit: Heathenry, New-Indigenes and the Imagined Past', in I.A. Russell (ed.), *Images, Representations and Heritage: Moving Beyond Modern Approaches to Archaeology*. London and New York: Springer, pp. 89–108.
———. 2009. 'Heathenry', in J.M. Lewis and M. Pizza (eds), *Handbook of Contemporary Paganism*. Leiden and Boston: Brill, pp. 413–32.
Daun, Å. 1998. *Svensk Mentalitet*. Stockholm: Rabén Prisma.
Eurobarometer Report for the European Commission. 2010. Retrieved 2 July 2013 from http://ec.europa.eu/public_opinion/archives/ebs/ebs_341_en.pdf.
Finke, R. and R. Stark. 1992. *The Churching of America: Winners and Losers in our Religious Economy*. New Brunswick: Rutgers University Press.
Gardell, M. 2003. *Gods of the Blood: The Pagan Revival and White Separatism*. Durham, NC: Duke University Press.
Gregorius, F. 2009 'Modern Asatro: Att Konstruera Kulturell och Etnisk Identitet'. Ph.D. dissertation, Lund University, Centrum for Teologi och Religionsvetenskap.
Hallgren, H. 2006. 'Ledare', *Mimers källa* 14: 3.
Hammar, O. 1997. *På Spaning efter Helheten: New Age en ny Folktro?* Stockholm: Wahlström and Widstrand.
Harvey, G. 2000. 'Heathenism: A North European Pagan Tradition', in G. Harvey and C. Hardman (eds), *Pagan Pathways: A Guide to the Ancient Earth Traditions*. London: Thorsons, pp. 49–64.
Hutton, R. 1999. *Triumph of the Moon*. Oxford: Oxford University Press.
Hyltén-Cavallius, G.O. 1921. *Wärend och Wirdarne: del 1*. Stockholm: Norstedt.
Kaplan, J. 1996. 'The Reconstruction of the Ásatrú and Odinist Traditions', in J.R. Lewis (ed.), *Magical Religion and Modern Witchcraft*. New York: State University of New York Press, pp. 193–236.
Lindquist, G. 1997. *Shamanic Performances on the Urban Scene: Neo-Shamanism in Contemporary Sweden*. Stockholm: Stockholm Studies in Social Anthropology.
Om Forn Sed. 2013. http://www.samfundetfornsed.se/om-forn-sed-1282539. Accessed 1 July 2013.
Samfundet Forn Sed Sverige. 2013. 'Vad vill vi?'. Retrieved 2 July 2013 from http://www.asatrosamfundet.se/omsamfundssidor/vadvillvi.html.

Spjut, S. 2012. *Stallo*. Stockholm: Albert Bonniers.

Sturluson, S. 1993. *Nordiska Kungasagor: Olav den Helige*. Stockholm: Fabel Pocket.

Svd Nyheter. 2009. 'Weak Support of Research'. Retrieved 2 July 2013 from http://www.svd.se/nyheter/idagsidan/svagt-stod-hos-forskningen_3747315.svd.

Svenska Kyrkan. 2014. 'Swedish Church in Figures'. Retrieved 5 May 2014 from http://www.svenskakyrkan.se/default.aspx?id=645562.

Sveriges Asatrosamfund. 2008. *Forn Sed i Nutid*. Nockeby: Sveriges Asatrosamfund.

Vanliga frågor. 2013. http://www.nordisksed.se/faq/1. Accessed 1 July 2013.

Von Schnurbein, S. 1993. *Religion als Kulturkritik: Neugermanisches Heidentum im 20. Jahrhundert*. Heidelberg: Winter.

Wall, J. 1992. '"Wilt tu nu falla nedh och tilbidha migh…": Folkets tro och kyrkans lära om djävulen', in U. Wolf-Knuts (ed.), *Djävulen*. Åbo: Folkloristiska Institutionen, pp. 21–36.

World Values Survey. 2013. http://www.worldvaluessurvey.org/wvs/articles/folder_published/article_base_54. Accessed 14 May 2013.

Znamenski, A. 2007. *The Beauty of the Primitive: Shamanism and Western Imagination*. Oxford: Oxford University Press.

4

The Brotherhood of Wolves in the Czech Republic

From Ásatrú to Primitivism

Kamila Velkoborská

> *Gagg im af wiga, aiththau gaggais mith im.*[1]
> Get out of their way; otherwise you'll be walking the
> path with them.
> (Motto of the Brotherhood of Wolves in Gothic, their
> sacral language)

Introduction

The Czech Pagan community is very small but highly diverse. Every contemporary Pagan tradition developed elsewhere is represented here: ethnic Pagan reconstructionists as well as eclectic Witches, Pagans searching for a connection with their ancestors and native land as well as those seeking initiation in the Western Mysteries traditions, self-initiated individuals and those seeking community within established traditions such as Wicca, ADF (Ár nDraíocht Féin/A Druid Fellowship), OBOD (Order of Bards, Ovates and Druids) and Native Faith. There is one group, however, that is unique and unlike anything known elsewhere.

The rise of the Brotherhood of Wolves dates back to 1998. The original impulses of its founders were apolitical nationalism, a search for ancient roots and a spirituality connected with these roots. When trying to join established groups, however, they found that nationalism tended to be connected with political radicalism, and a search for roots with reconstructionism. Moreover, both such directions lacked a connection with a living spirituality. They began to develop their own unique system of faith and practice based on worship of the Great Wolf of the Eddas and a lifestyle revolving around dogs – Czechoslovakian Wolfdogs – which most members breed. This cult, as they call it, is not a precisely delimited or finished system. It is susceptible to change and development. It is alive.

The Brotherhood of Wolves bears significant features common to reconstructionism in that it invokes Germanic/Old Norse paganism, but ethnicity is irrelevant and reconstruction goes beyond documented history. Rather than attempting to reconstruct ethnic Paganism as such, the Wolves creatively use its mythology, particularly the part connected with Fenris (the Wolf attested in the Eddas), and combine it with stories and legends about forest tribes, wolves and werewolves, along with visions of their imagination. The resulting Great Wolf religion serves as a connection to the period of human history when people still lived as part of nature; the 'golden age' of Wolf worship is seen as the era of hunters and gatherers. The shamanic aspect of the cult's practice is experienced mainly within the physical environment of the woods. However, this experience and knowledge is also brought into the urban environments where most members live, work and socialize. Their vision is to spread the message of how to connect to a deeper, animalistic self while living in the contemporary world.

The Brotherhood of Wolves is a small group[2] of Pagan believers who have adapted the Old Norse pantheon and modern Ásatrú beliefs to fit their unique practices,[3] which they call the 'Wolf mysteries'. Unlike many contemporary Pagans whose spiritual systems revolve around ritual practice and who call themselves 'practitioners', the Wolves put great emphasis on their faith as a body of central beliefs. Unlike other groups and individuals who reflect the postmodern tendency to explore the 'spiritual marketplace' and put together their own unique spiritual systems, the Wolves desire a set of common beliefs. Unlike Pagans and Witches who like meeting for rituals and other social events regardless of what they believe and how they live as individuals, the Wolves' goal is to create a community whose sharing and mutual interactions stretch beyond ritual. Ritual is important, but it is directed by their faith – one which has a much greater impact on their lifestyles than is the case for most other Pagans.

The Wolves' faith, obviously, is not something inherited or fixed by tradition. It had a beginning, is developing and changing and may decline. In my approach to the Brotherhood of Wolves I follow the lead of Lila Abu-Lughod in her article 'Writing against Culture' (1991) in which she suggests that 'cultural theories ... tend to overemphasize coherence', and this favouring of coherence 'in turn contributes to the perception of communities as bounded and discrete' (Abu-Lughod 1991: 146). To achieve a less neat but perhaps more accurate account of the community under study, Abu-Lughod proposes experimenting with what she calls 'narrative ethnographies of the particular' based on fieldwork carried out traditionally. An ethnography of the particular opposes approaches which favour generalizing, searching for the typical and notions of homogeneity, coherence and timelessness. Such connotations are, according to Abu-Lughod, problematic and scarcely 'make sense when one tries to piece together and convey what life is like' for individuals encountered in the field (Abu-Lughod 1991: 154). Using this approach this chapter will not present the Wolves as a coherent group uniformly doing things in a certain way, but rather as people constantly creating and recreating their faith and practice. The goal of this process is, paradoxically, a framed, fixed, fully functional and pleasing tradition. Nevertheless, this goal – more a desire than a goal – contains also the implicit *dis*belief that this is possible at all. The leader of the group often complains about people joining the group, becoming enthusiastic, then getting into arguments and leaving the group, thus blocking the path to achieving the 'bounded and discrete' tradition which he seems to strongly desire, and which Abu-Lughod claims does not exist. At the same time, however, when observing other groups with more or less fixed rituals and habits over several years, he considers such a situation as stagnation. Needless to say, these ongoing and indeterminate processes are seen only from the inside; to the outside world the Brotherhood of Wolves looks homogeneous and coherent: a unique and distinct tradition.

The task here, then, is to present the Brotherhood of Wolves not as a fully developed and framed tradition, which it is not, but as a tradition-in-the-making. This chapter outlines the process I have been a part of for a period and which will continue and undoubtedly change – aiming for an ethnography of the particular. At the same time, however, it is hoped that this will capture the general, typical features of the group that make it stand out in the Czech Pagan scene and that will make it recognizable for readers.

The Search: Idealism and Romanticism

Members of the Brotherhood of Wolves have different backgrounds and motivations for joining the cult.[4] Some are animists with no interest in ethnic religion, drawn by the image of the Great Wolf as an embodiment of nature's powers; some come for Ásatrú, the new religious movement inspired by the religion of northern pre-Christian Europe, and later discover a love for wolves and dogs; some are simply looking for an earth-based religion; and some join through a relationship with an existing member of the Brotherhood. To trace the group's origins, I asked the leader and priest of the cult, Adrian (Figure 4.1), who was there when the first Czech Pagans-to-be looked around for inspiration. Other voices and outlooks will be included, but the prevailing one will be his.

One of the inspirational contexts for some Pagan seekers during the 1980s was the skinhead movement, which attracted individuals drawn by militant nationalism and cherishing ideas about mythical heroes, powerful warriors and mighty pagan gods. The skinhead scene made a connection with the Nazis due to the SS interest in Norse mythology.[5] Adrian explained that imagery connected with Nazism has a strong impact on the subconscious because it operates with religious symbolism (interview, 28 January 2010). The impression it makes is different from, for example, the imagery of Soviet power. To understand the difference I was told to compare the image of a Hitlerjugend member with that of a Soviet soldier, which is incompatible with the idea of a 'noble warrior'. Despite affiliating

Fig. 4.1 *Adrian and his Wolfdog, Akeenah Runar Waawanyanka. Author's photograph.*

with Nazi imagery and the ethics of the Third Reich, not all skin-
heads were or are fascist; by the end of the 1980s the anti-fascist wing
of the skinhead subculture had been created. The Czech skinhead
scene also differed sociologically from that in the West: many Czech
skins were not working class, but university students. In spite of the
powerful visual form of the culture, however, those seeking spirituality found it superficial and left the movement.

The 1990s was a decade of searching abroad. The first contacts
were made within the White Power scene (which Adrian joined in
1995) and particularly the Blood and Honour movement because
it contained elements of Pagan revival. Blood and Honour is not
a Pagan organization, but a politically motivated group and music
promotion network. Within the skinhead movement in general, and
White Power in particular, roots and ancestry are key concerns, so
naturally elements of pagan mythology appeared in their texts as an
emotional expression of connection to a heroic mythical past and as
a legacy of the Nazi connection with paganism. Blood and Honour
was attractive to Czechs because, unlike the wider skinhead movement, it selected members who were supposed to be active in such
activities as producing music and printing journals. The Czechs who
joined met these criteria.

Within this organization Adrian and several others from the Czech
Republic and Slovakia gained access to information about Pagan
activities abroad and began searching for fellow believers at home.
In 1997 four core members agreed to either establish a local Pagan
group outside the skinhead subculture or to join established organizations elsewhere in the world such as the U.S.-based Ásatrú Folk
Assembly or WotansVolk, a branch of Nordic racial Paganism.[6] As a
result, a Czech Germanic Pagan scene emerged in 1998 with the creation of the Ásatrú group Fraternitas Ulfar (Gothic for 'Brotherhood
of Wolves'), founded by Adrian and Managarm. Fraternitas Ulfar initially contained two clans: the Carpathian Wolves (Adrian's clan) and
Managarm (named after its founder, but no longer in existence). They
began celebrating Ásatrú-style rituals attended by up to ten people.
The rituals were inspired by the texts of Stephen McNallen (2009), an
influential American writer and leader of the Ásatrú Folk Assembly
since 1972. The ritual scripts the Wolves used had been self-published
by McNallen in 1985 under the name *Ásatrú Rituals* and were translated into the Czech language for use by Czech practitioners.[7] These
rituals include *Sumbel*, where an alcoholic beverage is passed round
the circle in a drinking horn and three toasts are made: to the Norse
gods and supernatural beings, to heroes and ancestors, and finally to

others (Strmiska and Sigurvinsson 2005: 129). The other key element of Ásatrú ritual is the *blót*, an invocation of, and offering or sacrifice to, the gods.

At the same time as Fraternitas Ulfar was formed, a society known as the Heathen Hearts of Boiohaemum was formed by a person known as Green Man. (Boiohaemum, or Bohemia, was named after the Celtic tribe Boii which inhabited the area of the contemporary Czech Republic.) This was not a Pagan group but a civic society meant to serve as a platform for the exchange of contacts among Germanic Pagans. It organized common rituals and published a journal.

In 2000 the first *Althing* (gathering)[8] took place and the eight participants agreed on the fusion of Fraternitas Ulfar with the Heathen Hearts of Boiohaemum. The new group (named the Heathen Hearts of Boiohaemum) contained four clans: the two Fraternitas Ulfar clans mentioned above, along with Gabreta[9] and the only clan in Slovakia, Golden Hammer. There were some personal disagreements about matters such as the style of rituals and ritual clothing, but membership grew and twice as many people participated in the second Althing a year later. At the third Althing new clans were created – Villisvin, Wodan and Valknut – on the basis of geographical proximity of members, friendship and, in the case of Villisvin, the worship of a power animal, the wild swine. That year disagreements emerged between the Carpathian Wolves and the rest of the Heathen Hearts of Boiohaemum, based mainly on a power struggle over who was going to decide important matters. For Adrian the absence of spirituality was an issue; he also disliked the excessive amount of alcohol consumed during rituals and disagreed with the general leaning of the organization towards radical subcultures (especially skinhead culture). Because many members were former skins, the group still attracted these people. According to the Heathen Hearts' statutes, they were supposed to study the history and spirituality of the Germanic and Viking civilizations and organize meetings of contemporary adherents, but in practice, Adrian said, many 'just wanted to get drunk'.

This was also the year that the Carpathian Wolves began to shift away from 'orthodox' Ásatrú and began developing the Wolf cult, including the Wolf mysteries (see below) based on a mystical connection with the wolf as power animal. When asked about the idea behind the Carpathian Wolves clan, Adrian explained that because he came from the Hostýnské hills (central Moravia, eastern Czech Republic), a gateway to the Carpathians, 'the Carpathians are an obsession, the land of ancestors and myths. The wolf has been present in my mind always. I have never loved horses, but wolves' (sms conversation, 30 June 2013). Thus his motivations were forged by an emotional connection and intuitive sense of calling, rather than a political agenda.

At this time there were two tendencies within the Carpathian Wolves: a desire to create a distinctive image for the group with a particular faith and practice as a result of moving away from the wider Germanic Pagan scene, and at the same time a continuing desire to belong somewhere. After the disappointment with the Heathen Hearts, in 2003 the Wolves became involved in another attempt to create an umbrella Pagan organization in the Czech Republic named Old Faith, together with Native Faith Slavic Pagans and Wiccans. However, this also failed due to major disagreements, again over issues of control. Controversies between the Wolves and the Heathen Hearts culminated at the fourth Althing where participants, including the participating researcher Petr Jan Vinš, witnessed tensions verging on physical assault between the Wolves and other members of the Heathen Hearts. The Wolves were forbidden to practise the Wolf mysteries, which was the final straw leading to their decision to leave the organization. As Adrian commented (personal conversation, 21 April 2013):

> I wanted to practise rituals in the historicist style but they wanted just to get drunk and do something ... so in fact I travelled 500 km for a drinking session! I didn't like that. At that ritual someone toasted the death of the Wolves and that was the last straw.

The Carpathian Wolves then became allied with a Czech historical reenactment group, Donarian, and a society of old customs, Dunkelheim, was formed containing three guilds: craftsmen, warriors and Pagan priests (Vinš 2006). After a year, however, the Wolves left this organization because its other members emphasized the importance of historical accuracy of material culture and they felt that spiritual matters had become marginalized. In 2004 the project of constructing a living 'ancient village' in the Šumava Mountains commenced in cooperation with the town of Prášily. The Wolves performed religious activities as part of the reconstruction of pre-Christian rituals, mostly in the form of sacral dramas. These are documented on the Carpathiana web pages and included the mystery of binding and releasing the Great Wolf, a handfasting (wedding) ceremony, a Wild Hunt ritual and a ritual devoted to the goddess Hel connected with the journey to the underworld (Carpathiana 2013). More importantly for the future development of the Brotherhood, this was the beginning of long-term experiments with the transformation of their instincts with the help of wolf hybrids – the Wolfdogs. The first one, named Sigrid, was born that year.

By 2005 the Wolves had broken off all contact with the Heathen Hearts and the latter issued a warning that whoever came into contact with the Wolves would be excommunicated. That happened and the Wolves gained new members as a result. At Beltane[10] the Brotherhood of Wolves, which had existed under Fraternitas Ulfar as a part of Heathen Hearts for five years, was revived under the Gothic name Brothrjus Wulfe. Ethnicity was no longer important apart from in the liturgical language and terminology.

Thereafter the cult developed independently; some people left or were expelled and new people arrived, including some with a background in historical reenactment and Czechoslovakian Wolfdog breeding. Most newcomers already had – or acquired – one or more Wolfdogs. The mythical, divine Great Wolf encountered the dog of flesh and daily life. This changed the group's rituals and lifestyle. Previously members had lived more or less mainstream lives in the sense of having jobs, developing their spirituality in their free time, and practising rituals based on Ásatrú with an emphasis on Fenris, the monstrous wolf of the Eddas. By the end of the decade the Wolves' daily lives revolved around their dogs. Merging their lives with those of their companions, they turned to primitivism and what they imagined to be a culture akin to that of ancient hunters and gatherers, believing their lifestyle should be simple and as closely connected with nature as possible. This shift was marked by rituals which contained shamanistic aspects in the form of trance-inducing techniques such as drumming, spontaneous dancing and singing. Sometimes the Wolves refer to their practice as Seidr, the modern reconstruction of which is variously understood as trance-working, soul-journeying, magical practice and sorcery, 'but it is generally agreed that it should involve a complete shift of consciousness – perhaps even a loss of physical control' (Harvey 1997: 115). Mead is sometimes used for Sumbel, but more commonly milk with honey,[11] especially when children are around. Other psychoactive substances (mushrooms or marijuana) are used occasionally with the purpose of awakening the primitive, animalistic self.

In 2010 the 'wolf pack', as Brotherhood members sometimes refer to themselves, expanded through marriages and the birth of children, as well as a rapid rise in the number of dogs (Figure 4.2). The group began to cooperate with the Czechoslovakian Wolfdog Breeding Club (Czechoslovakian Wolfdog Club 2013). Members became more

Fig. 4.2 *Adrian, his daughter and Wolfdogs. Author's photograph.*

and more interested in gaining scientific information about dogs and wolves through books and personal friendship with the writer and wolf-lover Jaroslav Monte Kvasnica (2009, 2011). From 2008 they began to participate regularly in a European gathering of Wolfdog owners in Poland, thus interacting with people outside the spiritual scene, yet sharing on another level.

> Those who get Wolfdogs are romantic spirits, searching for spirituality although not talking about it. We brought in the spirit and began to speak about it. They got the Wolfdog because of spiritual kinship with nature. The Wolfdog stock is perfect for that; it doesn't work with other dog breeds. (Adrian, personal conversation, 21 April 2013)

With more dogs and family and their associated responsibilities, new challenges entered the Wolves' lives: problems with work, debt, mortgages, ill children and so on. As Adrian said: 'It begins to be real'.

The Wolf Cult

People need the cult – something they share and relate to. It may be motorbikes or dogs ... and from there proceeds all life, everything is subjugated to this – work; to be able to look after the dogs, you lose friends, family. (Adrian, personal conversation, 21 April 2013)

As described above, the journey leading to the Wolf cult as it exists today began with a search for a spiritual life. The reason for choosing Ásatrú was rarely a search for ethnicity or an ethnic religion; practitioners pointed to practical reasons, such as the availability of numerous sources on Nordic mythology. One informant, Zmije, did not understand my question about the importance of ethnicity in her faith and practice. When, in the course of the interview, she was told that Ásatrú is perceived as an ethnic religion by scholars, she understood the question, but insisted that ethnicity was irrelevant in her practice. When asked why she chose this particular religion, she replied: 'That's hard to answer, perhaps it is destiny, it just happened' (Facebook conversation, 20 May 2013). Such a view contrasts with the practice of Ásatrú in the U.S., where there is a significant emphasis on race and ancestry (Adler 2006: 284–99).

Scholars often speak about the element of choice when describing religion in modernity and postmodernity. According to this idea, people metaphorically select 'goods' from a religious 'marketplace' and use these to construct a personal religious system. This may apply to eclectic Pagans and Witches but rarely applies in the case of so-called 'ethnic Pagans'. From an emic perspective, 'there is not really any choice, a person hears some kind of call and replies … . I can choose not to reply, but then I would live in contradiction with myself' (Zmije, Facebook conversation, 20 May 2013). Likewise, other informants said that when they began practising Ásatrú they were not looking for their ethnic roots. As discussed above, the Wolves were first drawn to the skinhead movement and later went in search of spirituality and community. Ásatrú was conveniently at hand.

Like many Ásatrúars who adapt Ásatrú to the particular landscape in which they live, the Wolves did not want a 'museum exhibit' religion but one that could be lived in the Czech Republic in the twenty-first century. They were drawn to the most important power animal in Germanic mythology: the wolf. From an etic perspective, the terminology and parts of the Nordic pantheon were retrieved from the Ásatrú 'marketplace' while other aspects were ignored. This approach contrasts with that of U.S. Ásatrúars, who see the religion as a holistic, integrated system offering a complete worldview which 'is not and should never be "just another option" in the marketplace that anyone can try out one day and abandon the next' (Adler 2006: 294).

On the group's old web pages the wolf is presented as an animal worshipped and feared since ancient times as a symbol of wild and unbound power: 'There is no other creature that would be woven into so many legends, blood-curdling stories and superstitions charging from the depths of the human subconscious' (Carpathiana 2013).[12] The author of this text refers to a mythical past when people respected wolves and lived in harmony with them, tracing similarities between wolves and humans in terms of community structure and hunting strategies. Because of its unbound nature, the wolf was a guide and teacher to humans, unlike the dog who became their servant. As a symbol of freedom and solidarity, and because of its extrasensory perception, the animal attained divine status as the Great Wolf worshipped by ancient tribes, many of which, the group believes, derived their origin from wolves. There is no historical evidence of these tribes, but their existence is conjectured on the basis that prior to the development of agriculture – associated with humans' alienation from the wild – people were part of nature and made alliances with other beings both mystically and physically. 'I can see this in Wilmar', Adrian once told me. Whereas Wilmar was once perfectly at home in the woods, his feelings became ambivalent after acquiring domestic animals (Figure 4.3). Although still personally comfortable in the forest, he had also begun to see it as formidable – the *'selva oscura'* (dark forest of Dante's *Divine Comedy*) – and was afraid to locate his chickens near its boundary in case they were killed by predators. When describing this shift, Adrian used similar wording to that of Jacques Le Goff in *La Civilisation de l'Occident Médiéval* (1964),[13] where he explains that the forest, once the 'sanctuary of pagan gods', was cleared between the tenth and thirteenth centuries in the name of Christianity and progress and became a wilderness and place of exile for hermits, lovers, vagrant knights, bandits and outcasts (Le Goff 2005: 184). The Wolves inhabit both spaces: the world in which one drives a car and looks after chickens, and the wilderness, which for the mythical ancestors was a place of communion with both flesh-and-blood wolves and the divine Great Wolf.

According to the Carpathian Wolves the ancient tribes were connected to wolves because:

> at the dawn of ages some individuals on both sides [humans and wolves] crossed over the forbidden threshold of their kind on the journey following the voice of their heart, and with the help of ancient gods they sealed by blood a connection that gave rise to a new kind – Werewolves [those connected with wolves, worshippers of the Wolf] – those who were gifted

Fig. 4.3 *Wilmar. Author's photograph.*

by the favour of the gods with unusual powers that would often be taken as a stigma of damnation in times to come. But even today the legacy of the ancient connection still circulates in many a vein. It urges [those connected with wolves] to an unease that will never cease and they disappear into the night following the call which only few can understand. And so they then, bewildered, roam the moonlit land and search in vain for answers to something they had forgotten a long time ago. But the blood never forgets. (Carpathiana 2013)

The poetic language used here evokes the atmosphere of mythical stories set in time immemorial, but the liminal experience alluded to is something almost every Wolf I have spoken to has experienced. Almost always they speak about 'a call' they could hardly understand but were unable to resist. Meri, for example, who claims to have originally hated wolves, described an experience when, at the age of fourteen, he was roaming through Ostrava, his industrial hometown, when 'suddenly civilization fell on me and I ran away into the woods' (personal conversation, 25 November 2012). Following this experience he contacted the Brotherhood, began participating in their rituals and got himself a Wolfdog. He is now active in the ritual and social life of the group.

Hearing and following the call can be classified as a preliminal experience which is followed by an initiation ritual performed by the pack and initiation into the 'Wolf mysteries' (see below) and rules of the pack, which include, above all, the absolute solidarity of the group and a knowledge of, and respect for, the natural environment. The precise content of the initiation ritual is secret, but it includes tests of physical and mental fitness based on the theory of similarity between the wolf pack and human pack: survival depends on the strength of the weakest member. Wolves must be strong, resistant and fit. The initiatory period lasts about one year, during which time the initiand is observed and tested and after which the group decides whether the person will be formally initiated or not.[14]

On the mystical level, the true significance of the wolf is uncovered 'only by those who pass through all the gates until they stand in the circle of grey skins' (quoted from printed material distributed to pack members only). Initiation has two kinds of transformational effects. It reflects the irresistible beauty and free nature of the wolf as well as its dismal fate – both as animal species and mythical power animal. This refers to the persecution and mass killing of wolves in Europe and America as hated predators and vermin, and to the parallel fate of Fenris of the Eddas, who was bound and killed. The Wolves make clear from the outset that the life of a Wolf is not for everyone and after going through initiation there is no way back. As their motto says: 'Get out of their way; otherwise you'll be walking the path with them'. I have been warned several times that as a result of communing with the Wolves and their dogs I might also be affected by 'the power of amber eyes'.

The Wolf Mysteries

In the Prose Edda, Fenris-Wolf is the son of Loki and a Jötunheim giantess, Angrboda. His siblings are Jörmungandr (also known as the Midgard Serpent) and Hel, who rules the realm of those dead who die of sickness or old age (not in battle). Fenris grew so rapidly that the Æsir (gods) decided to bind him and as a result he bit off the right hand of the god Týr, the only god who dared feed him (Sturluson 2006: 42–43). According to prophecies, Fenris was to be the slayer of Odin, yet the Æsir did not kill him because '[s]o greatly did the gods esteem their holy place and sanctuary, that they would not stain it with the Wolf's blood' (Sturluson 2006: 45). Further, the prophecy says that at the final battle of Ragnarök, in which most gods will die and the world will finally be submerged under water after a series of catastrophes, Fenris-Wolf shall swallow the sun and break loose, but finally he will be killed.

That is how the story goes. According to Wilmar, a member of the Brotherhood of Wolves, the mystery to be drawn from this story is that:

> Every official religion tends to be a religion of law, [concerned with] order in the world, to lead people to acts that make their living together bearable. But even the dark sides of existence struggle for acceptance and respect. Tywaz [alternative spelling of the god Týr], the god of law, by specifying the law, creates the wolf and feeds him – defines him – he who plunders, murders and cheats. But in the end the wolf cannot be destroyed, it's only possible to bind him. (Personal correspondence, 21 May 2013)

On the profane level, wolves are not seen as evil killers but as capable of surviving even in difficult conditions, due to the solidarity of the pack. However, on the mystical level, the wolf is perceived as a symbol of darkness and death and is therefore associated with banishment and life in exile. By embracing this symbol the Wolves accept the dualism of light and darkness, but not in the sense of light representing good and darkness representing evil. Rather, the two form a dialectic of opposites which cannot exist without each other. By identifying with the wolf, long associated with evil, a particular life philosophy is created. The fact that people have been denying the darkness for centuries – and persecuting and killing the wolf – is the reason the world is in decline today. 'The wolf is killed so people may live in the world. But eventually they find out that it was the wolf who brought the world/light' (Wilmar, personal correspondence, 21 May 2013). (The words for 'light', *světlo*, and 'world', *svět*, have a common etymology in Slavic languages.)

Dedication to the wolf due to its association with darkness is also connected with human sacrifice. Physical killing is not essential and may be substituted by exile, or leaving for the wilderness. Members of the Brotherhood perceive themselves as voluntarily taking on the burden of being associated with the dark and living 'in exile' to help save the light/world. Understanding this philosophy is part of the initiation to the Wolf mysteries. Needless to say, there are other ways to understand the Wolf mysteries. In Meri's experience: 'For me it means possession by a wolf ... at least that's how I take it ... so it's a mystery during which you feel the wolf inside yourself and act like the wolf' (Facebook communication, 26 May 2013).

Although the Wolves do not live literally in exile, the expression is not purely metaphorical either. The core group (Adrian's family and Wilmar) lives in an old farmhouse located in the woods several kilometres from the village of Kovčín in western Bohemia. They are dependent on jobs in the village (Wilmar) and Prague (Adrian). Other members live in Prague or Brno. On another level, Wolves choose not to be part of the majority society, which they see as consumerist and ignorant, in decline and responsible for damage to the environment. They perceive themselves as the chosen ones, believing that after centuries of deliberate elimination of the wolf's people (in a literal and metaphorical sense) it is time to rise again: 'We are the wolf's kin and don't want to be part of a society crying in fear from a safe hide, severed from the ancient destiny of the children of Mother Earth' (Carpathiana 2013). This, however, brings consequences which are sometimes hard to accept. Life with a pack of dogs is incompatible with the eight-hour (or longer) working day. Student members supported by their parents do not feel this yet. Those liking a simple hand-to-mouth lifestyle do not care. But those responsible for families sometimes face serious financial problems. As well as practical challenges, living the Wolf's life may bring other difficulties, as Rowlana explains:

> No one can probably explain but it really seems that those connected with wolves on a deeper level attract troubles and he or she doesn't do very well for example in relationships and so on. Hard to say why it is so, maybe there is simply a kind of wolf atavism that's been accumulated during the centuries it's been suppressed. It's a bit paradoxical as regards the relationships as wolves are very faithful and create partnerships for

life. But I think it's also caused by the freethinking, unrestrainedness and this kind of thing … (Facebook communication, 10 June 2013)

In his book *Amber Eyes* Monte Kvasnica confesses to financial and psychological problems and claims that specialists on wolves seem to attract troubles of all kinds. Apparently this does not happen to biologists working with other animals. Kvasnica (2011: 14) wonders: 'The devil only knows … Are wolves carrying for their worshippers apart from joy and euphoria also a dark curse?'

The Wolves Today

This chapter now turns to the year when the first Czechoslovakian Wolfdog was born into the cult and a transformation of the Wolves' instincts began, bringing significant changes to their identities. As Adrian remarked, 'Until then people were only blabbing about the wolves … they were a symbol more than anything else … when one comes into contact with the animal, one finds out that the truth is elsewhere' (personal conversation, 5 May 2013). The perception of the wolf as a predator and fierce killer may have been prevalent among the general public until recently,[15] but this notion is very attractive for others. For admirers of Old Norse mythology and lovers of ancient warfare and the Vikings, the image of the wolf as fierce killer may appeal, but the reality of the wolf hybrid collapses this image completely: 'Everybody wants to be evil! But the Wolfdog is not such a hero and killer … he is actually quite cute' (Adrian, personal conversation, 1 April 2013).

The emotional and mental change this realization caused inevitably brought changes to both spiritual and everyday life. Members of the cult reported that people's behaviour changed as a result of the shift from worshipping the monstrous and powerful Wolf of myth to living with the friendly but cunning wolf hybrid:

He or she behaves less noticeably, communicates differently, not noisily, not talking big, not sorting out things by socking people on the jaw … not raising conflicts, rather being friendly … which actually means treacherous – a poor thing at first sight and then he bites … (Adrian and Rowlana, personal conversation, 21 March 2013)

Dogs participate in the group's rituals. The daily and ritual interaction with them intensifies the Wolves' relationship with nature. In a phenomenological sense, when people live and share with dogs, they *'participate* in one another's existence, influencing each other and being influenced in turn' (Abram 1996: 57). The Wolves' perception of the natural environment is implicitly animistic and dynamic. They draw inspiration from both mythology and nature: from the stories and poems about Fenris as well as the physical reality of their dogs. In rituals they invoke the Great Wolf, but much of this is done in a non-verbal or meta-verbal way, with the understanding that '[p]rior to all our verbal reflections, at the level of our spontaneous, sensorial engagement with the world around us, we are *all* animists' (Abram 1996: 57). Thus in parts of their ritual, and sometimes spontaneously, the Wolves howl. The utterances of the priest give an impression of trying to cross the boundary between verbal and non-verbal communication, between the worlds of people, animals and spiritual beings. For example, an invocation accompanied by rhythmical drumming and preceded by blowing a horn may begin with the priest's long-drawn-out 'aarhhaaa', while he collapses with his arms stretched upwards into the circle of Wolves all squatting 'with one leg underneath, a position learned from the dogs' (Adrian, sms communication, 6 June 2013). The invocation may end: 'We are calling the She-Wolf, the Great White Wolf, our mother … We are calling the She-Wolf, grey and beautiful … [pause] to be with us on this day, oohhh gods … aarhhaaa' (observation of Ostara ritual, Kovčín, 30 March 2013). This has a powerful effect on participants' psyches and emotions.

Participating in the cult's rituals, I have witnessed what Richard Schechner theorizes in *Performance Theory* (2003). Comparing Western drama and prehistoric (but also some contemporary) ritual theatre,[16] Schechner (2003: 69) claims that while in drama the 'scripts' are modes of thinking, in ritual they are patterns of doing: 'Talking does not appear first as configuration (words-as-written) but as sound (breath-noise)'. Similarly, drama's efficacy is achieved in a different way from ritual's efficacy. In ritual, efficacy is 'not "a result of" dancing the script but "contained in" dancing the script. In other words, in prehistoric ritual theatre, as in contemporary ritual, the doing is a manifestation more than a communication' (Schechner 2003: 69). It seems that using phatic cries and animal sounds helped the Wolves turn from well-organized Ásatrú-style rituals, which are intended to mean something, to primitivism, where the doing culminating in ecstasy is the meaning. Spontaneous sounds and movements are not intended to communicate, but rather manifest and rouse feelings; a strong sense of *communitas* is created within rituals.

This style of ritual was the result of a gradual shift, beginning about 2005, from the more or less established system of Ásatrú as it came, ready-to-use, from the U.S., to rituals of the Wolves' own making, which have a loose structure, are ecstatic and are intended to be evocative of contemporary hunters and gatherers. The idea behind following a philosophy of primitivism and lifestyle which cherishes hunting and gathering as an ideal is not to put the clocks back fifteen hundred years, but to create a new wolf tribe. There is little evidence of the ancient hunting and gathering lifestyle to be inspired by, but as the Wolves say: 'Where history ends, we begin to learn by practice' (Adrian, personal conversation, 11 July 2013). They aim to live as simply as possible – without electricity, running water or a flushing toilet in the case of Adrian's household, which is shared with Wilmar. Although not all members live like this, they try to follow ecological principles by not wasting, reusing and mending, as well as finding novel ways to get what they need. For example, they pick up roadkill and use the animals' skins. When killing their own animals, they use everything from the animal. All members are able to skin animals, dress the skin, work with wood and bone and kindle a fire without matches. They shop at second-hand shops and recycle clothing. They retrieve discarded Christmas trees to use the fir wood for their Yule fire. In a former farmhouse in western Bohemia set in the woods, food is cooked over the fire outside when the weather is good (Figure 4.4), and on the stove indoors during winter. The dishes and kitchen utensils include handmade wooden plates, old enamel pans, old porcelain plates and mugs recalling the Czech socialist regime, artistic handmade bowls with swastikas, chipped enamel cups and mugs with flower patterns, traditional Scandinavian drinking cups called *kuksa*, glass jars from pickles used as vases for meadow flowers … nothing is wasted. I have been asked to help cook, look after the fire, cut wood and disentangle an old wire fence to get wire for mending a goats' enclosure. In creating their lifestyle the Wolves have also changed the sources of information which help them build it. Instead of asking historians and archaeologists as they did in their Ásatrú period, they now talk to biologists, botanists and experts on animal breeding.

The Brotherhood's relationship to wolves is threefold. First, they have a mystical relationship to Fenris of the Eddas, a symbol of strength and darkness, temporarily bound but not killed. Together with Skadi, the White huntress, and Uller, the Black hunter, Fenris stands at the centre of the cult's worship. Second, they admire and study the grey wolf (*Canis lupus*), which once inhabited large areas

Fig. 4.4 *The Wolves cook outdoors during summer. Author's photograph.*

of North America and Eurasia and was demonized and almost eradicated. Wolves were 'cast as villains in stories almost since there were stories' but also represent the 'untamed call of the wild' (Dutcher 1997). The idea that following this 'call' is connected with the fate of an outcast resonates strongly in the cult. At the same time it contains the implicit belief that being an outcast but connected to the land is better than separation from the land while living in plenty. Absolute self-sufficiency is not the Wolves' goal, but rather a lifestyle which is more respectful of the living environment than that of the dominant society, which thoughtlessly consumes.

Being a symbol of survival is associated with another key quality of wolves: their social behaviour. A lone wolf is rare; survival depends on the pack (Dutcher 1997; see also Living with Wolves 2013). The wolf pack is seen as a model for the human pack. The togetherness and unity of the Brotherhood is evident in everyday behaviour, such as in dealing with a newborn baby, who is looked after by all members of the pack, including the participating anthropologist. It also reveals itself in extreme situations, such as one I witnessed on the night after the winter solstice (22 December 2012). The ritual was attended by guests, one of whom, after some alcohol consumption, verbally attacked one of the she-Wolves. The seemingly trivial incident culminated in a fierce physical fight that included dog bites and verbal threats like: 'No one offends members of the Brotherhood! I'll kill you, bastard!' and ended with banishment of the offender from the Wolves' territory. Following the Wolves' ethical code, there was a thorough investigation of the argument the next day, but in the heat of the moment this was irrelevant: the whole pack stood in unity behind one of its own.

Third, as discussed above, daily life with the Czechoslovakian Wolfdog, the wolf hybrid, brings an embodied dimension to the Wolves' spirituality. Just as the wolf pack mirrors the human family with its structure, hierarchy, mutual support, love for young ones and so on, the Wolfdog serves as a symbolic mirror. However, unlike the free, wild wolves, dogs – like modern people – are tamed and chained, unable to do what they want. As Adrian said, the Brotherhood represents a kind of 'desperado culture' (personal telephone conversation, 21 May 2013). Yet it is also a romantic life filled with beauty and joy experienced by those who yield to the charm of wolves and Wolfdogs. Both wolf and dog serve as mirrors to humans: the wolf represents the ideal picture, the dog the real one.

Conclusion

To be sincere, inspired by Native Americans, we sometimes tell the esoteric-lovers total bollocks that reflect what they want us to be, the best in this is Wilmar. (Adrian, sms communication, 16 November 2012)

After a glimpse into the history and life of contemporary practitioners of the Wolf mysteries and primitivism, it may seem that they are a voluntarily secluded, self-contained group of solemn people taking on the burden of saving the world. To correct this picture I would like to end with a story. On the day after the winter solstice ritual in 2012, the Wolves slaughtered a pig to supply themselves with meat for the winter. Their reasons were altogether mundane. Dogs participated, as they usually do, and received their portions. After everything was over, the human members of the pack realized that splashing the blood around the dogs created a perfect circle. An idea was born and the same day a photograph of the place with a sunlit circle of blood in the snow was put on the Brotherhood of Wolves Facebook page, entitled 'Solstice Sacrifice'. A stormy discussion erupted immediately with emotionally charged posts, such as:

> Discussant: 'What??? Why....?'
> Wolf: 'Because we want the sun to rise tomorrow!'
> Discussant: 'But this is practised only perhaps in black magic ... are you a sect or what? ... You obviously know nothing about harmony with nature and Mother Earth ...'
> Wolf: 'Dear ladies, here you have wandered into the territory of pre-Christian indigenous cults.... And we are truly afraid that the sun will not rise tomorrow!!! The night is unbearable'.

While the discussion was evidently taken very seriously by some participants, those who knew the Wolves well could hear their laughter behind the lines. Consistent with Schechner's (2003: 270) theories about the encounter between 'gullible ethnographers' – replaced by 'esoteric-lovers' in this context – and locals who delighted in describing 'incredible cruelties' and 'elaborate displays of fact-mixed-with-fantasy', the Wolves like to present themselves as primitives of a much harder core than they really are. Schechner interprets such behaviour as violence that is desired but not realized, or a cathartic display analogous to the Western delight in horror movies. In the case of the Wolves, the position is rather that of setting themselves apart from, and also provoking, those who follow spiritual paths they consider naive (especially those in the New Age movement), in that they ignore the darker parts of human nature. But it is also simply because they like having fun and believe this kind of fun corresponds with their spiritual path.

Notes

1 According to the Wolves' website, 'This sentence, used in the cultic book *Jiná Rasa*, 2007 [Other Race, by Jenny Nowak], became the motto for *Brothrjus Wulfe* [The Brotherhood of Wolves]' (http://www.carpathiana.wz.cz, accessed 31 May 2013). All translations into English in this chapter are by the author.
2 I was asked not to reveal the number of present members.
3 Ásatrú is a Pagan reconstructionist movement based on Old Norse religion. *Ásatrú* means belief in the Old Norse gods, or, more correctly, loyalty to the Æsir, a race of sky gods, one of two groups of gods in Norse mythology. (The other is the Vanir.) The Æsir consists of Odin, often seen as the high god; his wife, Frigga; his son Thor; Týr; Balder and many others (Adler 2006: 286–87).
4 The term 'cult' is used by group members; in the centre of the cult stands the Wolf.
5 Aspects of Norse paganism were introduced into Nazism by Heinrich Himmler, who was responsible for research into German roots and ancestry with the goal of teaching Germans about Aryan superiority. Himmler is believed to have loved Norse mythology.
6 VotansVolk is one of two organizations within Wotanism, a form of Paganism established in 1990 by David Lane, a U.S. American White-nationalist leader and criminal (sentenced to 190 years in prison for activities, including murder, connected with his White-nationalist group, The Order). He saw ethnic religion as a weapon against the alleged genocide of the White race. Wotanism differs from other kinds of Germanic Paganism in that it contains political overtones.
7 The official version of the book was published in 2009 as *Asatru Book of Blotar and Rituals – by the Asatru Folk Assembly*.
8 In the U.S. an Althing is a national gathering of Nordic Pagans 'from across the United States modelled on the *Althing*, the ancient Pan-Icelandic quasi-parliament that was held each summer in the spectacular natural landscape of Thingvellir in the early period of Icelandic settlement' (Strmiska and Sigurvinsson 2005: 132). Czech Althings included participants from the Czech Republic and Slovakia. They copied American Althings but were much smaller in size. In its heyday the Heathen Hearts of Boiohaemum had about twenty people. Most clans had two or three members.
9 'Gabreta' is another name for the Šumava Mountains in western Bohemia.
10 The Wolves have their own names for the Pagan holidays in the Gothic language, but are still developing the terminology. They use the well-known Celtic names for the seasonal rituals so as not to confuse people (Adrian, sms conversation, 1 July 2013).
11 Milk with honey is understood to be a traditional drink on the basis of a personal gnosis: milk is the first drink we are fed by our mothers; the

honey symbolism is connected with amber. Amber is a symbol of the sun and also the golden amber eyes of wolves and Wolfdogs. Many members wear amber necklaces.

12 These web pages (http://www.carpathiana.wz.cz) still exist but no longer reflect the current cult because the last update was in 2007. At present, due to busy lives filled with dogs and families, the Brotherhood has no official web pages, only a profile on Facebook: https://www.facebook.com/pages/Brothrjus-Wulfe/176511539106948?fref=ts.

13 References to this work here are to the Czech edition, *Kultura Středověké Evropy* (2005).

14 For obvious reasons (revealing the nature of initiation tasks to future initiands would spoil their effect), the initiation ritual has not been explained to me in detail, and I am unwilling to reveal my observations for the same reason.

15 Wolves and werewolves are gaining popularity evidenced by such films as the *Harry Potter*, *Twilight Saga* and *Vampire Diaries* series. Such popularity has no impact on the membership of the Brotherhood of Wolves.

16 Schechner speculates about the nature of prehistoric ritual theatre on the basis of cave art and the documented rituals of hunting societies.

References

Abram, D. 1996. *The Spell of the Sensuous*. New York: Vintage Books.

Abu-Lughod, L. 1991. 'Writing against Culture', in R.G. Fox (ed.), *Recapturing Anthropology: Working in the Present*. Santa Fe: School of American Research Press, pp. 137–54, 161–62.

Adler, M. 2006. *Drawing Down the Moon: Witches, Druids, Goddess-Worshippers and Other Pagans in America Today*, 4th edn. New York: Penguin.

Carpathiana, Brothrjus Wulfe. 2013. http://www.carpathiana.wz.cz. Accessed 21 May 3013.

Czechoslovakian Wolfdog Club. 2013. http://www.cswolfdog.cz. Accessed 21 May 2013.

Dutcher, J. (dir.). 1997. *Wolves at our Door*. Television documentary. Discovery Channel, U.S.A.

Harvey, G. 1997. *Listening People, Speaking Earth: Contemporary Paganism*. London: Hurst and Company.

Kvasnica, J.M. 2009. *Krajina s vlky* [Landscape with Wolves]. České Budějovice: Élysion.

——. 2011. *Jantarové oči* [Amber Eyes]. České Budějovice: Élysion.

Le Goff, J. 2005. *Kultura Středověké Evropy*, trans. J. Cermak, 2nd edn. Prague: Vyšehrad.

Living with Wolves. 2013. http://www.livingwithwolves.org. Accessed 6 June 2013.

McNallen, S., E. Odinsson, T. LeBouthillier, and B. Shelbrick. 2009 [1985]. *Asatru Book of Blotar and Rituals – by the Asatru Folk Assembly*. Published by the Asatru Folk Assembly, printed in the U.S.

Nowak, J. 2007. *Jiná Rasa*. Olomouc: Netopejr.

Schechner, R. 2003. *Performance Theory*. London and New York: Routledge.

Strmiska, M. and B. Sigurvinsson. 2005. 'Asatru: Nordic Paganism in Iceland and America', in M. Strmiska (ed.), *Modern Paganism in World Cultures*. Santa Barbara: ABC Clio, pp. 127–79.

Sturluson, S. 2006. *The Prose Edda: Tales from Norse Mythology*. Mineola: Dover Publications.

Vinš, P.J. 2006. 'Nejnovější vývoj germánského pohanství v ČR: Neúspěch jednotících tendencí soudobého českého pohanství a radikalizace klanu Karpatských vlků – terénní studie'. (Translation: 'The Most Recent Development of Germanic Paganism in CR: The Failure of Unifying Tendencies in Contemporary Czech Paganism and Radicalization of the Carpathian Wolves Clan'). Student scientific conference, Hussite Theological Faculty, Charles University, Prague.

5

Soviet-Era Discourse and Siberian Shamanic Revivalism

How Area Spirits Speak through Academia

Eleanor Peers

Introduction

The shamanic revival currently taking place in the Republic of Sakha (Yakutia), northeastern Siberia, bears much resemblance to the other Pagan and shamanic religious movements described in this volume: it too is heavily influenced by global forms of Neo-pagan spirituality and ethnic nationalism.[1] Like contemporary Paganism, it bears the stamp of pervasive contemporary post-Enlightenment epistemologies and social forms in that Sakha shamanic activity is infracted by paradigms, identities and practices associated with the quintessentially modern institutions of the nation state, universal education and the academy. And yet contemporary forms of Sakha shamanism are shaped by two legacies that are absent from the European context – that of the Sakha people's pre-Soviet shamanic tradition, which has survived both Christian missionization and Soviet-era repression, and that of the republic's experience of Soviet modernization in particular and subsequent post-Soviet national revival. As this chapter will show, traces of the various political, historical and social currents around Sakha shamanism are clearly manifested in its practice and development. Forms that have their roots in the pre-Soviet shamanic tradition have become adapted and assimilated into a social context that stands at the intersection of shifting nationalist, colonialist and globalizing power dynamics, in common with the shamanic revivals that are occurring in other parts of Siberia (c.f. Balzer 2011; Lindquist 2006).

This chapter sets out the main features of contemporary Sakha shamanism, and in doing so explores the role a strikingly consistent performance – the delivery of an authoritative lecture – has in Sakha shamanic practice, and, in particular, in the articulation of shamanic communities. Following Edward Schieffelin's interest in the power of performance to 'make present realities' (Schieffelin 1998: 194), I discuss here the impact a form of performance arising out of Soviet-era discursive practice has had on the way communities of shamanic healers and their clients emerge into Sakha (Yakutia)'s social reality. Ironically, this Soviet discursive form has also served to perpetuate aspects of Sakha community life that have their roots in pre-Soviet Sakha society and its shamanic heritage. It is an instance of the way in which the specificities of a given local context shape social forms with connections and equivalences all over the globalized world – such as modern Paganism, and its overlaps with academia, education and nationalism.

Sakha (Yakutia) is unusual, although not unique, among Russia's federal subjects, in that its titular ethnic group, the Sakha people, is numerically dominant over the Russian population: according to the 2010 census, 49.9 per cent of the population are Sakha, while 37.8 are Russian (*National Population Census, Russian Federation* 2010). The republic's capital city is Yakutsk. Like many other non-Russian Siberian cultures, the Sakha people experienced a revival of their cultural and religious tradition during the 1980s and 1990s after many decades of state-sponsored social transformation. The first section of this chapter discusses the shamanic movement this revival has generated and its links with academia. Shamanic communities and their practices are contextualized further in the second section, which addresses the particular shapes and conventions within Sakha society, and its hierarchies. The final section draws on Aleksei Yurchak's (2006) discussion of changing Soviet-era discursive practice to show how shamanic practitioners are taking their own places within Sakha society through adapting Soviet-era performative forms, thus harnessing their power to shape and articulate communities in the Sakha context.

Contemporary Sakha Shamanism and its Influences

During March 2011, I found myself temporarily coopted into my friends' efforts to build their careers as *Algyschyttar* – the Sakha shamanic specialists who heal through their capacity to interact with the higher spirits and gods in the Sakha shamanic pantheon. Yegor and Sardaana were travelling together through a province of Sakha (Yakutia), delivering lectures and demonstrating healing techniques at village halls around the region. Yegor spoke about his own skills as a masseur and spiritual healer, while Sardaana was publicizing her partner Vanya's revival of a Sakha tradition for ceremonially preserving the afterbirth. Yegor invited me to accompany them partly to give me an opportunity to collect ethnographic data on the region, but also because their village audiences would be interested to hear about England and the West, and to meet in person someone from a distant country. He hoped that my accounts of life in England would help to promote his own messages, in particular his personal campaign to discourage alcohol abuse. In addition, a public cooperation with a foreign academic would be likely to raise Yegor's own status.

And so Yegor, Sardaana and I would sit together behind a long table, facing our quiet and attentive audiences. Yegor directed the meetings; generally I started off, and then Yegor and Sardaana would explain in turn their particular healing techniques and the place these techniques had within the Sakha shamanic tradition. Sardaana told her audience about the ancient Sakha practice of preserving afterbirths in specially made containers, in order to build a beneficial connection between their children and their home territories. Yegor described the range of healing techniques he had developed, from traditional Sakha massage to the healing amulets he had made using wood from a tree that had been struck by lightning. Often a member of the village's administration would be present and would give a short speech to express the village's gratitude to us. These speeches, and the long table with its jug of water and three glasses, were part of the reason why I felt so at home during these occasions: in form they were identical to the academic conferences I often attended in Sakha (Yakutia), during the field trips I had made as part of my Ph.D. and postdoctoral research. The three of us could have been delivering a panel presentation – had the content of our talks been slightly different.

In fact, the practice of delivering instructive speeches about shamanism and Sakha culture is common within Sakha (Yakutia)'s emerging shamanic scene. For example, a fortune-telling festival in January 2011 began with a banquet, which several activists used as an opportunity to tell the assembled company about their insights into the Sakha heritage. One of them showed us a 'family tree' of the Turkic peoples, which has been circulating on the Internet since 2009 (Tengry 2013). According to this tree, the Turkic peoples are descended from the Huns, or the *Khunnar*, who themselves are a branch of the *Skif-Sakalar*, the tribe standing at the tree's base. The occasions of this type I attended combined several functions: they were therapeutic in that individuals came to seek help for a variety of physical, emotional and financial problems; they could often be entertaining; and they offered their Sakha audiences a combination of moral, philosophical and historical education through their discussions of past Sakha practices, values, beliefs and cultural origins. This combination of education, spiritual healing and entertainment reflects the place of contemporary Sakha shamanic practice within simultaneously the Sakha nationalist revival and the opening up of Sakha (Yakutia) to global cultural and economic trends following the political transformation of the Soviet Union.

The most recent Sakha nationalist mobilization occurred during the 1980s and 1990s, in tandem with similar non-Russian nationalist revivals throughout the former Soviet Union – and, like them, emerged out of a long history of Russian tsarist and Soviet colonization. Sakha populations first encountered Russian colonization during the first half of the seventeenth century. This colonization was to usher in a transformation of Sakha life and culture, which was accelerated during the Soviet period by the arrival of technologically advanced industry and infrastructure on the one hand, and a new determination on the part of the central government to incorporate non-Russian communities into its state project on the other.[2] Like the former Soviet Union's other non-Russian peoples, the Sakha experienced a range of policies designed to convert their then broadly Turkic, animist culture and worldview into the modernist, Marxist-Leninist and therefore materialist outlook of committed Soviet citizens. The Soviet-era policies have succeeded in radically changing the Sakha way of life, as they have integrated the Sakha population more closely into the Russian-dominated mainstream. By the 1980s, most of the Sakha population lived in Russian-style villages; younger Sakha people in particular could often regard their own cultural tradition as irrelevant within the new Soviet world of cars, pop music and technological advance (Balzer 1995; Crate 2006).

And yet the late 1980s saw a sudden awakening of interest in the Sakha cultural tradition, particularly among intellectuals and cultural workers (Balzer 1995). This reappearance of Sakha cultural practice within public consciousness combined political mobilization with a flurry of activism designed to promote, express and reinvigorate the Sakha cultural tradition and, in particular, shamanism. The acknowledgement of a predilection towards shamanic belief became in some important circles the mark of a laudable interest in Sakha traditional culture, instead of an embarrassingly backward, pre-modern world-view. The project to revive Sakha culture thus became closely linked to the practice of shamanism, to the extent that shamanic practitioners will often combine healing with explaining their own discoveries about the Sakha shamanic tradition, as in the examples above.

Many of Sakha (Yakutia)'s leading shamanic specialists came to prominence during the 1990s as nationalist activists, who had taken it upon themselves to research and revive their people's dying spiritual tradition. These individuals had at their disposal both a corpus of pre-Soviet and Soviet ethnographic data on Sakha culture and life, and the possibility of interacting with the small number of shamanic practitioners who had survived Soviet-era political repression. Indeed, many people suddenly found themselves able to perceive or acknowledge shamanic vocations that they had previously repressed – just as others could talk openly about the small shamanic rituals they had continued to perform throughout their daily lives, such as feeding Bayanai, the spirit master of the forest, before going hunting (see also Balzer 1993; Crate 2006). This vague consciousness of a spiritual presence in daily life had replaced the experience of a capacious and rich shamanic cosmos, divided into multiple dimensions and inhabited by gods, beneficial *ajyy* spirits, area spirits, ghosts and demons. A handful of people, generally living in the more remote parts of the republic, still performed classic shamanic rituals in which they went on journeys into the spirit world, or were possessed by spirits while in trance. More common, however, were and are the *ekstrasensy* – individuals who have varied psychic gifts, such as being able to tell a person's mental and physical state from looking at their eyes, but who do not go into a full shamanic trance.

I have encountered a huge variety of reaction towards the shamanic revival, including the shamanic discussion of Sakha cultural tradition, ranging from dismissal to a sense of excited discovery. A small community of people devote the bulk of their time, energy and money to attending shamanic lectures, for example, or visiting important ritual sites. However, this spectrum of activity is not as marginal as one might initially expect. There is a close interaction between Sakha (Yakutia)'s community of shamanic practitioners and sections of the republic's academic establishment – a legacy of the crucial role academics have had in the Sakha nationalist revival. The connections cut both ways, in that there are academics who have become shamanic specialists or their helpers – echoing the career of anthropologist-turned-shaman Michael Harner, for example

– and shamanic specialists who have published what they present as authoritative or academic texts. Some of the claims shamanic specialists have made about the Sakha cultural heritage echo or cite claims made by academics. For example, a history professor at Sakha (Yakutia)'s state university has published several works on the probable Iranian and Aryan origins of the Sakha people, and has noted similarities between Sakha and Sanskrit (Gogolev 2004: 101–102). One of Yakutsk's more extravagant shamanic specialists has taken this observation further, asserting that Sakha is in fact both an ancient form of Sanskrit and closely linked to English; this fact reflects the fundamental importance the Sakha cultural tradition has within the history of humankind (Bozhedonov 2008). (These contentions sit uneasily with the view taken by many foreign and local scholars that the Sakha culture and language are predominantly Turkic, the Sakha communities themselves having moved north, possibly from the Baikal region, in a series of migrations during the second millennium CE (see, for example, Crate 2006; Gogolev 1986; Jochelson 1933: 164; Maak 1994; or Seroschevskiy 1993).) It is this preoccupation with the Sakha cultural heritage, and its significance in world history, that distinguishes the work of Sakha shaman-academics from that of their American or European colleagues, such as Harner (who synthesized practices from various traditions to create his 'Core Shamanism'), while manifesting the impact post-Soviet identity politics have had in shaping contemporary Sakha shamanic practice.

As might be expected, shamanic specialists have a greater tendency to describe their educational material as inspired by supernatural forces, in addition to their own research in the archives. Shamanic practitioners, already steeped in knowledge about past shamanic forms from their attention both to older Sakha acquaintances and to the ethnographic data they have seen, can receive spiritual information (*informatsiya*) about the Sakha heritage and its significance. The lectures and books produced by shamanic specialists often incorporate quasi-academic rhetorical strategies and terms – a reflection of the lack of perceived boundary between the form of knowledge production commonly acknowledged as 'academic' in Russia, and the knowledge generated by spiritual insight, among many members of this community. Some shamanic practitioners have explained to me their need to use 'modern' language to describe shamanic experience, so that 'modern' people will understand – and so spirits have become 'energies' (*energetiki*), for example. However, many shamanic practitioners have gone beyond reframing their activities according to paradigms that are seemingly more palatable to the contemporary mindset, to produce extensive accounts of the world, humanity and existence. Vanya explained to me his view of the world, its people and its direction, and was keen to hear about my own philosophical system as a fellow intellectual. Many shamanic practitioners therefore do not feel that their spiritual gifts and skills are sufficient in themselves to justify their claims towards competence in their field. One shaman told me that, these days, shamanic practitioners have to be not only spiritual leaders but also businessmen and academics if they are to get anywhere. Hence, my public willingness to cooperate with Yegor was a significant addition to his authority: Yegor himself had not yet published any books; but my presence showed that he was capable of earning respect and friendship from qualified academics.

Thanks to the rapid introduction of contemporary information technology, Sakha people now have access to cultural forms from around the world – and hence contemporary Sakha shamanic practice can assimilate aspects of other religious or philosophical traditions from the wider Russian Federation and beyond. Sardaana's own shamanic practice is a particularly clear example of the new possibilities a greater connection with the outside world can afford. She has found her shamanic vocation to lie in the Hawaiian shamanic massage tradition, *Lomi Lomi Nui*: she learned the art at courses run by a Russian who had himself visited Hawaii. Other leading shamanic activists have toured countries such as India, Tibet, China and Mongolia, returning to share their experiences via lectures and magazine articles.

However, the sudden exposure of the Sakha people to globalizing social and cultural trends, following their history as a community colonized by successive Russian state administrations, has created a profound insecurity about the value and meaning of the Sakha heritage. This uncertainty has been exacerbated by a massive migration of Sakha people to Sakha (Yakutia)'s capital, Yakutsk, over the past decade, which is causing the rapid decline of practices and relationships that previously had been understood as central to Sakha culture and identification (Argounova-Low 2007; Ventsel 2006). In addition, the Russian Federation's central government has succeeded in whittling away the autonomy Sakha (Yakutia)'s regional administration gained during the early 1990s, turning Sakha (Yakutia) back into a peripheral part of a larger, Russian-dominated state.

The role I had in Yegor's lecture tour illustrates the ambivalent relationship Sakha people can have towards Europeans in particular, and its roots in the Sakha people's longstanding position as an ethnic minority subject to cultural, social and economic interventions from a distant and dominant European power. On the one hand, my attraction and authority as a guest and speaker was increased significantly by my belonging to what is locally known as a 'civilized people': Yegor would interject during my account with comments on the practices and conventions of my 'developed nation'. On the other, Yegor and Sardaana were emphasizing the value of traditional Sakha practice and the healing techniques it had to offer. The far-reaching claims about the Sakha cultural heritage described above are in fact an extreme case of a general tendency to affirm the worth of a Sakha identification in the face of the perceived contempt evinced by 'civilized Europeans'. Contemporary shamanic practice is thus influenced simultaneously by a motivation to promote or satisfy Sakha national pride and, paradoxically, the attractive cultural and religious forms from outside Sakha (Yakutia) that seem to threaten its heritage. This tension is also manifested in the controversies that can surround an interest in or engagement with foreign forms of Pagan spirituality. The pages of *Kisteleng Küüs*, Sakha (Yakutia)'s specialist esoteric/shamanist magazine, contain some Russian-language articles about eastern, first-nation American, ancient religious and ancient cultural traditions, reflecting a widespread curiosity about foreign cultural forms. However, during my fieldwork I also encountered the opinion that Sakha people should reserve their most profound level of commitment for Sakha shamanism in particular: some healers disparaged or mocked colleagues with too profound an interest in foreign healing traditions (Peers 2014).

Unsurprisingly, the renewed popularity of shamanism among the Sakha people, in combination with the rapidity of recent social and political change, has generated a huge variety of techniques and approaches among shamanic practitioners. There are plenty of shamanic healers who are less keen on delivering talks and publishing books, and whose practice takes the form of private, intimate encounters with their clients. In fact the most famous and respected shaman in Sakha (Yakutia) – an elderly reindeer-herder who is ethnically Eveny rather than Sakha – is prevented from making his own public speeches by his heavily accented Russian. Hence, the efficacy of shamanic specialists is not regarded as dependent on their capacity for public presentation. Many Sakha acquaintances have insisted that traditionally the most powerful shamans do not seek to attract attention to their work and achievements. Why, then, do so many of Sakha (Yakutia)'s up-and-coming shamanic healers invest so much time and effort into their status as outstanding authority figures?

Why is their authority understood to accrue from the production and dissemination of expert knowledge about the Sakha cultural tradition in particular – especially when some prominent shamans have no university education whatsoever, like the Eveny reindeer-herder mentioned above? And why are the people who seek spiritual and physical benefit from shamanic healers also content to devote considerable amounts of time and money to attending these lectures and buying these books?

Public Speaking, Achievement, Authority and Community in Sakha (Yakutia)

Sakha communities – and the power dynamics within them – have been shaped by their integration into an overarching Russian state for the past three hundred years. The forms of social differentiation among Sakha groups and the way these forms emerge and are negotiated closely resemble patterns that exist all over the Russian Federation and the former Soviet Union. After all, the population of Sakha (Yakutia) was incorporated into the Soviet Union's system of government, along with the overlapping clientelist networks that co-existed with the Soviet Union's state institutions (Ledeneva 1998; Verdery 1996; Yurchak 2006) and have come to succeed them (Ledeneva 2013). The Sakha population was likewise drawn into the network of cultural and educational institutions that existed throughout the Soviet Union and the varying perceptions of status and hierarchy they generated. Sakha academics, musicians, artists, actors, war heroes, party officials and sports champions enjoyed the high status within Sakha (Yakutia) that such figures had all over the Soviet Union, even if their provincial background could make it difficult for them to compete with their colleagues from central Russia.

And yet, variations existed in the power dynamics within the different communities that made up the Soviet population, which continue to exert an influence; these variations could arise from the interrelationship of particular personalities and circumstances; but they could also make manifest lingering cultural differences among the former Soviet Union's ethnic groups (Humphrey 1998; Iğmen 2011; Vitebsky 2005). In Sakha (Yakutia) it is noticeable that rural Sakha populations seem to form more tightly knit territorial communities than Russian or mixed populations. Some scholars have pointed to the continuing importance of kin relationships, to the extent that life in both rural and urban communities is conditioned by the presence of powerful family networks (Argounova-Low 2007) – although Csaba Mészáros has pointed out the ways in which surnames can be exchanged, or even bought or sold, as part of the power dynamics within some villages (Mészáros 2013).

During my visits to Sakha (Yakutia), I found that the presence of a strong sense of affiliation to the home region and village, especially among older generations, is manifested in many different ways – whether in common conversational patterns, such as detailing one's home region and its defining characteristics on being introduced to a stranger, or in institutional practice, and especially cultural production (c.f. Ventsel 2009). It is conventional for the influential members of a particular regional population to stage lavish concerts in Yakutsk, which are opportunities for the region's Yakutsk-based diaspora to come together and celebrate their region and its most prominent inhabitants. Musical entertainment, performed by the region's leading singers and dancers, is interspersed during these concerts with long speeches from both the concert organizers and performers and the members of the audience whom they call onstage to receive prizes or certificates. These speeches generally consist of praise for the region and for the achievements, talents and value of specific individuals – in addition to the expression of the speaker's good wishes for the region and its people.

Rural communities also display and celebrate their members and cohesion through building museums (Cruikshank and Argounova 2000). Many of the regional centres and villages in Sakha (Yakutia) can boast museums about the locality, which contain large exhibitions of photographs of the region's families, often detailing their education and professional careers. A stranger visiting one of these museums is likely to learn a great deal about the region's individual inhabitants and their activities, in addition to what they might glean about local history, flora and fauna. These exhibitions display a galaxy of talented, hard-working, competent individuals, often grouped into their family units. Some of the stars shine more brightly than others, as the outstanding sports champions, singers, musicians, academics or politicians are displayed more prominently. However, there were no signs of envy or competitiveness in the way that museum guides or others spoke about their regions' leading inhabitants: they seemed rather to take pride and pleasure in praising their fellow country-men. I encountered people who were willing to praise local heroes, even when these individuals had controversial reputations in other parts of the republic. For instance, the teachers in one rural school were keen to emphasize the sterling qualities of their local member of parliament (*deputat*) and what he had achieved for their school, despite the fact that this politician has been involved in some prominent scandals.

As the example of this *deputat* shows, much of Sakha (Yakutia)'s republican political establishment is integrated into its regional communities. Sakha politicians and businessmen can act as patrons for their home regions and villages, as in this example: the politician concerned had provided his hometown with a new school. The expectation that Sakha (Yakutia)'s *deputaty* will further the interests of their region of origin is integrated into the republic's governance, in addition to its complex relationship with the federal government in Moscow (Peers 2009). The federal government may now have a decisive level of control over the republic's natural resources and policies, but it cannot ignore the fact that a considerable number of the republic's politicians and government officials maintain their authority, and hence their capacity to govern, through their patronage of their home regions. A felt need for cohesiveness and loyalty in fact extends to the Sakha people as an ethnic group: many Sakha people have expressed to me a layered sense of identification, first with their home region and then with the Sakha people as a whole. There is thus an onus on Sakha politicians to further the interests of the Sakha population in particular, which they have to balance with the federal government's interest in minimizing the significance of a Sakha identification.

Of course, systems of patronage connected to territorial, kin and ethnic affiliation exist throughout the Russian Federation and the wider world. What is notable about the Sakha case is the role of publicly acknowledged and celebrated personal achievement in the delineation and reproduction of both regional communities and the Sakha people as a whole. While high-achieving individuals are lauded at public gatherings, in the mass media and through the books they publish about themselves, the more ambitious community members are busily seeking to record and display their own initiatives and achievements. There are various arenas and genres of performance that index achievement; one example is the practice of running competitions at public events throughout the year. These competitions might be sports tournaments or beauty contests, or they might test their participants' aptitude at handicrafts, traditional Sakha music, cooking, fishing or psychic healing. Success in these competitions enhances the prestige of the individual and their home region, while renewing the possibilities for their home community to praise and feel proud of its outstanding members – and, in doing so, to reassert and affirm its cohesion and worth. The competitions provide the context for a selection of conventionalized performances, which in turn act to 'make present' both the successful individual and their lucky associates (Schieffelin 1998).

The forms within which achievement now is recognized are conditioned by the technological, political and social changes that have taken place in Sakha (Yakutia) over the past century – and, in particular, Soviet practices of competitive self-improvement have left a prominent trace (Habeck 2011). However, the eagerness with which Sakha communities have adapted these practices into their relationships suggests that competitive achievement had a significance in pre-Soviet Sakha social life. And in fact, the well-known late nineteenth-century ethnographer Vatslav Seroschevskiy notes that the Sakha people he saw were 'passionately' interested in the sports competitions held at their *Yhyakh* festivals; these large gatherings generally occurred on the pretext of feeding the local area spirits, although they also involved dancing, eating, drinking and games (Seroschevskiy 1993: 446). The Sakha concern with talent and status I have encountered over the years evokes the Sakha folk legends collected by Gavriil Ksenofontov during the 1920s and 1930s – and in particular, the interaction they represent between the human and spirit worlds (Ksenofontov 2004). These stories describe the superhuman feats performed by the teller's forebears or prominent Sakha historical figures such as the Sakha king Tygyn. Some of them mention the talents or abilities bestowed upon individuals by particular spirits. For example, according to one account the goddess Ajyysyt gave Tygyn's grandson a son 'of solid and persistent morals', who became his father's 'favourite', an 'unusually strong and powerful person'; Omogoy describes his servant Elley, the exceptionally strong and wise forefather of the Sakha, as 'a person with a divine protector' (Ksenofontov 2004: 89, 30). The belief that personal attributes are donated by spiritual entities, and therefore that an individual's outstanding ability demonstrates their high standing among specific powerful spirits, explains the close attention the narrators pay to the physical prowess of their heroes.

The idea that talent or achievement manifests a benevolent attitude on the part of the world's more mysterious forces continues to crop up in various circumstances. Sakha acquaintances have confirmed to me that evidence of personal talent indicates the presence of a spiritual protector, while a leading academic has described his senior colleague, the blind Sakha ethnographer Semyon Somogotto, as 'more penetrating … [and able to see] farther and more piercingly than sighted people. The powers that be gave him only the internal vision of a perspicacious researcher, a clairvoyant-prophet, possessing an outstanding heuristic gift' (Yakutsk History 2013). A newspaper report of a 2004 Yhyakh dedicated to the memory of an influential regional policeman and bureaucrat described the event as a 'great success', 'whether it was because the population of Tyungyulyu pleased the spirits of the Earth and nature by dedicating the *Yhyakh* to a good person, or simply because they had made an effort ...' (*Yakutia*, 24 June 2004: 6). The importance that publicly acclaimed achievement has within the power dynamics of Sakha community relationships seems therefore to have its roots in pre-Soviet Sakha social and religious life – even if the ways achievement is understood and recognized have changed radically under the influence of Soviet modernization. The powerful, valued and authoritative are now sportsmen, businessmen, academics, politicians or pop singers, rather than knights or princes; their feats occur and are recorded through Soviet-style modernist categories of worth and attainment, such as those that define the value of 'perspicacious' academic researchers. The hierarchical communities that form around these figures shape modernist institutions that are integrated into the wider Russian state, such as municipal or regional administrations, schools and university departments.

Following the post-Soviet nationalist revival, the demonstration of shamanic ability is now also an important manifestation of talent and achievement. There may not be many shamanic healers among the republic's leading businessmen and politicians, but there are several individuals who cite their attainments as lying within a continuum of shamanic practice, academia (as I have mentioned) and cultural production. Perhaps the most prominent example of this kind of crossover is Andrey Borisov, Minister of Culture and Spiritual Development (*ministr kul'tury i dukhovnogo razvitiya*) since 1990, and a leading director in Yakutsk's Sakha-language film and theatre scene, who often emphasizes the influence his spiritual insights have over his work (cf. Balzer 2011).

The respect now accorded to people who can boast an ability to interact with spiritual forces both generates and is reinforced by the political establishment's attempts to co-opt them into negotiating a hegemonic balance between a centralizing federal government and the Sakha population. Shamanic healers have mentioned an inconvenient pressure to cooperate with 'bureaucrats' (*chinovniki*) over public events, and particularly over Yhyakh festivals. The Yhyakh has become one of the republic's most important yearly events; several are held over the end of June and the beginning of July, the largest being the Yhyakh staged by Yakutsk's municipal administration. Large Yhyakh festivals last for two days and incorporate pop concerts, exhibitions, sports tournaments, fashion shows and markets, in addition to the shamanic ritual – which itself is accompanied by lengthy speeches from prominent politicians. The republic's political establishment demonstrates its commitment to the Sakha cultural heritage by funding lavish Yhyakh rituals in an effort to ameliorate the discontent its subordination to centralizing federal government policies may be causing. The Yhyakh cannot take place without the shamanic specialists, cultural workers and academics who design and perform its various rituals – and hence the uneasy collaboration between politicians, shamanic healers, cultural workers and intellectuals that generated the nationalist revival of the 1990s has to continue.

Since Sakha shamanism is so closely integrated into the republic's governance, academia and cultural production, it is perhaps unsurprising that the workings of shamanic hierarchical communities should map onto the power dynamics that exist in broader Sakha society. One important common facet of the production of power within both shamanic and mainstream Sakha communities is the crucial role public speaking has in articulating and demonstrating personal achievement, and the communities it generates. The lectures delivered by Yegor and his colleagues are echoed in the impromptu speeches made at the regional diaspora concerts mentioned above, the speeches made by politicians at the Yhyakh ritual and the requirement that every guest at an official banquet be given an opportunity to make their own speech, in order of precedence.[3] Teachers can readily acknowledge the necessity of training children to present themselves effectively through public speaking, to the extent that they make great efforts to organize competitions in speech-making. I found myself at one of these in March 2011.

The content of these speeches varies across a spectrum of praise, information, personal opinion and occasionally condemnation – but their form is remarkably consistent. In every case, a single person steps out of the company to impart their communication to a passive audience, which itself temporarily comes into being through the action of the speech-maker in addressing the group. On finishing their speech, the speaker is again absorbed into the group, as it re-forms into a new configuration of speaker and audience. The discursive forms in which knowledge or opinion are expressed are also remarkably similar. Yegor and his colleagues express their contentions about the Sakha cultural heritage as authoritative experts, just as an academic delivers their paper as an authoritative specialist – even if the contentions themselves arise out of varying forms of knowledge production. The act of temporarily assuming the centre of an audience's attention has become a performance that enables both the display of personal achievement in the form of expertise and the acknowledgement and celebration of personal talent that serves to define a given community. And yet the actions and purposes of these communities vary widely. How is it, then, that a single communicative form can act as the basis for so many different groups – ranging from regional community networks to groupings of academic colleagues, to an organization of shamanic healers and their clients – within the Sakha community as a whole?

Speech-making and Community in Sakha Shamanic Practice

I would like to suggest that the consistent role speech-making has within different Sakha communities, and within the shamanic community in particular, arises out of a specific configuration of performance convention and power that emerged during the Soviet era, and its continuing influence over the ways community and agency are both shaped and made manifest. As Aleksei Yurchak (2006) contends, changes in the production, dissemination and effects of the Soviet Union's authoritative discourse created a social context that accorded a huge importance to a relatively well-defined and conventionalized set of expressive forms. The imperative to reproduce exactly the range of performative, discursive and aesthetic forms that were approved by the Party leadership was eventually to enable these forms to be incorporated into the articulation and maintenance of a wide range of communities, whose interests, activities and values did not necessarily correspond to those promoted by state propaganda.

Yurchak draws on John Austin's distinction between the performative and the constative in language – that is, the distinction between speech acts that have the power to achieve change within a given context and those that communicate meaning (Yurchak 2006: 19). As Yurchak (2006) describes, authoritative discourse began to lose its literal meaning, or constative force, after Stalin's death, as it became incorporated into practices of community formation that the Soviet political elites had not envisaged. Authoritative discourse – whether communicated directly as propaganda or via state-sponsored cultural production – consisted more and more of repeated poetic and aesthetic forms, rather than substantive messages, as the 1960s and 1970s progressed (Yurchak 2006: 77–125). The importance of reproducing the correct verbal or visual forms and sounds came to take precedence over transmitting arguments, ideas or information. The production of authoritative discourse thus became the performance of a number of clear and well-understood formulae. As part of this, cultural production became so conventionalized that artists would produce portraits of Lenin according to a series of set poses, each with its own number; for example, a 'sixer' (*shestyorka*) showed Lenin in his office, while a 'sevener' (*semyorka*) was Lenin sitting on a tree stump (Yurchak 2006: 55).

As the relevance of the substantive content of authoritative discourse decreased, the various performances and conventions its production entailed became assimilated into both signalling and establishing the communities and relationships that constituted Soviet society, and enabled its members to act within it. As Yurchak describes, when the members of the Soviet youth organization, the Komsomol, were asked to vote on a resolution they knew had to be passed,

> they collectively responded not to the constative meaning of this question ('Do you support the resolution?'), but to its performative meaning ('Are you the kind of people who understand that the norms and rules of the current ritual need to be performatively reproduced, that constative meanings do not necessarily have to be attended to, who act accordingly, and who, therefore, can be engaged in other meanings?'). It is this latter address that the audience at the meeting recognized with an affirmative gesture and that therefore brought into existence the public of *svoi* [ours, in Russian]. (Yurchak 2006: 117)

Authoritative discourse and its rituals thus became incorporated into a set of expressive practices which enabled communities to emerge among and within the Soviet state institutions that pervaded every aspect of life. Their members knew what the official agenda was in relation to their own and how to balance a degree of conformity, mutually supportive cooperation and the resources their own positions offered, in order to achieve their personal ends. Hence the participants at the Komsomol meeting could 'vote' to support the resolution without even looking up from the book they happened to be reading, and certainly without having understood the resolution itself. Their duty was to raise their hands so that the resolution could be approved, releasing the Komsomol members to get on with whatever else they wanted to be doing – and, in doing so, affirming their commitment to the informal community of *svoi,* or 'ours'. These communities did not necessarily correspond to the working collectives that officially constituted Soviet institutions, instead forming the complementary networks that were integral to late Soviet social differentiation, agency and morality. Individual Soviet citizens could formulate and express their personal values and ideals through these relationships, as well as using them for more pragmatic purposes.

The array of officially approved poetic and aesthetic formulae had become integrated into a wider and more complex spectrum of knowledge, skill and practice, and, in doing so, had developed into a selection of performances whose meaning and effect depended on the interests, values and understanding of the people directly involved. A range of expressive practices – such as raising one's hand to express one's support, or delivering a speech in the appropriate tone of voice – had become incorporated into strategic acts with effects that transcended their literal meaning. Meanwhile, the significance of the relationships, values and interests that coexisted with the officially recognized institutions and collectives increased as time went on. Yurchak contends that the cohesiveness of svoi communities intensified in the larger population centres during the 1960s, 1970s and 1980s, creating small networks of people who sought to emphasize their detachment from mainstream Soviet culture (Yurchak 2006: 126–57). These small groups were able to exploit the Soviet system in order to create the time and resources they needed to interact with each other, and pursue activities that were self-consciously idealistic and external to everyday Soviet life – such as researching ancient history, foreign systems of writing, literature or religions (Yurchak 2006: 151). This trend could well have provided the conditions for the non-Russian national revivals: in the late 1980s it was clearly possible for like-minded Sakha intellectuals to think of indulging their curiosity about their own cultural and religious heritage, distinguished as it then was from 'modern', everyday Soviet life by its status as 'traditional', and therefore obsolete.

The prevalence of a conventionalized form of speechmaking in Sakha community life could well be a continuation from the Soviet era, which has also acted to reproduce a pre-Soviet Sakha emphasis on personal achievement in the articulation of status. Soviet-era Sakha communities became accustomed, first, to measuring and acknowledging personal achievement according to Soviet categories of expertise, and second, to incorporating a small range of expressive forms into their daily communicative practice. The force of these expressive forms lay in the conventionalized ways they were interpreted by the communities involved in their performance, rather than in the substantive content they purported to communicate – and one particularly prominent expressive form was the act of standing up to deliver an authoritative speech. Therefore, the practice of lecturing to an audience has acquired a force beyond its origin in Soviet-era education, to become an important index of attainment – and hence also community in the Sakha context – whether the content of the lecture concerns local policy, new technologies for teaching English to schoolchildren or traditional shamanic healing. Yegor, Sardaana and Vanya were investing so much into their speeches because it is precisely this expressive act that serves to articulate and affirm both the shamanic communities of healers and clients and their personal capacities to act within them.

A Soviet-era discursive practice has become an integral part of contemporary Sakha shamanism, meshing with such disparate cultural phenomena as global neo-shamanisms, post-Soviet identity politics and early twentieth-century shamanic belief. Its emergence and importance indicates the difficulty of separating out local from global: it is undeniably Sakha, undeniably post-Soviet, undeniably modern, and yet serves to anchor Sakha shamanism into a context that has been swept into social transformations with parallels all over the world. Its incorporation into contemporary shamanic practice reveals the way Sakha shamanic practitioners are negotiating the balances of power and hierarchy in Sakha (Yakutia), and the opportunities and hazards they afford – including the tortuous entanglement of political interests and personal identification that surrounds the Sakha nationalist revival.

Notes

1 I would like to thank the Max Planck Institute of Social Anthropology for the financial and intellectual support I received while writing this chapter.
2 C.f. the various discussions of the Soviet Nationalities Policy that have appeared since the late 1980s. Their authors include Francine Hirsch (2005), Andrei Slezkine (1994) and Timo Vihavainen (2000).
3 The convention of making long and elaborate toasts exists in other former Soviet regions, such as Georgia. However, this practice varies according to local circumstance and cultural heritage, in common with other former Soviet cultural forms such as workers' competitions and regionally

produced pop music. Hence Russian visitors to Sakha (Yakutia) did not necessarily expect to be handed a microphone and told to speak at an important dinner.

References

Argounova-Low, T. 2007. 'Close Relatives and Outsiders: Village People in the City of Yakutsk, Siberia', *Arctic Anthropology* 44(1): 51–61.

Balzer, M.M. 1993. 'Dilemmas of the Spirit: Religion and Atheism in the Yakut-Sakha Republic', in S. Ramet (ed.), *Religious Policy in the Soviet Union*. Cambridge: Cambridge University Press, pp. 231–51.

———. 1995. 'A State within a State: The Sakha Republic (Yakutia)', in S. Kotkin and D. Wolff (eds), *Rediscovering Russia in Asia: Siberia and the Russian Far East*. London: M.E. Sharpe, pp. 139–59.

———. 2011. *Shamans, Spirituality and Cultural Revitalization: Explorations in Siberia and Beyond*. New York: Palgrave Macmillan.

Bozhedonov, A.I. 2008. *Törükü tyl, Törük omuk* [Eternal Language, Eternal People]. Yakutsk: Saydam.

Crate, S.A. 2006. *Cows, Kin and Globalization: An Ethnography of Sustainability*. Plymouth: AltaMira Press.

Cruikshank, J. and T. Argounova. 2000. 'Reinscribing Meaning: Memory and Indigenous Identity in Sakha Republic (Yakutia)', *Arctic Anthropology* 37(1): 96–119.

Gogolev, A.I. 1986. *Istoricheskaya Etnografiya Yakutov: Voprosy Proiskhozhdeniya*. Yakutsk: Sakhapoligrafizdat.

———. 2004. *Etnicheskaya Istoriya Narodov Yakutii*. Yakutsk: Izdatel'stvo YaGU.

Habeck, J.O. 2011. 'Introduction. Cultivation, Collective, and the Self', in B. Donohoe and J.O. Habeck (eds), *Reconstructing the House of Culture: Community, Self, and the Makings of Culture in Russia and Beyond*. New York: Berghahn, pp. 1–28.

Hirsch, Francine. 2005. *Empire of Nations: Ethnographic Knowledge and the Making of the Soviet Union*. Ithaca: Cornell University Press.

Humphrey, C. 1998. *Marx Went Away but Karl Stayed Behind: Updated Edition of Karl Marx Collective: Economy, Society and Religion in a Siberian Collective Farm*. Ann Arbor: The University of Michigan Press.

Iğmen, A. 2011. 'The Emergence of Soviet Houses of Culture in Kyrgyzstan', in B. Donohoe and J.O. Habeck (eds), *Reconstructing the House of Culture: Community, Self, and the Makings of Culture in Russia and Beyond*. New York: Berghahn, pp. 163–88.

Jochelson, W. 1933. 'The Yakut', *Anthropological Papers of the American Museum of Natural History* 33(2). New York.

Ksenofontov, G. 2004. *Elleiada*. Yakutsk: Bichik.

Ledeneva, A. 1998. *Russia's Economy of Favours*: Blat, *Networking and Informal Exchanges*. New York: Cambridge University Press.
———. 2013. *Can Russia Modernise?* Sistema *Power Networks and Informal Governance*. Cambridge: Cambridge University Press.
Lindquist, G. 2006. *The Quest for the Authentic Shaman: Multiple Meanings of Shamanism on a Siberian Journey*. Stockholm: Almqvist and Wiksell International.
Maak, R.K. 1994. *Viliyuskiy Okrug*, 2nd edn. Moscow: Yana.
National Population Census, Russian Federation. 2010. http://www.perepis-2010.ru/results_of_the_census. Accessed 18 November 2013.
Mészáros, C. 2013. 'Surnames and Genealogies in Central Yakutia.' Paper presented at the History Making in Central and Inner Asia conference, Martin Luther University, Halle, Germany, 22–23 February.
Peers, E. 2009. 'Sakha Community Leaders and their Historical Mission: The Relevance of Soviet Ideology to Contemporary Sakha Politics', *Sibirica* 8(1): 75–81.
Peers, E. 2014. 'Are they *energetiki* or *ichchi*? Shamanic Performance and Modernity in Sakha (Yakutia)'. Paper presented at the British Association for Slavonic and East European Studies annual conference, University of Cambridge, 5–7 April.
Schieffelin, E. 1998. 'Problematizing Performance', in F. Hughes-Freeland (ed.), *Ritual, Performance, Media*. London: Routledge, pp. 194–207.
Seroschevskiy, V.L. 1993. *Yakuty: Opyt etnograficheskogo issledovaniya*. [Yakuts: The Experience of Ethnographic Research.] Moscow: ROSSPEN.
Slezkine, Y. 1994. *Arctic Mirrors: Russia and the Small Peoples of the North*. Ithaca, NY: Cornell University Press.
Tengry. 2013. http://tengry.org/site/index.php?cstart=3&newsid=18. Accessed 6 June 2013.
Ventsel, A. 2006. 'Sakha Pop Music – a Celebration of Consuming', *Anthropology of East Europe Review* 24(2): 35–43.
———. 2009. 'Sakha Music Business: Mission, Contracts, and Social Relations in the Developing Post-Socialist Market Economy', *Sibirica* 8(1): 1–23.
Verdery, K. 1996. *What Was Socialism and What Comes Next?* Princeton: Princeton University Press.
Vihavainen, T. 2000. 'Nationalism and Internationalism: How Did the Bolsheviks Cope with National Sentiments?', in C.J. Chulos and T. Piirainen (eds), *The Fall of an Empire, the Birth of a Nation: National Identities in Russia*. Aldershot: Ashgate, pp. 75–97.
Vitebsky, P. 2005. *Reindeer People: Living with Animals and Spirits in Siberia*. London: Harper Collins.
Yakutsk History. 2013. http://www.yakutskhistory.net. Accessed 9 February 2013.
Yurchak, A. 2006. *Everything Was Forever, until it Was No More: The Last Soviet Generation*. Princeton: Princeton University Press.

6

In Search of Genuine Religion

The Contemporary Estonian Maausulised Movement and Nationalist Discourse

Ergo-Hart Västrik

Introduction

This chapter focuses on the contemporary Estonian *maausulised* movement whose members claim to be adherents of the Estonian native or ethnic religion *maausk*.[1] In Estonian *maausk* literally means 'the faith/belief of the land/earth'. The derivative *maausulised* means 'followers of maausk'. From a scholarly or etic perspective, maausk may be identified as a new religion and a manifestation of modern Paganism (Strmiska 2005a; Magliocco 2009: 104). However, it should be acknowledged that from an emic perspective members of the movement do not agree with such labelling and stress the genuineness of their religious tradition. In English translations they call it the Estonian native or indigenous religion and underline their essential differences from Western Paganisms. In public statements maausulised spokespersons constantly highlight the continuity and local specificity of this religion, its essential relationship with vernacular languages and its roots in indigenous ethnic traditions and customs. Invoking linguistic affinity and common origin, maausulised relate their religious principles to the analogous traditions of kindred peoples – ethnic groups whose languages belong to the Finno-Ugric and Uralic language families – and have not sought connections with similar contemporary Baltic, Slavic and Germanic Pagan movements in neighbouring countries.

The upsurge of the maausulised movement was connected with aspirations relating to a search for cultural roots during the turbulent

changes of the mid 1980s to early 1990s. Since its institutionalization two decades ago, members of the movement have been active
in public discussions on such issues as religious freedom and religious education, safeguarding historical sacred sites, and evaluating
Estonia's national and cultural heritage using opportunities offered
by the Internet and mass media. Despite the fact that the movement
represents a quite specific nationalist discourse in public statements,
it has generally received positive media coverage and the ideas of
the maausulised have enjoyed unprecedented popularity in recent
national surveys. As an alternative religious movement, maausulised
make up the largest and fastest growing non-Christian denomina-
tion in Estonia today (Vakker and Rohtmets 2008: 48; RA 2013). The
religious studies scholar Lea Altnurme (2010: 21) claims that these
developments no longer allow the conceptualization of maausulised
as a marginal, new religious group and challenges researchers to study
the meanings that maausk has in contemporary Estonian society and
its messages and functions in the wider cultural context.

Compared with studies on analogous initiatives in other Baltic
and neighbouring states, the maausulised have not received special-
ized scholarly attention until recently.[2] In addition to some early
attempts to conceptualize this emergent phenomenon in the mid
1990s (Västrik 1996), there have been only a few studies published in
English that have concentrated exclusively on the ideas and activities
of the movement (for example, Kuutma (2005) on maausulised in the
context of Finno-Ugrism and Estonian identity politics).[3] The movement's status and role in framing the religious landscape of post-
socialist Estonia has been mentioned briefly in two recent doctoral
monographs in the discipline of religious studies (Altnurme 2005;
Ringvee 2011) and in several reviews of religious diversity in Estonia
since the 1990s (Au and Ringvee 2000, 2007; Plaat 2002; Altnurme
2011b, 2012). Maausulised activities have been analysed, among
other phenomena, in the context of relationships between the state,
new religious movements and mainstream religions (Ringvee 2012;
Vakker and Rohtmets 2008), and in the framework of New Age religiosity (Kõiva 2011). This chapter focuses on the self-presentation of
the contemporary maausk movement in public media by its spokespersons. The aim is to provide a wider historical and cultural context
for the movement's emergence, as well as to discuss its relationship
with nationalist discourse and earlier initiatives to create an Estonian
(pagan) religion.

The empirical research material that this article draws on consists of articles, interviews, press releases and other forms of public

self-presentation by members of maausk in the media, as well as news about their activities where members were cited. The Web archives of three Estonian dailies (*Postimees, Eesti Päevaleht* and *Õhtuleht*) were searched, followed by the Web archives of two weeklies (*Eesti Ekspress* and *Maaleht*). In addition the home page of the official umbrella organization for the maausulised was consulted:[4] this serves as a digital repository for a wide range of materials related to the endeavours of the movement made available online by its members and published, in addition to the dailies and weeklies mentioned above, in a variety of thematic periodicals (among them monthlies dedicated to culture and nature such as *Vikerkaar, Kultuur ja Elu, Maakodu* and *Loodusesõber*). Together the analysed texts constituted a corpus of more than 350 articles published between 1987 and 2012.

The Cultural, Political and Religious Context of Estonian Nationalism and Paganism

Estonia, together with Latvia and Lithuania, is one of the three Baltic states in northeastern Europe that regained their independence in 1991 as a result of the dissolution of the Soviet Union.[5] From the thirteenth century up until 1918 the present-day territories of Estonia and Latvia were governed by foreign powers (Denmark, the Livonian and Teutonic Orders, bishops of the Roman Catholic Church, Sweden, Poland and Russia). The ruling elite during that time was comprised, both in urban centres and in the countryside, mainly of Baltic German nobility (Ringvee 2012: 94–95).[6] During the centuries of foreign rule ethnic Estonians, together with other indigenous peoples of the region (Livonians, Latvians), gradually lost their rights and the former local elite was apparently eradicated or Germanized. By the sixteenth century the majority of Estonians belonged to the rural peasantry (referred to as *Undeutsch*), who were serfs of their landlords (Raun 2001: 20). Foreign rule also brought Christianization; the territory of Estonia, like that of Latvia, was Christianized in the course of the Northern Crusades at the beginning of the thirteenth century by the Roman Catholic Church.[7] In all probability earlier religions existed for some time parallel to the newly introduced practices of the Catholic creed resulting in various manifestations of religious syncretism, as indicated in historical sources. The Protestant Reformation reached the area in the 1520s and since then the Lutheran Church has been the majority church in Estonia (Ringvee 2012: 95). Through the Lutheran religion, which gradually introduced literacy, and especially through the spread of Pietism from the 1730s, the essentials of Christianity were generally accepted among Estonian peasants by the nineteenth century (Jansen 1998: 811).

At the turn of the eighteenth and nineteenth centuries, ideas of Enlightenment and Herderian Romanticism spread among Baltic German Estophile intellectuals who started to idealize local peasants and valorize their pagan past (Jonuks 2013: 146). The most influential piece of this kind was Garlieb Helwig Merkel's (1769–1850) *Die Vorzeit Lieflands* (1798), which depicted a 'golden age' of local peasants before Christianization and referred to Estonia as an autonomous nation (Raun 2003: 144). As written sources about the ancient religion of Estonians were scarce, it was Baltic German scholars and pastors who formulated the initial ideas about the local pagan religion. The most disputed pagan god in that period was Tharapita, who was mentioned in the thirteenth-century work *Henry's Chronicle of Livonia*, the most prominent written source on the history of medieval Estonia.[8]

Serfdom was abolished in the Baltic provinces of the Russian Empire in 1816–1819, when peasants were allowed to own land or move to the cities (Raun 2001: 45–48). In the 1820s and 1830s the first intellectuals of Estonian ethnic origin with a keen interest in Romantic ideas and the existence of Estonian pagan gods appeared. The most well known and influential attempt to reconstruct an Estonian pagan pantheon was made by a pioneer of the Estonian national movement, Friedrich Robert Faehlmann (1798–1850), in his eight pseudo-mythological legends (*Estnische Sage*) published for the first time in German between 1848 and 1852 in the proceedings of the Learned Estonian Society. In these scholarly compilations, Taara or Vanaisa ('Grandfather') was depicted as the main Estonian god, assisted by several minor deities whose names and functions were apparently adapted from the Finnish national epic *Kalevala*. This 'pantheon' was widely popularized and disseminated through the publication of the Estonian national epic *Kalevipoeg* ('Kalev's Son'), finalized in 1862 by another pioneer of the Estonian national movement, Friedrich Reinhold Kreutzwald (1803–1882), in which Taara, for example, was mentioned around fifty times (Viires 1991: 139).[9] These invented gods and deities were accepted by the emergent nationalist movement as symbols of national mythology, but no contradiction arose with the prevailing Christian identity of the people leading the national awakening, several of whom were members of the Lutheran clergy.

The national epic *Kalevipoeg* played an extremely important role in the process of constructing Estonian nationhood in the second half of the nineteenth century.[10] This was in 1850 when the ethnonym *eestlane* ('Estonian') was used for the first time in an Estonian publication, marking the beginning of national consolidation for a people who had earlier referred to themselves as *maarahvas* ('country people') (Raun 2001: 55–56; Gross 2002: 344). In the course of the national awakening, several important keywords of the national narrative were formulated, accepted and cemented as elements of the dominant national discourse during the first period of the independent Republic of Estonia (1918–1940). The national narrative included ideas such as an idealization of the ancient past of Estonians, the Christianization of Estonians with 'fire and sword' accompanied by hostility against Germans as conquerors, and the persistent resistance of the nation to the '700-year night of slavery' (Karo 2007: 16–27; Jonuks 2013: 151). The latter was conceptualized and developed after the establishment of the Republic of Estonia as 'The Great Battle for Freedom' that combined 'into one coherent plot all of the prominent conflicts with Germans that Estonians have preserved in their cultural memory, from the crusades of the thirteenth century to the so-called War of Independence of 1918–1920' (Tamm 2008: 505–506).

Despite the fact that Lutheranism played its part in shaping Estonian national identity, Christianity was not incorporated into the nationalist narrative. As Altnurme (2011a: 79) states, it was treated 'as an ideological weapon and a tool for the subjugation of the people' introduced and disseminated by foreigners, meaning that since the 1920s and 1930s the Estonian national myth was hostile to Christianity because it was based on the struggle between classes (the Estonian peasantry versus the Baltic German elite).[11]

Nationalism in Practice: The Taarausulised of the 1920s and 1930s

The peculiarities of the national narrative mentioned above resulted in the establishment of the modern Estonian (Pagan) religion *Taara usk* ('Taara faith') during the first period of independence.[12] The principles of this new national religion were worked out in the 1920s by a group of intellectuals, among them several officers of the Estonian army. Leading figures among its followers (known as *taarausulised, taaralased* or *hiielased*, from *hiis*, 'sacred grove') were Major Kustas

Utuste (1884–1941), the main ideologue, and his wife Maarda Lepp-Utuste (1883–1940), a writer and teacher who worked out the majority of the movement's rituals and ceremonies (Vakker 2012: 176–77, 194). The religious organization of the movement, the Hiis, was officially registered in 1931 and by 1940, when the organization was shut down by the Soviet regime, it had three regional branches and sixteen local committees of national culture spread throughout Estonia (Arjakas 1987). Registered members of taarausulised organizations numbered by that time around seven hundred, but the estimated number of supporters was around twenty-five times larger (Arjakas 1987).

Spokespersons of the movement opposed Christianity and cosmopolitanism, suggesting that Estonian spiritual and cultural independence could be accomplished only through a sovereign Estonian religion. Taarausulised criticized the mainstream Estonian cultural elite who were, according to their views, too Western or European (that is, Baltic German) oriented. Instead, somewhat paradoxically, they proposed following patterns of Romanticism mediated by Baltic German intellectuals in order to stick to their forefathers' intellectual legacy and developing a religion that followed the 'true nature of the Estonian soul' (Vakker 2012: 175, 197). However, in their search for a genuine religion the taarausulised did not turn to folklore collections containing abundant material on vernacular religion (as they realized the ancient Estonian religion had ceased to exist during the period of foreign powers), but started to construct a new religion on the basis of earlier scholarship and national literature in order to meet the needs of the contemporary society. Eventually many ideas formulated and disseminated earlier within the nationalist discourse were taken over in this process and modified to form a coherent religious system.

According to the statutes of the Hiis organization, Taara usk was conceived as a developing and changing phenomenon, with something similar applying to its ideas about deities. Taara, popularized through the national epic and textbooks (Viires 1991), was conceptualized as a monotheistic supreme god. The religious doctrine of Taara usk recognized only a positive moral absolute (leaving aside evil or negative absolutes) and the foremost sins according to the teaching were mistakes against natural laws. Its moral teaching held that each person bore responsibility for his or her own actions, which would influence their good health and luck (Vakker 2012: 182–84).

The movement's rituals, accepted by taarausulised as obligatory, were designed to celebrate important events in the human life cycle (birth, initiation, wedding, funerals) and national holidays. The compulsory element of rituals was the sacrificial fire (*urituli*) which was made on a sacrificial stone (*urikivi*), a natural or artificial rock which had a cavity for a flammable liquid. Rituals were carried out indoors or outdoors in a special ritual space decorated with fresh flowers, green branches or 'beloved mementos' (Vakker 2012: 194–95; cf. Deemant 1988). All adult members were allowed to carry out rites in their home shrine, but common and public ceremonies were performed by the movement's spiritual leaders, called *asko* and *hiislar*.[13] Ritual garments included stylized folk costumes, mostly in white and grey, and the movement was also active in popularizing so-called national costumes where elements of regional folk costumes were combined with modern fashion trends to meet the needs of contemporary people. Rituals and celebrations were accompanied with zither playing and choral singing of the common patriotic repertoire (Vakker 2012: 184–88, 190).

Holidays observed by taarausulised were partly taken from the list of public holidays, such as Estonian Independence Day (24 June), which is celebrated as the most important of the movement's holidays.[14] The movement also initiated partly new holidays, among them St George's Night (23 April), which was celebrated to commemorate the St George's Night Uprising in 1343, one of the venerated events of 'The Great Battle for Freedom'.[15] Many holidays were adapted from the Estonian folk calendar with the aim of giving these holidays new national meaning, at the same time avoiding appellations with Christian connotations. For example, the end of the summer working season, Michaelmas (*mihklipäev*, 29 September), which was adapted to the Estonian folk calendar from the Catholic tradition, was celebrated among taarausulised as the Day of Acknowledgement to acknowledge the merits of all living Estonians (Vakker 2012: 186).

Despite the fact that the core group of the taarausulised movement was not numerous and that the mainstream cultural and political elite did not accept some of their ideas, they were active in sociopolitical discussions. Taara usk organizations were banned in 1940 by the Soviet regime and the movement's adherents were repressed, although activities continued to some extent in exile and secretly in small groups in Estonia throughout the Soviet occupation. The first newspaper articles about the Taara religion were published during the Soviet regime at the end of the 1980s (Arjakas 1987; Deemant 1988) and these ideas found fertile soil in the atmosphere of spiritual disenchantment on the eve of the collapse of the Soviet Union.

Redefining Nationalism and Paganism:
The Contemporary Maausulised Movement

Soon after the national reawakening at the end of 1980s and the regaining of political sovereignty in 1991, a new form of modern Paganism was developed and disseminated in Estonia (see Figure 6.1). It adapted many ideas from the pre-Second-World-War movement of the taarausulised, but also introduced alternative keywords and utilized different strategies and rhetoric taken from national discourse.

The wider ideological framework of the maausulised movement was formulated during the Soviet occupation, in the 1960s and 1970s, when essays criticizing the mainstream Western orientation of Estonian national culture were disseminated among students and the literati. The most outstanding ideological manifesto of this kind was the essay entitled 'Maarahvast' (About the People of the Land) by Kalle Istvan Eller, a teacher who had studied English and Estonian philology at the University of Tartu. His essay was first circulated unofficially as a machine-typed manuscript and then published in

Fig. 6.1 *Prayer meeting of maausulised at Kunda sacred hill in Mahu (Viru-Nigula) parish, north Estonia, November 2009. Homemade bread was placed on the white cloth. Beside it is a cauldron of porridge which was boiled at the site while folk songs were sung. Prayer elders addressed their prayers to the ancestors, Maaema, Uku and other deities. Image used with the kind permission of the photographer, Mana Kaasik.*

1972 in the weekly of the Estonian Agricultural Academy where it initiated heated debate on Estonia's cultural orientation (Eller 1972; Sarv 1990).[16] Eller and a group of alternative intellectuals, several of whom were descendants of the taarausulised and had inherited this tradition through family lineages, started to advocate the use of vernacular personal names instead of international borrowings (Sarv and Eller 1987) and at the end of the 1970s introduced an alternative calendar in runic symbols based on the traditional agrarian calendar but promoting non-Christian vernacular terms to designate holidays and calendar months (Koostajad 1988) (see Figure 6.2). The initiators of this 'refined' traditional calendar also presented an alternative time division:

> The rejection of the so-called Indo-European influence or Western civilization by *maausulised* also found expression in their invention of an indigenous definition and reckoning of time. In the runic calendar *Sirvilauad*, the vernacular 'creation of the world' was dated to 8213 BC, based on the occurrence of the Billingen catastrophe. (Kuutma 2005: 64)

As explained by the compilers of the calendar, the Billingen catastrophe, dated by Swedish scholars according to tests with varved clay, 'demarcates the breakthrough of the Baltic Glacial Reservoir into the ocean at the site of the present-day Lake Mälar' (Kuutma 2005: 64; cf. Koostajad 1988: 50). As a result of this, the greater part of Estonian terrain rose above sea level. (Following this reckoning of time, the year 2015 is considered to be 10228.) Both the alternative time division and vernacular month and holiday designations have been popularized on the movement's home page and in publications. With these endeavours maausulised follow the example of their pre-Second-World-War forerunners, although they have changed the zero-point in their time reckoning. The Sirvilauad do not contain invented national holidays, only those that have an equivalent in the Estonian (or in some cases kindred peoples') folk calendar (Kuutma 2005: 65).

The terms *maausk* and *maausulised* appeared in the Estonian press for the first time in the early 1990s, when two members of the initial group, the aforementioned Eller and Kaido Kama, publicly confessed their inherited traditions and religious preferences (Heinapuu and Kama 1990: 70; Pohla and Eller 1991: 14–15). Both Eller and Kama were at that time active in politics and became founders of the Conservative People's Party of Estonia (1990–1992), which later united with other conservative parties. Kama was elected to the Congress of Estonia (an innovative grassroots parliament

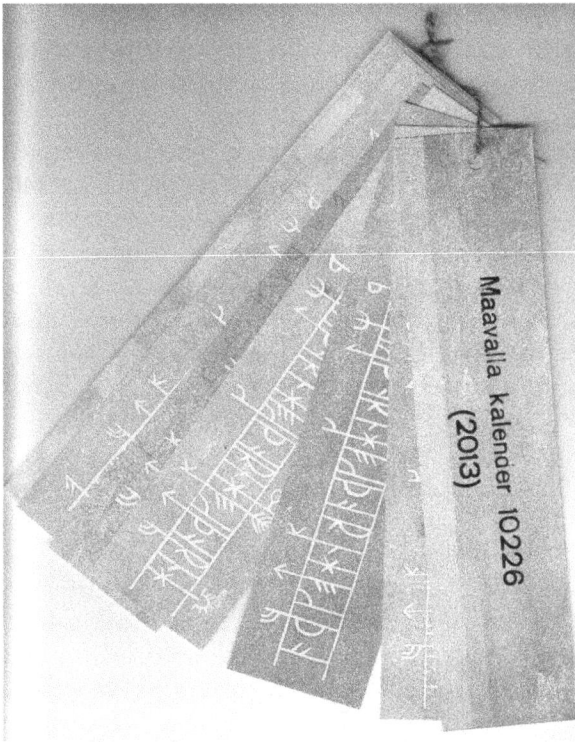

Fig. 6.2 *Calendar of Maavald 10226 (2013), an alternative calendar in runic symbols introduced and popularized by maausulised. Photograph by the author, used with the kind permission of Ahto Kaasik on behalf of Maavalla Koda.*

established as part of the process of regaining independence from the Soviet Union), and later to the Estonian parliament where he served as Minister of Justice (1992–1994) and Minister of Internal Affairs (1994–1995). At the end of the 1980s and in the early 1990s Eller was among the officers of the newly reestablished Estonian Defence League.

The compound *maausk* and its derivatives *maausuline* (sing.) and *maausulised* (pl.) are, however, not vernacular concepts but were invented on the basis of compounds such as *maarahvas* ('people of the land' or 'country people') and *maakeel* ('language of the land'), denoting Estonians and the Estonian language before the terms *eesti rahvas* ('Estonian people') and *eesti keel* ('Estonian language') were introduced and accepted among Estonians in the middle of the nineteenth century (Kaasik 2003). Among new 'old' vocabulary was the toponym *Maavald* (genitive: *Maavalla*, see below) denoting in the movement's ideology the territory populated by maarahvas, the Estonians. All these terms were reintroduced by spokespersons of the movement as more genuine appellations to be favoured over designations of foreign origin.[17]

Ideas of cultural independence and religious sovereignty, promoted by the pre-war taaralased movement, were picked up and developed between 1987 and 1995 within the Heritage Protection Club Tõlet,[18] which mobilized a small group of young people, mainly students at the University of Tartu, who were interested in religion, history, ethnology and folklore. Members of Tõlet initially had a keen interest in the activities of the taarausulised and were themselves initially called *noortaaralased*, 'young adherents of the Taara faith' (Kaasik 2000). Tõlet explored Estonian folk religion and Finno-Ugric cultures, sharing their views in the club's publications and in a variety of events such as open discussion evenings, the club's spring school, public rituals and so on (Västrik 1996).

Since 1992 members of the club have used public debate to popularize maausk and maausulised (Toimetus 1992) instead of taarausk, and in the process took the initiative to institutionalize the movement as an officially recognized religious organization. This was manifested, among various other ways, in a public appeal published in *Postimees*, one of the main Estonian dailies (Kaasik and Sarv 1992), and in a detailed essay by Ahto Kaasik about the essence and basic assumptions of maausk published in the club's journal (Kaasik 1993). Kaasik has been part of the maausulised leadership since the 1990s and was one of the founders of Tõlet, later becoming the movement's most active spokesperson.[19] Although his essay was based on an earlier nationalist narrative that was hostile to Christianity, it reflected several differences from the principles of the taarausulised, and stressed cultural continuity and the importance of folklore. Kaasik described maausk as a 'conception of the world and the frame of mind of our ancestors', which is reflected in a particular way of life and culture. According to Kaasik, no one ever constructed maausk; it developed 'together with our ancestors' and for at least five thousand years adjusted traits of other cultures. These fusions took place according to certain principles that include the ideas that everything that exists has power, nature is animate, the ancestors are holy, all deeds have consequences (everyone is responsible for his or her deeds) and one's creed is one's personal business (Kaasik 1993: 3–8).

Maausk is conceptualized as an animistic nature religion in which attention is paid to a variety of forces and deities. Each member of the maausulised community has the freedom to interpret any deity as either a spiritual entity or a natural force (Lipp and Kaasik 2008). The most important and well-known deity is Maaema ('Mother Earth'), who is perceived as the source of all living beings and natural resources (Kerge 2007; Aitsam 2009; Kaasik 2012: 65; Maavalla Koda 2012). Other popular deities mentioned in public media texts are those related to thunder (Uku, Pikne, Vanaisa) and various regional deities (for example, Peko, Tõnn, Pell) who are linked to specific domains and venerated on particular calendar holidays. According to the interpretations of contemporary maausulised, Taar (the appellation preferred instead of 'Taara') is the only deity with no specific domain and can thus be interpreted as the 'vastest and all-compassing force' (Aitsam 2009). In this respect the maausulised have taken a different approach from that of the taarausulised of the 1930s. The deities named above have been adapted from Estonian folklore collections representing a variety of local traditions. However, there are no descriptions of maausulised rituals in relation to these deities in media texts.

Institutionalization of the Maausulised Movement and Numbers of Followers

The umbrella organization of the maausulised movement was officially registered on 14 March 1995 as 'Taarausuliste ja Maausuliste Maavalla Koda', translated by its members as 'The Estonian House of Taara and Native Religions'.[20] The shortened variant of the name, Maavalla Koda, is used below. Official recognition of maausulised was made possible due to the fact that Kaido Kama was at that time Minister of Internal Affairs and responsible for issues related to religion (Ringvee 2011: 109). As indicated in the name of the organization (which has the status of a 'union of churches and congregations' according to the Estonian Churches and Congregations Act), it represents both the maausulised and taarausulised movements.[21] The first public announcement about the newly registered organization, published in May 1995 in *Postimees*, stated that the organization represented both movements on equal terms and that each had its own particular ideology and cultic activities. Despite the fact that taarausulised had first position in the official name of the organization, from the beginning the maausulised groups dominated in Maavalla Koda and make up the majority in its regional member organizations.[22] However, it is important to note that the maausulised movement is in no way homogeneous. Despite the fact that within the movement there are tendencies towards a doctrinal mode of religiosity which underlines the importance of traditions and continuity, there are also followers who prefer an imagistic mode which allows spontaneous reflections and diverse individual interpretations (Leete 1995; Whitehouse 2004: 65–75; Sammelselg 2011: 32–35).

The numbers of people belonging to Maavalla Koda member organizations have not been numerous. Membership numbers vary considerably in different public sources. At the beginning of the year 2000, for example, Maavalla Koda estimated its membership at around two hundred (Au and Ringvee 2000: 140), while in one of its official appeals to the Prime Minister of the Republic of Estonia (November 2002) membership was stated to be approximately one hundred (MK Press Release 2003). In interviews and articles Maavalla Koda spokespersons have refused to reveal data about registered members of their organization, because this would be against the principles of religious freedom (Ringvee 2011: 78).

Maausk is conceptualized within the movement as an indigenous nature religion that needs no formal affiliation or formalized organization. Today the basic unit for practising maausk is considered to be the family (Altnurme 2012: 53). Maausulised have stated repeatedly that Maavalla Koda and regional organizations are needed only to represent their values and needs in communication with the state (Kasemets, Barkalaja and Eller 1995). Therefore they have no intention of mobilizing all followers and they accept that the majority have not joined the movement's official organizations. Furthermore, in their public statements maausulised deny any missionary activities (thus evidently contrasting themselves with the Christian mission) and emphasize the free will of followers – becoming a maausuline should be one's personal choice and a free option (Koppel and Kaasik 2001: 12).

According to various censuses and public opinion polls on religious matters, the movement's popularity has increased considerably since its institutionalization in 1995. The Population and Housing Census of the year 2000 indicated that the number of people who identified as adherents of taarausk and maausk was in total 1,058 (PHC 2002: 292). The idea that these movements are the fastest growing non-Christian religious groups in Estonia was supported in the results of the latest Population and Housing Census from 2011, according to which the number of adherents of maausk was 1,925 and of taarausk 1,047 (RA 2013). The total was 2,972, meaning an almost threefold increase in ten years. The generally positive attitude towards the movement is also reflected in recent national surveys. Public opinion polls conducted in 2010 revealed that 51 per cent of respondents declared support for the principles of the maausulised and 37 per cent indicated positive feelings towards this religion (Altnurme 2010: 21).

Indigenous Values and Alternative National Discourse

The specific rhetoric of indigeneity and continuity used by followers of the movement to legitimize their religious ideas and practices came to the fore in public media texts about maausk. Maausulised spokespersons referred to family lineages of inherited oral traditions that were kept secret (Holvandus and Eller 1995; Eller 2000; Liiv and Eller 2003), and were 'passed on ... from generation to generation during the centuries of the Christian occupation' (Kaasik n.d.). Similar ideas were also spread among the taarausulised (Kaasik 1993: 4; Kasemets, Barkalaja and Eller 1995: 19). Thus the movement's in-group mythology includes the idea that there has been a sporadic, conscious and continuous tradition of indigenous religion 'unpolluted' by Christianity since time immemorial. It is highly probable that this idea goes back to the early Romantic authors, such as Faehlmann, who used similar constructs to glorify the nation's past.

In explanations of maausk much attention is paid to linguistic matters as well as to folklore and local cultural traditions. The movement's ideologues stress the idea that traits of indigenous religion have survived in vernacular language(s), earlier folklore records and traditions which have survived in contemporary folk culture. According to Kaasik (n.d.): 'The tradition of the native religion can be fragmentarily traced in the Estonian culture. In our customs, beliefs, attitudes, but most of all our language, there are many elements similar to those of our ancestors'. This idea is developed further in the claim that all Estonians who follow some traditional customs are unconsciously maausulised. This has been constantly articulated in interviews with Ahto Kaasik and in newspaper headlines such as: 'Yuletide is an ancient maausk holiday', 'A person who makes a fire on St John's day is a follower of maausk', and so on. Newspaper articles contain lists of practices that can be labelled 'age-old traditions' of maausulised, thus reflecting contesting claims about the ownership of elements of traditional culture. On the other hand, such claims create a huge virtual community of followers (a kind of virtual inclusion) that allows people to easily identify with the movement.

At the same time, maausulised spokespersons suggest that foreign influences should be avoided or dropped:

> Everything in the tradition is not acceptable for us. Quite a big part of it has been borrowed from different cultures at different times and is in ... opposition with the native religion. Thus the studying of ... tradition based on the native religion is like gold washing [panning for gold] – only the important and valuable part must remain. (Kaasik n.d.)

In this way they clearly differentiate the movement from Christianity (labelled in some articles as 'the native religion of Jews'), which has had a long-term impact on Estonian folk culture, as well as from modern manifestations of Western and Eastern esoteric traditions and New Age thought:

> The adherents of the native religion don't create new traditions or borrow them from other peoples. Should ... borrowing in some cases be necessary, the missing fragment of tradition is taken from a kindred people. Our native religion forms one family with the nature worship ... of ... other Uralic peoples. (Kaasik n.d.)

Maausk is thus located and interpreted from the perspective of Uralic (or Finno-Ugric) linguistic and cultural affinity, which generally refers to kindred peoples living in present-day Russia. This shows a clear eastward orientation and is based on a long-term inclination toward pan-Finno-Ugric ideas (cf. Kuutma 2005). Connections with Finno-Ugric peoples were also stressed in the Declaration of Uralic Communion, a document signed by Estonian, Mari, Erzya-Mordovian and Finnish representatives of native and indigenous religions, who, in 2001, founded the International Uralic Communion of Native Religions (Declaration 2001).

As indicated above, in recent years a positive image of maausulised and their aspirations has been created by print and online media. Maavalla Koda has addressed issues that have reached the public media and has been quite successful in presenting the movement's ideas to wider audiences. Maausulised have been active in debates about religious freedom in relation to legislation concerning religious education in public schools. Maavalla Koda has consistently been against any religious instruction in public schools, claiming that this violates a person's inherent religious rights (Vakker and Rohtmets 2008; Ringvee 2011). In 2004 Maavalla Koda, together with other non-Christian religious organizations, managed to change the legislative act that allowed registration of only those religious associations that had Christian vocabulary in their name (such as 'church', 'congregation', 'monastery' and so on).

In addition, Maavalla Koda has been successful in several court cases and public debates concerning sacred natural sites – primarily holy groves, but also other types of 'historical sacred natural sites' considered the main ritual venues of the maausulised (Kaasik 2012; Sepp 2012). These cases have mainly addressed the movement's objections to the construction of modern buildings (such as windmills, sports and leisure centres, dwelling houses) in or near sacred groves that depend on destruction of national heritage and violation of the religious needs of the maausulised. Maavalla Koda has skilfully used discourses of heritage protection and wilderness preservation, yet this is constantly combined with discourses of religious freedom and human rights (Sammelselg 2011).

In the 2000s the maausulised managed to influence legislation and state politics in such a way that in 2008 a state-financed development plan was launched to register and study sacred natural sites, and a special research centre was established by the University of Tartu to fulfil the aims of the programme (Sepp 2012). Maavalla Koda is the official partner in this project and their representatives participate in the work of the research centre. Since then, the topic of natural sacred sites has been continuously discussed in the public media. In May 2011 a political 'support group of natural sacred sites' was formed in the Estonian parliament after a recent case in which logging was carried out in one of the 'indigenous sacred groves' in Maardu, near Tallinn (Simson 2011).

Conclusions

A consideration of the historical background, earlier initiatives to create an Estonian national religion and articles about maausulised and maausk in the Estonian press over the last two decades indicates that a coherent and functioning alternative religious movement – or a wider cultural and religious worldview – has developed. It combines elements of taarausk of the 1920s and 1930s, pan-Finno-Ugric ideas, knowledge drawn from folklore collections and modern nationalist discourse. Apart from the forerunners of the pre-Second-World-War period, the spokespersons of maausk oppose, at least in their rhetoric, the idea of creating new concepts, rituals and holidays. They rely instead mainly on folkloric resources (in the form of texts) and living cultural traditions, which have been taken up selectively. Practices and ideas are chosen only when they fit with a nationalist narrative that is opposed to foreign influence (including Christianity), stress continuity and sovereignty, and value linguistic and cultural affinity with kindred peoples. A clear institutionalization of the movement has taken place with spokespersons tending to develop it towards a doctrinal mode of religiosity. In their umbrella organization, maausu-lised have a dominant position and their opinions and activities have received generally positive media coverage. The movement's ideas have apparently found support because they are based on a national narrative that is intermingled with rhetoric and activities related to religious freedom, indigenous rights, natural sacred sites and cultural heritage. The preconditions for the creation of a positive media image have been created through the rich and well-maintained home page of Maavalla Koda, effective use of social media, and spokespersons' conscious and active networking with journalists, in both the main-stream media and alternative online publications.

Acknowledgements

Research for this chapter was supported by the institutional research project 'Tradition, Creativity and Society: Minorities and Alternative Discourses' (IUT2–43), Estonian Research Council (grant no. 9271) and the European Union through its European Regional Development Fund (Centre of Excellence in Cultural Theory, CECT).

Notes

1 In Estonian the word *maa* has multiple meanings including 'Earth', 'land', 'ground', 'soil', 'earth', 'country(side)' and 'state'. The second part of the compound, *usk*, means 'belief', 'faith', 'trust', 'creed' and 'religion' (TEA 2005: 355, 698).
2 There are studies on various aspects of modern Paganism available in English about Lithuania (Strmiska 2005b, 2012b), Latvia (Strmiska 2012a) and the Russian Federation (Aitamurto 2011).
3 In Estonian, students of semiotics, theology and ethnology have pro-duced three pieces of research dedicated to modern Paganisms in Estonia. In a seminar paper Auli Kütt (2002) explored maausk as a manifestation of deep ecology; Triin Vakker (2007) wrote her M.A. dissertation on attempts to construct a national pagan religion in the 1920s and 1930s (see also Vakker 2012); and Kaisa Sammelselg's M.A. thesis (2011) dis-cussed the movement's views on natural sacred sites.
4 See the English version of the site, Maavalla Koda, which contains, how-ever, much less information than the pages in Estonian. http://www.maavald.ee/eng/ (retrieved 15 August 2013).

5 The territory of the Republic of Estonia is 45,277 square kilometres. According to the latest census in 2011, there were 1,294,455 permanent residents, making the country one of the least populous member states of the European Union. Ethnic Estonians make up around 69 per cent of the total population and the largest minority are Russians, making up approximately 25 per cent. Http://en.wikipedia.org/wiki/Demographics_of_Estonia (retrieved 15 August 2013).

6 Estonian history evidently shares more similarities with Latvia than Lithuania. However, it should be mentioned that the Latvian and Lithuanian languages belong to the Baltic branch of the Indo-European language family, while Estonian, together with Finnish, Ingrian, Karelian, Livonian, Ludic, Veps and Votic, belongs to the Finnic branch of the Uralic language family (Marcantonio 2002).

7 For a general overview of the crusade in the Baltic area, see Murray (2009).

8 On the historiography and etymology of Tharapita (referred to as Taara in later interpretations), see Sutrop (2005). For a recent collection of articles on the chronicle, see Tamm, Kaljundi and Jensen (2011).

9 For the most up-to-date translation of the epic into English, see Kreutzwald (2011).

10 For details on this process, labelled as 'national awakening' in Estonian historiography, see Gross (2002) and Raun (2003). Campaigns to collect folklore in order to study the 'true national history' of Estonians, including material about pagan religion, were initiated by principal figures of the nationalist movement (Västrik 2007: 3–8).

11 Nationalist ideas led to secularization and this process escalated rapidly during the Soviet regime (1940–1991) when the clergy was repressed and many religious organizations were banned. This is vividly illustrated by the statistics of church affiliation: while in the 1934 census 78 per cent of Estonia's population designated themselves followers of the Lutheran faith and 19 per cent the Orthodox, by the year 2000 these figures had dropped to 14.8 per cent and 13.9 per cent respectively (Altnurme 2011a: 77–78). The situation has not changed much since Estonia regained independence: according to recent surveys Estonia is considered one of the most secularized and unchurched countries in Europe (Ringvee 2012: 96).

12 The term has also been used in the forms *taara usk* and *taarausk*, both translated as 'Taara belief' or 'Taara religion'. To date no extensive study of this movement has been published in English; in Estonian see Arjakas (1987), Deemant (1988), Vakker (2007, 2012) (the last contains a short English summary).

13 These terms were both neologisms: *asko* derived from *ask* ('magic', 'enchantment') and *hiislar* from *hiis* ('sacred grove') (Kaasik 2003).

14 Independence Day commemorates the declaration of Estonia's independence in 1918. Within their organization taarausulised introduced their own reckoning of time according to which each year started with

Independence Day, and 1918 was the starting point for counting the years (Vakker 2012: 187).

15 This celebration was introduced by the movement in 1928 and later popularized by the Estonian World Youth Organization (1919–1940), which was under the influence of taarausulised (Deemant 1988).

16 Eller's essay was republished in print and online several times in the 1990s and 2000s, and can be treated as one of the core texts of maausulised ideology (Eller 1990, 1998).

17 For criticism of this kind of ideological statement see Beyer (2007). Beyer showed that compounds such as *maarahvas* and *maakeel* were translations of Western legal vocabulary, introduced by foreign conquerors, which gained specific meaning over the course of centuries.

18 The name of the club refers to the insignia of Taara usk – *tõlet* (a neologism formed with the words *tõde* 'truth', *elu* 'life' and *tee* 'path'), a silver medallion containing a piece of earth from a sacred site – worn by the members of Hiis.

19 Kaasik was the main initiator of the national development plan 'Sacred Natural Sites in Estonia: Study and Maintenance 2008–2012' (Kaasik 2012; Sepp 2012) and since 2008 has acted as the project leader and head of the Centre of Sacred Natural Sites at the University of Tartu.

20 This name, from the English version of the organization's homepage (Maavalla Koda 2013), has been carried over to scholarly literature (Vakker and Rohtmets 2008; Ringvee 2012).

21 In 2014 there were five regional member organizations united under Maavalla Koda: Maausuliste Viru Koda, Emajõe Maausuliste Koda, Emujärve Taarausuliste ja Maausuliste Koda, Härjapea Taarausuliste ja Maausuliste Koda, and Maausuliste Saarepealne Koda (*Kohalikud Kojad* 2014).

22 Since 2003 three independent congregations of taarausulised which do not belong to Maavalla Koda have been officially registered (Ringvee 2011: 78). These are Tarbatu Hiis, Mäe Hiis and Päikese Hiis (Au and Ringvee 2007: 136). This development reflects a gradual move towards sovereignty within both movements. The taarausulised independently publish the journal *Hiis* although their ideas and activities have not attracted as much attention as the maausulised in the mass media and Internet.

References

Aitamurto, K. 2011. *Paganism, Traditionalism, Nationalism: Narratives of Russian Rodnoverie*. Helsinki: University of Helsinki, Department of World Cultures.

Aitsam, V. 2009. 'Kus on maailma kõige uskmatuma rahva jumalad?' [Where are the Gods of the Most Faithless People?], *Maaleht*,

26 December. Retrieved 15 July 2013 from http://www.maaleht.ee/
    archive/article.php?id=28063447.
Altnurme, L. 2005. *Kristlusest oma usuni. Uurimus muutustest eestlaste
    religioossuses 20. sajandi II poolel* [From Christianity to Own Belief:
    A Study of Changes in the Religiosity of Estonians in the Second Half
    of the Twentieth Century]. Dissertationes Theologiae Universitatis
    Tartuensis 9. Tartu: Tartu Ülikooli Kirjastus.
———. 2010. 'Religiooni uurimise probleemidest
    sotsiaalkonstruktsionistlikust perspektiivist' [On the Problems of
    Religious Studies from the Perspective of Social Constructivism],
    Usuteaduslik Ajakiri 60(1): 4–22.
———. 2011a. 'Changes in Mythic Patterns in Estonian Religious Life
    Stories', *Social Compass* 58(1): 77–94.
———. 2011b. 'Eestlased usulises pöördes' [Estonians in the Religious
    Turn], *Postimees*, 20 March. Retrieved 15 December 2012 from http://
    arvamus.postimees.ee/405074.
———. 2012. 'Maavalla Koda', in L. Altnurme et al. (eds), *Uued usulised
    ja vaimsed ühendused Eestis* [New Religious and Spiritual Unions in
    Estonia]. Tartu: Tartu Ülikooli Kirjastus, pp. 52–59.
Arjakas, K. 1987. 'Taaralastest ja Kustas Utuste kirjakogust' [About
    Followers of the Taara Religion and K. Utuste's Collection of Letters],
    Looming 7: 999–1001. Retrieved 31 July 2013 from http://www.maavald.
    ee/prindi.html?id=26.
Au, I. and R. Ringvee. 2000. *Kirikud ja kogudused Eestis* [Churches and
    Congregations in Estonia]. Tallinn: Ilo.
———. 2007. *Usulised ühendused Eestis* [Religious Associations in Estonia].
    Tallinn: Allika.
Beyer, J. 2007. 'Ist "maarahvas" ("Landvolk"), die alte Selbstbezeichnung
    der Esten, eine Lehnübersetzung? Eine Studie zur Begriffsgeschichte
    des Ostseeraums', *Zeitschrift für Ostmitteleuropa-Forschung* 56:
    566–93.
Declaration 2001 = *Declaration of the Uralic Communion*. Retrieved 18
    September 2011 from http://www.maavald.ee/prindi.html?id=362.
Deemant, K. 1988. 'Taarausulistest' [About the Followers of the Taara
    Faith], *Edasi* 101: 4; 106: 5. Retrieved 3 August 2013 from http://www.
    maavald.ee/prindi.html?id=29.
Eller, K.I. 1972. 'Maarahvast' [About *Maarahvas*], *Põllumajanduse
    Akadeemia* 4–7 (27 January: 9; 9 February: 12; 17 February: 14–15;
    24 February: 18–20).
———. 1990. 'Maarahvast' [About *Maarahvas*], *Vikerkaar* 3: 72–77.
———. 1998. 'Maarahvast' [About *Maarahvas*], in Asser Murutar
    (comp.), *Maarahva elujõud* II. Tartu: Elmatar, pp. 199–216.
    Retrieved 15 December 2012 from http://www.maavald.ee/koda.
    html?rubriik=17&id=34&op=lugu.
———. 2000. 'Noatera jutt. Omauskudest tänapäeva maailmas' [Talk on a
    Razor-Edge: On Vernacular Religions in the Contemporary World].

Retrieved 15 December 2012 from http://www.maavald.ee/prindi. html?id=36.

Gross, T. 2002. 'Anthropology of Collective Memory: Estonian National Awakening Revisited', *Trames* 6(4): 342–54.

Heinapuu, A. and K. Kama. 1990. 'Olla enese moodi. Kaido Kama intervjuu Andres Heinapuule' [To Be Like Yourself: A. Heinapuu's Interview with K. Eller], *Vikerkaar* 9: 69–73.

Holvandus, J. and K. Eller. 1995. 'Eestlasest ja maarahvast. Intervjuu Kalle Elleriga' [About Estonians and *maarahvas*; J. Holvandus' Interview with K. Eller], *Kultuur ja Elu* 2: 6–9.

Jansen, E. 1998. 'Muinaseesti panteon: Faehlmanni müütide roll eestlaste rahvusteadvuses' [Ancient Estonian Pantheon: The Role of Faehlmann's Myths in National Identity of Estonians], *Keel ja Kirjandus* 12: 801–11.

Jonuks, T. 2013. 'Der estnische Nationalismus und sein Konzept der prähistorischen Religion: Die Nation als Gestalterin des Religionsbildes', *Forschungen zur baltischen Geschichte* 8: 145–64.

Kaasik, A. 1993. 'Ahto jutt' [Ahto's Talk], *Hiis. Tõleti ajakiri* 6: 2–8.

———. 2000. 'Mis oli Tõlet?' [What Was Tõlet?]. Retrieved 15 December 2012 from http://www.maavald.ee/prindi.html?id=43.

———. 2003. 'Old Estonian Religions', *Estonian Culture* 2. Retrieved 13 July 2013 from http://www.estinst.ee/publications/estonianculture/ II_MMIII/ kaasik.html.

———. 2012. 'Conserving Sacred Natural Sites in Estonia', in J.- M. Mallarach, T. Papayannis and R. Väisänen (eds), *The Diversity of Sacred Lands in Europe: Proceedings of the Third Workshop of the Delos Initiative – Inari/Aanaar 2010*. Gland: IUCN; and Vantaa: Metsähallitus Natural Heritage Services, pp. 61–73. Retrieved 13 July 2013 from http:// data.iucn.org/dbtw-wpd/edocs/2012–006.pdf.

———. n.d. 'The Estonian Native Religion'. Retrieved 18 September 2011 from http://www.maavald.ee/prindi.html?id=253.

Kaasik, A. and T. Sarv. 1992. 'Eestlastele Eesti maausk' [For Estonians Estonian *maausk*], *Postimees* 100 (4 May): 7.

Karo, K. 2007. 'Rahvuslikud narratiivid ja religion' [National Narratives and Religion], in L. Altnurme (ed.), *Mitut usku Eesti II. Valik usundiloolisi uurimusi: kristluse eri*. Tartu: Tartu Ülikooli Kirjastus, pp. 13–46.

Kasemets, A., A. Barkalaja and K. Eller. 1995. 'Maavalla Koda – mis see on?' [Maavalla Koda – What Is It?], *Postimees* 109 (15 May): 19; 110 (16 May): 13.

Kerge, R. 2007. 'Maausuline Ahto Kaasik: maausuliseks ei saada üleloomulike kogemuste abil. Selleks kasvatakse' [Maausuline Ahto Kaasik: It Is Not Possible to Become Maausuline through Supernatural Experiences. You Have to Grow], *Õhtuleht*, 6 December. Retrieved 16 September 2013 from http://www.ohtuleht.ee/257422.

Kohalikud Kojad [Local Houses]. 2014. Retrieved 29 October 2014 from http://www.maavald.ee/koda.html?op=rubriik&rubriik=23.

Kõiva, M. 2011. 'Women's Holidays and Porridge Rites', *The Ritual Year: The Inner and the Outer. The Yearbook of the SIEF Working Group on The Ritual Year* 6: 83–106.

Koostajad [Kama, K.] 1988. 'Kymme aastat nyydisaegseid sirvilaudu' [10 Years of Modern Runic Calendars], *Vikerkaar* 1: 49–54. Retrieved 13 July 2013 from http://www.maavald.ee/prindi.html?id=44.

Koppel, M. and A. Kaasik. 2001. 'Omausk ja omailm' [Vernacular Religion and Vernacular Worldview; M. Koppel's interview with A. Kaasik], *Kultuur ja Elu* 4: 8–12. Retrieved 10 July 2011 from http://www.maavald.ee/prindi.html?id=96.

Kreutzwald, F. 2011. *Kalevipoeg. The Estonian National Epic.* Translated by Triinu Kartus. Tartu, Tallinn: Estonian Literary Museum, Kunst.

Kütt, A. 2002. *Ökoloogilised aspektid maausuliste eneseväljendustes* [Ecological Aspects in the Self-Presentation of *Maausulised*]. Unpublished seminar paper, Department of Semiotics, University of Tartu. Retrieved 12 July 2013 from http://www.scribd.com/doc/25656058/.

Kuutma, K. 2005. 'Vernacular Religions and the Invention of Identities behind the Finno-Ugric Wall', *Temenos: Nordic Journal of Comparative Religion* 41(1): 51–76.

Leete, A. 1995. 'Maausk – rahvalik salakäik kristluse ja satanismi lähistel?' [Maausk – Vernacular Hidden Passage in the Vicinity of Christianity and Satanism], *Postimees* 15 February: 13.

Liiv, P. and K. Eller 2003. 'Kalle Eller: Meie rahvas on olemas kristliku Õhtumaa kiuste' [Kalle Eller: Our People Exists in the Teeth of the Christian Occident; P. Liiv's interview with K. Eller], *Päiksetuul* 11. Retrieved 29 October 2014 from http://www.maavald.ee/press.html?rubriik=33&id=331&op=lugu.

Lipp, K. and A. Kaasik. 2008. 'Ahto Kaasik: Maausk on lahutamatu osa meie keelest, meelest ja kultuurist (III osa)' [Ahto Kaasik: Maausk is an Inseparable Element of our Language, Mind and Culture (3rd part); K. Lipp's interview with A. Kaasik]. Retrieved 16 August 2013 from http://www.bioneer.ee/bioneer/arvamus/aid-1676/.

Maavalla Koda. 2012. 'Maaema sünnipäeval mullatöid ei tehta ega niideta' [It is not Allowed either to Dig or Mow on the Birthday of Maaema], *Maaleht* 17 May. Retrieved 13 July 2013 from http://www.maaleht.ee/archive/article.php?id=64409000.

———. 2013. 'Maavalla Koda'. Retrieved 13 July 2013 from http://www.maavald.ee/prindi.html?id=251.

Magliocco, S. 2009. 'Pagans', in G. Harvey (ed.), *Religions in Focus: New Approaches to Tradition and Contemporary Practices.* London: Equinox, pp.101–120.

Marcantonio, A. 2002. *The Uralic Language Family: Facts, Myths and Statistics.* Oxford and Boston: Blackwell.

MK Press Release 2003 = '27.01.10216 (2003) Peaminister ei soovi koostööd maausulistega' [The Prime Minister Does not Wish to Cooperate with

Maausulised]. Retrieved 17 November 2011 from http://www.maavald. ee/prindi.html?id=145.

Murray, A.V. (ed.). 2009. *Clash of Cultures on the Medieval Baltic Frontier.* Aldershot: Ashgate.

PHC 2002 = *2000. aasta rahva ja eluruumide loendus. 2000 Population and Housing Census* IV. Tallinn: Statistikaamet. Retrieved 16 December 2012 from http://www.stat.ee/26287.

Plaat, J. 2002. 'Christian and Non-Christian Religiosity in Estonia and East-Virumaa in the 1990s: Comparison of Estonians and other Ethnic Groups', *Pro Ethnologia* 14: 97–134. Retrieved 18 November 2011 from http://www.erm.ee/pdf/pro14/ plaat.pdf.

Pohla, T. and K. Eller. 1991. 'Intervjuu Kalle Elleriga' [T. Pohla's interview with K. Eller], *Kultuur ja Elu* 3: 12–17.

RA 2013 = 'Religious Affiliation'. Retrieved 13 July 2013 from http://pub.stat.ee/px-web.2001/I_Databas/Population_ census/PHC2011/01Demographic_and_ethno_cultural_ characteristics/08Religious_affiliation/08Religious_affiliation.asp.

Raun, T.U. 2001. *Estonia and the Estonians.* Stanford: Hoover Institution Press, Stanford University.

———. 2003. 'Nineteenth- and Early Twentieth-Century Estonian Nationalism Revisited', *Nations and Nationalism* 9(1): 129–47.

Ringvee, R. 2011. *Riik ja religioon nõukogudejärgses Eestis 1991–2008* [State and Religion in the Post-Soviet Estonia from 1991 to 2008], Dissertationes Theologiae Universitatis Tartuensis 23. Tartu: Tartu Ülikooli Kirjastus. Retrieved 18 November 2011 from http://hdl.handle.net/10062/17525.

———. 2012. 'Dialogue or Confrontation? New Religious Movements, Mainstream Religions and the State in Secular Estonia', *International Journal for the Study of New Religions* 3(1): 93–116.

Sammelselg, K. 2011. *Maausulised 21. sajandi alguse Eestis: analüüs läbi hiie problemaatika* [*Maausulised* at the Beginning of the 21st Century in Estonia: Analysis via the Problematics of Hiis-Sites]. Unpublished M.A. thesis, Department of Ethnology, University of Tartu.

Sarv, T. 1990. 'Ehkki 70ndate aastate alternatiivseid...' [Commentary on Eller 1990], *Vikerkaar* 3: 77.

Sarv, T. and K.I. Eller. 1987. '200 maakeelset nime' [200 Vernacular Names], *Kultuur ja Elu* 9: 21–22.

Sepp, A. 2012. 'National Plan on Natural Sanctuaries in Estonia 2008–2012: Challenges and Perspectives', in J.-M. Mallarach (ed.), *Spiritual Values of Protected Areas of Europe. Workshop Proceedings.* Bonn: Federal Agency for Nature Conservation, pp. 149–55. Retrieved 15 July 2013 from http://www.bfn.de/fileadmin/MDB/documents/service/Skript322. pdf.

Simson, K. 2011. 'Riigikogus loodi looduslike pühapaikade toetusrühm' [Support Group of Natural Sacred Sites Established in Parliament], *Maaleht* May 2. Retrieved 15 July 2013 from http://www.maaleht.ee/ archive/article.php?id=45169099.

Strmiska, M.F. 2005a. *Modern Paganism in World Cultures: Comparative Perspectives*. Santa Barbara: ABC-CLIO.

———. 2005b. 'The Music of the Past in Modern Paganism', *Nova Religio: The Journal of Alternative and Emergent Religions* 8(3): 39–58.

———. 2012a. 'Modern Latvian Paganism: Some Introductory Remarks', *Pomegranate: The International Journal of Pagan Studies* 14(1): 22–30.

———. 2012b. 'Romuva Looks East: Indian Inspiration in Lithuanian Paganism', in M. Ališauskienė and I.W. Schröder (eds), *Religious Diversity in Post-Soviet Society: Ethnographies of Catholic Hegemony and the New Pluralism in Lithuania*. Surrey: Ashgate, pp. 125–50.

Sutrop, U. 2005. 'Taarapita – the Great God of the Oeselians', *Folklore: Electronic Journal of Folklore* 26: 27–64. Retrieved 15 December 2012 from http://www.folklore.ee/folklore/vol26/sutrop.pdf.

Tamm, M. 2008. 'History as Cultural Memory: Mnemohistory and the Construction of the Estonian Nation', *Journal of Baltic Studies* 39(4): 499–516.

Tamm, M., L. Kaljundi and C.S. Jensen (eds). 2001. *Crusading and Chronicle Writing on the Medieval Baltic Frontier: A Companion to the Chronicle of Henry of Livonia*. Farnham and Burlington: Ashgate.

TEA 2005 = *Eesti-Inglise sõnaraamat. Estonian-English Dictionary*. Tallinn: TEA Kirjastus.

Toimetus [Editorial Team]. 1992. 'Alustuseks' [Foreword], *Hiis. Tõleti ajakiri* [Sacred Grove: The Journal of Tõlet] 5: 2–3.

Vakker, T. 2007. *Taaralastest ja nende tegevusest okupatsioonieelses Eestis* [About *Taaralased* and their Activities in Pre-Occupation Estonia]. Unpublished M.A. thesis, Faculty of Theology, University of Tartu.

———. 2012. 'Rahvusliku religiooni konstrueerimise katsed – taara usk' [Efforts to Construct National Religion in Estonia in the 1920s-30s – Taara Religion], *Mäetagused* 50: 175–98. Retrieved 15 December 2012 from http://www.folklore.ee/tagused/nr50/vakker.pdf.

Vakker, T. and P. Rohtmets. 2008. 'Estonia: Relations between Christian and Non-Christian Religious Organisations and the State of Religious Freedom', *Religion, State and Society* 36(1): 45–53.

Västrik, E.-H. 1996. 'The Heathens in Tartu in 1987–1994: Heritage Protection Club Tõlet', in M. Kõiva (ed.), *Contemporary Folklore: Changing World View and Tradition*. Tartu: Institute of Estonian Language and Estonian Museum of Literature, pp. 86–101.

———. 2007. 'Archiving Tradition in a Changing Political Order: From Nationalism to Pan-Finno-Ugrianism in the Estonian Folklore Archives', in *Culture Archives and the State: Between Nationalism, Socialism, and the Global Market* (Working Papers of the Center for Folklore Studies, vol. 1). Retrieved 15 July 2013 from http://hdl.handle.net/1811/46903.

Viires, A. 1991. 'Pseudomythology in Estonian Publicity in the 19th and 20th Century', *Ethnologia Europaea* 21(2): 137–43.

Whitehouse, H. 2004. *Modes of Religiosity: A Cognitive Theory of Religious Transmission*. Walnut Creek: AltaMira Press.

7

Emerging Identity Markets of Contemporary Pagan Ideologies in Hungary

Tamás Szilágyi

Introduction

An important upswing of religious variety could be observed in Hungary by the end of socialism. The changes involved a double tendency: the destruction of cultural traditions along with the arrival of new religious ideas. This upswing brought with it the expansion of an 'identity-market' whose religious dimensions cannot be disregarded. Although secularization theory seems to have been disproved, in the case of some groups religious characteristics have been combined with political orientations. Religious and national identities merge, especially in the post-communist context. Amidst the growing religious diversity, Pagan groups began establishing themselves from the early 1990s. Lacking a missionary agenda, they tended to have exclusive membership and lower numbers than other religious movements. Among the Pagan communities which emerged were Wicca groups deriving from Western traditions and which were registered as churches, communities aiming to revitalize ancient Hungarian Paganism, and modern shamanic groups. Because none of these groups had significant numbers, they did not become the focus of media attention or scholarly interest during the decade of their inception. Increased interest in these groups occurred only from the mid-2000s, when several mass events were organized, Pagan teachers and healers started to appear in the media and the first scientific papers were published (Szilágyi and Szilárdi 2007). This chapter offers an insight into the post-transitional history of contemporary Paganism in Hungary, focusing on its characteristics, sources and myth-making tendencies[1]. It concludes with a case study of one Pagan group: the Yotengrit Church.

Characteristics of Hungarian Paganism

Several researchers have recently examined the distinctiveness of the contemporary Hungarian Pagan milieu (Szilárdi 2007, 2009, 2013; Povedák 2010; Bakó and Hubbes 2011; Hubbes 2011; Szilágyi 2011, 2012). These studies highlight some key characteristics: a strong attachment to the issue of national identity and syncretic worldviews as a result of integrating various other religious ideas and beliefs, including, somewhat paradoxically given Hungarian Pagans' feelings about Christianity, some local Christian elements. These tendencies are closely related to the regional characteristics of eastern-central European Paganism (Wiench 1997; Simpson 2000), though specific patterns are identifiable in a number of areas.

The first notable characteristic of contemporary Hungarian Paganism is its countercultural nature. After the political transition in Hungary, modern Paganism – with its tendencies of myth-making, sacralization of the nation and invention of new traditions based on national folklore – has defined its ideology broadly in contrast to the globalized mass culture and Western-oriented political and cultural ideologies. Besides the role it plays in giving a distinctive religious identity, embracing Paganism is for many a symbolic expression of political and ideological resistance to modernity, capitalism and a generally Western cultural orientation. Linking this orientation to political ideologies – especially to right-wing radicalism – has resulted in Paganism's emergence in Hungary as a kind of total counterculture.

Hungarian Paganism's second general characteristic is its exclusivity and ethnocentrism: religious and national identities are closely intertwined in a way that makes them complementary and inseparable. Ethnicity and blood bonds acquire a sacral character and become especially important in the question of origins and continuity. There is a general rejection of other religious views and political ideologies. Another characteristic is Paganism's opposition to views represented by official history sanctioned by academic scholars. Pagans often claim that scholars distort 'true' Hungarian history, acting as agents of 'foreign' external forces. Numerous (often conflicting) alternative theories of history and linguistics held and represented by key figures within Paganism coexist without difficulty and play a role in strengthening identity.

A fourth element, already referred to above, is Paganism's tendency towards syncretism, particularly the incorporation of local Christian and indigenous elements. While there is an ambivalence towards the Christian churches among Hungarian Pagans, open opposition to Christianity is not typical. Rather, there is an integration or merging of traditional Christian elements with elements of Hungary's 'ancient religion', including, for example, claims regarding the Hungarian origin of Jesus Christ and the Christianity of early Hungarian Christians, the Virgin Mary as the Holy Mother of Hungarian Pagans, the Paulines[2] as 'white shamans' (Szilágyi and Szilárdi 2007) and so on.

The revitalization of ancient Hungarian traditions is another key characteristic. Pagans attach great importance to widely disseminating information about traditions that can be associated with Hungarians and the ancient Hungarian religion, such as shamanic drumming, the use of a runic script and traditional archery.[3] These have a certain symbolic role: they indicate the status of their practitioners as positioned outside the majority culture, the practitioners' conscious acceptance of this separation and consequently their particular ideological orientation. Another characteristic of Hungarian Paganism is ideological flexibility: elements of Pagan belief appear in a wide variety of religious and political ideologies and Pagans are capable of incorporating widely differing views. In this way Paganism may appear as a kind of political religion (Szilágyi 2010) or as a cult which absorbs New Age elements. Finally, anti-pluralism and anti-modernism should be mentioned: contemporary Hungarian Paganism is strongly resistant to liberalization and cultural pluralism. The globalized world is felt to threaten the traditional, indigenous worldview.

In the context of this general characterization of Hungarian Paganism, it should be noted that the Pagan scene in Hungary is highly diverse and fragmented. Thus the elements listed above capture only broadly the characteristics of Pagan groups with Hungarian roots (see also Szilárdi 2013: 244–45). While Baltic and Slavic Paganisms are well defined in their organizational, ritual and ideological characteristics, there is no single strand which typifies Hungarian Paganism. Whereas Romuva in Lithuania or Dievturība in Latvia clearly define indigenous forms of Paganism, in Hungary's case this is very difficult to do. As a unified ideology cannot be identified, in a recent study groups were categorized using a strictly functional approach (Szilágyi and Szilárdi 2007); primarily, the movements active as officially registered churches in Hungary were included in the research's field of inquiry.

The Law on the Freedom of Conscience and Religion and the Churches introduced in Hungary in 1990 regulated the activities of, and benefits enjoyed by, religious communities; it also established the criteria for legal designation. To register, religious groups were required to submit a statement to a county court declaring they had at least one hundred followers. The requirements were easy to meet and registration essentially was pro forma. While any group is free to practise its faith, formal registration grants rights, imposes obligations on educational and social institutions and provides access to several forms of state funding.

The above-mentioned study (Szilágyi and Szilárdi 2007) researched officially registered Pagan groups' teachings, beliefs and social presence, constructing a general methodological framework because of the diversity of the communities. A significant portion of these officially registered communities – which could be considered 'Pagan' at a definitional level – had become 'phantomized' by the middle of the first decade of the twenty-first century: that is, following their registration they apparently did not have any religious activities, the public could not easily gain access to them and they could not be found at their registered address. The definition of Neopaganism applied in this study was: 'a collective term which stands for the many different religious groups that can be traced back to varied archaic (mostly nature-oriented) religious traditions, reviving and reconstructing ancient beliefs, habits and religious practices by adapting them to the challenges of the modern world' (Szilágyi and Szilárdi 2007: 21). These communities could be studied using content analysis methods exclusively through publications and published materials on communities' web pages, in cases where they were available. Besides these registered communities, groups fitting the definition of Neopaganism set out above that were involved in actual religious activities but were not officially registered were also studied. Most of the time these did not act as religious communities (for example, drum circles or naturopathy groups). However, they bore characteristics of a sort of 'Pagan metaculture' which included a particular intellectual orientation, alternative medicine, a renewed interest in ancient religious traditions, nature-centred thinking and so on.

Through studying the distinctiveness of this Pagan metaculture it became evident that its effects went beyond the field of religion and spilled into the wider culture. Beyond Pagan groups with no

organizational background or unified ideology, the metaculture vigorously manifests, for example, in the fields of politics and popular
culture. Its intellectual orientation is determined by a few trends that
can be grouped around key figures; modern Hungarian Pagans draw
inspiration from these individuals and cite them as the sources of
their religious views. When speaking of Paganism in the Hungarian
context, it is important to make a clear distinction between this
'Pagan orientation' and the officially registered groups or those
functioning as informal (unregistered) circles. The distinction can be
measured mainly in their influence on society, culture and politics.
Religious groups classifiable as Pagan are situated on the periphery
of Hungarian religious life: their situation is marginal and public
support and knowledge of them are barely measurable.

In contrast with this, a Pagan intellectual orientation has been
spreading dynamically since the early 2000s in the wider cultural
field, and especially in the political arena (Szilágyi 2012). Its appearance in the political field is closely connected with the rise and successful political performance of radical right-wing movements at the
end of the first decade of the 2000s. Although these groups consider
themselves to have Christian roots in terms of ideology, their symbolism goes back to the traditions of the pre-Christian era, tracing
the legitimacy of their views to ancient times. As Szilárdi (2009: 55)
writes: 'The concept of the sacred nation, the consecrated (alternative) history of the nation and the language, the emerging xenopho-
bia, along with the anti-pluralist and anti-globalist approaches, seem
to strengthen the idea that the concepts of Pagan organizations and
the concepts articulated by the far right wing adjoin each other'. The
Pagan opposition to 'foreign' Christianity is a recurring element in
radical right-wing media. Political figures in mainstream politics
also refer regularly to ideas connected to Paganism; for example, a
parliamentary representative of the (2013) governing party Fidesz,
Mária Wittner, analysed one of the prophecies of the founder of the
contemporary Hungarian Yotengrit Church on a national television show. In popular culture topics bearing the influence of a Pagan
metaculture regularly appear in connection with national rock bands,
popular among teenagers. Popular mass events bearing characteristics
of a Pagan metaculture also exist. *Kurultaj* is one such event. With
approximately 150,000 participants each year, it is one of the largest
tradition-preserving events in Europe. The National Gathering of
Hungarians is a similar mass event with 100–150,000 participants each
year. Its code can be described in terms of a Pagan intellectual orientation which is Hungarian in origin and has an influence extending

far beyond the members and supporters of religious communities that can be regarded as 'Pagan'.

Sources of Hungarian Paganism

As noted above, two of the main features of Hungarian Paganism are ideological flexibility and syncretism. The roots of these characteristics can be found in sources which appear as constant reference points among Pagan groups. These sources fall into three main types: (1) alternative linguistic and histographical sources; (2) the organic-traditionalist school; and (3) modern myth-creators and syncretic teachers.

Alternative linguistic and histographical sources are a recurring element in Pagan communities with Hungarian roots. These sources draw upon theories which typically arose in the first third of the twentieth century offering alternative conceptions of the origin of the Hungarian nation and Hungarian language in a spirit of romantic nationalism. One of the most popular authors, Ferenc Badiny-Jós, in his book *Jézus király: A pártus herceg* [*King Jesus: The Parthian Prince*] (1998), states that Jesus Christ did not belong to the Jewish nation, but originated from the Parthian ethnic group, which was at the time present everywhere in Galilee, and was a royal prince. The Parthians were an ancient Iranian people, who built up an empire that controlled all of the Iranian Plateau, the Tigris–Euphrates River Valley and much of Syria. Badiny-Jós's argument, based on conspiracy theories, reached its peak when he claimed that the Hungarian royal dynasty is descended directly from Jesus Christ – the dynasty of the Adi-Aban Parthian royal prince (Szilágyi and Szilárdi 2007; Szilágyi 2010). Most similar theories have one common feature, namely, the attempt to shift the Hungarian nation from its central-European reality and locate it in the realm of 'great' historical events, even if this means the reinterpretation of world history (Bobula 1961; Badiny-Jós 1998; Baráth 2002). Such authors as Badiny-Jós, Bobula or Baráth treat historical facts in a rather arbitrary way, often tending to interpret historical reality in a way that justifies their own views (Szilágyi and Szilárdi 2007).

The authors that could be classified as belonging to the organic-traditionalist school (Gábor Pap, V. József Molnár and Lajos Szántai) have primarily defined themselves as scholars of folkloric traditions and special national and cultural characteristics (Pap 1997, 1998, 1999, 2007; Szántai 2001, 2007; Molnár 2005, 2010). They have published widely in the areas of history of art, iconological analyses, historical research and linguistic studies and also regularly propagate their views in public lectures in regions where large numbers of Hungarians live outside the borders of present-day Hungary, such as Romania, Slovakia and Serbia. Their theories emphasize the sacred role of Hungarians as a chosen nation with a spiritual mission demonstrated through Hungarian folk art, traditions and culture.

The third group are modern myth-creators and syncretic teachers. These people have gained widespread publicity and become well known since the end of the communist era. Some syncretic teachers ('Magyar' András Kovács, Zoltán Nagy Sólyomfi)[4] have adopted an esoteric system drawing on diverse doctrines and religious systems enriched with shamanic views, where common rituals and healing activities are given a significant role. The leaders identify themselves and their roles with the figure of the *táltos*, a figure from ancient Hungarian religion similar to a shaman, possessing magical powers (Kovács 1992, 2000; Nagy Sólyomfi 2004, 2007). Most contemporary Hungarian Pagan groups are organized around such spiritual teachers, whose eclectic views define the group's orientation. Christian elements may be included. For example, the followers of 'Magyar' András Kovács participate in Catholic celebrations and regularly participate in the most significant Hungarian Catholic pilgrimage of Csíksomlyó.[5] The religious eclecticism of the founder is reminiscent of New Age beliefs, whose common elements include a holistic worldview, pseudoscientific practices and a belief in channelling and communication with the dead, clairvoyance and reincarnation. However, group members claim to be following the ancient Hungarian religion.

The most significant figures of this third group are Zoltán Paál (2003) and Imre Máté (2004, 2005, 2006, 2008). Paál wrote a work of more than one thousand pages in the 1970s and 1980s – *Arvisura* (meaning 'clear speaking', according to Paál) – summarizing his belief system. Paál claimed that what he described in his work he had heard from a partisan called Szalaváré Tura during the Second World War. Szalaváré Tura was the grandchild of a Mansi shaman who, fulfilling the will of his grandfather, revealed the common ancient history of the Hungarian and Mansi nations to Paál. (The Mansi are a Finno-Ugric people living in areas west of the Urals in Russia.) *Arvisura* tells the alternative history of Hungarians, describing their beliefs, social relations and culture covering more than a thousand years. The stories contradict widely accepted historical, linguistic and ethnological knowledge, though their complexity reveals their author as a great myth-creator. Hungarian Pagans are not unified in their evaluation of *Arvisura*, but the impact of the books goes beyond Pagans, with several groups forming to propagate Paál's alternative history.

Another religious cosmological system is Yotengrit, founded by Imre Máté (discussed below). This religion is an excellent example of the construction of an entire religious universe, which, stepping out of its own constructed framework, is positioning itself as an authentic religious tradition.

Myth-Making after the Collapse of Communism

The decline of traditional forms of religiosity and religious practice in the eastern-central European region during the decades of state socialism did not bring about extensive secularization, but rather the weakening of church-based religiosity, overshadowing the earlier social role of Christian churches. Unlike secularization processes in the West, in the communist bloc secularization was a centralized, forced project (Tomka 2005). After the end of communism in 1990, the Christian churches were unable to rebuild their base to the level prior to the communist regime, and their social and political role did not again become significant in Hungary. The decrease of institutional religiosity, however, did not contribute to an increase in the number of non-religious people. The ideological vacuum following the fall of communism significantly increased the number who sought some kind of transcendental answer for the anomie surrounding them. The numbers of religiously non-committed ('religious in their own way') followers of new religious movements and membership of small churches grew (Tomka 1996).

As a consequence of increasing unemployment and the general insecurity generated by the economic and political crisis, the popularity of non-traditional religious interpretations began to increase. These were closely connected with the necessity to redefine individual and collective identities, a characteristic of transition societies. According to Hobsbawm (1992), where a sociopolitical system fails (as happened in Hungary after the end of communism), the ethnic group or nation is seen to provide ultimate security. This is consonant with the Hungarian situation after the end of communism. Due to the inadequacy of existing religious explanations, many people turned to new sense-giving sources and nationalist narratives appeared in religious packaging. 'Belonging somewhere' provides a remedy for anomie – belonging to an imagined community (Anderson 1991) which exists sui generis and whose framework provides a framework for individual existence.

It is worth mentioning here that the appearance of 'the nation' as political and social reference point in the context of post-socialist countries is not self-evident (Niedermüller 1996). The cultural representation of the past is at the centre of this process; the starting point was the deliberately distorted historiography of the communist dictatorship. The main goal of the evolving national discourse was the redemption, reproduction and placing in context of a suppressed national history. Three interrelated strategies can be observed in the creation of this national discourse: reconstruction, restoration and the nationalization of history. These strategies can also be perceived among Pagan groups. Researchers have identified these characteristics of the national discourse through content analysis of historical textual sources compiled and made available electronically by Hungarian Pagans (Vincze and László 2010; László 2012; Szilárdi 2013).

During restoration various historical events were viewed from new perspectives contributing to a symbolic recreation of history. Historical events were deliberately selected to represent the past in the light of a particular political-ideological space and aims. The reconstruction of history, after all, always starts with demythologization and ends with remythologization. The process of nationalization aimed to place this reconstructed history in a wider political and ideological context and to create myths of origin which were able to justify for the post-socialist society its own existence. The focal point of cultural myths of origin is the authenticity and continuity of an archaic culture; hence an assortment of culturally inherited symbols and rituals can be constructed and adapted to represent the national identity.

As highlighted in my earlier study (Szilágyi 2010: 21–22), a common history and memory are the most important elements in the construction of national identity. This common memory expresses itself in specific mythological constructions. In the case of Hungary in the nineteenth century, during the process of becoming a nation, these mythological constructions formed a relatively coherent narrative; however, the traumas of the twentieth century crushed this narrative. The nationalist intellectual elite which appeared following the system change started a process of remythologization for strengthening national identity, which led to a radical revision of the Hungarian past. As Daniele Conversi (1995) points out, this type of ethnic history-writing aims for the reconstruction of an imaginary past. The historian creates a fiction which underpins a programme of national revival. Arguably the ethnic historian is nothing more than the modern successor of the one-time myth-creator, and, as such, their role is similar to those who establish religions.

The traditional religious narratives offered by Christian churches apparently failed to offer a plausibility structure which was broadly acceptable amidst the pervasive anomie, which led to the emergence of new, private and common myths and new plausibility structures. Some Christian traditions and ideas were transformed and incorporated into the emerging new ideas, in some cases producing absurd theories (such as the Hungarian origin of Jesus Christ proposed by Badiny-Jós). The Pagan intellectual orientation referred to above gained strength in this milieu, offering what might be described as a non-institutionalized, transcendent worldview.

As in many countries of eastern-central Europe, in Hungary Paganism appears as a religious reconstruction of an existing ethnic or native faith. Hungarian Pagan groups uniformly refer to the continuity between ancient religious knowledge and contemporary forms of Paganism. However, it has to be acknowledged that some elements within this reconstruction are neither ancient nor indigenous. In a significant study of ancient Hungarian religion Vilmos Voigt (2003) points to the scanty and problematic nature of sources, emphasizing that 'an understanding of history and its theories' is important. Research into Hungarian ancient religion began in the seventeenth century and since then various authors have proposed various theories, refining the description of Hungarian religious views (Diószegi 1954, 1978, 1998; László 1976; Hoppál 1982; Ipolyi 1987). The available academic works serve as important sources for contemporary ethnic Paganism, although while some theories have become popular others have been neglected and marginalized according to their perceived usefulness for particular groups. For example, using elements of shamanism, which can be verified from a religious historical perspective, is generally accepted. However, incorporating Tengrism, the ancient belief system of central Asian nomadic peoples, for example, can be considered an extemporaneous stage of Hungarian religious development (Fodor 2004) and is not embraced by every group. Essentially, for the major groups, defining Hungarian Paganism relies on folkloric and historical research to create a religious cosmos and body of belief and practice. Thus it resembles revival and construction processes within Western Paganism; as Magliocco (2004: 4) says, 'For Pagans, folklore becomes an important tool to discover the past and bring authenticity to contemporary spiritual practice'.

Besides the elements which can be verified from a religious-historical perspective, as in Western Paganism the constructed nature of Hungarian Pagans' religious views is evident. Elements from historical sources are continuously augmented by other and newer theories, including aspects of Western esotericism, elements of New Age spirituality, the results of research on Hungarian folklore and the theories of widely accepted iconic figures (Paál 2003; Máté 2004). All of these components are drawn on variously by different groups. As Michael York (1999: 138) says in relation to Western Paganism, it 'can be seen as a multiple conflation of numerous traditions or sources, many of which were patently contrived or even erroneous'. However, Lonnie Kliever (1981: 658) points out that 'seeing religious beliefsystems or life-worlds as "fictions" involves more than the mere claim that they are imaginative fabrications or symbolic constructions'. Their 'fictional' status does not mean at all that they are valueless or inconsequential; their constructed nature does not influence their 'reality'. In the case of Hungarian Paganism, elements of folk culture only contribute to the constructed worldview of individuals' belief systems, strengthening their bricolage nature.

Similar to all non-conventional belief systems, the worldview of Hungarian Paganism is inherently fragile (Snow and Machalek 1982). Through the mirror of modernity, the constructed religious tradition cannot work as meaning and sense-giving nor as a world explanatory system in all cases, so to fulfil this function it is continuously altering in an ongoing process of adaptation. This is why the issue of authenticity is emphasized among Hungarian Pagan groups: the notion of an authentic, ancient origin compensates for the diversity of views and the flexibility of worldview. Legitimacy is sought in the national myth beyond the realm of religion. As mentioned above, the Pagan intellectual orientation points beyond the groups considered to be explicitly religious; some elements appear as views accepted by broad segments of society, especially because they are related to national identity narratives. These narratives themselves are built up from religious elements in several cases (sacralization of the Hungarian nation, the idea of a chosen nation) so they easily integrate with Pagan interpretations. The interaction of ideas sustaining the plausibility structure is not only present in the religious sphere, but moves beyond this small community to the broader social, cultural and political space. This results in the situation whereby even though the number of followers of Pagan traditions in Hungarian society is very low, their plausibility structure is easily sustainable due to their compatibility with a broader social and political environment. Under the umbrella of a fictive authenticity the plausibility structure can remain intact and Pagans' religious views are able to be rebuilt through their adaptivity. Together with the widely accepted narratives related to nation, this strengthens the validity of believers' worldviews.

Case Study: Yotengrit as a Unique Face of Hungarian Paganism

The plausibility of constructed religious worldviews raises an exciting question in the case of Yotengrit, the Pagan community which was becoming popular in the early 2000s. The founder of the community, Imre Máté, was born in 1934; he studied linguistics in the 1950s at Eötvös Lorand University in Budapest. In the Hungarian Uprising of 1956 he was a leading figure of the revolutionary student group[6] and he also participated in armed combat. After the revolution he had to flee Hungary, immigrated to Germany and continued his studies in Göttingen and Munich, where he studied history, ethnology and archaeology.[7] From 1986, he published materials in Radio Free Europe about the ancient Hungarian belief system with the title 'Hungarian Prehistorical Religion' and the public presence of Yotengrit beliefs can be dated from this time. In 2004 Máté began publishing the doctrines of Yotengrit; currently four complete volumes have been published (Máté 2004, 2005, 2006, 2008). The popularity of Yotengrit is based on these volumes and Imre Máté is a significant figure in the Hungarian Pagan scene. In 2012 a new 'Law on the Freedom of Conscience and Religion and the Churches' came into force in Hungary and three-quarters of the previously registered churches lost their legal status and became, in legal terms, NGOs. Thus Yotengrit – together with some other religious communities – lost its registered legal status in 2012 and also suffered internal conflicts: there was a split between the founder and some close colleagues. Imre Máté died in the summer of 2012 after a long illness and his work is now continued by his followers.

In his writings Máté presented to the public the so far unknown 'authentic' form of Hungarian Paganism, which according to him is identical with the primordial ancient Hungarian religion. The founder's versatile skills and interests basically defined the developments of the movement's religious doctrines. Máté intended to synthesize popular but often contradictory views, to integrate the elements of other religious worldviews matching his system and represent these as elements of Hungarian ancient culture. According to him, he did not add anything to the *táltos* traditions of Rábaköz (a geographically enclosed region of northwestern Hungary), but researchers can find few ethnographically and religiously verifiable elements. Their analyses detect the impact of several other religious traditions. The linguistic and historical mistakes in it make clear the constructed nature of Yotengrit and similarities to the above-mentioned *Arvisura* can be recognized (*Renhirek, The Nyirkai Prediction and Yotengrit* 2013).

With Yotengrit's appearance on the scene, according to Máté a new religion did not come into existence, but rather an ancient faith was renewed. Yotengrit is the revival of a pre-Christian faith, the so-called *Büün*, which was preserved by the táltoses or shamans of Rábaköz. According to Máté the spiritual legacy of this ancient religion had been kept alive by a unique shamanic subculture which called itself the 'Order of the Cormorant'. This organization was established in the thirteenth century and until the twentieth century the tradition of the Hungarian táltos faith survived within the framework of this secret society. The members were 'sages', both men and women, and the general of the Order was called Master *Bácsa* (religious leader). Imre Máté made contact in his early years with the Order and claimed to have been initiated into their belief system. A member of the Order – József Bendes – later sent him the symbol of initiation of Master Táltos or Bácsa, a hand-anvil, and Máté became the general of the Order. Yotengrit was founded on this background. There is a hierarchical system in the Order: the head of the church is the high priest who is 'traditionally' called a bácsa and appoints other office holders.

According to Máté the name *Yotengrit* means 'first God' and also 'first ocean'. Máté's position is that Yotengrit is etymologically connected with Tengri, the chief deity of the early Turkic peoples, primarily a sky God, who is mentioned in Altaic languages. (Altaic is a language family that includes the Turkic, Mongolic, Tungusic, Koreanic and Japonic languages.) In the ancient Hungarian belief system, Yotengrit is a primordial spiritual being – it is also the pristine state of all things. The Yotengrit religion is not a 'táltos-belief', but a religion with a positive attitude derived from the ancient shamanic religion. Yotengrit has a philosophical background and sets of dogmas, liturgies, rituals and ethics. The connections between Yotengrit and other religions are not regarded as the results of borrowing, but every similarity is deemed to be the legacy of a primordial revelation.

The basis of Yotengrit is the equalizing of feminine and masculine. In the Yotengrit system femininity and masculinity both contain activity and passivity; their characteristics are not opposite, but complete each other. The symbol of this philosophy is a so-called Twin-Vortex or Twin-Whirlwind. This basic duality determines everything in the world: social teachings, the legal system, even the relationship between life and death. The ancestors of the people of the Steppe distinguished a female Goddess called *Ukkó* (Mother Earth) and a male God called *Gönüz* (Spirit-Sky). The symbol of the Goddess Ukkó is the moon; the male God Gönüz was created by Her and is symbolized by the sun. Ukkó and Gönüz together constitute the 'Old God' Tengri of the Altaic mythologies. In Tengri there exist two persons: a masculine and a feminine, at both a material and a philosophical level. They are the driving forces of the World Vortex which stabilize each other. In the spirit of this worldview men and women are equal and the essence of Divine Duality is sexuality: the trio of affection, love and lovemaking.

The main ethical teaching of the Yotengrit Church is: 'You can do anything, but do not harm others' – 'others' include not only humanity but other beings in living nature too. This is virtually identical to the Wiccan Rede which underpins Wicca's moral system: 'An it harm none, do what ye will' ('Wiccan Rede' 2013), meaning 'Do what you want to, so long as it harms noone'. While there are no express references for this borrowing, it is presumed that Máté took his ethical tenet from Western Pagan sources. In Yotengrit the individual cannot be submitted to the society or sacrificed for community, and based on this idea there is no collective redemption. Máté summarized his teachings as follows:

> The philosophical basis for the theology of *Büün* is a non-polarized, dualist worldview. *Yotengrit* is a force which contains both female and male, good and bad, but Its nature is inherently female.... According to the teachings of *Büün*, the spirit is material, possesses quantity and quality as well. This doctrine is the theory of 'spiritual-quantum' which states that the spirit is divisible, addable and subtractable. In this 'spiritual-quantum' theory, the materials of spirits are addable, and powerful new spirits can be created....
>
> The theology of *Büün* supports the philosophically reasoned tenet that the individual person, as the smallest cell of society, is an independent social being. Therefore, there is no collective crime, no redemption, no collective responsibility.... Sexuality in this theological system is not an offence but a 'lure' and a divine model devised by Gods to assure reproduction. The only way to offend is by the manner of lovemaking, not by the act. In the trio of love, affection and lovemaking, affection makes the lovemaking love.

In this theological system exists the idea of rebirth (reincarnation), but it does not work automatically. According to teachings only those can be born again who develop their spirituality to a certain level during their lives and are thereby able to remain independent entities in the spirit world. To reach this level – besides increasing one's knowledge – it is necessary to enrich one's emotional experiences and do good deeds. In the relationship between God and men there is a celestial hierarchy: men do not worship their Gods by falling on their knees, but respect Them as ancestors, and they are called respectfully protectors, honoured guests, participants in men's lives. The Gods of *Büün* religion are not omnipotent Gods....

The conception of the other-world in *Büün* differs from every other religion: the other-world is not a place but a state. The simple souls who have not reached a higher spiritual level in their earthly existence 'return to God' – those who have achieved a higher level become independent as spiritual beings. (Yotengrit Theology 2013, author's translation)

In terms of Yotengrit's relationship to other Pagan groups in Hungary or internationally, Yotengrit clearly differs significantly from a 'Pagan orientation'. The countercultural nature of Yotengrit is not accentuated. Imre Máté was trying to direct the church towards institutionalization and an established position within society, instead of the marginalization commonly experienced by Pagan groups. As he wrote on the church's home page: 'The main aims of Yotengrit are spiritual and missionary: to propagate a modern belief system for people who are not interested in conventional churches or New Religious Movements or sects' (Yotengrit Theology 2013). Perhaps owing to Máté's years spent abroad, Yotengrit's exclusivity and ethnocentric attitudes are not stressed at all. Máté's intention is to popularize the religion not only in Hungary, but also in the whole of Europe. In service of this promotion, a German translation of the first Yotengrit book has been made.

Certain circles of Pagans and the radical right wing in Hungary have attacked Imre Máté and Yotengrit, accusing him of falsification and stigmatizing him as a supporter of Finno-Ugrism instead of 'real' historical and linguistic theories.[8] For his part, Máté stood up in protest against 'business-shamans' and the betrayal of national traditions. He criticized others for 'polluting' the ancient Hungarian faith, for example, by integrating Christian elements into Pagan practices, symbols and rituals. This point of view – the espousal of a 'pure' Paganism and refusal of syncretic tendencies – separated him from the Hungarian Pagan mainstream.

From the beginning Imre Máté emphasized that Yotengrit was primarily a religion and marked it off from the political field: 'Our Church is not a political organization and does not have any political background, but our doctrines can be sources of healthy, non-aggressive national policy' (Yotengrit Theology 2011).[9] In keeping with this statement, Máté regularly commented on international and Hungarian politics on the official web page of Yotengrit. In the doctrine of the church one does not find any excluding elements: Yotengrit accepts different belief systems and ideologies and is not hostile towards them. Thus the expressly anti-modernist attitude which characterizes other Pagan groups in Hungary is not evident in the case of Yotengrit. The perception of sexuality and gender roles, along with ideas about living nature within Yotengrit, are more closely connected to Western Paganism than to some other Hungarian Pagan groups.

Conclusion

The aim of this study was to show how Hungarian Pagan movements appear in the world of postmodernity and globalization, by what means they strengthen their position and what other dimensions they combine. Narratives of these movements present them as a response to the uncertainties and fragmentation of modernity. In an age of multiculturalism Pagan communities react to the fragmentation by creating a collective identity typical of ethnic groups, constructing a plausibility structure which aids their survival. What is described here as a Pagan orientation is an outward form of a Pagan metaculture which pervades modern Hungarian politics, and its increasing effect can also be observed in contemporary popular culture. Evidence for this are the mass events mobilizing hundreds of thousands of people each year, the growing number of publishers which provide opportunities for new authors and theories to be presented, and the táltoses or healer-teachers promoting their views on both state-owned and commercial television channels. Across Hungary every week several presentations and lectures are organized in clubs and cultural centres, providing space for the promotion of alternative views. A dozen festivals exist in Hungary connected to different branches of Paganism. Beside these, there are many associations and clubs, as well as several periodicals and almost one hundred websites in Hungarian, proving the popularity of this phenomenon. In addition, ancient Hungarian elements are appearing on clothing; several companies manufacture national brands (for example, Harcos or Botond) employing Pagan symbols. Several companies specialize in making souvenirs bearing Pagan motifs.

Contemporary Hungarian Paganism is a diverse phenomenon which includes modern, organized religious groups – such as Yotengrit – as well as traditional drum circles and mass programmes and camps with hundreds of thousands of visitors. What does Paganism really mean in this context? As a religious phenomenon Paganism might be best described as a 'traditional rebellion' caused by consumerism and materialism, a response to the alienation of society and the individual. The question remains: in future years will the effects of a modern Pagan orientation become more visible in the religious or sociopolitical field?

Notes

1 This research was supported by the European Union and the State of Hungary, co-financed by the European Social Fund in the framework of TÁMOP 4.2.4. A/1–11–1-2012–0001 'National Excellence Program'.
2 The Paulines in the Hungarian '*Pálos*' order (Ordo Fratrum Sancti Pauli Primi Eremitae, the Order of St Paul the First Hermit) are a male monastic order in the Roman Catholic Church founded by the Blessed Eusebius of Esztergom. The Paulines are the only Hungarian-founded religious order.
3 Traditional archery also became a widespread phenomenon in the majority culture following the change of political system, but among Pagans it is even more popular.
4 Zoltán Nagy Sólyomfi is a spiritual teacher, founder of the Tengri Community, popular healer, shaman and musician. 'Magyar' András Kovács is an eclectic spiritual teacher, the founder of the Ancient Hungarian Táltos Church which disbanded in 2012.
5 Although Csíksomlyó is primarily a sacred place connected with Catholicism, it is also very important for some Pagan groups. Within the traditions around the Csíksomlyó pilgrimage – which are mainly connected to the *Mária*-cult – certain elements of the ancient pre-Christian faith are mixed with elements of Catholicism. The Hungarian cult of the Virgin Mary is based on the pre-Christian deity Boldogasszony (Blessed Mother), who was worshipped as Magna Domina Hungarorum (the Great Queen of Hungary) (Szilágyi 2010).
6 The uprising of the Hungarian people against the Stalinist dictatorship and Soviet occupation took place in the autumn of 1956, and was ended by the military intervention of the Soviet army.
7 This information is given in the autobiography of Máté published on the website: http://www.mateimre.hu/web/index.php Accessed 4 November 2014.

8 For example, in a Hungarian periodical called *Dobogó*, which popularizes alternative historiography and other theories connected to the Pagan orientation, Máté was attacked by some authors for his liberal worldview and 'Finno-Ugric' commitments, and was accused of creating a religious system which was pure construction.
9 This document, together with other texts, was removed from the official Yotengrit website (http://www.yotengrit.hu) after Máté's death.

References

Anderson, B.R. 1991. *Imagined Communities: Reflections on the Origin and Spread of Nationalism.* London: Verso.
Badiny-Jós, F. 1998. *Jézus király: A pártus herceg* [King Jesus: The Parthian Prince]. Budapest: Ősi Örökségünk Alapítvány.
Bakó, R. and L.-A. Hubbes. 2011. 'Religious Minorities' Web Rhetoric: Romanian and Hungarian Ethno-Pagan Organizations', *Journal for the Study of Religions and Ideologies* 10(30): 127–58.
Baráth, T. 2002. *A magyar Népek őstörténete* [The Ancient History of the Hungarian Nation]. Budapest: Püski kiadó.
Bobula, I. 1961. *A sumér-magyar rokonság kérdése* [Questions of Hungarian-Sumerian Relativity]. Buenos Aires: Esda.
Conversi, D. 1995. 'Reassessing Theories of Nationalism: Nationalism as Boundary Maintenance and Creation', *Nationalism and Ethnic Politics* 1(1): 73–85.
Diószegi, V. 1954. 'A honfoglaló magyar nép hitvilága (ősvallásunk) kutatásának módszertani kérdései' [Belief System of the Hungarian Conquerors: Methodological Questions of Research on Ancient Religion], *Ethnographia* 65: 20–68.
———. 1978. *Az ősi magyar hitvilág. Válogatás a magyar mitológiával foglalkozó XVIII–XIX. századi művekből* [Ancient Hungarian Beliefs: A Selection of Hungarian Mythology from Eighteenth- and Nineteenth-Century Sources]. Budapest: Gondolat Kiadó.
———. 1998 [1958]. *A sámánhit emlékei a magyar népi műveltségben* [Memories of Shamanic Beliefs in Hungarian Folklore]. Budapest: Academic Press.
Fodor, I. 2004. *A magyarok ősi vallásáról* [About Ancient Hungarian Religion]. Budapest: Magyar Vallástudományi Társaság.
Hobsbawm, E.J. 1992. 'Ethnicity and Nationalism in Europe Today', *Anthropology Today* 8(1): 3–8.
Hoppál, M. 1982. 'Az összehasonlító mitológia-kutatás és a magyar őstörténet' [Ancient Hungarian History and Comparative Mythology], *Új Írás* 22(9): 44–51.

Hubbes, L.-A. 2011. 'A Comparative Investigation of Romanian and Hungarian Ethno-Pagan Blogs'. Reconnect Working Papers No. 2. Retrieved 3 March 2013 from http://ssrn.com/abstract=1984597.

Ipolyi, A. 1987. *Magyar mythologia* [Hungarian Mythology]. Budapest: Európa Könyvkiadó.

Kliever, L.D. 1981. 'Fictive Religion: Rhetoric and Play', *Journal of the American Academy of Religion* 49(4): 657–69.

Kovács, A. 1992. *Gyógyító táltosok nyomában* [In the Footsteps of the Healing Táltos]. Budapest: Energia Klinika.

———. 2000. *Nagy Táltoskönyv* [The Great Táltos Book]. Budapest: Energia Klinika.

László, G. 1976. 'Különvélemény ősvallásunkról' [Minority Report on the Ancient Hungarian Religion], *Új Írás* 16(6): 59–68.

László, J. 2012. *Történelem történetek. Bevezetés a narratív szociálpszichológiába* [Stories from History. Introduction to Narrative Social-Psychology]. Budapest: Akadémiai Kiadó.

Magliocco, S. 2004. *Witching Culture: Folklore and Neo-Paganism in America*. Philadelphia: University of Pennsylvania Press.

Máté, I. 2004. *Yotengrit I*. Budapest: Püski kiadó.

———. 2005.*Yotengrit II*. Budapest: Püski kiadó.

———. 2006. *Yotengrit III*. Budapest: Püski kiadó.

———. 2008. *Yotengrit IV*. Budapest: Püski kiadó.

Molnár, V.J. 2005. *Világ-Virág A természetes műveltség alapjelei, és azok rendszere* [Earth-Flower. The Basic Elements of Natural Literacy and its System]. Budapest: Örökség Könyvműhely.

———. 2010. *A magyar lélek képe* [Image of the Hungarian Spirit]. Budapest: Hun-Idea.

Nagy Sólyomfi, Z. 2004. *Csillagsólyom* [Starhawk]. Budapest: Hun-Idea.

———. 2007. *Göncöl szekerén* [title is a wordplay, untranslatable]. Budapest: Püski.

Niedermüller, P. 1996. 'A nacionalizmus kulturális logikája a posztszocializmusban' [The Cultural Logic of Nationalism in Post-Socialism], *Századvég* 16: 91–109.

Paál, Z. 2003. *Arvisura (Igazszólás)* [Arvisura. Clear Speaking]. Budapest: Püski Könyvkiadó.

Pap, G. 1997. *Angyali korona, szent csillag: Beszélgetések a magyar szent koronáról* [Angel Crown, Sacred Star: Conversations on the Hungarian Holy Crown]. Jászberény: Jásztel Rt.

———. 1998. *Nézz egy kicsit a fejembe: A hagyományörökítés útjai a szkítautód népeknél* [Look Into My Mind: Ways of Inheriting Traditions]. Debrecen: Dél-Nyírség Bihari Tájvédelmi és Kulturális Értékőrző Egyesület.

———. 1999. *Hazatalálás: Művelődéstörténeti írások* [Find a Way Back Home. Essays on Cultural History]. Budapest: Püski.

———. 2007. *Száll az Isten házadra: Ősvallási elemek téli napfordulós népi szertartásainkban* [God is in the House: Ancient Religious Elements in

Rituals Connected to Winter Solstice]. Debrecen: Dél-Nyírség Bihari Tájvédelmi és Kulturális Értékőrző Egyesület.

Povedák, I. 2010. 'Árpád és a gepárd: A magyar "civil vallásosság" dimenziói címmel' [Árpád and the Cheetah: Dimensions of Hungarian 'Civil Religion'], *Voigtlorisztika. Tanulmányok a 70 éves Voigt Vilmos tiszteletére*, ATU 503. *Folcloristica* 11: 267–80.

Renhirek, The Nyirkai Prediction and Yotengrit. 2013. Retrieved 9 March 2013 from http://www.nyest.hu/renhirek/a-nyirkai-joslat-es-a-yotengrit-a-tengervegtelen-os-szellem-egyhaza.

Simpson, S. 2000. *Native Faith: Polish Neo-Paganism at the Brink of the 21st Century*. Krakow: Nomos.

Snow, D. and R. Machalek. 1982. 'On the Presumed Fragility of Unconventional Beliefs', *Journal for the Scientific Study of Religion* 21(1): 15–26.

Szántai, L. 2001. *A két Hollós: Mátyás király és a Pálos Rend* [The Two Ravens: King Matthias and the Pauline Order]. Budapest: Sáros és Fiai.

———. 2007. *Szent őseink nyomában maradva – Szent korona, népmese, mítikus történelem* [In the Footsteps of Our Sacred Ancestors – Holy Crown, Folktale, Mythical History]. Debrecen: Dél-Nyírség Bihari Tájvédelmi és Kulturális Értékőrző Egyesület.

Szilágyi, T. 2010. 'Sacred Characteristics of the Nation: Religion and Politics in Contemporary Hungary', in T. Szilágyi (ed.), *Religious Transformations in Contemporary European Societies*. Szeged: SZTE-BTK Vallástudományi Tanszék, pp. 18–35.

———. 2011. 'Quasi-religious Character of the Hungarian Right-Wing Radical Ideology: An International Comparison', in A. Máté-Tóth and C. Rughinis (eds), *Spaces and Borders: Current Research on Religion in Central and Eastern Europe*. Berlin: De Gruyter Verlag, pp. 251–65.

———. 2012. 'The Neopagan Intellectual Orientation and its Effects on Contemporary Hungarian Mentality and Politics: Some Remarks', in B. Gábor and O. László (eds), *Hereditas*. Szeged: Gerhardus kiadó, pp. 111–21.

Szilágyi, T. and R. Szilárdi. 2007. *Istenek ébredése. A neopogányság vallástudományi vizsgálata* [Awakening of Gods: A Study of Contemporary Paganism in the Field of Religious Studies]. Szeged: JATEPress.

Szilárdi, R. 2007. 'Posztmodern identitás kultúra a magyarországi neopogány közösségekben' [Postmodern Identity-Culture in Hungarian Neopagan Communities], *Debreceni Disputa* 5: 71–76.

———. 2009. 'Ancient Gods – New Ages: Lessons from Hungarian Paganism', *The Pomegranate: The International Journal of Pagan Studies* 11(1): 44–57.

———. 2013. 'Neopaganism in Hungary: Under the Spell of Roots', in K. Aitamurto and S. Simpson (eds), *Modern Pagan and Native Faith Movements in Central and Eastern Europe*. Durham: Acumen, pp. 230–48.

Tomka, M. 1996. 'A felekezeti struktúra változása Kelet- és Közép-Európában' [Changes to Ecclesiastical Structure in Cee], *Szociológia Szemle* 1996(1): 157–73.

———. 2005. *Halálra szántak, mégis élünk. Egyházüldözés és az ügynökkérdés, 1945–1990* [We Deserved to Die. The Persecution of Churches and the Question of Agents, 1945–1990]. Budapest: Szt. István Társulat.

Vincze, O. and J. László. 2010. 'A narratív perspektíva szerepe a történelemkönyvekben' [Role of the Narrative Perspective in History Books], *Magyar Pszichológiai Szemle* 65(4): 571–95.

Voigt, V. 2003. *A magyar ősvalláskutatás kérdései* [Questions of Research into Hungarian Ancient Religion]. Budapest: Magyar Vallástudományi Társaság.

'Wiccan Rede'. 2013. Retrieved 18 November 2013 from http://en.wikipedia.org/wiki/Wiccan_Rede.

Wiench, P. 1997. 'Neo-paganism in Central Eastern European Countries', in I. Borowik and G. Babinski (eds), *New Religious Phenomena in Central and Eastern Europe*. Krakow: Nomos, pp. 283–92.

York, M. 1999. 'Invented Culture/Invented Religion: The Fictional Origins of Contemporary Paganism', *Nova Religio: The Journal of Alternative and Emergent Religions* 3(1): 135–46.

Yotengrit Theology. 2011 and 2013. The official web page of the Yotengrit community. http://www.yotengrit.hu/hu/article/teologiaja. Accessed 21 August 2011 and 24 May 2013.

8

Hot, Strange, Völkisch, Cosmopolitan

Native Faith and Neopagan Witchcraft in Berlin's Changing Urban Context

Victoria Hegner

Introduction

This chapter is about Neopagan witches in Berlin (Germany) and the complex ways they make use of the Germanic or Norse pantheon and Teutonic alphabet within their religious practice.[1] The focus is the role of the immediate urban context and how this inscribes interpretations of witchcraft, mythology and symbolism, and thus gives shape to a Native Faith – a faith based on a specific idea of belonging to a certain territory and ethnicity predicated on history and ancestry.[2]

Studies of Neopaganism, witchcraft or (new) religion are usually framed by a national context and the contingencies this produces for the development of religious practices and cosmologies. This approach can be highly informative because it makes explicit the fact that in times of intense globalization, the category of 'nation' still holds strong discursive value, particularly in view of what 'native' and 'indigenous' in different areas of social life are supposed to (or can be made to) mean (Magliocco 2004; Rountree 2004, 2010; Strmiska 2005). By narrowing the focus further, the individual city can be seen as an emblematic site as well as an important laboratory for the development of religious movements. Cities – with their cultural openness, diversity, highly individualized residents and accessibility to niche lifestyles – give impetus to religious innovations which may later manifest more openly and diffuse into wider social settings (Cox 1984; Greverus and Welz 1990; Orsi 1999; Livezey 2000;

MetroZones 2011; Becci, Borchardt and Casanova 2013). The specificity of the city, its cultural and historical singularity, surely leaves its
imprint on religions and, in the case of Berlin, on Neopagan witchcraft. As an American scholar of religious studies, Robert Orsi, has
pointed out (1999: 46): 'What people do religiously in cities is shaped
by what kinds of cities they find themselves in, at what moments in
the histories of those cities'.

In order to reveal what kind of city Berlin is and how its unique
context and history are inscribed in Neopagan and Native Faith practices, the chapter is divided into two parts. The first gives an insight
into the beginnings of the Berlin Neopagan witch-scene during the
early 1980s. It will be shown that the story of Neopagan witchcraft
in Berlin is clearly a tale of a divided city. Hence, it is significant that
Neopagan witches started off in *West* Berlin. Arising from the unique
situation of being 'locked in by the Wall', the question of space and
a place for worship became critical. For modern witches the celebration in and of nature is central; such religious practice is seen
as pre-Christian and an important ideal. The goal is to deepen their
connection with every natural thing, with community, and thus with
the divine overall. However, 'surrounded by the zone' – as Neopagan
witches now describe the situation of the early 1980s – they seldom
performed their religion 'in nature' away from the city. Instead they
remained within the urban confines and made use of Berlin's prehistoric sites for their rituals. In relation to the practice of a Native Faith,
therefore, some central questions emerge: What religious significance did Neopagans and Neopagan witches ascribe to those sites?
How did they reflect upon the local, German and European past and
thus construct an historical continuity, with all the ambivalence that
carries within the German context? Finally, which impulses from the
larger (national and global) Pagan movement reached and became
influential within this political island?

Following the historical analysis, the focus of this chapter will
shift to the contemporary period. More than twenty years after the
Berlin Wall came down the city had changed tremendously, and so
had the witch-scene. Even so, the historical beginnings left their
mark on Neopagan witchcraft in Berlin and are well remembered
collectively. Using ethnographic data and concentrating on a particular group of Neopagan witches, this section will describe how
Native Faith practices changed specifically in relation to the altered
urban context. Like the historical section of the chapter, this concentrates on the sites of rituals. Where are they situated nowadays? How
do witches today find out about sites, or – to be analytically more

precise – how do they construct them? What kind of understanding of history comes into play? And last but not least, how do different strains of Pagan traditions worldwide become reinterpreted within the urban setting of Berlin? By combining an historical analysis with a contemporary ethnography of witchcraft and Native Faith in the city, the chapter aims to draw a complex picture of Neopaganism in relation to the urban. It asks to what extent Neopaganism in itself becomes an expression of the urban.[3]

Neopagan Witchcraft and Native Faith in the Frontier City: An Exception to the Rule

Since the early 1980s Berlin has developed into one of the centres of Neopagan witchcraft in Germany. The term 'witch' refers to a variety of manifestations of Neopagan religiosity. It comprises neo-Germanic groups as well as practitioners of a feminist spirituality (often termed 'Goddess spirituality'). Some witches are followers of Wicca – a specific interpretation of Neopagan witchcraft first created by the British occultist Gerald B. Gardner (1884–1964) during the 1950s (Schnurbein 1993; Hutton 1999: 205–40; Bötsch 2005; Rensing 2006). The basic organizational principle of Wicca is the coven – a circle of witches into which one has to be ritually initiated (Gardner 1959).

When self-acclaimed Neopagans and Neopagan witches first appeared in Berlin – in West Berlin – they were part of the boom in 'alternative' forms of religiosity the city was witnessing at that time. Throughout West Berlin various groups were being established that based their religiosity on sources which ventured far beyond the dominant Christian theology and practices. New Age centres began opening their doors, teaching tantra and Buddhism. Esoteric book-shops sprang up and occultists of diverse strains seemed to reach more people than ever before. Encircled by a socialist and officially atheist state, this urban democratic island seemed to intensify spiritual or religious experimentation. Some activists within the emerging spiritual scene even declared Berlin 'a spiritual Mecca' and published what they claimed was 'The First Esoteric City Guide of the World' (*'Berlin Okkult: der erste esoterische Stadtführer der Welt'*). This rather boastful title reflects the dynamics felt at that time. The publishers stated: 'Berlin is the secret capital of esoterics and occultists. Clairvoyants, fortune-tellers, astrologists, seers, mystics, dervishes … fairies and magicians work in this metropolis.… In no other

European city do we find so many different religious communities and groups. Indeed, Berlin is a spiritual Mecca' (Scharna, Flamm and Lux 1985: 7).

In this 'spiritual Mecca' one can locate the various beginnings of Neopagan witchcraft. A small advertisement posted by the then 24-year-old student of graphic design Géza von Neményi could count as one of the initial sparks. The advertisement appeared on the noticeboard of an esoteric bookshop called 'Yggdrasil' (the 'world-tree' in Norse mythology). The name of the shop suited the content of the note well. Handwritten in Gothic lettering, it read (Figure 8.1):

> Germanic Mythology! Interested members wanted for the purpose of founding an association. The association's mission: spreading mythological knowledge. For that purpose we will celebrate together the old festivals (i.e., Yule, solstice ...) and cultivate old customs; we will also engage in Runology, travel to the gods of Asgart or to the elves of Alfheim. A get-together for real witches (*Hag* = *Idisen*, Valkyries, wise women ...). Maybe folkdances, folksongs ... (Autumn 1982, author's translation)

As Géza explained during my interview with him, he had tried to be a devoted Christian but always felt something missing in Christianity. 'I missed nature', he said, and went on to describe how he discovered he was actually a Pagan: 'Well, for me there was simply too much desert [in descriptions in the Bible].... I started to buy books about runes and ... the Eddas[4] as well ... These things spoke much more to my soul. It was the descriptions of nature which I found more interesting.... I need nature; it was ... missing in the Bible. Regarding my spiritual feeling, I was a Pagan' (interview, 22 October 2012). In saying there was 'too much desert' in Biblical descriptions, Géza takes up the topos of Christianity as a 'desert religion' – a topos which has its roots in nineteenth-century Romantic nationalism and which became more manifest in the *völkisch* orientalism of the early twentieth century (Wiedemann 2007: 126).[5] As a 'desert religion' – it was and is argued – Christianity is spatially, culturally and racially alien to Europe and Germany. Géza illustrated this point with an allegory: 'Religion is like a jacket', he said, 'and the jacket Christianity is not really made for our climate. We fixed it, we mended the holes ... but it is not ideal. The jacket is not a made-to-measure suit.... Paganism is our made-to-measure suit, congenial to our nature' (interview, 22 October 2012).

As he began to practise as a Pagan, Géza looked upon the Eddas as the basis of his religious cosmology and an inspiration for ritual performances. With a group of like-minded people he hoped to

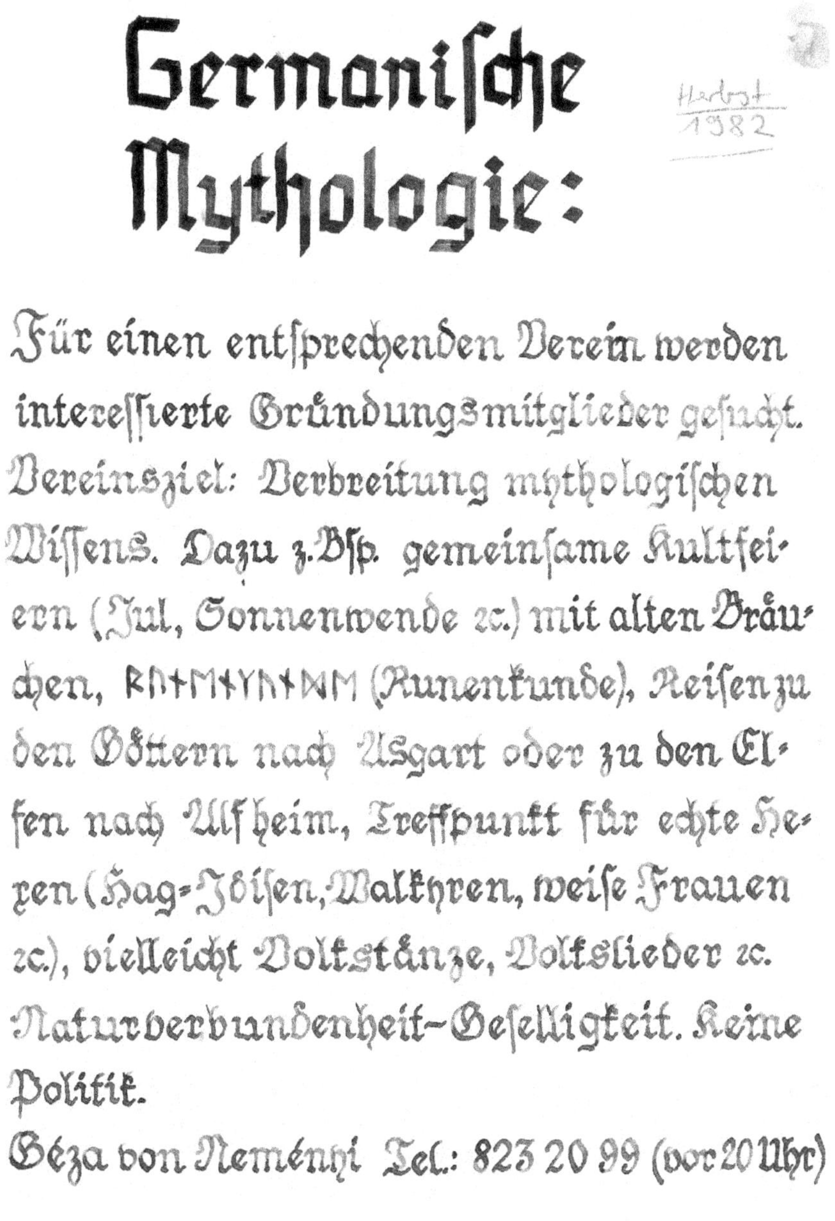

Germanische Mythologie:

Herbst 1982

Für einen entsprechenden Verein werden interessierte Gründungsmitglieder gesucht. Vereinsziel: Verbreitung mythologischen Wissens. Dazu z.Bsp. gemeinsame Kultfeiern (Jul, Sonnenwende xc.) mit alten Bräuchen, ᚱᚢᚾᛖᚾ (Runenkunde), Reisen zu den Göttern nach Asgart oder zu den Elfen nach Ulfheim, Treffpunkt für echte Hexen (Hag-Idisen, Walküren, weise Frauen xc.), vielleicht Volkstänze, Volkslieder xc. Naturverbundenheit-Geselligkeit. Keine Politik.

Géza von Neményi Tel.: 823 20 99 (vor 20 Uhr)

Fig. 8.1 *The 'initial spark': handwritten advertisement for the purpose of founding an association to practise and cultivate 'old customs'. Image used with the kind permission of the photographer, Géza von Neményi.*

meticulously reconstruct, as he called it, 'our faith' – a faith based on territory, ethnicity and ancestry. His goal was to revive a 'Germanic priesthood' – the so-called *Godentum*.[6] In line with this kind of reconstructionist approach, Géza refused and still refuses the term 'Neopagan', because for him there is nothing new about 'our faith' and the Godentum (see Strmiska (2005: 18–22) for an instructive discussion of definitions of 'Reconstructionist' and 'Eclectic').

After publishing some more advertisements in journals and city magazines a small group of women and men gathered together. They all called themselves Pagan. Only the female members also adopted the term 'witch'. The identification as a witch was based on an image which again went back to the nineteenth century and was introduced mainly by the folklorist Jacob Grimm, who reinterpreted the figure of the witch as a 'wise woman' of pre-Christian times who knew the 'art of healing' and worshipped the Germanic pantheon (Wiedemann 2007: 60–70). As the group started to meet, they were keen to learn more about the Eddas, read them together and begin to celebrate the 'old festivals' and perform rituals as their predecessors supposedly did. Some of them hoped to finally become a *Gode* or a *Gydja* (priest or priestess), going through an initiation process designed by Géza and a friend. The process comprised an oral and written examination on pre-Christian German history before being ordained into the priesthood. The worship of nature as a divine force was, overall, central to the group.

But how does one worship nature within the city, a place often envisioned as the opposite of nature, where nature is diminished and people often described as 'rationalized', 'intellectualized' and detached from the sacred (Simmel 1903; Weber 1994 [1919])? How does one get away from a city like West Berlin – walled in the heart of the Eastern Bloc – to worship in nature? Undoubtedly one *could* leave West Berlin and access the nearby Marc of Brandenburg with its legendary forests, but doing so entailed a strenuous bureaucratic procedure. One had to apply for a temporary passport (*Passierschein*) two to three days in advance. For each day spent in the German Democratic Republic, one had to pay a mandatory fee of twenty-five Deutschmarks. Once in East Germany, visitors from the West had to register with the socialist authorities, leave a visitor's address and sometimes explain the purpose for their visit. Ritualizing – perhaps 'skyclad' (naked) with no valid address – in the forest and worshipping gods and goddesses would probably have sounded degenerate (at best) to the socialist regime and politically too problematic to serve as a legitimate reason for a visit. 'You could get out', Matthias

Wenger, one of the first group members, emphasized. 'However, it was troublesome. That's why we hardly got away from the city, and if we did, we went straight to West Germany.[7] But this rarely happened – only three or four times a year' (field notes, 13 January 2010).

Instead of trying to retreat from the city, the group, and particularly Géza, turned to history and started to thoroughly study Berlin's Slavic and Germanic past in search of 'ancient cult-sites'. In doing so they drafted a Pagan spiritual topography of the city, which they hoped to revive. As Géza proudly noted, 'I found out about more than forty ancient cult-sites in Berlin. We surely had no undersupply of ritual places'. The rationale underlying the use of these sites for worship, and thus of this spiritual topography, was that 'our predecessors used these holy sites ..., because there are specific forces there'. Géza further explained:

> Esoterics would call them ... 'cosmic forces' ... 'magnetism' ... whatever. We say: these are ... divine forces. Germanic and Celtic people simply knew, felt, where the gods live, where the divine forces are particularly strong. At those places they performed their cults. In doing so, they intensified the forces ... Today we can use them. When we go to these places, the forces are still there. (Interview, 22 October 2012)

As the group began to celebrate their rituals at these sites, they tried to use only those which were, at least to some extent, withdrawn from the city's hustle and bustle and located in recreation areas within the urban setting, like spacious parks or lakes on West Berlin's outskirts. All those places were public spaces – officially designed to be open to all city dwellers for recreation and taking time out from hectic urban life. In this sense such places were deeply urban.

It did not take long for city officials to notice the group and its rituals. Local journalists were alerted and began reporting on these 'Pagans and witches', aligning them with religious groups like Jim Jones's People's Temple. The Berlin city magazine, *Tip*, for example, opened an article about Géza von Neményi saying: 'after the most spectacular mass suicide in history in Jonestown, sects have not lost their appeal. Berlin is no exception.... Fun [German: *Heidenspaß*, literally 'heathens' fun', an idiom for 'great fun'] must stop somewhere' (Herrmann 1988: 240). Such rhetoric has to be seen within the context of the anti-cult movement and its heyday during this decade. In West Germany, and particularly in West Berlin, however, it was strongly politicized. Because the group apparently founded their religious practice on Germanic roots and territory, they were immediately suspected of being neo-Nazis or neo-fascists. Use of symbols like the Teutonic alphabet and the claim of, and pride in, German(ic) ancestry reminded political activists and church and media representatives painfully of the National Socialist regime and its references to Teutonism as well as its 'blood and soil' ideology. In Berlin, as the former political centre of the Nazi regime and with its post-war division, the West German collective memory of the Nazi period was particularly intense and always physically (in the most literal sense) present. Conflicts between Pagans, the church and the media were accordingly unique in their fierceness.

Public interest in this small group grew enormously. In the view of the national West German media, Géza, Matthias and the other group members became probably the most famous Pagans in the German context. Some of the most popular dailies, including *Der Spiegel* and the widely read national tabloid newspaper *Bild-Zeitung*, wrote about them, warning against a religion apparently based on Nazi ideology (*Bild-Zeitung*, 24 February 1984; *Der Spiegel*, 7 January 1985: 71, 74). When the group began to hold rituals at the Teufelsberg (in English, the Devil's Mountain), which is not an ancient cult-site but a rubble mountain, and by that time rather secluded, the *Bild* sensationally headlined: 'Beer and Rune-Oracle: Sacrificial Feast at the Teufelsberg'. West Berlin's evangelical advisor on sects[8] lamented: 'These neo-Germanics are starting to become a firm association, preaching the call of blood and pure-bred ancestry. Our society cannot be neutral when occult groups abuse the people in our city's need for religion'. Sharply, he concluded, this practice of 'Divine knowledge … can be interpreted as a … canonization of Nazi ideology' (*Bild-Zeitung*, 24 February 1984: 4). (Quotations in this paragraph are my translations from the German.)

It is important to note that the group of Pagans and witches, which later became a non-profit association calling itself the Heidnische Gemeinschaft (Pagan Community), in fact did contain a few people who were under the surveillance of the regional intelligence service because they were right-wing extremists (Schnurbein 1993: 42; Wiedemann 2007: 210–14). Furthermore, the group and its later rival offshoot, the Gemeinschaft für heidnisches Leben (Community for Pagan Life), were in contact with völkisch, racist neo-Germanic associations in West Germany like the Armanen-Orden or the Artgemeinschaft (field notes, 13 January 2010; interview with Géza, 22 October 2012; Schnurbein 1993: 36–45). Nevertheless Géza vehemently tried to distance himself and the Heidnische Gemeinschaft from all racism, fascism and Nazism. He made it explicit in the association's statutes that only those people who 'repudiate Fascism or racism' could be accepted as members (quoted in Schnurbein 1993: 40). He made use of runes carefully: for example, basing their use on literature which was 'unstained' by the National Socialist period. Time after time, Géza appeared at public events in the city, trying to explain Paganism.[9] Because the Heidnische Gemeinschaft grounded its religion in territory and ethnicity, however, it remained highly problematic for the German public. Furthermore, Géza could never satisfactorily show politicians, academics and other Neopagans that he was not a member of the Armanen-Orden.[10]

For several years to come the political debates about this group of Pagans and witches and its Germanic practices maintained their intensity. For the media in particular, the Heidnische Gemeinschaft and subsequently the emerging Neopagan scene in Berlin often served to represent the growing Neopagan and Native Faith phenomenon in the whole of West Germany. And yet, at the same time, it was a special case. Reports and essays on Neopagan groups in the national context almost exclusively turned to West Berlin, where important issues seemed to catalyse.[11] However, in its intense political dynamics, the Berlin Neopagan scene remained an exception to the rule. Berlin being a characteristic yet different site of Neopaganism in West Germany, Berlin's Pagans and witches mirrored the city as a whole – a city which on the one hand functioned as 'a window display of the West', and on the other hand appeared to be an island of incomparable political and socio-cultural conditions. In short, Berlin's Neopagan witchcraft and the city alike worked as an unrepresentative case of representation (Lindner 1993: 105).

Considering the context of the entire city, it is significant that the decade before the Berlin Wall came down was politically and culturally highly dynamic in general. Isolated from the West, Berlin became a space for experimentation and a laboratory of social fantasies (Lindner 1993). City guide books of that time – which always condense and fashion the cultural characteristics of a city – described Berlin as *the* place to be, as 'strange' and 'hot' (Schweinfurth 1986: 39), and as a place that 'was ahead of all the smug West German cities' (Rosh 1986: 37). 'This is mirrored in the city's music, art, writing, theatre, fashion, off-scene, punks', as one author explained and went on: 'Every detail taken by itself might be found somewhere else as well.... Still, nowhere else all those things come together' (ibid.). The emerging witch-scene was a product and part of the city's socio-cultural dynamics. It depicted a further 'spiritual' expression of Berlin's walled hot-and-strangeness.

The practice of witchcraft and ideas on Native Faith proliferated accordingly fast in the city, particularly during the second half of the 1980s. Within this context, 1986 and 1988 became important years. In 1986 Starhawk – the internationally famous author of *The Spiral Dance* (1979) and founder of the 'Reclaiming Tradition' of witchcraft in the United States – travelled to Berlin. (The German translation of *The Spiral Dance* had been published in 1983.) 'Reclaiming' originated in San Francisco and is a form of witchcraft that puts emphasis on feminism, the Goddess and the political aspects of magic and ritual (Salomonsen 2001). Two years later traditional British Wicca arrived in the city. Vivianne Crowley, one of the best known and mostly widely read British Wiccans worldwide, visited West Berlin in 1988 and began to initiate people into this tradition of witchcraft.

Like Starhawk, Vivianne Crowley clearly had an impact on the local Neopagan witch-scene. Due to the city's isolation, the community remained tightly knit. Almost all of the scene's activists met up with these two internationally well-known witches. However, Géza and Matthias were greatly disappointed. From their Reconstructionist approach they looked upon Wicca and Reclaiming witchcraft as forms of 'fantasy religion' with questionable historical grounding (interview with Géza, 22 October 2012). Remembering his conversation with Starhawk, Matthias stated: 'I had read a lot of pre-Christian sources and I gained the impression that this ... witch-cult was too generous in its interpretation of these sources. Everything [different historical sources] was lumped together. I did not like that' (interview, 10 November 2011). For him, as well as for Géza, Wicca and Reclaiming did not 'fit' the German territory and ethnicity, and thus the idea of 'our faith', because they were highly Eclectic (see Strmiska 2005: 19). Not least, the feminist interpretation of the witch as an emancipated modern woman did not work for them and in their view seemed to be without any historical base. Ancient matriarchy, as it was particularly advocated by the Reclaiming witches, depicted a myth to them. Other Pagans in the city, however, were excited. As Natol, a close friend of Matthias Wenger during the 1980s and a regular guest of the Heidnische Gemeinschaft and later the Gemeinschaft für heidnisches Leben, even claimed: 'It was Starhawk ... and Vivianne. It all started off with them, when they came to Berlin in 1986 and 1988' (conversation with Natol, 24 February 2011).

Considering today's practice of witchcraft in the city, one might share this perspective. Reclaiming and Wicca have become inspiring sources for Berlin witches, and the dominant Reconstructionist approach has gradually been superseded by a rather Eclectic understanding of Neopaganism. Völkisch elements are however still present. The following section provides insight into this contemporary conglomerate of ideas on witchcraft and Native Faith in the city. The 'ancient cult-sites' of Berlin are long left behind. When witches choose ritual sites today, it is no longer important for them whether their ancestors might have already worshipped there; instead the decisive question is to what extent they want to perform ritual in public, or should rather remain secretive in the city.

The 'Old Wisdom' in the United City: A Practice with Cosmopolitan Flair

Today the German capital can apparently claim numerous superlatives. According to *Körper, Geist, Seele* (Body, Spirit, Soul) – one of Berlin's two major esoteric magazines – this is also true for the city's Neopagan witch-scene. Hence Berlin is not only one of the centres of witchcraft in Germany, but it possesses 'the highest concentration of witches in all of central Europe' (Schäfer 2010: 32). There are no official statistics available which could confirm this statement. Careful estimates range from three hundred to four hundred Neopagan witches who live in the city (Perschke 2003: 525). In view of the figure for the whole of Germany, which ranges from two thousand to eight thousand (Rensing 2007: 99; interview with Natol, 24 February 2011), the number of witches in Berlin appears comparatively high. Overwhelmingly they are 'solitary';[12] some are Wiccans. They mainly get to know each other via the Internet these days. Facebook appears to be one of the most relevant sources. These groups of self-acclaimed witches and Neopagans advertise regular face-to-face meetings, called *Hexenstammtische* ('witches' round-tables'). Currently three of Berlin's *Hexenstammtische* are active and well attended. They take place at restaurants, corner-bars or neighbourhood cafés and thus become an expression of urbanity and urban lifestyle in themselves.

At these get-togethers, people talk about their spiritual experiences. Some let others read the tarot cards for them. Someone might want to discuss a newly published book on witchcraft. Some simply want to talk about their everyday life, their work, vocation or their children while having a drink and a meal with like-minded people. In other words, people get to know each other better. A basis of trust is created, which witches see as necessary to celebrate religious festivals, organize rituals together and open up to the individual experience of ecstasy and trance. Although most groups do not constitute an exclusive coven, it is essential to them that nothing that happens during a ritual becomes known – unauthorized – to the 'world outside', to people who are not part of the witch-scene. This form of enclosure provides, not least, protection against social discrimination – a common experience of Neopagans worldwide. Significantly, in Germany witches are particularly careful about the people they ritualize with when they want to employ Norse or Germanic mythology and symbols for their religious performance and advocate the idea of a Native Faith. As a result of the German National Socialist history, Native Faith continues to be highly controversial more than sixty years later, and in particular since unification and a thus reinvigorated German nation. Ideas about what 'native' means in terms of faith and what kind of historical references are legitimate to constitute the discursive field are again being contested, especially in the united Berlin, a central place and strong symbol of the united – new – Germany. The resulting new dynamics of the practice of witchcraft become particularly obvious in one of the most active groups of witches in the city: the Moon-Women, whose leading figure is Xenia.

When I first met Xenia she was watchful when she explained witchcraft and her ideas of an 'old wisdom', as she calls her form of Native Faith practice. Xenia is a professional actress, but since the beginning of the new millennium has worked as a 'full-time witch'. She opened a centre called *Löwenmond* (The Lion's Moon) in the apartment building where she lives. There she offers her spiritual healing abilities to interested people. Most importantly, she organizes the eight Neopagan festivals of the year and exclusively invites women to celebrate the moon as a symbol and the embodiment of the Great Goddess. The group is accordingly called the Moon-Women. One of Xenia's main sources of spiritual inspiration is Starhawk. *The Spiral Dance* (Starhawk 1979) was a revelation to her. 'Right away I was caught by her [Starhawk's] ideas', she once exclaimed to me. 'I knew. That's it. I had done some tarot before. But Starhawk described what I really wanted to be: a witch' (field notes, 22 October 2010). Xenia is particularly fascinated by Starhawk's radical feminist and socialist interpretation of witchcraft. She intertwines it with her ideas of the 'old wisdom'. The old wisdom, as Xenia explained, has been transmitted genetically through the generations via DNA and is inscribed in our 'blood and bones'. It is thus a deeply physical experience and part of our subconscious, something we cannot always express verbally, yet our body knows and moves and reacts accordingly. Most importantly, it belongs to a certain territory.

When Xenia introduced me to these ideas, she paused in the middle of her speech and right away felt the need to refer to the Nazi times as well as to the 1980s in Berlin and the era of the Heidnische Gemeinschaft. 'Well, parts of the wisdom – the runes in particular – were deeply misused during Nazi times and then again during the 1980s, as we all know', she said.

> It was discredited. Thus it is a thorny issue to bring up. However and despite that, these are real energies, forces. They are connected to this area, the trees, to the stones. The Christian god is imported from the desert. It does not belong here. We have our Hulda [Germanic Goddess of the Underworld]. Our ancestors did not suffer from the heat but from the cold. I have to say, it is such a beneficial experience for the whole body as well as for your own cultural identity to remember Germanic mythology. (Interview, 30 September 2010)

The use of Germanic mythology and the Teutonic alphabet is seen as an act that 'purifies' them from their misuse during the Nazi period, returning them to their 'original, authentic meaning'. For Xenia and her group, this does not mean thoroughly reconstructing the ways people in pre-Christian times apparently worshipped the pantheon, or the magical significance they ascribed to the runes. As Xenia says, you should know about these things. But most important for a ritual, as well as for choosing sites for rituals, is your intuition. Your individual feeling, experience and need are significant and always prior to any religious reconstruction.

Hence the group's favourite ritual site, the lake Krumme Lanke in one of Berlin's public parks, is not an ancient cult-site, as would have been preferred for rituals by, for instance, Géza and his group back in the 1980s. Instead it is a place where Xenia used to go swimming during her childhood. Over the years Xenia has sensed a growing 'interconnection' with the lake, which makes it for her an ideal place for ritualizing (Figure 8.2). She and the other Moon-Women feel that the lake is sometimes calling them to tidy the site up when it is (again) littered with cigarettes and beer bottles. It almost 'cries out' for a ritual. When the Moon-Women gather and invoke the Germanic goddesses or perform runes, they interpret it as a 'beneficial experience' not only to themselves, but to all Berlin residents. Such performances constitute what Xenia calls 'super signs' within the urban context. They are created, she explained, 'in order to evoke ... within

Fig. 8.2 *Xenia casts the circle and invokes Germanic deities at the ritual site at Krumme Lanke, thus creating a 'super sign' in the city of Berlin. Image used with the kind permission of Xenia and the photographer, Manuela Schneider. Copyright 2013.*

the archaic consciousness of people the feeling of reconnection with the earth' (interview, 30 September 2010).

However, references to runes and calling upon Germanic gods and goddesses as well as ideas of a wisdom that is in 'our blood and bones' remain problematic. They always necessitate intense reflections upon Germany's specific history of racism and nationalism. Xenia and her group are aware of the historical and political ambiguities and tensions their spiritual performances still evoke. For rituals within the city's confines, the Moon-Women thus came up with the rough and ready rule: in private, when the Moon-Women do rituals at night by the Krumme Lanke unseen by other Berlin residents, they prefer to call upon their (female) ancestors, invoke the Germanic pantheon and dance and sing the Teutonic alphabet. Those rituals are hidden, secretive and exclusive. In public places when they want to be seen, when they do not avoid being seen, or when there is a chance of being seen, they simply 'switch' the code of religious performance and become highly Eclectic. They call upon Hindu and Buddhist deities, such as Kali, perform yoga or sing songs from North- and Latin-American indigenous peoples. Those rituals are open and inclusive.

This 'switch of code' and its peculiar interplay with the urban context of Berlin, its culture and history, were catalysed when Xenia was playing with the idea of organizing a ritual at an historically highly sensitive place in the city: the Topography of Terror. The Topography of Terror is one of the central memorials of the horrendous crimes of the National Socialist regime. It represents the historical site of the Gestapo headquarters, with its so-called house-prison, as well as the Reichsführung SS, the SS Leadership's Main Office. Today the memorial includes a newly built documentation centre which presents an exhibition on the Nazi security apparatus. The Topography of Terror is one of several monumental memorials to remember the Nazi period and the Holocaust, which were to be built and prominently located in the government district. They symbolize Germany's commitment to 'accept the burden of German history' and to enact the signal that the unified state and – as its symbol – the new capital, the city of Berlin, avow peaceful cohabitation and cosmopolitanism (Till 2005: 177).

When I asked Xenia why she wanted to do a ritual at the Topography of Terror, of all the other possible sites, she explained: 'When you drive by the Topography of Terror it makes you tremble. It is horrifying.... [W]e should do a ritual for the poor people who died there [in the house-prison] and whose energies are still there and can be felt. We should send them some peace and lay them to rest' (interview, 30 September 2010). For her it represented 'a healing ritual' which would be 'great and beautiful'. Poignantly Xenia concluded: 'Somehow we have to heal the past'. When I asked her what such a ritual to 'heal the past' would look like and whether one could use the 'old wisdom' in such a case – that is, calling upon the Germanic pantheon – she replied: 'Well, certainly not. To invoke Germanic deities in this place, at the "Topography", would be a no-go. It could easily be misunderstood and it does not suit the place'. Then she paused for a moment and went on: 'In general it should be a quiet ritual. No spectacle. No pranksters. The best way to do it would probably be to sit there like a Buddha, in silence. One could do a yoga exercise and get to feel the energies there and develop and bring one's own energy of an inner and outer harmony and happiness' (telephone call, 15 March 2012). This process would be equivalent to 'healing' for her and it could not be achieved through ritual practice that is bound to 'blood and bones' and ancestry. The latter might be appropriate at some geographical sites, but would seem antagonistic to 'harmony' and 'happiness' at this specific historical place.

According to Xenia, Buddhist or Hindu practices are not only suitable for the Topography of Terror because they appear historically 'unstained'. Interestingly, Xenia looks upon them and their underlying spiritual and philosophical cosmologies as belonging here – to the area of Berlin – like the 'old wisdom'. Within this context, she takes the city's international migrants into account. When people come from abroad and make their home in Berlin, Xenia explained, they bring their spirits, ghosts and divinities along, which gradually settle down here too. 'They came with the people', she said to me. 'Through fragrances, joss sticks and different ceremonies, people established their gods, goddesses, divine forces – whatever you call it – here. Those forces we can use.... The city and this land are now home to them'. To a certain extent, she thus makes migrants' religious practices 'native': they might not (yet) be part of the 'old wisdom' but they already 'fit' the territory.

Although the Moon-Women have still not realized the healing ritual at the Topography of Terror, this does not mean that they would rather stay away from urban public places for ritual practice and thus from potentially becoming visible to other city-dwellers. On the contrary, they want to gain publicity. For example, they organized a witch-demonstration against the Pope in 2011 (Hegner 2013) and hold regular weekend rituals in the Tiergarten – Berlin's second largest urban garden – during the daytime. However, when witches go public, they still mostly avoid elements of the 'old wisdom'. Yet sometimes the Moon-Women bravely introduce the latter into a public performance – like calling upon Freya – and thus slowly and publicly make it legitimate within the urban context of Berlin. Sporadic references to German(ic) roots at carefully chosen spaces appear less problematic than wholesale attempts at reconstruction. The united Berlin with its urban culture of tolerance and cosmopolitanism, as well as its staged sensitivity towards German national history, opens a space for spiritual experimentation with forms of Native Faith.

Native Faith and the City: A Summary

It has long been acknowledged that today's cities are headquarters for a wide range of religions and their practitioners. Still religious developments in the city remain a marginal field within qualitative social research. This is particularly true in regard to Native Faith movements. Most research focuses on the national context and how it gives shape to specific concepts and practices. However, in times when national images, identification and boundaries are not only becoming more fundamental, but also apparently crumbling fast, it appears to be the postmodern city, with its staged (national) history and urban culture, that becomes more and more significant in forming, practising and spelling out ideas on Native Faith. This chapter has tried to bring the category of the urban to the fore by focusing on Neopagan witchcraft in Berlin and offering an historical analysis as well as a contemporary ethnography. It becomes obvious that as radically as Berlin changed, so too did the practice and the concepts of Native Faith.

In the 1980s it was a small group of Neopagans and witches in West Berlin who started to follow – as they called it – 'our faith' by being very Reconstructionist in their approach. Their search for religious identification has to be read within the context of a boom of alternative forms of religiosity in the city. West Berlin during this decade in general developed into a social laboratory. Self-acclaimed Pagans and witches were part of this. Their practice of a Native Faith was largely confined to the city's territory due to its political status. Out of this peculiar situation, they creatively designed a Pagan spiritual topography of the city. Practising at 'ancient cult-sites' and preaching a faith bound to the land produced a highly controversial expression of ideas about Germany's national past, about German(ic) tradition, ancestry and ethnicity. Since the end of the Second World War, German national identity had been a highly contested discourse of guilt, which made spiritual references to Teutonism and Germanic gods and goddesses problematic. This was particularly the case in West Berlin – one could argue – because the divided city with its Wall presented the very emblem of Germany's difficult past and burden of history.

Today the once dominant Reconstructionist approach has been superseded by a rather Eclectic way of practising and thinking about Native Faith. As was shown in the case of the Moon-Women and their idea of an 'old wisdom', völkisch elements are still present, for example, by thinking of their religious practice as bound to 'blood and bones' and declaring Christianity a 'desert religion'. Yet those historically sedimented thoughts intermingle intensely with a very new understanding of what 'native' might mean. By declaring, for example, Buddhist and Hindu practices at 'home' in the city, because 'they came with the people' from abroad, Xenia and the Moon-Women reflect on an urban experience par excellence – international migration – in terms of which Berlin today is a hotspot.

Although it still appears problematic to make reference to German(ic) ancestry and territory in one's spiritual practice, some socio-cultural spaces that carefully establish the legitimacy of such references within the urban context are beginning to be ritually created. The united Berlin, as a created symbol of the new Germany that accepts, rather than negates, the Nationalist Socialist past as an integral part of German identity and fashions itself as cosmopolitan, playfully opens the way to this process.

Notes

1 Norse and Germanic mythology overlap considerably. They have the same origin; their basic source is the Eddas, comprising the Poetic Edda and the Prose Edda. The Prose Edda – or Snorri's Edda – is a collection of poems containing tales of Norse mythology claimed to be Icelandic in origin and originally written in Icelandic in the thirteenth century, apparently by Snorri Sturluson. During the eighteenth century the Edda began to be interpreted as the basis of the Germanic pantheon.

2 In his study 'Belonging in the Two Berlins', Borneman (1992: 28–35) discusses concepts of belonging. He sees the category of the nation/national as central.

3 This chapter uses the terms 'Neopaganism' and 'modern Paganism/witchcraft' synonymously. In doing so, it follows the usage common in academic literature. The terms 'Heathenry' and 'Heathens' are seldom used here. Some researchers reserve these for religious practitioners who worship the Norse/Germanic/Celtic pantheon(s). This form of worship was predominant during the 1980s in Berlin, but is not any longer. For reasons of clarity, all strains are summarized under one term here. However, in the first part of this chapter the term 'Pagan' is used, complying with the protagonists' own terminology. See Strmiska (2005: 6–9) on the issue of terminology.

4 Runes are letters of the Teutonic alphabet, which was used to write European languages before the introduction of the Latin alphabet. In Norse mythology runes are of divine origin and help one do magic. See endnote 1 regarding the Eddas.

5 The word 'völkisch' refers to an ethnonationalistic ideology. There is no direct English equivalent. The German word 'Volk' (noun of the adjective völkisch) refers to a metaphysical entity and implies a common language, culture and the idea of a genealogical bond through blood (Wiedemann 2007: 119). Völkisch orientalism is decisively shaped by anti-Semitic sentiments. As a religion originating in the Semitic Orient,

Christianity is seen as Jewish at its roots. It thus represents the emblematic 'other' within this ideology.

6 In 1991 he was elected head of all *Goden – Allsherjargode* – in Germany by the *Goden* assembly. The assembly is an organisation that brings together representatives of Goden and Gydjas from the whole of Germany. It is difficult to provide a definitive meaning for Gode and the Godentum. Depending on the sources one consults, assumptions and historical references vary. Géza defines the Godentum as an old-Germanic priesthood and interprets several written sources, among them Tacitus, accordingly (http://www.allsherjargode.de/, link: 'Goden und Gydjas'). The so called Goden-Order, founded in 1957 in Germany, defines the Godentum as a 'religion with a racial base'; although anticlerical, the Goden-Order still acknowledges Jesus as one of its prophets: 'the ever returning incarnation of the Aryan Christ, the most beloved creature of the divine' (Schnurbein 1993: 48, my translation). The *Reallexikon der Germanischen Altertumskunde* (Hoops 1913: 262–63) defines Gode as an Icelandic 'temple-owner', who is the spiritual and political leader of a community called the 'Goðorð' (first attested in written sources in the thirteenth century).

7 They left West Berlin, drove through East Germany (GDR) with few stops along the so-called 'transit route' to the West (because they were only permitted to stop at a few designated sites), and arrived in West Germany.

8 An advisor on sects was employed either by the Church (both Protestant and Catholic) or by the state. He or she kept religious and spiritual groups outside the dominant monotheistic religions under intense surveillance. Such advisors are still employed today, though often under different names, for example, as a 'contact person for questions on worldviews (*weltanschauung*)'. Presently, the focus is on Scientology.

9 On Géza's home page (Allsherjargode 2013) he lists dates of his public appearances on television and radio. He regularly gave lectures at the city hall of Berlin-Schöneberg.

10 Schnurbein (1993) provides data that he was a member of the Armanen-Orden. Géza repudiates Schnurbein's sources.

11 Géza von Neményi became well known to the extent that Neopagans of later years composed a satirical pop song about him: http://www.raben clan.de/attachments/Magazin/gezablues.mp3. Accessed 30 October 2014.

12 A 'solitary' is the term commonly used within Neopaganism to describe an individual who chooses to practise their spirituality or religion privately, rather than belonging to an established coven or group. Solitaries are likely to take inspiration from books (some Pagan literature is specifically directed to the solitary practitioner), online resources and other Pagans, and they may participate in some communal activities.

References

Allsherjargode. 2013. http://allsherjargode.beepworld.de/ projekteundmedien.htm. Accessed 31 May 2013.
Becci, I., M. Borchardt and J. Casanova (eds). 2013. *Topographies of Faith: Religion in Urban Spaces.* Boston, MA: Brill.
Borneman, J. 1992. *Belonging in the Two Berlins: Kin, State, Nation.* Cambridge and New York: Cambridge University Press.
Bötsch, B. 2005. *Leben mit der großen Göttin: Biografien, Glaubensweisen, Hintergründe zur Göttinreligion in Deutschland.* Regensburg: Lipa.
Cox, H.G. 1984. *Religion in the Secular City: Toward a Postmodern Theory.* New York: Simon and Schuster.
Gardner, G.B. 1959. *The Meaning of Witchcraft.* London: Aquarian.
Greverus, I.-M. and G. Welz (eds). 1990. *Spirituelle Wege und Orte: Untersuchungen zum New Age im urbanen Raum.* Frankfurt am Main: Institut für Europäische Ethnologie.
Hegner, V. 2013. 'Hex and the City: Neopagan Witchcraft and the Urban Imaginary in Berlin', *Ethnologia Europaea* 43(1): 88–97.
Herrmann, K. 1988. 'Sekten im Anzug', *Tip* 17(24): 240–41.
Hoops, J. 1913. *Reallexikon der Germanischen Altertumskunde.* Vol.2. Straßburg: K. J. Trübner.
Hutton, R. 1999. *The Triumph of the Moon: A History of Modern Pagan Witchcraft.* Oxford and New York: Oxford University Press.
Lindner, R. 1993. 'Zone in Transition', *Anthropological Journal on European Cultures* 2(2): 99–111.
Livezey, L. (ed.) 2000. *Public Religion and Urban Transformation: Faith in the City.* New York: New York University Press.
Magliocco, S. 2004. *Witching Culture: Folklore and Neo-Paganism in America.* Philadelphia: University of Pennsylvania Press.
MetroZones (eds). 2011. *Urban Prayers: Neue religiöse Bewegungen in der globalen Stadt.* Berlin and Hamburg: Assoziation A.
Orsi, R. (ed.) 1999. *Gods of the City: Religion and the American Urban Landscape.* Bloomington: Indiana University Press.
Perschke, R. 2003. 'Neuheidnisches Hexentum: Wicca, Pagan, Freifliegende', in N. Grübel and S. Rademacher (eds), *Religion in Berlin: Ein Handbuch.* Berlin: Weißensee Verlag, pp. 525–29.
Rensing, B. 2006. *Der Glaube an die Göttin und den Gott: Theologische, Rituelle und ethische Merkmale der Wicca-Religion, unter besonderer Berücksichtigung der Lyrik englischsprachiger Wicca-Anhänger.* Ph.D. dissertation, Friedrich-Schiller-University, Jena.
———. 2007. *Die Wicca-Religion: Theologie, Rituale, Ethik.* Marburg: Tectum-Verlag.
Rosh, L. 1986. 'Der wunde deutsche Punkt', *Geo Special Berlin* 6 (3 December): 36–37.

Rountree, K. 2004. *Embracing the Witch and the Goddess: Feminist Ritual-Makers in New Zealand*. London and New York: Routledge.

———. 2010. *Crafting Contemporary Pagan Identities in a Catholic Society*. Surrey: Ashgate.

Salomonsen, J. 2001. *Enchanted Feminism: Ritual, Gender and Divinity among the Reclaiming Witches of San Francisco*. London and New York: Routledge.

Schäfer, H. 2010. 'Kreativ oder reaktiv?', *Körper, Geist, Seele* 17(2): 31–33.

Scharna, M., W.M. Flamm and C. Lux (eds). 1985. *Berlin Okkult: der erste esoterische Stadtführer der Welt*. Berlin: Frieling.

Schnurbein, S. von. 1993. *Göttertrost in Wendezeiten: Neugermanisches Heidentum Zwischen New Age und Rechtsradikalismus*. Munich: Claudius Verlag.

Schweinfurth, R. 1986. 'Schön schräg und schrill und scharf', *Geo Special Berlin* 6 (3 December): 38–44.

Simmel, G. 1903. *Die Grossstädte und das Geistesleben*. Dresden: Zahn & Jentsch.

Starhawk. 1979. *The Spiral Dance: A Rebirth of the Ancient Religion of the Great Goddess*. San Francisco: Harper & Row.

———. 1983. *Der Hexenkult als Ur-Religion der Grossen Göttin: Magische Übungen, Rituale und Anrufungen*. Freiburg im Breisgau: Hermann Bauer KG.

Strmiska, M. 2005. 'Modern Paganism in World Cultures: Comparative Perspectives', in M. Strmiska (ed.), *Modern Paganism in World Cultures: Comparative Perspectives*. Santa Barbara: ABC-CLIO, pp. 1–53.

Till, K.E. 2005. *The New Berlin: Memory, Politics, Place*. Minneapolis: University of Minnesota Press.

Weber, M. 1994 [1919]. *Wissenschaft als Beruf: 1917/1919. Politik als Beruf: 1919*. Tübingen: J.C.B. Mohr.

Wiedemann, F. 2007. *Rassenmutter und Rebellin: Hexenbilder in Romantik, Völkischer Bewegung, Neuheidentum und Feminismus*. Würzburg: Königshausen und Neumann.

9

Paganism in Ireland

Syncretic Processes, Identity and a Sense of Place

Jenny Butler

Introduction

This chapter is an exploration of Irish Paganism and the interrelationships between identity, nationalism and cultural context. An examination of some cultural elements that are brought to bear on the construction of Irish Pagans' identities reveals much about how the local socio-geographical and cultural context impacts on the shape this globalized religious movement takes within a specific country. The beliefs and practices of Irish Pagans are informed by the vernacular cultural context, indigenous religious traditions, 'Celtic' heritage and the pre-Christian past. The cultural setting shapes the form Paganism takes: the Irish language, the local natural environment, sacred sites, mythology and history all strongly influence the formation and maintenance of identities. All of these cultural threads lend a feeling of authenticity and a sense of place to contemporary Pagans. Different Pagan traditions ascribe and assert their own 'authentic' Irish identity.[1] The chapter also pays attention to the socio-cultural impulses, such as Romantic Nationalism, that inform contemporary Pagan culture as it exists in Ireland.

Paganism and the Irish Socio-Political Context

Irish Paganism has emerged from a complex historical and socio-political milieu. Ireland is renowned for being one of the stalwart locations for Christian thought and is regarded as rich in Catholic traditions. The national identity is inextricably linked with Christianity. Ireland is famously known as the 'Island of Saints and Scholars', with 'the tradition of Irish scholarship as an adjunct to sanctity' (McMahon and O'Donoghue 2004: 403). The political framework is unavoidably entangled with issues of both religion and nationhood. Modern Ireland is known for its religious disputes between Protestants and Catholics and the 'troubles' of Northern Ireland. Religion has always been an important part of Irish identity and the Catholic Church has, since the nineteenth century, had a strong influence over the lives of Irish people. Catholicism still keenly influences contemporary Irish culture and the country has a hegemonic Catholic ethos. The predominance of Catholicism in the country has affected the character of modern Irish Paganism in various ways. The anthropologist Kathryn Rountree remarks that even if Pagan practitioners in Malta, where she conducted her study, 'identify spiritually as Pagan, they are, unavoidably, culturally Catholic' (2010: 80) and a similar situation exists in Ireland.

Irish Paganism is shaped by meanings and symbols which are drawn from the Irish cultural repository. Myth and folklore are utilized as inspirational resources, the same reserves from which historical patriotic as well as more nationalistic movements drew their inspiration. This shared cultural background for the development of Irish national identity during the founding of the Irish nation-state makes it especially interesting to see how contemporary Paganism relates to nationalist sentiment and political orientation.

The utilization of traditional Irish cultural elements is part of the creative impulse in Paganism, while also being a way for the newly established (in a historical sense) religious community to embed itself in the wider socio-cultural context. Irish Pagan identities are negotiated through the cultural aspects that inform Irish national identity in a general sense. On the whole, there does not seem to be a militant or politically activist bent to Irish Paganism, as there is in some branches of Paganism elsewhere; that is not to say, of course, that there are no nationalistic Irish Pagans at all. Rather, it appears that xenophobic and racist ideologies are not to the fore and therefore the tensions between nationalistic Pagans and other Pagans may not be as pronounced in Ireland as elsewhere in Europe. Irish Paganism is less politicized than that of elsewhere, particularly Eastern Europe. There are various reasons why the social situation is different in Ireland and why Paganism is not so politically driven. The main reason explored here is the gravitation of Paganism towards the values of Romantic

Nationalism, which results in particular expressions of identity. Romantic Nationalism draws much from the notion that what unites a particular socio-geographical group is shared culture, and subsequently mythology and folklore become important as the expressive forms which display a putative shared culture.[2] As a consequence of having Romantic Nationalist themes as a point of reference, the main concern of modern Pagans comes to be identity politics rather than national politics.

Romantic Nationalism seems to be the most influential philosophical strand when it comes to Irish Pagans' conceptualization of their national identity. This kind of nationalism has its basis in nineteenth-century European intellectual currents and philosophies espoused by prominent writers of the time: 'Romantics ... drew a distinction between nationality and nationalism, between the nation as the vehicle of moral and spiritual values and the nation as a political power tending to aggression and imperialism' (Costigan 1973: 141). As well as being influenced by Romanticism, itself influenced by antiquarianism, the Irish Pagan worldview is inspired by ideas found in contemporary fantasy art and literature. These sources and associations combine to colour the perspective of the Pagan movement. As Alan Gailey (1988: 65) states, 'it is clear that different social groups adhere to different corpuses of tradition in defining their identities or in ascribing their identities to themselves'.

Sidestepping the Modern: Paganism and 'Celtic' Religiosity

For Irish Pagans, dialogues of national identity are often circumvented, and sometimes deliberately evaded, by a concentration on a broader 'Celtic' identity. Focusing on this more inclusive 'Celtic-ness' is a way of circumventing the political wrangling over the concept of 'Irishness', with its associated religious and geopolitical cultural baggage. The fact that it is the distant past and ancient heritage that is evoked most often by Pagans makes the symbolic manoeuvrings around identity and place less challenging and contentious than if recent or contemporary history and heritage were at the forefront of their discourse. As Frykman and Löfgren (1996: 17) state:

> Customs always tell us about the present. By seeing what has become tradition, what is considered worth preserving, we can learn something about how different groups nowadays present themselves, building up an

identity of their own with the aid of references to the old days. The interesting question is not whether this tradition-building gives a true or false picture of the past, but why this particular version of a shared history is chosen.

The idea of shared 'Celtic' history is important for many Irish Pagans. 'Celtic' has become a contemporary buzzword, with many different meanings attributed to it. A specialist in Cornish studies, Amy Hale, takes note that 'a number of scholars now realize that, rather than emphasizing the lack of continuity between the ancient Celt and contemporary Celts and focusing on the "inauthenticity" of contemporary Celtic traditions, the ambiguities and complexities surrounding the Celts and various expressions of Celtic identity are in themselves worthy of study' (2002: 157). For many Irish Pagans and Pagans of foreign nationality living in Ireland, it is Celtic identity that provides a sense of legitimacy for their religion as well as a feeling of belonging to the land of Ireland.

For most Pagans, pre-Christian religions are a precursor to their own belief-system and spiritual practices. In the Irish context, the endeavour of reconstruction is tenuous as relatively little evidence exists of the precise religious beliefs and practices of people in the country prior to Christianity. While there are archaeological, mythological and Early Irish literary sources (mediated through Christian authors), no first-hand accounts are extant from the pre-Christian Irish themselves. Pagans are aware that it is not possible to 'revive' ancient religious practices per se, or even to reconstruct accurately what pre-Christian religions might have been like based on disparate pieces of historical information. Rather, Pagans collate various bits of available information and use them as a foundation to design their own rituals. The folklorist Henry Glassie (2003: 176) describes the process of defining an emergent tradition: 'Tradition is the creation of the future out of the past. A continuous process situated in the nothingness of the present, linking the vanished with the unknown, tradition is stopped, parcelled, and codified by thinkers who fix upon this aspect or that, in accord with their needs or preoccupations'.

The lack of detail of Irish life prior to Christian influence has compounded a romanticized view of indigenous culture and quixotic notions of pre-Christian populations as having had a deep spiritual connection to the land, living in harmony with the natural cycle and worshipping the 'Old Gods'. The Romantic influence is apparent in how Pagans are more receptive to mythic history and imaginative versions of the past, especially to the idea of a Golden Age of the Celts. The Romantic Movement did much to idealize indigenous Irish culture by connecting it to a Celtic heroic past. Similarly, Pagans engage with spiritual aspects of Irish culture that are sifted through the notion of 'Celtic'. There is a selective process involved in the creation of this 'Celtic' identity and an intentional engagement with what are often hackneyed ideas. The wistful, dreamlike notions attached to the Celtic world are purposefully reiterated in Pagan discourse.

The concept of Celtic spirituality is hugely popular and has attached to it particular perceptions of the religion of the Celtic peoples as mystical and special. 'The popularity of the subject', says the Celticist Donald Meek (2000: 4), 'has created an expectation which anticipates a glowing portrait of the "Celts" and their spirituality'. It is the religious ideals associated with the Celts that are most important to Pagans. The folklorist Marion Bowman (2000a: 88) remarks: 'A variety of spiritual seekers consider that the Celts are providing inspiration, motivation and exhilaration in their religious lives. The "spiritual Celt" is real, whether or not he or she exists/ existed'. James Lewis (2009: 480) acknowledges that 'an aspect of the present [Celtic] revival that sets it apart from its predecessors is the extent to which Celtophiles are appropriating Celtic identities and, as part of this appropriation, engaging in religious practices perceived to be Celtic'. There are attempts to connect with the past and give modern Paganism a foundation in Ireland's history; the traditions of Druidry and Wicca achieve this Celtic connection by engaging with mythology, landscape and language in specific ways (see Figure 9.1).

Druidry is a revivalist tradition that makes claims to native cultural heritage. Some of Ireland's Druids believe that certain traditions they practise stretch back to the ancient Druid priests of Celtic Ireland (Butler 2005). The 'Celtic' identity of modern Druids is problematic and there are difficulties with the definition of the term 'Celtic' in these contexts. The folklorist Leslie Ellen Jones (1998: 1) remarks that 'the simplest answer to the question, "Who were the Druids?" is to reply, "The Druids were the priests of the pagan Celts". But this leads to the question, "Who were the Celts?" or perhaps, "Who *are* the Celts?" Even a simple answer to a simple question opens a bottomless can of worms'. Modern Druid identities may be constructed on the basis of scant historical evidence but the historical aspect still serves as an authenticator for the practices of today; 'all invented traditions, so far as possible, use history as a legitimator' (Hobsbawm 1983: 12).

Fig. 9.1 *Druid sensing energy from a stone. Image used with the kind permission of Druid Fred Mathews and the photographer, Melvyn Lloyd.*

Some Irish Wiccans have also assumed a 'Celtic' identity. In view of the fact that Wicca originated as a British initiatory tradition that was 'imported' into Ireland, there is some anxiety around the subject of Irish Wicca and national identity. Perhaps indirectly a response to this, Wicca has taken on local inflections to suit the Irish cultural landscape and the tradition of 'Celtic Wicca' has emerged as a subset of the wider Wiccan path. One practitioner defines what 'Celtic Wicca' means:

> The Celtic part is more that we take account of the energies of this land here, which are quite specific; they're quite different from what you get on the Continent or say, in the States, and also some of the traditions in both worship and belief. We also only worship the Celtic deities. We wouldn't worship Egyptian deities or Norse deities.... We worship all of them [Celtic deities] and not just the Irish ones. Also, say, Welsh deities. For example, our Coven goddess is Arianrhod who's a Welsh deity of rebirth. But my personal patron deities are Brigit and Herne the hunter. (Interview with Sarah, 14 February 2002)[3]

For both Wiccans and Druids, spiritually connecting with the Celtic past and articulating a 'Celtic' identity are ways to authenticate their religion as well as position themselves within the Irish cultural inventory.

Paganism, Folklore and Local Cultural Traditions

The desire Pagans have for affiliation with practices that have their roots in Irish historical contexts has led to the incorporation of various traditional Irish customs into Pagan practices. The reinterpretation of older Irish customs and beliefs has led to the formation of new traditions. The historian David Gross speaks of traditions that come into being 'because they satisfy some internal, psychological, even visceral "need for tradition"' (1992: 64). This seemingly inherent need for tradition is palpable in the relationship Pagans have with cultural heritage.

Pagans make links with native Irish 'magical' and healing traditions. They assimilate folklore connected to these traditional practices into their worldview and ritual practices. Irish Pagans often identify with traditional healers, such as 'wise women' and 'cunning men', or 'fairy doctors' as they were more often known in Ireland. Given that Wicca was formed in England, and other Pagan paths have been imported into Ireland, some practitioners prefer to follow practices that have a precedent in Irish tradition. In Pagan discourse, there is the notion of hidden magical knowledge being passed on in folk customs. As Helen Cornish (2005: 365) states, 'Despite criticisms of claims to continuous religious Witchcraft, a crucial feature has been re-invoked – namely, that folk magic employed by cunning folk as a repository of hidden and surviving knowledge has been transmitted through oral traditions'. The idea of knowledge concealed in oral traditions is another reason why Pagans consider folklore material an invaluable resource.

The Pagan tradition of Hereditary Witchcraft features prominently as an indigenous practice, as it is believed to be transmitted through familial lines and can be traced back, it is claimed, through the generations. Pagans allude to rural popular practices in the belief that it validates their own practices by providing them with spiritual roots in the country. For example, one Witch states: 'Essentially I think of myself as a Witch, as an earth-Witch, not as a Wiccan, more cunning craft, the old – ancient – tradition of the country wise. You know, I'm a herbalist, I'm a country craftsman, I have a lot of country skills....

Wicca is a hierarchical, hermetic tradition' (interview with Benjamin, 6 June 2002). This process of identifying with rural practices of an older time reveals the importance to Pagans of ancestry and continuous tradition.

The techniques of traditional magical practitioners of various cultures and geographical locations are blended together by Pagans. Eighteenth- and nineteenth-century Romantic imagery and historical customs that are often disconnected are melded together to create certain conceptions of the past. 'A survey of popular Pagan texts', Ann-Marie Gallagher (2009: 578) remarks, 'turned up an arrestingly unproblematized relationship with ethnic, historical, national, social and political boundaries. Amongst the very popular titles surveyed, there was a markedly lackadaisical attitude towards historical periodicity'. Paganism globally makes attempts to connect with the 'old religion'. For Irish Pagans, the manner of connecting with the folk culture of the past is often ahistorical, thus allowing a disregarding of historical contexts as well as evasion of political contexts.

Folkloristics, Nationalism and Paganism

Prior to the academic discipline devoted to the study of folklore, there were antiquarian and seminal folklore collections. In Ireland, as in many parts of Europe, early folklore collection was motivated and spurred on by nationalistic agendas. The Romantic Movement was a motivating factor for the interest in and assembly of folklore material in the late eighteenth and early nineteenth centuries, especially for use as an artistic resource. Connections were made at this time between the culture of the European peasantry and the culture of ancient peoples, as the folklorist Roger Abrahams (1993: 3) points out: 'The study of folklore was formulated by antiquarian scholars.... These men of learning saw in the study of antiquities the possibility of obtaining political and social advancement by identifying scarce remains of past cultures, and calling attention to their strange status as dislocated remnants that carried with them a certain mystery and power'. The 'Celtic culture' that was constructed for Ireland was largely a creation of antiquarian Romantic writers. The movement that became known as the 'Celtic Revival' centred on the notion of 'survivals' of Celtic culture being extant in the traditions of the ordinary people.

In the late nineteenth century, the writers of the Irish Literary Revival enhanced these notions of the 'Celtic'. Perhaps most notable is the work of William Butler Yeats: the literary renaissance in Ireland is nicknamed 'The Celtic Twilight' after his work of the same name. The Romantics concentrated on the northwest edge of Europe, regions known as the 'Celtic fringe', particularly the west of Ireland and Highland Scotland, as inspirational locations for their artwork and 'with Romanticism the ancient Celts were idealized as were the landscapes inhabited by the modern speakers of Celtic languages' (Ó Giolláin 2000: 25). The mostly English-speaking writers created an image of the Celtic world for a literary audience yearning for something exotic. This recreation of Celtic-speaking peoples meant that cultural and historical realities were distorted to suit an imaginative picture; 'Celticism served to define Ireland and the Irish in partly exotic and partly romantic terms' (Ó Cadhla 2007: 56). The Romantic conceptualization of Ireland in the work of Yeats and his circle of literary figures including George William Russell (also known as Æ) and Douglas Hyde (a folklorist and the first president of Ireland) served to spur on Irish cultural nationalism.

It is the folklore collections of this era of Romanticism, as well as earlier antiquarianism, that are used by Pagans as an inspirational source:

> Many of the images in Pagans' ecstatic visions come from folklore and mythology: goddesses and gods, fairies, nature and animal spirits, ancestors. These elements are part of our shared cultural register; but they also emerge because they were preserved by the folklore collections of the 19th and early 20th centuries, with their Romantic re-evaluation of what appeared to be disappearing rural lifeways rooted in an ancient past. (Magliocco 2009: 231)

Seeing as many of the Irish Romantic writers and artists were reimagining the vernacular culture for a new audience and adding a quixotic tinge to their portrayals, it is interesting to consider that Irish Pagans in turn draw upon this reimagining of Irish culture as a way of engaging with Irish history and folk culture.

Despite the refutations of academic historians that historically traceable antecedents for modern Pagan traditions exist, Pagans are still receptive to the idea of secret, underground magical practitioners who have carried on certain traditions right through until the present day. There is a tendency for Pagans to equate the folklore and customs of the early modern period and the court proceedings of the witch trials with that of pre-Christian times; this reflects a notion of magical knowledge passed on through time but hidden in popular practices. While the vast majority of Pagans by now reject the idea of a continuous lineage going back to pre-Christian times, they are, as mentioned above, still attracted to the idea of hidden magical knowledge. The repository for this knowledge is believed to be the popular customs, oral traditions and beliefs of the ordinary people of past eras.

The use of such folkloric material, particularly the collections of the nineteenth century, brings the issue of authenticity to the fore with regard to the notion of historical antecedents for tradition. Regina Bendix (1997: 216), examining the intellectual history of the discipline of folkloristics, points out that 'ethnicity, the conceptualization of tradition, and the history of the discipline, all turn in one way or another around dearly held beliefs in authenticity'. The history of folklore study itself involves notions of 'survivals' or 'remnants' of ancient tradition, believed to have continued from ancient cultures into 'authentic' folk culture. The Pagan yearning to connect to traditions of people in the recent past, in the belief that they contain knowledge passed down from the remote past, is quite similar to the mindset of early folklorists who followed a theory of cultural evolution.

Land, Language and Ideology

Ideas about land, language and the nation are interconnected in ways that can give rise to emotive and controversial discourses. Land as homeland, 'native soil' or territory has obvious nationalist overtones and various symbolic associations which can be provocative. For Pagans, the land on which one lives is extremely important to one's spirituality. Pagans have an emotional relationship with land because of its symbolic connections to ancestral religion and culture. For many Pagans, the Irish landscape is represented as the land of the 'Old Gods', the deities of Celtic mythology. Some Pagans venerate deities from a range of pantheons without being geographically, historically or culturally specific about the gods and goddesses they work with in ritual. On the other hand, there is a strong view among some Pagans that only the gods of one's own land should be invoked in ritual, and in Ireland there are those who only invoke deities that have their origin in Celtic myth and not any other pantheons that are 'alien' to Irish culture.

For Pagans who are animists, the natural landscape is a connection to the spirit realm and the location where it is possible to commune with the divine. Graham Harvey (2007: 287) remarks on the relationship between landscape and constructed memory: 'While already a fluid term, "nature" among "ethnic Pagans" has to refer to landscapes of ancestry and memory (neither of which should be taken as straightforward terms, but refer to creative and constructed relationships and knowledges)'. While ethnicity is not a focal point for most Irish Pagans, the landscape is of exceptional importance in the construction of identity and the remembrance of the past. As Paganism gives primacy to embodiment and that which is perceived and ecstatically felt, a relationship with the local natural environment can be created. The personal spiritual connection to land, locality and the *genii loci* (local spirits), deities and energies, is key in terms of Pagans' identity and sense of having roots in the country (see Figure 9.2). For Pagans who move to Ireland from elsewhere, a prominent theme in their discourse is the experience of connecting to the local landscape, adapting to its different energies and spirits.

The Irish landscape contains many megalithic monuments, such as the well-known Newgrange in County Meath, and stone circles, and these are sacred sites for Pagans. There are meaningful connections made by Pagans between these sites and ancient religious observances and, for many Pagans, the perceived lineage to an ancient religious tradition is extremely important. Some Pagans claim it is possible to sense and attune to spiritual energies that are thought to permeate sacred sites, the idea being that the sites 'hold' energies that were raised during rituals of the distant past (see Figure 9.1). For Pagans, the idea of magical energies permeating these sites is important and it somehow transcends documented information in that it is based on intuitive feeling; carrying out rituals at these sites could mean that they are practising ritual in the same sacred space as ancestral peoples. As David Lowenthal (1979: 121) observes, 'monuments and memorials locate the remembered or imagined past in the present landscape. Their function is not to preserve the past but to recall and celebrate it'.

These megalithic sites became symbols of the ancient world as imagined by the antiquarian writers and artists of the eighteenth and nineteenth centuries. The Pagan symbolic use of the sites seems to connect with their use as antiquarian romantic symbols. These sites are hyper-symbolic with many different associations: modern Pagan ritual, ancient cultures, 'Celtic', mythic history and so on. As David Harvey has noted, ancient monuments often play an important role as iconographic symbols of place and heritage that are evocative of national identity; he remarks that 'ancient monuments, by definition, comprise a set of structures for which the original meaning is

Fig. 9.2 *'Boann', from the painting series* The Ever-Living Ones *by Jane Brideson. Copyright 2013. Reproduced with the kind permission of the artist.*

not (and, indeed, can never be) known. This allows for endless re-interpretation by later societies' (2003: 475). The land of Ireland and the archaeological structures upon it have a certain ideological asso-ciation for Pagans, which can often be emotionally charged.

Tied in with issues of place, land and belonging is the matter of language. The Irish language is nowadays a minority language and a second language for only a small percentage of the population; this makes the issue of present-day linguistic nationalism as a social force or cultural power a complicated one in Ireland's case. Added to this complexity, the Irish language has a bearing on the notion of Celtic identity. Academic definitions of 'Celtic' rest on the language group (including Irish, Scottish Gaelic, Welsh, Breton, Manx and Cornish), so that 'Celtic countries' include modern nations or regions in which a Celtic language is, or was historically, spoken. Irish nationalist movements and cultural nationalist organizations, such as the Gaelic League (founded 1893), have focused on the spoken Irish language as a basis for cultural continuity and means of preserving the Irish native traditions and way of life (Mays 1996: 6–7). There are Irish Pagans who are native speakers of Irish and others who have learned the language to fluency. There are others who are not Irish speakers, but feel that they should include Irish-language words or phrases in their rituals. Some ritual groups have a mixture of Irish and non-Irish speakers:

> Interviewer: Do you usually do rituals through Irish?
> Eadaoin: For me personally, particularly with key words like that, I feel better calling them through Irish. And again, when I'm speaking my own name, I speak that through Irish as well … that's something that is in many ways personal to me. But I know that the other people who meet here and celebrate here very much want the Irish language used and heard. And there is something that resonates with people even if they don't understand the literal meaning of the word. The physical sound of the word resonates very strongly with the people who share these celebrations with us. (Interview with Eadaoin, 3 February 2002)

Some feel that by speaking Irish words in their rituals, they are connecting to their Celtic heritage, or to their heritage as Irish people. This has to do with continuity between past generations and the present inhabitants of the land of Ireland. Others believe that Irish is the language of the gods of the land and others go further still to suggest that the deities of old would speak Old Irish. As one Druid states:

> Any circle that affirms its identity with the Celtic path, or any circle that says, like, 'We're part of the Celtic continuum, we're invoking Celtic gods here', can't evade the language issue and I feel very strongly on that point. It really is a matter of respect for the land and Druidry teaches us to respect the land, to love the land, to speak the language that is of the land. Now we can keep refining that and saying 'you should speak Old Irish' and 'maybe you should speak something that was there before that again'. We can go back until we were all grunting [*laughs*] like cavemen, you know? But it's the thought that counts, if you know what I mean. It's the actions, it's the intent, that we want to speak a language that is native to this land, native to the people, the culture and the heritage of this land. And in doing this, and in going to the trouble of translating my – 'cause I'm no fluent Irish speaker – but in going to the trouble of translating my rituals into Irish, it's another act of love and a token gesture of love to the land and, you know, hopefully, the Goddess will smile on us for that. (Interview with Ronán, 29 March 2002)

Others disagree with the view that language, or even verbal communication, is necessary to commune with deities, as another Druid comments:

> [Having been] born in Germany and come to live in Ireland for the last sixteen years, I have connected to my Celtic roots through living a simple life close to nature. I do not speak Irish apart from a couple of *focal* [words] and even though I'd like to know Irish, I don't think it's necessary to speak Irish to connect with gods and goddesses or the fairy folk. Communication with deities and entities lies far beyond human languages, but I also do believe that an old language [such] as Irish is a good medium for the human to get in touch with other realms, if that is their way to connect. The way I connect is not so much with words, but rather with feelings and senses and images. (Interview with Martha, 2 August 2003)

For some Pagans, language is firmly tied up with poetic notions of Celtic affiliation or a sense of ancestral belonging, while for others it is not a barrier to connection with land or history. While the Irish language can play a significant part in ritual, it is not central to Irish Pagan identity and does not appear to be employed in an exclusionary way. The instances of Irish Pagan immigrants learning Irish phrases to use in ritual looks as if it is a token of respect to the Irish culture and, as some believe, the language of the gods of the land. The fact that there is not an obvious resistance to this use of the Irish language by foreigners also suggests inclusiveness within the wider Irish Pagan community. Once again, 'Celtic' identity and spiritual unity is to the fore, rather than modern Irish national identity. It is believed that one can connect to Celtic spirituality regardless of whether one has ancestral roots in a Celtic country or speaks a Celtic language. Marion Bowman highlights this phenomenon and states that 'there are increasing numbers of people who might be described as "Cardiac Celts"; they feel in their hearts that they are Celts. For Cardiac Celts, spiritual nationality is a matter of elective affinity' (2000b: 246). 'Celtic self-identity' itself, James Lewis (2009: 484) observes, 'is a modern phenomenon' and evidently is a way for some Pagans to integrate into Irish spiritual communities.

There are indeed Irish Pagans who put great emphasis on ethnicity, land, language and local indigenous traditions. However, Irish Paganism in general does not seem to be exclusionary or to have overtly political leanings. The Irish situation is in stark contrast to the nationalistic 'blood and soil' forms of Paganism in other parts of Europe. In some countries, Pagan groups with fascist agendas are on the rise and 'Paganism is being pressed to the cause of spiritual

Aryanism in Europe' (Gallagher 2009: 585). Speaking on the connections between some Pagan groups in Britain and neo-Nazism, as well as the hijacking of Pagan symbols and identities by those with neo-Nazi agendas, Ann-Marie Gallagher (2009: 585) states: 'There are a number of neo-fascist initiatives operative in most parts of Britain and some of these appeal to what they perceive as Pagan "values" within the extreme right. These values are those mobilized around notions of history, race and nationhood'.

The language issue comes into play with concepts around homeland for nationalistic movements, particularly when it becomes a tool of exclusion and segregation of foreign nationals who do not speak the native and thus 'authentic' language of a country or region. Bendix (1997: 98), discussing the 'Nazification' of the German discipline of folkloristics, observes how 'the central inclusion of authenticity into definitional practices' is 'an invitation to exclusionary politics'. It seems that a similar process of exclusionary politics is at work in parts of Europe in regard to the commandeering of Pagan symbols for fascist agendas, or the use by nationalistic Pagan groups of an exclusionary ideology based on notions of authenticity entwined with ideas about ethnicity, language, 'true religion' or cultural heritage. It is clear that, for the Irish Pagans encountered during this study at least, it is the identity as Pagan that is foremost, rather than national or ethnic lineage or language; for these Pagans, self-referential dialogues do not normally contain perceptible expressions of national pride but much evidence of pride in being Pagan.

Pagans, Catholics and Religious Syncretism

The idea of Celtic influences on Irish folk religion also affects Pagans' relationship with popular Catholicism. Historians generally agree that the transition from paganism to Christianity was a more harmonious process in Ireland than in other areas of the world. Due to Ireland's peripheral location, and because Christianity was not enforced in the same way as it was in Britain by the Roman state, there was accommodation between the pagan religion and the incoming Christian faith. The indigenous people in due course converted to the new religion, and 'apparently many of the Druids and *filid* (members of the traditional order of poets), the traditional guardians of Celtic religion, converted to Christianity and simply continued many of the same practices under the name of a different god' (Jestice 2000: xiv). This syncretism and blending of the pre-Christian and Christian traditions meant that older pagan elements survived in popular religiosity. The folklorist Diarmuid Ó Giolláin describes the hybrid nature of Irish popular religion and states 'we can speak of syncretism from an early period, of pre-Christian phenomena being Christianised and of surviving non-Christian phenomena taking on a Christian frame of reference' (1997: 203).

A synthesis of pagan and Christian elements is revealed in popular religious practices, such as devotions at holy wells, which are reminiscent of older religious rites. Many believe that the wells dedicated to Christian saints were previously markers of sacred springs that were used for druidical rites. Holy wells are also sacred sites for Pagans. Visiting a holy well on the 'pattern-day' was a widespread custom in Ireland in the past and still exists to a lesser extent in contemporary times. The word 'pattern' comes from the pronunciation of the word 'patron' in Hiberno-English due to the usual association of the pilgrimage with a holy well dedicated to a patron saint, but many scholars have observed that the pattern ritual contains vestiges of pre-Christian practices. The pattern is often held close to the major seasonal festivals and as Patrick Logan (1992: 35) points out, 'some pre-Christian practices associated with these festivals were continued when Christianity had become the religion of the Irish and some of them are still seen after fifteen hundred years'. During a pattern, the tradition is a circumambulation which proceeds clockwise round the well, known colloquially as 'doing the rounds'.

In contemporary Pagan cosmology, circling is a meaningful ritual act, as is the direction of this rotation, that is, deosil, which is a Pagan term for 'clockwise'. The word 'deosil' is an anglicized form of the Irish-language word *deiseal*, meaning 'clockwise'. *Deiseal* has the meaning of turning to the right and derives from the word *deas*,[4] which also has connotations of 'positive', 'appropriate', 'auspicious' and 'pleasant'. In Irish popular religious practices and 'folk' magic, there are many ritual actions that involve clockwise rotation in order to attain positive outcomes and, conversely, anticlockwise motions to attain nefarious outcomes. It has been acknowledged that, in many cultures, rituals that involve making a circuit of a sacred focal point can be interpreted as symbolically encompassing the cosmos; it is a microcosmic ritual act that reflects the macrocosmic order of the universe. Moving clockwise means turning in accordance with the sun's trajectory and thus has associations with the progression of the cosmic order; as a ritual act this 'movement [is] in harmony with the sun's diurnal course and was thought from ancient times to be auspicious' (Ó Cadhla 2002: 11).

Traditionally, the Catholic pilgrimage involves saying prayers while circling the well a certain number of times and it is interesting to note that 'the number of circuits – three, seven, nine, twelve and seventeen – is commonly associated with magic and the supernatural' (Menefree 1985: 6). Some of these numbers resonate with Pagans as magical (three, seven and nine). Modern Pagan acts of veneration at holy wells are to the spirits of place and not to a saint or the Christian god. Pagans might circle the well three or seven times as part of a ritual but this is to do with raising 'magical energy' rather than a devotional act, and there are chants rather than prayers.

It appears that specific elements of popular Catholic devotions are incorporated into Pagan rituals because they are viewed as the 'pagan' elements of what Christians are practising. Contemporary Pagans view this as acceptable given that Christians appropriated ancient pagan practice to begin with, a process that features in Paganism in other Catholic contexts. Kathryn Rountree (2010: 4–5) compares Irish Pagans to those in Malta as regards their relationship with Catholicism: 'In both countries some Neo-Pagans incorporate Christianity into their personal spiritual paths and identities. Overall, Irish and Maltese Pagans are perhaps less antagonistic towards the prevailing Catholicism of their societies than many of their counterparts elsewhere are towards Christianity'. Irish Pagans are agreeable to integrating aspects of popular Catholicism they deem to be pagan but conversely, the elements of popular religious practices that they view as Christian are omitted, so Pagans do not view this as including Christianity in their practices. Pagans consciously incorporate aspects of belief and ritual from a wide range of indigenous religions and different magical systems, but pass over anything that they consider to be Christian or to belong to another Abrahamic faith.[5] This exclusion has to do with the Pagan view of the monotheistic faiths as destructive of, or threatening to, the indigenous religions. The syncretistic religious background and identification of 'pagan' elements of Catholic practices results in a less hostile relationship between Paganism and Christianity than elsewhere in Europe.

Concluding Remarks

Ireland's socio-cultural context has shaped a specific kind of Paganism. Meanings are pulled together from history as well as an imagined past to provide an impetus for modern practices. Writers of the Romantic Movement have largely compiled the folklore sources Pagans consult and the modern Pagan movement has itself been strongly influenced by Romanticism as well as cultural nationalism. Folk practices, indigenous religious traditions and local sites are embraced and absorbed into Pagan practices, which situates Pagan identity in a particular niche on the Irish cultural landscape. Engaging with history and cultural traditions in specific ways results in a unique formation of ideological Irish Paganism. Discussing globalization, cultural hybridization and Paganism, Dave Green (2003: 80) remarks: 'Traditions, therefore, are reflexive in the sense that individuals are able to simultaneously adopt and adapt, shape and be shaped by tradition. Such historical *bricolage* allows occultist philosophies, especially forms of Pagan spirituality, to constantly reinvent themselves'. Irish Pagan spirituality is shaped by a variety of Irish cultural elements. The cultural capital employed by nationalist movements of the past – land, ancient monuments, language, mythology, folklore – is used by Pagans in the interpretation of the past as well as in the assemblage and articulation of their identities. Despite this and perhaps unexpectedly – in that the identity politics of cultural movements historically turned into political agendas – the resulting spiritual movement of Irish Paganism is not manifestly nationalistic. Rather, the cultural threads of history, Celtic heritage, myth and folklore lend a feeling of authenticity and a sense of place to contemporary Irish Pagans.

Notes

1 This examination focuses on the Pagan 'traditions' or 'paths' of Druidry and Wicca. While Shamanism, Heathenism and various other forms of Paganism exist in Ireland, they were not included in this study.

2 This idea of the *volksgeist*, 'spirit of the people', or 'national spirit' that is somehow contained in folklore comes from the work of Johann Gottfried von Herder (1744–1803).

3 Pseudonyms are used to protect the identity of research participants.

4 The Irish word for 'ritual' is *deasghnáth*, literally 'correct custom'.

5 It should be noted that there are Christo-Pagans for whom Paganism and Christianity are not mutually exclusive – for example, Christian Druids – but given that the study on which this chapter is based deals only with Druids who identify as Pagans, this was not investigated. Christo-Pagans were not encountered in the Irish Pagan community, but again, this may have been due to the specific focus in this study.

References

Abrahams, R.D. 1993. 'Phantoms of Romantic Nationalism in Folkloristics', *The Journal of American Folklore* 106(419): 3–37.

Bendix, R. 1997. *In Search of Authenticity: The Formation of Folklore Studies*. Madison: University of Wisconsin Press.

Bowman, M. 2000a. 'Contemporary Celtic Spirituality', in A. Hale and P. Payton (eds), *New Directions in Celtic Studies*. Exeter: University of Exeter Press, pp. 69–91.

———. 2000b. 'Cardiac Celts: Images of the Celts in Paganism', in C. Hardman and G. Harvey (eds), *Pagan Pathways: A Complete Guide to the Ancient Earth Traditions*. London: Thorsons, pp. 242–51.

Butler, J. 2005. 'Druidry in Contemporary Ireland', in M.F. Strmiska (ed.), *Modern Paganism in World Cultures: Comparative Perspectives*. Santa Barbara: ABC-CLIO, pp. 87–125.

Cornish, H. 2005. 'Cunning Histories: Privileging Narratives in the Present', *History and Anthropology* 16(3): 363–76.

Costigan, G. 1973. 'Romantic Nationalism: Ireland and Europe', *Irish University Review* 3(2): 141–52.

Frykman, J. and O. Löfgren. 1996. 'Introduction', in J. Frykman and O. Löfgren (eds), *Force of Habit: Exploring Everyday Culture*. Lund: Lund University Press, pp. 5–19.

Gailey, A. 1988. 'Tradition and Identity', in A. Gailey (ed.), *The Use of Tradition: Essays Presented to G. B. Thompson*. County Down: Ulster Folk and Transport Museum, pp. 61–67.

Gallagher, A. 2009. 'Weaving a Tangled Web? Pagan Ethics and Issues of History, "Race" and Ethnicity in Pagan Identity', in J.R. Lewis and M. Pizza (eds), *Handbook of Contemporary Paganism*. Leiden: Brill, pp. 577–90.

Glassie, H. 2003. 'Tradition', in B. Feintuch (ed.), *Eight Words for the Study of Expressive Culture*. Urbana and Chicago: University of Illinois Press, pp. 176–97.

Green, D. 2003. 'Opposites Attract: Magical Identity and Social Uncertainty', *The Journal for the Academic Study of Magic* 1: 75–101.

Gross, D.L. 1992. *The Past in Ruins: Tradition and the Critique of Modernity*. Amherst: The University of Massachusetts Press.

Hale, A. 2002. 'Whose Celtic Cornwall? The Ethnic Cornish Meet Celtic Spirituality', in D.C. Harvey, R. Jones, N. McInroy and C. Milligan (eds), *Celtic Geographies: Old Culture, New Times*. London and New York: Routledge, pp. 157–70.

Harvey, D.C. 2003. '"National" Identities and the Politics of Ancient Heritage: Continuity and Change at Ancient Monuments in Britain and Ireland, c.1675–1850', *Transactions of the Institute of British Geographers* 28(4): 473–87.

Harvey, G. 2007. 'Inventing Paganisms: Making Nature', in J.R. Lewis and O. Hammer (eds), *The Invention of Sacred Tradition*. Cambridge: Cambridge University Press, pp. 277–90.

Hobsbawm, E. 1983. 'Introduction', in E. Hobsbawm and T. Ranger (eds), *The Invention of Tradition*. Cambridge: Cambridge University Press.

Jestice, P.G. 2000. *Encyclopedia of Irish Spirituality*. Santa Barbara: ABC-CLIO.

Jones, L.E. 1998. *Druid Shaman Priest: Metaphors of Celtic Paganism*. Middlesex: Hisarlik Press.

Lewis, J.R. 2009. 'Celts, Druids and the Invention of Tradition', in J.R. Lewis and M. Pizza (eds), *Handbook of Contemporary Paganism*. Leiden: Brill, pp. 479–93.

Logan, P. 1992. *The Holy Wells of Ireland*. Buckinghamshire: Colin Smythe.

Lowenthal, D. 1979. 'Age and Artifact: Dilemmas of Appreciation', in D.W. Meinig (ed.), *The Interpretation of Ordinary Landscapes: Geographical Essays*. New York and Oxford: Oxford University Press, pp. 103–28.

Magliocco, S. 2009. 'Reclamation, Appropriation and the Ecstatic Imagination in Modern Pagan Ritual', in J.R. Lewis and M. Pizza (eds), *Handbook of Contemporary Paganism*. Leiden: Brill, pp. 223–40.

Mays, M. 1996. '"Irelands of the Heart": The Ends of Cultural Nationalism and the Limits of Nationalist Culture', *The Canadian Journal of Irish Studies* 22(1): 1–20.

McMahon, S. and J. O'Donoghue. 2004. 'Island of Saints and Scholars', in *Brewer's Dictionary of Irish Phrase and Fable*. London: Weidenfeld & Nicolson, pp. 402–403.

Meek, D.E. 2000. *The Quest for Celtic Christianity*. Edinburgh: Handsel Press.

Menefree, P.S. 1985. 'Circling as an Entrance to the Otherworld', *Folklore* 96: 3–20.

Ó Cadhla, S. 2002. *The Holy Well Tradition: The Pattern of St. Declan, Ardmore, County Waterford, 1800–2000*. Maynooth Studies in Local History, No. 45. Dublin: Four Courts Press.

———. 2007. *Civilizing Ireland: Ordnance Survey 1824–1842*. Dublin: Irish Academic Press.

Ó Giolláin, D. 1997. 'The Fairy Belief and Official Religion in Ireland', in P. Narváez (ed.), *The Good People: New Fairylore Essays*. Kentucky: The University Press of Kentucky, pp. 199–214.

———. 2000. *Locating Irish Folklore: Tradition, Modernity, Identity*. Cork: Cork University Press.

Rountree, K. 2010. *Crafting Contemporary Pagan Identities in a Catholic Society*. Surrey: Ashgate.

10

On the Sticks and Stones of the Greencraft Temple in Flanders

Balancing Global and Local Heritage in Wicca

Léon A. van Gulik

O goat-foot God of Arcady!
This modern world is grey and old,
And what remains to us of thee? ...

Then blow some trumpet loud and free,
And give thine oaten pipe away,
Ah, leave the hills of Arcady!
The modern world has need of Thee!

– Oscar Wilde, *Pan: Double Villanelle*

Introduction

During the 1960s and 1970s what today is referred to as British Traditional Wicca (BTW) was spreading through the Anglo-Saxon world. In the early 1980s the main strands also got a foothold in continental Europe. From its original dissemination the movement always retained a strong connection with its source through stressing the fundamental importance of a lineage of initiates. Originating with Gerald Gardner and Alex Sanders, who each founded a strand of BTW – called Gardnerians and Alexandrians, respectively – the new nature religion quickly developed a steady, albeit somewhat conservative core that even nowadays is seen as Wicca proper. The emphasis put on pedigree and orthopraxy implied a high fidelity of the culturally transmitted elements of Britishness that gave rise to the movement in the first place.

When in the 1970s American feminism and deep ecology fused with Wicca, reactionary forces within BTW were quick to dismiss what they saw as unwarranted straying from the original path. The new movements, in turn, did away with what they perceived as the rigid structures of BTW and became theologically eclectic and organizationally egalitarian. Much in the spirit of this age of liberation, new, often non-initiatory groups emerged and freely reassessed and 'reclaimed' the spiritual heritage of what they referred to as 'the old religion' or 'the craft'. More widely, people attracted to earth-based spirituality felt free to appropriate European myths and traditions. Thus Wicca brought forth a broader association of nature spiritualities that go under the umbrella term of contemporary Paganism. These developments, in a nutshell, explain the complex relationship between BTW and strands of the broader Pagan movement that it originally helped to develop. As a consequence, a tension between the perspectives of eclecticism and traditionalism now exists on two levels simultaneously. Firstly, a disparity exists between the original take on Wicca as developed by the British traditionalists and its derivations in both structure and content (Van Gulik 2010). Secondly, both eclecticism and traditionalism seek to root themselves in appropriate ethnic pasts that are as yet too underdetermined and too ill-fitting to easily transpose to cater for the spiritual needs of contemporary individuals. In Wicca this amounts to the reclamation of a pan-European fertility cult, whereas other Pagans paths like Druidry (contemporary Celtic Paganism), Ásatrú (contemporary Germanic Paganism) and Rodnovery (contemporary Slavic Paganism) emphasize a specific ethnicity.

Focusing on religious creativity in the predominantly Flemish Wiccan community called Greencraft, this chapter explores this double tension between eclecticism and traditionalism. The group represents a particularly interesting case with regard to the development and diversification of contemporary Pagan witchcraft on the European continent. On the one hand, Greencraft can be argued to be a part of BTW, in that Greencrafters consider themselves part of the Alexandrian lineage and all follow the original system that comes with this tradition. On the other hand, they have moved far beyond Alexandrian orthodoxy.[1] That is, the network of covens explicitly draws from Celtic mythology and its literary embellishments, and hence maintains a strong link with the ethnic past of the British Isles. Yet Greencraft has also moved beyond exploring this ethnic base by seeking to uncover what are believed to be the universal roots of ancient European nature religions in a way that far exceeds the practices of BTW. Creatively negotiating between ethnic inspirations and cognitively appealing reconfigurations, then, Greencraft represents a compelling case in support of a functionalist perspective on cosmological renewal. The movement thus supports a view on the notion of neo-colonialism that can be recast as a field of tension between traditionalism and eclecticism. The attempted reconciliation between the two can best be illustrated by contributions in the form of Greencraft's Tree Calendar and its correspondences on the one hand, and their experiments and experiences with stone circles on the other. Together, these practices and the system of thought form the 'sticks and stones' of the 'temple' Greencrafters are building in Flanders.

Greencraft

Greencraft Traditional Craft Wicca, as participants call it, was founded in 1991 by Arghuicha and Hera, both initiates of the Dutch branch of Alexandrian Wicca. Important to Greencraft is its manifest, which consists of nine objectives, dubbed the principles of tradition, freedom, ecology, ethics, polarity, pluriformity, non-dogmatism, psychology and folk (Greencraft Creations n.d.). Even though most objectives are in line with BTW, two stand out immediately as particular to Greencraft. Firstly, regarding the principle of ecology, humans, animals, plants and megaliths are explicitly mentioned as Gaia's children, amongst whom Greencraft seeks to 'restore the pact' (Van Gulik 2012a). Secondly, the folk principle refers to Greencraft's objective to create a religion that is open not only to 'priests and priestesses, but also to those that convert to the religion without aspiring to priesthood' (Greencraft Creations n.d.). In addition, the folk principle suggests a motivation to appeal to a larger group of people, seeking to serve and promote the Pagan way of life. Greencraft, then, is more than an association of covens. In Flanders the organization is arguably the primary source of information for anyone with an interest in Wicca, whether these are spiritual seekers, journalists or the general public. Greencraft has helped found what now is her sister organization in the U.S., the Sacred Well Congregation, which is aimed at exclusively supporting the Wiccan community and offers training for priests to conduct open rituals. Nowadays, Sacred Well is also active in Belgium, and seeks to inform non-initiates about Paganism, Wicca and Greencraft, while in Greencraft proper, emphasis is placed on the initiated witches.

In the first five years of the new millennium, Greencraft, like many other Wiccan organizations, noticed a growth in the number of people who wanted to become Wiccans. With the 'witchcraft' hype at a high, mostly youngsters started tinkering with magic. Often ill-informed and without the perseverance to learn the Wiccan ways, the enthusiasm of many a youngster in retrospect seems to have been nothing more than a fad. The leaders of Greencraft, who wanted to keep secure their own enhanced version of Wicca from the untrained but prying eyes of the aspirant new members, responded by introducing one extra hurdle in the three-grade initiation system: the neophyte initiation. Rather than becoming a neophyte after being accepted as an apprentice, as in most initiatory Wiccan traditions, in Greencraft new members first become 'roedies' (that is, rudimentary 'stones'), and get a general Wiccan training with conventional material (De Zutter 1997: 80–81; 2003: 115–16). Only after their initiation as neophytes, to which they must have been invited by their coven leaders, will they have access to the basics of the Greencraft system, which is further developed in the neophyte course. In this fashion, course material and the specific Greencraft system of correspondences are better protected from dissemination by dropouts. However, in the past, when sometimes whole covens left the tradition, Greencraft material was pirated occasionally. This course of affairs has led Greencraft to turn itself into a non-profit corporation that protects its intellectual property as a trademark. Consequently, all Greencraft coven leaders have to apply for a renewable licence to be allowed to teach the Greencraft material.

What sets Greencraft apart from BTW, besides its organizational structure, is its attempt to reconcile Celtic ethnicity with pan-European universalism. This is discussed in the section below and refers to Greencraft's employment of Robert Graves's Tree Calendar (Van Gulik 2012a) and R.J. Stewart's Tree of Life–Tarot correspondence (Stewart 1992).[2] The latter, which is discussed in the subsequent section, concerns the long-standing interest in stone circles, which not only led to frequent visits to sites all over Europe by members of the group, but also inspired them to experiment with these and create their own circles and labyrinths. The discussions of the Tree Calendar and the interest in stone circles are then related to the traditionalism/eclecticism dichotomy with which I seek to deconstruct the term 'neo-colonialism' in the contemporary Pagan context. Finally, the chapter concludes with a discussion of how, on a psychological level, (re)claimed material is internalized and consequently experienced as either collectively or privately owned.

Twisting and Turning Celtic Roots and Branches

In his book *The White Goddess* (1966) the visionary British poet and writer Robert Graves used his literary skills and imagination to lend support to the supposed existence of a Celtic Tree Calendar. Although the calendar itself was not entirely his own invention – the amateur Celtic historian Edward Davis first constructed it on the basis of rather speculative research (De Zutter 1997: 80) – Graves developed the concept according to what he called 'a historical grammar of poetic myth' in an attempt to explain its origin, significance and relation to the Ogham alphabet.[3] In the calendar native European trees and other plants stand as symbols for each synodic month, and Graves expounded on the order of the trees by explaining their folkloric signification in relation to the time of year. Birch, for instance, is placed at the beginning of the year, when the days begin to lengthen. Graves (1966: 166) explains:

> Birch is the tree of inception. It is indeed the earliest forest tree, with the exception of the mysterious elder, to put out new leaves (April 1st in England, the beginning of the financial year), and in Scandinavia its leafing marks the beginning of the agricultural year, because farmers use it as a directory for sowing their spring wheat. The first month begins immediately after the winter solstice, when the days after shortening to the extreme limit begin to lengthen again.

In Greencraft a Celtic Tree Calendar has been adopted with only minor differences from Graves's version (Van Gulik 2012a). Already in Graves is the graphic display of the Tree Calendar in the form of a dolmen, with two standing stones that represent the first four and last four months of a year and the capstone as the middle five months (Figure 10.1).[4] The dolmen, or trilithon, symbolizes the cycle of life, death and rebirth, just as the original stone structure would have been a burial chamber in which a dead hero would await rebirth (Graves 1966: 213). In Greencraft this reference to a personal life cycle has been developed further. Thus the biological and folkloric properties of the trees are partly transformed into spiritual lessons:

> The birch is the pioneer among trees and has its roots in the lunar world of the personal unconscious, but its crown reaches to the solar world of the personal consciousness. The power of Beith [Birch] can help us to

Blackthorn
Ztraiff
Z (SS=Z); IX
Heron, Nuada

expansion and flourishing →

Apple
Quert
Q (CC=Q), V
Swan, Llvr

exploration and introspection

transcendence and introspection

	6	7	8	9	10	
5	**Willow** *Saille* S, XVIII Wolf, Kerridwen 4/4 – 12/5	**Hawthorn** *Huath* (Whitethorn) H, II Bull, Morgaine 12/5 – 9/6	**Oak** *Duir* D, III Horse, Epona 9/6 – 7/7	**Holly** *Tinne* T, XV Ram, Kernwn 7/7 – 4/8	**Hazel** *Koll* K/C, I Raven, Myrddin 4/8 – 1/9	11
4	**Alder** *Vaem* V (F), XXI Bee, Bran 17/3 – 4/4				**Blackberry** *Muin* (Vine) M, XX Ibex, Arianrhod 1/9 – 29/9	12
3	**Ash** *Nion* N, XI (or VIII) Boar, Kreiddvlad 17/2 – 17/3				**Ivy** *Gort* G, XVII Eagle, Brigid 29/9 – 27/10	13
2	**Rowan** *Luis* L, [none] (or XXII) Stag, Nimue 20/1 – 17/2				**Reed** *Peith* P (NG), IV Salmon, Manawyddan 27/10 – 24/11	14
1	**Birch** *Beith* B, XIX Lion, Lush 23/12 – 20/1				**Elder** *Ruis* R, XIII Dragon, Rhiannon 24/11 – 22/12	15
22	**Silver Fir** *Ailm* A, XVI Grouse, Math	**Broom** *(Furze)* *Onn* O, VII Hare, Beli	**Heather** *Ura* U, X Fox, Bloddeuwed	**Poplar** *Eodha* E, VI Owl, Mabon	**Yew** *Iodha* I, XII Salamander, Macha	16

Beech *Fagos* (Palm) F (AA), XIV Otter, Danu	21	20	19	18	17	**Mistletoe** *Ychelwydd* J/Y (II), VIII (or XI) Bear, Gwydion 22/12 – 23/12

Fig. 10.1 *Greencraft's Tree Calendar. Drawn by the author based on Graves (1966: 252) and Delaere (2010: 10). In each square first the English tree name is given in bold, followed by the Celtic name (in italics), then the letter associated with the tree, followed on the same line by the number of the associated tarot card. On the next line are the corresponding animal and deity and finally, where appropriate, the date range of the particular tree. Where trees and letters differ from Graves's system, the latter are provided in parentheses.*

discover possibilities within us and become aware of the hidden talents that we still have to develop. (Hera et al. 2005: 13)

The references to the lunar and solar worlds give away another elaboration of Graves's Celtic Tree Calendar, namely the connection with the Tree of Life from the hermetic Kabbalah that Greencraft has worked out. It should be noted here that although the calendar only comprises thirteen trees, the adapted Ogham alphabet of Graves consists of twenty-two letters. The extra corresponding trees are included in the calendar through the addition of a foundation stone and four trees at the corners. Each of the trees is then related to a path in the Kabbalistic Tree of Life, which consists of twenty-two paths between its ten spheres or sephirot (Figure 10.2). This mapping of one esoteric system onto another is not new. A closely related operation, for instance, was the Tree-of-Life/Tarot interrelation as originally devised by the French occultist Eliphas Levi (1856) in his book *Le Dogme et Rituel de la Haute Magie*. Although Greencraft followed suit, it was on the basis of another correspondence altogether: one that is most often attributed to R.J. Stewart.

The Merlin Tarot developed by Robert J. Stewart (1992) presents another obvious reference to Celtic mythology. With regard to the imagery on the Major Arcana,[5] Stewart's deck resembles the quintessential esoteric tarot deck of Rider-Waite. Only two cards differ between the two systems: the card of the Hierophant in Rider-Waite's deck is replaced with that of the Innocent (represented by a lady on a throne) in Stewart's deck, while the Devil has been replaced by the Guardian (represented by Pan). In the Greencraft Tarot, these cards are called 'Innocence' and 'Horned One' respectively, while Death has been replaced by the White Goddess (see Delaere 2010). Most importantly, however, Greencraft adopted the correspondences between the cards and the paths of the Tree of Life that Stewart used as a whole. These correspondences are entirely different from those originally proposed by Levi and, unbeknownst to most Greencrafters, were originally created by Stewart's one-time mentor, the English occultist William Gray. He argued that the original attributions according to their sequential numbering, regardless of their meaning, was amiss and needed to be recreated from scratch (see Figure 10.2 for an overview of the original and altered path-card associations).

Suppose we start sorting out the Tarot Trumps into sets of homogenous ideas entirely apart from their official numbering. For instance, the Sun, Moon, and Star would go together as astronomical or cosmic phenomena.

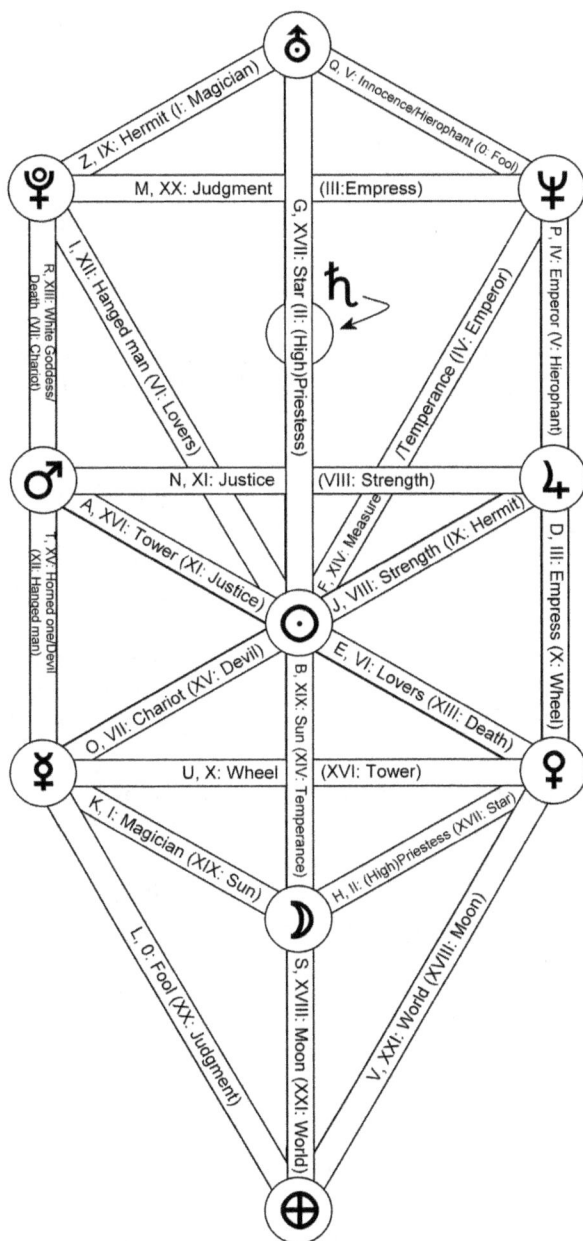

Fig. 10.2 *Tree of Life–Tarot correspondences. Drawn by the author based on Gray (1984: 223) and Delaere (2010: 14). On each path, first the letter of the tree is given, then the (numbered) card according to the Greencraft/Gray system (with the original names, if different, after a slash). The original path-card associations are given in parentheses.*

So would the Emperor, Empress, and Hierophant as external rulers of temporality and religion. Justice, Judgment, and the Wheel of Fortune seem to connect as the workings of karmic laws of compensation and balance. Let us set up a skeleton of the Tree and see if any of these ought to fit anywhere quite naturally. (Gray 1984: 215)

Thus Gray started out by combining the three central vertical paths with the three cosmic cards, while he placed the 'cards of balance' on the three horizontal paths that cross this middle axis. This horizontal/vertical configuration constitutes the skeletal structure of a tree and thus represents a logic of coherence. Then he proceeded to associate the rest of the cards to the remaining paths on the basis of a relationship between the meaning of the card and the field of tension between the sephira that each path forms, which represents a logic of correspondence. Thus, for instance, he put the Blasted Tower on the path between Severity and Beauty 'as anything upsetting balance and harmony in our universe [would be on that path]' (Gray 1984: 219).

Greencraft replaced the Hebrew names of the sephirot with the names of the celestial bodies of our solar system, but both Greencraft and Stewart retained Gray's Tree–Tarot correspondence. Arghuicha explained to me that contemporary Wiccans are often no longer acquainted with the original concepts of the sephirot. Without any prior study of the mystic Kabbalah, terms like Malkuth, Yesod and Hod would just remain abstract notions.

The complete transposition of the nine sephirot into what basically is an astrological model saves the Tree of Life from what is perceived as misguided traditionalism, and becomes an esoteric way to understand the human psyche and its potential developmental paths more easily. With this operation, Greencraft has also rendered the Tree of Life compatible with its elaborate system of archetypal correspondences between various trees, power animals and Celtic runes. The Greencraft Tarot deck is a clear indication of this, since the hermetic symbolism on each of the cards that was present in conventional decks has been changed to fit the Greencraft system, even if most of the ideological meanings have not been altered that much.

What, then, is the appeal of the Tree of Life as a visual system? In an interview (17 January 2012), Arghuicha told me that '[t]he structure of the Kabbalistic Tree of Life is something you find very often. For example, there are pictures from the Norse-Germanic tradition where you find the structure with the different worlds connected by paths. Perhaps that is something that is hard-wired in our brain or consciousness, as a result of which it appeals [to us]'. With the transposition of the sephirot to represent our solar system, the Tree of

Life can also be divided into three parts: the lunar, solar and stellar worlds, which are linked to the respective Jungian terms of personal unconscious, personal conscious and collective conscious. The belief in 'hard-wired' preferences for specific structures resonates well with the Jungian preformist notion of archetypes that has been widely accepted in Wiccan circles. The latter is often employed, as will be discussed below, both to objectify cosmological systems and to validate personal belief.

Stone Circles and Pan-European Universalism

Stone, or rather stones, play an important role in Greencraft. Stones are the oldest children of the Earth Goddess, but humans are the midwives who released them from their bedrock, quarried them, knapped them and erected them or polished them and thus granted them their individuality (Van Gulik 2012a). Although, as with trees, the human–stone relationship must be understood in terms of human agency (that is, what actions can be performed with, through or on trees and stones), both the ethics of these actions and their experiential significance are central. For instance, with regard to ethics, when roedies are asked to make a magical wand from a willow tree, their first task is to make contact with a specific willow and ask permission by meditating at the tree. In addition, when a suitable branch is chosen, it will have to be cut off with a knife that has never been in contact with blood (Hera and Arghuicha 2005). So even though the action is instigated by the person, the tree is treated with respect and an offering is expected to be given in return. Experiential significance, in turn, can be gleaned for instance from the stone-singing ritual. Here participants hold a hand-sized stone near their mouth and sing to it in such a manner that, when one finds the right pitch, the sound is experienced as originating from the stone rather than the person (Van Gulik 2012a).

Arguably more than trees, which can easily be represented as an idea, the significance of stones can best be appreciated outdoors, and mostly in situ where they either have been incorporated into sacred structures in which they have retained their individuality, like stone circles, or have become carriers of artwork and symbols. Place-bound, then, in both cases the stones are thought to either embody or equal the dwelling places of the *genii loci*. Interestingly, when Greencrafters erect new stone circles in permanent places they create for ritual, often located on private land, some make an effort to

Fig. 10.3 *Stone circle on private land created with stones and pebbles gathered from various locations by coven members. The fence was erected for privacy because the ritual space can be partly seen from a nearby road. Photograph by Aria, used with kind permission.*

assemble stones from various locations they have visited (Figure 10.3). Note, however, that the stones they take home are either picked up, or removed from rock beds near the sites, not taken from the structures themselves. The stones vary in size from mere pebbles (5–10 cm diameter) to small rocks (30–40 cm diameter). Following Frazer's law of contagion, this practice is motivated by the idea that a connection with the original location is thus maintained. In addition, soil from each of the newly built stone circles will be distributed among the others, thereby interconnecting Greencraft's own ritual places.

These practices hint at an unresolved tension between topophilia and idealism. Topophilia manifests itself as an implicit belief in what could be called the formal integrity of stones, which refers to their embeddedness in a specific circle in a specific landscape. With regard to substantive integrity, stones are understood as embodying their own essence, which allows for novel arrangements of single stones to create distinctly new structures. Illustrative with regard to this tension are Arghuicha's narratives about his visits to ancient sites. Take, for instance, this quote from his *Pilgrimage to Alba* (Alba is the Scottish Gaelic name for Scotland):

> Alas, the understandable preoccupation of the people of Alba with the traumas of their recent past often blinds their eyes to the true greatness of Alba and the heritage from a far remoter past, the glory of DalRiada and

the Picts and beyond that, the Stone Circles and Standing Stones from the people of the Oceanic Rim whose building only enhanced the sacredness of Alba's landscape instead of destroying it. (Arghuicha 2002: 9)

Here is an example of how Greencrafters position themselves between the imagined builders of specific structures in the landscape, which have since become cultural heritage, and the people who now inhabit the vicinity of these sacred places. I have heard numerous other instances of this self-appointed stewardship: from criticizing the building of a shed near the ancient stones to observing the neglect of sites where trees have been allowed to grow inside the circle, and even in Greencrafters' description of the out-of-place-ness of partying youngsters and their loud music. In the rare cases that locals are mentioned specifically in relationship to the sacred structures, their misguided care is emphasized – the local priority is to preserve the materiality of the stones somewhat like a museum exhibit, rather than allow them to be a place for pilgrimage or other contemporary sacred purposes.

When visiting the thirteen stone circles of Węsiory in Poland, for instance, a small group of third-degree Greencrafters resorted to bribing a local caretaker with 100 złoty to gain access to the site at night. They locked the fence, so as not to be disturbed while engaging in ritual and meditation. In an interview, Arghuicha told me that '[y]ou are not allowed to do much with the stones, because lichen grows on them, and these are delicate and protected, and therefore you are not allowed to touch [the stones]. And of course we did want to touch them!' One of the things Arghuicha and his fellow Greencrafters did was meditate on the stones to see if they could learn something about their purpose or history. Arghuicha explained what he experienced:

There were many stories locally about so and so has been [at these circles] during the night, and [ran] away screaming because he or she suddenly saw the shade of a Gothic warrior.... [The Goths] were there for a few years on their trek from Gotland to the Black Sea.... So there was a lot of fear, many people told us that they wouldn't dare to walk there at night.... The strange thing was that we didn't ... feel any fear. I had an [encounter] with what I like to call a Gothic princess, for lack of a better description, and the only thing that emanated from her was an enormous feeling of wistfulness [as if she said]: 'My people have moved away and I have remained here because of circumstances. I don't know what happened to them.' ... I had a strong feeling that ... the Goths, when they were there[,] ... used the stone circles [to bury] their kings and important people in such a manner that their spirits are bound to that spot, and remain there. Which is handy, if you want to consult them.

Quotes like these suggest that although the locals take care in preserving the site, according to the Greencrafters they do so for the wrong reason, because the stones need to be used for communication: in this case, making contact with the deceased. Important in this respect is the fact that while the Goths were not the builders of the circles, they put them to use in a similar manner to that which Greencrafters believe was intended by their original creators.

Besides ritual and meditation, Greencrafters also engage in various experiments using circles like these and other stone structures. At Węsiory they noticed in one circle that what had been thought to be the position of a missing stone was in fact too small to have held one. Arghuicha explained (interview, 17 January 2012):

> Typical [of some stone circles in Poland] is that there is a sort of circular pavement round each stone made from smaller rocks. [There is such a frame] around all the stones in the circle, also at the place where the stone is missing.... Only that frame is too small to have held a stone of the same size.... There must be a reason for that.... So we experimented ... [w]ith a few people round the omphalus activating it, with one person standing at the place of the so-called missing stone, who has to pass the energy of the stone next to him to the stone on his other side.... Something that kept happening was that the person who stood there could hardly get out of it afterwards.

These and many other experiments they conducted have led to the Greencrafters' theory that the stone circles across Europe can be used as giant centres of telepathic communication. Together with the Sacred Well Congregation, Greencrafters have even built various structures in the U.S., including a stone circle and a Cassini oval on private land in Texas.[6] The most important observation to make is that the experimentation with stone circles implies not only a revived usage of these ancient structures and the construction of new ones, but also a complex relation between the motives of traditionalism and eclecticism. This clash between the formal and substantive integrity of the stones is best showcased in an excerpt from *Pilgrimage to Alba* (Arghuicha 2002: 11):

> [T]heir only hope lies in forming a bond with the Stone Circles that are our own: so that they can be part of this great adventure that is our magnum opus. So I promised them [the stones] songs and dances and the sharing of souls and asked for their alliance in our undertaking. And as I opened my soul to them I felt the flux of their soul flowing into me, binding me to Alba forever: for that is the price that must be paid. And so my song became the song of Alba. I pleaded with them and cajoled

them, I sang and I cried and I howled. And went around once more in zigzag, slapping them and shaking them fully awake in sacred exhortation. And from this time on, with every Stone Circle we visited, I projected a mental image of our own Stone Circles, binding them to it: for through this bond, whenever we sing and dance in our Stone Circles, they can be part of it.

From the observation that the 'only hope' for the stone configurations to release their power is to recreate their essences in the newly built structures of Greencraft, while in the process the 'activating' person becomes bound to the original location of the circle, it must be concluded that this very act of transposition cannot bring closure. On the other hand, the observation helps us understand how neo-colonialism might be deconstructed into a complex of beliefs and motives that can be traced back via their collective manifestation of criteria of eclecticism, to which this chapter now turns, to their individual disposition, with which the chapter will conclude.

Criteria of Eclecticism and Implications for Neo-colonialism

So far this chapter has offered an overview of Greencraft's additions to the original Alexandrian lineage in Wicca with an eye to explaining the two-layered field of tension between traditionalism and eclecticism. The first layer of tension has to do with different takes on orthodoxy in Wicca. Greencraft cannot be pigeonholed into either perspective, since, as explained above, they both observe the practices of the Alexandrian branch and are developing their own system, which, even if it includes what is considered initiatory Wiccan material, belies a broad but ethnically sensitive Pagan outlook. Greencraft's system, then, belongs to the second layer as well. To specify the role of ethnicity, the perspectives of traditionalism and eclecticism are expounded on here as reconstructionism and revivalism respectively.

Bowman (1996: 244) suggests that whereas reconstructionists seek to replicate the past with high fidelity, revivalists aim at reinvigoration by any means necessary. In Greencraft the adoption of the Celtic Tree Calendar and the Tree-of-Life/Tarot correspondences have been shown above to rely as much on already developed innovations to both esoteric and Celtic material as on the novel recombination of these. Analogously, I have also discussed the unresolved position toward stones as 'individuals' that are featured in both the megalithic

stone circles of Europe and Greencraft's own newly created structures. In other words, with regard to both the 'sticks' and 'stones' of
the 'temple' Greencrafters are building, elements of reconstructionism and revivalism can be found in both the cosmological system and
the refiguring of ethnic roots.

I have discussed the traditionalism/eclecticism dichotomy previously (Van Gulik 2010), but here this tension will be discussed on
a collective, rather than individual, level and limited to initiatory
Wicca. Consequently, the emphasis has shifted from the motives
derived from the personal 'true Will' as the driving force behind religious renewal to consensual efforts after meaning[7] and protocols for
the adoption of novel elements in the shared cosmological system.
Where, then, should the line be drawn between traditionalism and
eclecticism in Greencraft, and how do Greencrafters' motives relate
to neo-nationalism and neo-colonialism?

At first glance, one would assume that Greencraft is engaged in
the discovery and reconstruction of purported esoteric aspects of
traditional Celticism. A prime example would be the adoption of
the so-called 'Celtic runes' that were featured in a course from the
'Temple of Danann', a contemporary Pagan group led by Michael
Ragan. Both these runes and their explanations were seen as material
for internal use only, but later Greencrafters were granted permission
to use them in their own system. According to Arghuicha, Ragan
assumed these runes were hinted at in ancient Irish texts and were
allegedly used strictly by the Celtic priesthood as a sacred counterpart of the secular Ogham script (Delaere 2010: 198–99). However,
there is no evidence for these runes from an academic perspective and
even some emic sources seem to frown upon what is regarded as a
blatant invention.

Regardless of this critique, though, most coven leaders in
Greencraft would argue that they are not after literal, but spiritual
truths. I have treated this line of argument elsewhere (Van Gulik
2012a), referring to it as the need for the suspension of disbelief in
order to secure attunement with the sacred world, which, after all,
is mediated through these symbols. Beside the notion of spiritual
truths, a second limitation of traditionalism has been put forward
in Greencraft: the dynamism of myth. Since myth is argued to be
subject to historical contingency, attributes and characteristics of
the Gods shift as a function of their growing or diminishing importance. As a result, in the absence of a single 'correct version' of the
story, the system builders in Greencraft feel relatively free to redis-
tribute the stones, runes, animals, Gods, tarot cards and objects in

their structure – relatively, because there are criteria both explicit and implicit that limit the degrees of freedom in the system.

After careful scrutiny, these criteria prevent the conclusion being drawn that Greencraft would count as purely revivalist. Where the two limitations of traditionalism may have contributed to justifying the creative invention of cosmological material, the criteria to which these are subject can be thought of as restrictions on eclecticism. Firstly, Greencrafters aim at making their system ethnically commensurate in that they combine elements that are either allegedly Celtic in origin (for example, the Gods, the runes) or at least indigenous to northern Europe (for example, the animals, the stones). This aspect encompasses perhaps the most blatant link with neo-colonialism, considering the various responses of critics of this kind of postmodern bricolage of cultural material. In the literature about contemporary Pagan use of ethnic material, often the case of Native American cultures is discussed (e.g. Magliocco 2004: 215–18; Pike 2001: 134–37). Depending on the Native American group, allegations of cultural imperialism by Pagans are phrased as 'borrowing', 'appropriating', 'strip-mining' or even 'stealing' (Magliocco 2004: 216).

In Europe, however, the relationship between the appropriated culture and the appropriating group is vastly different. A two-sided relationship between the guardians of Celtic heritage and Greencraft exists. Insofar as the guardians are themselves contemporary Pagans from the areas that are mostly associated with Celtic culture – Scotland, Ireland, Wales, Cornwall, the Isle of Man and Brittany – these 'ethnic' Pagans could accuse any foreigner of cultural imperialism. Be that as it may, their own ethnic links with the Celts may be conveniently assumed, rather than established beyond reasonable doubt, for these geographical areas have, to different extents, been subject to centuries of migration. As well as favouring the particular, postmodern rendition of Celticity of these Pagans, this neo-nationalist claim of ethnicity seems like an argument dusted down for the occasion, for in no way could they uphold an image of authentic Celticity, since that culture has long since vanished. Also, the position of these 'Celtic' Pagans relies on the implicit assumption that the Celtic world coincides only with these six remaining Celtic countries, whereas the original area of distribution of the Celtic tribes encompassed the greater parts of western and central Europe.

In turn, another group of outspoken stakeholders, Celtic scholars, attests that what constitutes Celtic culture proper belongs to the past – a past whose correct interpretation is monopolized by this very group. Celticity, then, can be considered as foremost a matter of the heart, rather than the mind, a position most aptly named by Marion Bowman (1996: 246) as that of the 'cardiac Celt', where 'spiritual nationality is a matter of elective affinity'. Still, the emphasis put by Greencraft on their system in its entirety suggests that the Celtic elements in it merely represent a pleasing aesthetic of ethnic unity. Being closely linked to the history of the English-speaking world, with its vast impact on popular culture, the appropriation of Celtic heritage since the 1970s created a lock-in effect, in that its look and feel have now become the leading aesthetic in Pagan practice.

Moving beyond ethnic commensurability as the external logic of coherence in Greencraft's system, the second restriction on eclecticism is an internal logic: the need for the cosmology to be systematically consistent within Greencraft by elaborating on mythic, etymological, logical and/or traditional connections between its various elements.[8] The term 'cosmology' here refers to the whole of the religiously acknowledged elements that make up a specific level of reality, their interrelations, and, in turn, the interrelations among (what are believed to be) multiple levels of reality. Thus a cosmology constitutes a rationale for both the emergence and development (and perhaps even dissolution) of the reality of our life world. Among the guiding principles of the reformation of these bits and pieces of source material into a coherent cosmology are aesthetics of symmetry, elegance, parsimony and balance on different levels. Thus when there were twenty-two – no more, no fewer – deities chosen for the Greencraft system, they needed to be divided equally into eleven males and eleven females to balance gender, while still remaining fit to be superimposed on the paths of the Tree of Life.

Matters become even more complicated since within the (super) system each deity also needs to become associated with a tree, an animal and a rune. Each (sub)system of these various elements, however, is different, and also the mythic, etymological, logical and/ or traditional connections between the elements across the various subsystems often point in different directions. Integrating these in a coherent supersystem, then, is not unlike trying to solve a Rubik's Cube. For instance, alder now is associated with bee, whereas it could also have been associated with raven, given the fact that linguistically 'raven' is identical to (the deity) 'Bran'. However, in that case 'bee' would have to go with another tree and there might be no mythological justification for that. Examples like this show that much of the work in building the cosmology consists of looking for an optimum fit between incompatible choices, while aiming for an elegant yet complete superstructure.

The internal logic of coherence here turns into one of correspondence, which is the third restriction on eclecticism. The supersystem as a whole needs to become cosmologically exhaustive. That is, even if the chosen elements in the system cohere and amount to an intelligible structure, the structure as a whole must represent a complete cosmology in that it constitutes a well-rounded whole in which systemic elements such as the different levels of consciousness, attributes, challenges, professions, social relationships, class, bodily functions, ways of knowing and so forth have their place. A one-dimensional example would be the four trumps of the Tarot as representative of the four traditional social classes: farmers, craftsmen, clergy and nobility. Another straightforward illustration is that of the four elements – earth, water, fire and air – that together make up the whole of the physical universe.

In turn, this internal logic of correspondence is mirrored by its external counterpart. That is, whereas a cosmology needs to be exhaustive, in that it offers a complete perspective of sacred reality, it also needs to correspond to the mundane world without. An infinite number of relationships between humans and their world, then, need to be expressible with this finite set of cosmological elements by the latter being representationally generative. In Greencraft's case, for instance, any name can be related to the system by means of numerological transposition, whereas each date can be linked to a specific animal and tree: for example, 'the Bear in the moon of Hawthorne', which in turn has an astrological bearing. To conclude this chapter, the process of coupling the collective sacred world to the personal mundane world will be discussed.

Conclusion: Towards a Cultural Psychology of Appropriation

Although both internal and correspondence-based criteria for eclecticism are sympathetic to a psychological understanding of the eclecticism/traditionalism dichotomy, representational generativity in particular has the potential to cross the bridge between a shared cosmology and a single person. Herein lies the key to the deconstruction of neo-colonialism into motives of eclecticism and traditionalism. The notion of neo-colonialism implies a sympathy for the 'victim' of appropriation, or at least puts an emphasis on the out-of-place-ness of the used cultural material. While this is a valid anthropological argument, it may prevent an understanding of the culprit's rationale for the appropriation.

Interestingly, the charges of 'strip-mining' and 'stealing' mentioned earlier, made by Native Americans with regard to cultural appropriation, imply that in an economic sense, culture consists of both rivalrous and excludable goods. In contrast, the other two forms of cultural imperialism of which Pagans have been accused – 'borrowing' and 'appropriating' – at least leave room for non-rivalry, meaning that the goods still can be 'consumed' by the original owner. In that sense, these charges brought against the contemporary use of ethnic material belie the dual understanding of culture as both a possessable and as a possessing entity, as Magliocco (2004: 216) also suggests. These two understandings are analogous to the fundamental distinction made in cultural psychology between substantive ('What does it consist of?') and formal or functional ('How does it work?') definitions of culture. The dichotomy of transmitted and evoked culture (see, e.g., Nettle 2009) is of particular interest here. Whereas culture may be seen as the body of transmitted information, what ultimately will spread, and how, is argued to depend on the specific sociocultural context, perennial human needs and/or our evolutionary heritage. For the present purposes I will focus on the contemporary Pagan context of the two-way relationship between transmitted and evoked culture.

First, the creation of a unique configuration of existing and cultural material as a way for minority groups like Wiccans to carve a niche in society entails a move from transmission to evocation. That is, the systematization of this appropriated material often involves processes of reassessment, bricolage, socialization and, eventually, concealment. In the institutionalization of secrecy, the system of beliefs and practices in which the once freely accessible material is incorporated becomes guarded or 'oath-bound' (that is, available only to initiates), and by that very act the appropriated material it is comprised of will eventually become perceived as being owned by the group (Van Gulik 2012b).

This process of 'mesocolonization' creates a cultural landscape where various traditions simultaneously may seek to distinguish themselves from society at large, and from each other. In turn, adherents are required to show allegiance to the tradition of their choice either implicitly or explicitly by upholding secrecy, or by socialization into a logic narrative of justification of the particular adaptations of the appropriated material in their group. In the case of Greencraft, a well-developed socialization process of gradual disclosure, oaths of secrecy and creating emotional attachments to the religious material prevents or limits deviation from acceptable interpretations of the system. Eventually, the whole becomes self-referential, when new experiences or material become related to the incumbent system. Moving towards a state of immunity to alternative understandings or critique, the group can create its own conditions for the emergence, transmission and transformation of culture.

Secondly, the movement from evoked to transmitted culture is typically framed in the language of Jungian archetypes. A reference to archetypes is perhaps the strongest means of objectifying, and thereby 'microcolonizing', religious material and justifying its particular usage. The concept of collective unconscious as the repository of archetypes turns culturally specific material into public property. In addition, the archetype is a 'quality check'. This holds for both group and individual. For instance, when the material surfaces in dreams, meditations or religiously inspired interpretations of life events, a successful explanation in terms of Jungian archetypes not only enhances the value of the personal life (one is living one's own myth), but also grants validity to the system in which the material is incorporated. In Greencraft, new material that cannot be incorporated logically will typically become the subject matter of a guided meditation to check its appropriateness. As part of the shared endeavour, having a shared understanding of the significance is important. Perhaps here a logic of consensus applies. However, archetypal objectification of mental states may also introduce the problem of self-validation of belief, which might lead members astray. Here the delicate fabric of collectively established meanings and interrelations that defines a unique and intricate combination of eclecticism and traditionalism can easily be torn apart and turn into the idiosyncrasies of capricious and striding individuals.

While the relationship between neo-colonialism and contemporary Paganism seems evident (just as the relationship between neo-nationalism and ethnic Paganism can be assumed), Greencraft presents a somewhat difficult case. Even if its Alexandrian lineage, and thus relationship to BTW, is maintained, Greencraft has steered clear of a closely knitted social structure and Wiccan imperialism. Instead, Greencrafters have developed into a spiritually semi-independent group with a keen interest in building their own complementary system. Even if their borrowing of Celtic material looks like cultural imperialism, Greencraft's deepest interests reach far beyond ethnic association. While their extensive bricolage of Celtic culture and elements from esoteric cosmologies may be mistaken for random appropriation, their reconstructions are in fact coherent and do not solely rely on either rationality or experience, but on the creative intermarriage of the two. On the tightrope between eclecticism and traditionalism, then, Greencraft's relationship with religious and cultural material is multifaceted and not without unresolved tensions. Colonizers themselves as much as colonized, collectors of material but subject to a system of their own making, a collective as much as a group of individuals, Greencrafters perpetuate a creative imbalance they can constantly feed off while building their 'temple' in Flanders.

Notes

1 Greencraft's alleged membership of BTW is not undisputed. However, as there is no central authority in Wicca, no definitive claim for or against membership can be made.

2 For reasons of brevity, only one of the two other important aspects of the Greencraft system will be discussed, in passing, towards the end of the chapter: the acceptance of Michael Ragan's 'Celtic runes', which were presented by him to be used esoterically within Greencraft (Delaere 2010: 199). Greencraft's profound revision of the Thirteen Treasures of the Island of Britain will not be treated here.

3 The alleged connection between the trees of the calendar and the letters of the script, however, had already been suggested in early modern times by scholars in the so-called arboreal tradition. While some of the letters indeed have a link with the tree names, modern scholarship has only established this link for eight trees at most, while all the other etymological explanations are considered too far-fetched (see, for example, McManus 1988).

4 The idea of thirteen months is derived from Graves's (1966: 166) argument that a true lunar month is 28 days long. This would allow for thirteen months per year, leaving one (or two) so-called 'Day/s of Liberation' (ibid., 249) designated to a 'tree that is no tree, on a day that is no day, at an hour that is no hour, at a place that is no place: Mistletoe' (Hera, Arghuicha, Kara, and Lupus 2005: 4).

5 The Tarot consists of the Major and Minor Arcana. The latter, sometimes called suit cards, are divided into the court cards and the numeral cards and together much resemble modern playing cards. In the Major Arcana, sometimes referred to as trumps, each card contains a symbolic or allegorical picture, the meaning of which is sometimes considered secret (Kaplan 1978).

6 A Cassini oval is a geometrical figure that is (in this case) closely related to the lemniscate (∞), a symbol of infinity.
7 'Effort after meaning' is a psychological term coined by C.F. Bartlett.
8 C.f. Brach and Hanegraaff (2005). They argue that a religious cosmology extends both vertically and horizontally. An example of a vertical extension or universal analogy is the idea that the microcosmos of humanity is a mirror image of the macrocosmos of the divine order. Horizontal extensions, which are also called correspondences, entail the associations between sets of elements like animals, deities, attributes, numbers and so forth.

References

Arghuicha. 2002. *Pilgrimage to Alba*. Hulst: Greencraft Creations.
Bowman, M. 1996. 'Cardiac Celts: Images of the Celts in Paganism', in G. Harvey and C. Hardman (eds), *Pagan Pathways: A Guide to the Earth Traditions*. London: Thorsons, pp. 242–51.
Brach, J.-P. and W.J. Hanegraaff. 2005. 'Correspondences', in W.J. Hanegraaff (ed.), *Dictionary of Gnosis and Western Esotericism*. Leiden: Brill, vol 1, pp. 275–79.
De Zutter, J. 1997. *Abracadabra: Lexicon van de Moderne Hekserij* [Abracadabra: Lexicon of Modern Witchcraft]. Antwerp: Hadewijch.
——. 2003. *Eko Eko: Een Halve Eeuw Wicca* [Eko Eko: Half a Century of Wicca]. Antwerp: Houtekiet.
Delaere, R. 2010. *Greencraft Tarot*. San Antonio: New Gaia Press.
Graves, R. 1966. *The White Goddess: A Historical Grammar of Poetic Myth*, Amended and enlarged edn. New York: Farrar, Straus and Giraux.
Gray, W.G. 1984. *Concepts of Qabalah*. York Beach: Samual Weiser.
Greencraft Creations. N.d. *Greencraft Manifest*. Retrieved 5 April 2012 from http://www.greencraftwicca.org/englishgreencraftmanifest.html.
Hera and Arghuicha. 2005. *Greencraft Wicca Course Roedi*. Hulst: Greencraft Creations.
Hera, Arghuicha, Kara, and Lupus. 2005. *Greencraft Handleiding Boomwandelingen* [Greencraft Manual Tree Walks]. Hulst: Greencraft Creations.
Kaplan, S.R. 1978. *The Encyclopedia of Tarot*, Vol. 1. Stamford: U.S. Games Systems.
Levi, E. 1856. *Dogme et Rituel de la Haute Magie*. Paris: Germer Baillière.
Magliocco, S. 2004. *Witching Culture: Folklore and Neo-Paganism in America*. Philadelphia: University of Pennsylvania Press.
McManus, D. 1988. 'Irish Letter-Names and their Kennings', *Ériu* 39: 127–68.

Nettle, D. 2009. 'Beyond Nature Versus Culture: Cultural Variation as an Evolved Characteristic', *Journal of the Royal Anthropological Institute* 15(2): 223–40.

Pike, S.M. 2001. *Earthly Bodies, Magical Selves: Contemporary Pagans and the Search for Community*. Berkeley: University of California Press.

Stewart, R.J. 1992. *The Merlin Tarot Handbook*. London: Aquarian.

Van Gulik, L.A. 2010. 'On the Pagan Parallax: A Sociocultural Exploration of the Tension between Eclecticism and Traditionalism as Observed among Dutch Wiccans', *The Pomegranate: The International Journal of Pagan Studies* 12(1): 49–70.

———. 2012a. 'The Scholar versus the Pagan on Greencraft Tree Walks: Attunement, Imagination, Interpretation', *Traditiones* 41(1): 47–63.

———. 2012b. 'Cleanliness is next to Godliness, but Oaths are for Horses: Antecedents and Consequences of the Institutionalization of Secrecy in Initiatory Wicca', *The Pomegranate: The International Journal of Pagan Studies* 14(2): 233–55.

11

Iberian Paganism

Goddess Spirituality in Spain and Portugal and the Quest for Authenticity

Anna Fedele

Introduction

On a warm autumn day in 2009 I was taking some pictures of the small building in a suburb in Lisbon where I had been attending workshops and rituals during my fieldwork about Goddess spirituality in Portugal. I had arrived too early for a workshop on the Sacred Feminine and was using the occasion to take some pictures of the spiritual centre and its surrounding neighbourhood. I became gradually aware that two elderly women I had passed on the street some minutes before were watching me from a distance and talking animatedly. After some time a third, somewhat younger woman joined their conversation, looked intently at me and then walked towards me with a gentle smile on her face. Pointing towards the workshop building, she asked me: 'You are one of the folks of this house, aren't you?' Somewhat puzzled I explained that I had arrived early for a workshop and that as I liked the paintings on the walls of the centre and also the surrounding area I was taking some pictures. Relieved and triumphant, the woman exclaimed: 'I knew it, I could tell from the way you are dressed! And I told those two ladies, "She is one of these girls from that house; they are peaceful people"'. While I was self-consciously looking at my long skirt and the long shawl I had resolved to wear for the occasion, the woman continued: 'I know them; one of the girls who leads this centre grew up in the neighbourhood; they do harmless activities, such as yoga and belly dancing; they are very friendly'. After some small talk about my being Italian and my Portuguese improving, the woman added that she was sorry about the older women's behaviour. She added that I had to understand that their neighbourhood was like a small village where everybody knows everybody and people worry about strangers, possible robberies and foreign religious habits.

This ethnographic vignette offers a good example of the difficulties faced by groups practising forms of contemporary spirituality not only in Portugal, but also in other countries of southern Europe such as Spain or Italy where Catholicism is still considered the official religion and new religious movements are easily labelled as dangerous sects.[1] This chapter draws on fieldwork about the Goddess spirituality movement in Spain and Portugal to analyse the peculiarities of Iberian Paganism.[2] The tensions between local forms of Goddess worship and Pagan traditions imported from the United States and Britain are discussed. Taking as an example the case of the Goddess Conference in Spain, I will argue that in order to be accepted by Iberian Pagans these 'Anglo-traditions' need to be adapted through a process of cultural and religious translation that takes into account different factors, such as their Catholic background, their need for secretiveness and their fear of criticism and even stigmatization.[3]

This adaptation process usually happens through local leaders who act as cultural and religious mediators and transform Goddess spirituality theories for their southern European public. An analysis of their adapted theories and rituals and their criticism of imported British and American Paganisms offers insights into processes of religious colonization and resistance at an historical moment when contemporary Pagan movements are gradually gaining increased public visibility in mainland Europe, and yearly 'Goddess Conferences' are being celebrated not only in Glastonbury (in the United Kingdom), but also in Germany, Spain, Hungary, Sweden, the Netherlands, Australia and Argentina.

The way in which the Goddess Conference package is transplanted from Britain to other countries offers a good example of the way in which Pagans negotiate the tensions between local, cultural or national identities and wider, international and increasingly globalized influences. There are constant efforts to construct forms of Paganism that are perceived as indigenous and therefore authentic, but there is also the wish to connect with a wider, international Pagan movement (see Bowman 2009; and Rountree 2010 and this volume). This phenomenon is particularly interesting in the context of traditionally Catholic countries such as Spain and Portugal, where English is not widely spoken and there seems to be a well-developed resistance towards what is often perceived as an Anglo-imperialism that does not take into account local specificities. As will be discussed, this process of resistance is particularly evident among 'heterodox' Pagan groups that are loosely structured and do not identify with a specific international Pagan tradition.

Iberian Paganism

As the religious historian Ronald Hutton has shown (1999), even if most contemporary Pagans consider themselves as part of a revitalization process of pre-Christian nature religions, their beliefs and practices are more recent and started to circulate in the 1960s in Great Britain and North America. Contemporary Pagans tend to criticize institutionalized religions, and particularly Christianity, as patriarchal and misogynist and believe that the conceptualization of the body as sinful has led members of Judaeo-Christian religions to despise the material world and perceive their sexuality as sinful. This rejection and denigration of body and matter is, according to Pagans, one of the principal causes not only of the current ecological disaster, but also of widespread sexual perversions such as child abuse and the rape of women. In order to create a safer world and foster an environmentally friendly attitude, Pagans advocate a sacralization of the body and sexuality and a conceptualization of planet Earth as inhabited by divine forces.

Pagans want to create non-hierarchical, gender-equal communities, based on a deep respect for nature and for each other's beliefs and choices. For analytical purposes contemporary Pagan movements have sometimes been united by social scientists and religious historians under the umbrella term 'Neopaganism', but so far no consensus about terminology has been reached. Movements considered under the umbrella range from neo-shamanic groups revitalizing Native American or other shamanic traditions,[4] to groups that have been described as part of a 'feminist spirituality' movement (Eller 1993), to a variety of witchcraft groups, as well as contemporary Druids and Isis fellowships.[5]

Not all social actors described by social scientists as Neopagans or contemporary Pagans would necessarily call themselves 'Pagans' and this is particularly the case in southern Europe (Fedele 2013b). Those following Pagan theories and practices in Italy, Spain or Portugal do not seem to share with their North American equivalents the need to form associations (see Berger, Davie and Fokas 2008: 14); they often do not belong to any religious organization and refuse to identify with a precise religious movement.

My Iberian interlocutors had been brought up as Catholics and many of them stated that they were not 'religious' but 'spiritual'.[6] They did not like the idea of joining an established religion again and seemed thereby to follow a trend in contemporary religiosity also common in North America and Europe (Heelas and Woodhead 2005; Berger, Davie and Fokas 2008: 14).[7] The women and few men I encountered during my fieldwork had been disappointed, and sometimes even wounded (Fedele 2013a: 191–216), by what they described as 'the Church' and therefore preferred the word 'spirituality' to 'religion' (Fedele 2009; Knibbe 2013; Fedele and Knibbe 2013). In fact, as can easily be deduced from the ethnographic vignette that opens this chapter, many of my interlocutors preferred to be secretive about their spiritual theories and practices. They often felt watched and judged by their colleagues or neighbours and found that their spirituality could be easily misunderstood by their Catholic families and by the wider social environment. For all these reasons my interlocutors preferred to describe themselves as part of 'Goddess spirituality' rather than a religion called 'Paganism'. My latest findings show that my interlocutors' fears were well founded. Between 2011 and 2012 some spiritual leaders I had interviewed in Italy and Spain told me that their groups had been investigated by the police to determine whether they were sects and to make sure that their activities were not related to Satanist rituals or did not include brainwashing methods.

Workshops related to Goddess spirituality in Portugal and Spain tend to be organized in an informal way (that is, having no legal visibility). Once the workshops start attracting a significant number of people and gaining social visibility, the most common solution is to create a non-profit organization. A good example of this constant need for discretion is the group whose workshop I was about to attend in the vignette that opens this chapter. It had a very general name that did not reveal its relationship with religion or spirituality, let alone Paganism. I will call it here: 'international association fostering human creativity'. The group's activities took place in an area of Lisbon where people still have small gardens in their backyards, know each other and stop to talk with neighbours on the street. The members of the association were attentive not to upset the neighbourhood and tended to describe their activities with labels such as 'yoga' or 'belly dancing' that were more related to leisure and health than spirituality.

I found that even though in Portugal there were some spiritual leaders who openly stated their commitment to the international Goddess movement and promoted their rituals and celebrations online, other groups and solitary practitioners of Goddess spirituality tended to be very protective, especially when promoting their events or describing their associations. They tend to use neutral terms such as 'cultural association' or 'development seminar', and it is only by reading in detail the description of an event, visiting a group's website or participating in their activities that one can see how the contents are clearly related to the Goddess movement.

In Spain I was mainly in touch with a women's spirituality group based in Barcelona that here will be called Goddess Wood (Fedele 2013a, 2013c, 2014a). It had been founded in 2002 by an Argentinean woman in her early fifties called Dana and was one the largest and fastest growing in Catalonia, and probably in the whole of Spain. At the start of this fieldwork in 2004, Goddess Wood comprised up to three hundred women from different areas of the Spanish state who participated now and then in rituals or workshops organized by Dana. A group of thirty to forty committed members regularly attended the group's activities. Goddess Wood had monthly gatherings for the celebration of each new moon and the most important ceremonies were the annual initiation ritual at the beginning of February and the 'pilgrimage of the blood' (Fedele 2013a, 2014a) organized every second summer. At the beginning, the group's activities were organized in an informal way, but the group has grown both in terms of participation and of social visibility and Dana has therefore created a cultural association that gives a legal background to the group. Goddess Wood members are spread all over Spain and monthly gatherings to celebrate the new moon are regularly held by local groups in a number of Spanish cities and towns.

Dana often observed that even though she enjoyed reading English 'classics of Goddess spirituality' such as Starhawk's or Diane Stein's books, she did not feel at ease using terms such as 'witch' or 'Pagan'. She felt that the rituals they described could offer a starting point, but needed to be adapted to the Iberian context. Talking about her book project, Dana observed that there were English books about the Goddess and that since the late 1990s Spanish authors had also written about women's spirituality, but she wanted to write about the 'Christian Goddess'. In her opinion women in Europe, especially those living in traditionally Catholic countries such as Spain, could not and should not dismiss their 'Christian cultural heritage'. According to Dana, women with an important Christian background

244 ◆ Anna Fedele

in Europe and also in Latin America could reinterpret it and thereby use it to create their own personal contact with the Goddess.[8] While refusing the negative concepts related to gender, corporeality and sexuality they had received in childhood, the Iberian women I encountered did not entirely refuse their Catholic background and reinterpreted Christian figures such as Jesus, the Virgin Mary and Mary Magdalene (Fedele 2013a). They found that Goddess spirituality allowed them to address problems related to sexuality and gender that were considered taboo in the Catholic environment in which they grew up.

Inversions of Christianity and the Importance of Uncertainty

Since 2002 I have been researching the spread of contemporary spirituality in Italy, Spain and Portugal with a particular focus on Goddess spirituality. For my doctoral dissertation I focused on pilgrimages to Catholic shrines in France related to Saint Mary Magdalene or to 'Black Madonnas' (Fedele 2013a). Although their pilgrimage leaders (from the United Kingdom, Italy and Argentina) had quite different spiritual backgrounds and approaches, the pilgrims I accompanied (coming from Spain, Italy, the United Kingdom and the United States) shared spiritual ideas and practices related to contemporary Paganism internationally, but also to contemporary spirituality more generally, or what is often referred to as 'New Age' spirituality.[9] My research was based on participant observation, informal conversations, loosely structured interviews and the recollection of life stories. I found that many of my interlocutors initially tended to have a defensive attitude because they were conscious of common critiques about their kind of religiosity as self-indulgent and consumerist. Because of this I believe that it is only through participant observation, the recollection of life stories and in-depth, open interviews that social scientists can gain access to the complexities of contemporary spirituality (see Bender 2010).

As Marion Bowman observed in her long-term research about 'integrative spirituality' in Glastonbury (2009; see also Bowman 1993, 2004a, 2004b, 2005 and 2008), although they often fiercely criticize Christian religion and established religions more generally, Goddess spirituality practitioners incorporate many Christian and especially Catholic elements. I found that Catholicism, with its many saints, its emphasis on the cult of the Virgin Mary and its complex

rituals and colourful processions, is particularly apt for Pagan rein-
terpretations. In this context the Virgin Mary appears as the Goddess
disguised under Christian robes, and Black Madonnas appear as survivals of ancient Goddess figurines and ultimately as the representation of Mother Earth (Fedele 2013c). My interlocutors considered
Christian saints to be Christianized Pagan gods and goddesses; thus
female saints such as Mary Magdalene (Fedele 2013a) and Bridget[10]
(Bowman 2004a, 2007, 2009) appeared in this context respectively as
the equivalents of the Greek goddess Aphrodite and the Celtic Brigid
(or Brigit).

In the adaptation process of Christian sites, figures, rituals and
symbols I found that my interlocutors often used strategies of
re-volution, in the original sense of the term. They did not refuse
Christian elements *in toto*, but incorporated them into their ritual
practices, turning their meaning upside down. Just two examples:
Mary Magdalene is no longer a repentant prostitute turned into a
saint by Jesus's intervention, but the sacred lover of Jesus helping
him in his difficult mission; menstrual blood, considered impure
and sinful, is sacralized by offering it to Mother Earth in a chalice,
thereby attaining a sort of ritual inversion of the Eucharist where
male blood is offered to a male God Father in the sky (Fedele 2013a:
145–90; 2014a).

Even if Goddess spirituality practitioners believe that they are
creating a spirituality that is radically different from, and often
directly opposed to, established religions of the past and present, a
close analysis of their theories and rituals shows that they have many
elements in common with other religious groups of the past and
present (Fedele and Knibbe 2013; Fedele 2013a, 2013c). An examination of recent and older anthropological studies of local Catholicism
(Christian 1972, 1981, 1996, 2011), historical analyses of Christianity
(Bynum 1987, 1991) and anthropological studies of other religious
groups (for example, Badone 1990; Lambek 1993) reveals that lived
religion (McGuire 2008), sometimes also described as 'vernacular
religion' (Primiano 1995; Bowman and Valk 2012) or 'folk religion'
(Yoder 1974; Bowman 2004b), and its multiple and sometimes ambiguous interpretations are not so different from those of contemporary
spirituality. I believe with Bowman that when analysing contemporary Paganism, its crafted rituals and its 'integrative spirituality', we
should bear in mind that 'although some scholars give the impression
that this is a particular feature of modern/post-modern "alternative"
spirituality, it is nothing new. This pragmatic, incorporative aspect
is common to "traditional" religion as well as to contemporary

spirituality, as countless ethnological studies have shown' (Bowman 2009: 197). I would add that what is new is the explicit legitimization of such an incorporative approach and the extent to which it is used (see also Fedele and Knibbe 2013).

Following Élisabeth Claverie's analysis of French pilgrims travelling to Medjugorje (2003) and influenced by French pragmatic sociologists, during my research I did not consider social actors to be passive victims of their social or religious milieu or of the spiritual theories and practices they had embraced. I believe they are equipped to engage with the social and religious realities they encounter and tend to be critical. Before accepting theories and rules, they find their own ways to put them to test and this also happened in the case of my interlocutors in Spain and Portugal. In my research I paid particular attention to the way in which spiritual practitioners accepted or refused certain theories and the processes that led them to the creation of their own spirituality.

Social scientists have often described religion as providing a remedy for uncertainty and the anxieties related to it. In this context uncertainty and doubt are regarded as undesirable and there has been a tendency to emphasize religion's capacity to offer a reassuring sense of continuity and certainty. Little attention has been paid so far to the role uncertainty plays in religious experiences.[11] I found that my southern European interlocutors saw doubts as allies rather than as needing to be neutralized. In fact they were constantly encouraged by their spiritual leaders not to take anything for granted, to put theories and spiritual practices to the test and see whether they 'worked for them' (Bell 1997; Fedele 2013a, 2014b). If they found that a certain theory or ritual was not useful for their process of spiritual growth, they should feel free to dismiss it or adapt it in order to make it work. In this context the capacity and willingness to challenge religious knowledge emerged as an ally in the face of dogmas imposed from above that were considered typical of monotheistic, patriarchal religions (Fedele 2014b).

These Iberians had managed to distance themselves from the Catholic dogmas they had received from their families, in the Catholic schools they had attended or more generally from their Catholic milieu. Having embraced a (Goddess) spirituality they perceived as opposed to (Catholic) religion, most were not willing to risk becoming 'religious' again. Putting to the test theories and practices they found in books or learnt about in workshops was therefore an important element in their defence against institutionalized and potentially disempowering religions.

Given their resistance to dogmas and refusal to become involved again in hierarchical and potentially controlling religious communities, their attitude towards Pagan theories and practices coming from Britain and the United States is particularly interesting. As will be discussed, they did not accept passively the rituals and ideas they found in English books (or Spanish translations of Pagan literature originally written in English), but evaluated whether they 'worked for them' in their local contexts. In their quest for an authentic Iberian Goddess tradition they often resisted what they perceived as a sort of Anglo-imperialism and preferred Spanish authors and spiritual leaders who did not simply follow established international traditions, but crafted their own Iberian tradition taking existing international traditions as sources of inspiration and blending them with local pre-Christian elements along with Catholic elements.

The Goddess Conference in Spain

In February 2010 I participated in the *Pantheacon*, the most important Pagan meeting in the United States (Pantheacon 2013).[12] There I discovered that in autumn of the same year the first Goddess Conference in Spain would be held in Madrid, and that it would be modelled on the Goddess Conference in Glastonbury. Surprised and curious, I contacted some of my informants in Spain only to find that they did not know about this upcoming event. They did not seem particularly interested and one of them commented rather sceptically that this was probably 'some big thing that was being organized by disciples of Kathy Jones in Spain'.

Glastonbury is one of the most important centres of contemporary spirituality and also a traditional pilgrimage site for Catholics and Anglicans (Prince and Riches 2000; Ivakhiv 2001; Bowman 1993, 2004a, 2005, 2007, 2008, 2009). The annual Glastonbury Goddess Conference is a five-day event that was founded in 1996, and Kathy Jones is probably the most important figure in the Goddess spirituality movement in Glastonbury and a central figure of the conference (Jones 2000; Bowman 2009; Trulsson 2010; Goddess Conference 2013). Glastonbury is believed to be the physical site of the mythical Avalon, described in Marion Zimmer Bradley's novel *The Mists of Avalon* (1983) as the home of the priestesses of the Goddess. There is a training programme for priestesses and priests of Avalon that produces ritual celebrants schooled in what is commonly referred to as 'the Glastonbury tradition' or 'the Avalon tradition'.

The Glastonbury Goddess Conference has been studied by Marion Bowman and others (for example, Trulsson 2010) and it would take too long here to describe it in detail. The following will refer to those elements of the Glastonbury conference that have influenced its Iberian equivalent. Bowman (2009) has also analysed how the 'Glastonbury Goddess package', which is being transplanted to different parts of Europe, is taking root in Hungary. The way in which this package has been adapted to the Hungarian context has many similarities with the Iberian case. However, in the Iberian case, apart from the influence of Kathy Jones and her Goddess training programme ('the Avalon tradition'), there was also the intervention of the 'Reclaiming' movement, which has Starhawk as its central figure.[13] This was the invitation I received by e-mail (on 20 February 2010) to the first Goddess Conference in Madrid to be held on 24–27 September 2010:

> We have the pleasure to inform you, that we, a small Group of Priestesses and Priests of the Goddess, in union of two traditions – Avalon and Celtic-Reclaiming, are preparing the first GODDESS CONFERENCE in Madrid, Spain! This Conference has been happening for many years in Glastonbury, England, nurtured by its founder Kathy Jones and the Priestesses of Avalon, visited by hundreds of people each year. Speakers such as Starhawk from Reclaiming San Francisco or Anique Radiant Heart from Australia have been attending for many years to encourage and support the Wiccan tradition in its multiple ways.
>
> We feel that the moment has come to reclaim the Goddess in Spain, and so we got together as the weavers of the Spanish Goddess Conference. We are pioneers venturing into the unknown, discovering treasures of this land: its sacred places, the names of the ancient Goddesses honoured in Hispania, traces of Her worship in old traditions. Little by little we start to know that Madrid is a whole Goddess city; that our ancestral Goddesses are eager to be found; to wake up [and come] to life again.

Several important elements of this first Iberian Goddess Conference were directly related to its British equivalent:

- The ritual celebration of each ancient local goddess was related to a cardinal direction, a colour and a priestess (the goddesses associated with the Iberian peninsula in the first conference were Ama Lur, Ataecina, Tanit, Belisama, Diana, Potnia Hippon, Noctiluca and Cybeles).
- A 'Goddess procession' with banners to important local sites (in this case, the fountain of Cybeles situated at the heart of Madrid).[14]

- A 'Goddess masked ball'.
- Fringe events to be paid for separately.
- The figures of the *melissas* ('bees' in Ancient Greek) as helpers during the conference.

Continuity with the Glastonbury Goddess Conference tradition was granted by the presence of its founder, Kathy Jones, and central figures connected with the Goddess Conference in Argentina (Sandra Román) and Australia (Anique Radiant Heart). Other high-profile figures of the international Pagan movement who joined this first occasion were Starhawk, Sally Pullinger, Steve Wilkes and Vicky Noble. To further emphasize continuity with Glastonbury's conference, Kathy Jones lit a ceremonial candle and ritually invoked the power of the 'flame of Avalon' – and thereby the power of the Avalon tradition – to ignite the 'flame of Iberia'. With this ritual she wanted to bring back to life the veneration of the Goddess in the Iberian peninsula. She reminded conference participants that after this ritual they all 'carried inside themselves the flame of Avalon and of Iberia'; they were now connected with both the Avalon and the Iberian traditions of Goddess worship.

When I asked my Portuguese interlocutors whether they would attend the first Goddess Conference in Spain, many of them did not know about it and once they had gathered information about it they all at first commented that it was too expensive for them. Some added that they felt that the conference organizers should also contact Portuguese Pagans in some way; although on the conference website the organizers addressed the whole Iberian peninsula, as far as my interlocutors knew, no direct contact had been made with Portuguese Pagans to see whether they wanted to contribute. In the second year of the Iberian conference, it became explicit that Portuguese Pagans were also invited to identify with the conference through the goddess Iberia. One of the speakers at the second conference in 2011 came from Portugal and she described herself as having a special link with Glastonbury.

Iberia is a goddess who was 'born' during the first Goddess Conference in Madrid and is a sort of Iberian equivalent of the Roman goddess Britannia venerated in Glastonbury. The birth of the goddess Iberia, representing the Iberian peninsula, also allowed another feature of the Glastonbury conference to be incorporated: the veneration of a different aspect of the fourfold Goddess (Maiden, Lover, Mother, Crone) (c.f. Bowman 2009: 209). This emerged in the announcement of the second Iberian conference, which was celebrated on 7–10 July 2011:

IBERIA, THE MAIDEN

The Goddess of Iberia, born at the Goddess Conference last September, has been maturing. Our baby girl is no longer asleep in the arms of the Great Cosmic Mother. Our blessed girl is a free maiden, joyful and expressive. She runs through the fields, shaking the still sleeping earth with her little feet....

The Maid of Iberia was known by many names: The Gala Belisama (clearly a cousin of the English Brigit), the Basque Ekhi (the healing light of the mild winter sun), Carmenta (one of the Roman Matres, who was in charge of receiving babies, oracles, edges and spells), the Greek Aphrodite Phosphoros (Aphrodite, bringer of light), the Iberian Cabar Sul (Matron Goddess of healing through water) amongst others. Like Brigit of England, she had two common characteristics: healing through the purification of fire and through the purification of the crystal-clear waters, therefore at our Conference we will honour her and ourselves with the purification of fire and water. They are all Divine expressions of the girl that once lived in each one of us. All of them a Divine expression of our inner child. They are all incarnated again as the children who are in our lives now and therefore will be honoured at the Second Iberian Goddess Conference, in early July in Madrid.

You are welcome to join us and share laughter, innocence and inspiration from the Maiden of Iberia.[15]

As we can see from this announcement there is a clear effort to find common elements between Iberia and Brigit (or Brigid), the Celtic goddess assimilated with the Christian Saint Bridget venerated in Glastonbury. Something similar happened in the Hungarian case analysed by Bowman (2009: 214).

In the third Iberian Goddess Conference the second aspect of the fourfold Goddess was to be venerated, and the reference to Iberia the Lover allowed the introduction of another feature of the Glastonbury conference, the association of each aspect of the Goddess with certain colours and the association of each conference with a prevalent colour (c.f. Bowman 2009: 210). This is the announcement of the third Iberian conference, which was to be held on 27–30 September 2012:

Iberia the Maiden went out to dance to the world at the Second Iberian Goddess Conference. Spinning joyfully She fell in love with the whole creation, She fell in love with Herself reflected in the mountains, in the valleys, in the rivers and the sea, in all creatures ... So She became Iberia the Lover.

Join us to celebrate the Third Iberian Goddess Conference in Madrid from 27th to 30th September 2012. Please wear red, pink and fuchsia in all possible shades to honour the fourfold Goddess of Love of our lands:

Iberia of the Birds, the Horses, the Snakes and the Crystalline Depths, Iberia the Lover manifesting Self-Love, Sacred Pleasure, Pure Heart Love, and Divine Love. (Conferencia de la Diosa 2013)

With every Iberian conference more elements of the Glastonbury conference were incorporated. Gradually an Iberian mythology was being created that also incorporated the Dama de Elche (Lady of Elche), a polychrome stone bust discovered in 1897 near Elche (Valencia, Spain) that has been at the centre of many controversies about its authenticity and is a popular image in Spain. After the first Iberian conference efforts were increasingly made to incorporate not only priestesses from the (British) Avalon and (American) Reclaiming traditions. In 2011 there was also a priestess from the Iberian tradition in the ceremonial *équipe* and several invited local speakers were heterodox priestesses or spiritual leaders.

However, the Glastonbury package failed to properly take root in Spain. In 2011 the organizers experienced a shortage of subscriptions and had to lower the price three weeks before the event so as to allow those affected by the economic crisis to participate.[16] This created discontent among those who had not been accorded a similar discount the year before and those who had already paid the full price for 2011. In 2012 the third Iberian Goddess Conference was significantly more affordable, but nevertheless it had to be cancelled because of a 'lack of subscriptions'.[17] Those interested were invited to participate in 'the next one' (Conferencia de la Diosa 2013).

Why Did the Goddess Conference Fail to Take Root in Spain?

At the time of this writing, in November 2014, the Spanish website of the conference no longer exists and there is no Goddess Conference scheduled for 2014 in Madrid. What were the reasons that led to the failure of this event? Why did the Glastonbury package not work in Madrid? The reasons are surely manifold and the financial crisis in southern Europe certainly was an important factor. However, some other elements played an important role in this process.

As described above, the Iberian Goddess Conference was organized by a number of priestesses belonging to the Avalon tradition or the Reclaiming tradition and they consciously modelled the event to reproduce some of the main features of the Glastonbury conference.

The organizers made an effort to adapt the Glastonbury package to the local context and announced that all Pagan groups of the Iberian peninsula were invited to participate and that they aimed to include all Pagan traditions.[18] However, this may have been more complicated than they thought, and they failed to involve in the creation and organization of the first Iberian conference other heterodox spiritual leaders and priestesses who had been practising Goddess spirituality all over Spain. The organizers of the first conference all belonged to one of the two traditions related to the conference and indicated their lineage in their biographical descriptions on the website (Conferencia de la Diosa 2010). Some of my Spanish informants complained that those from other local groups who wanted to participate and who offered to contribute by celebrating a ritual were welcomed, but unlike the invited celebrants they would not be paid for their ritual performance and would have to pay a registration fee. They were thereby considered on the same level as all other participants. This created several misunderstandings and conflicts, additionally because the price was considerable by Iberian standards and Iberians are not so familiar with early-registration discounts.

As I have explained elsewhere, in Spain and Portugal the cost of workshops and retreats tends to be quite inexpensive compared with other European countries, and this often allows younger participants or those with little income to attend at least some events (Fedele 2013a; see also Fedele and Knibbe 2013). The Glastonbury scheme that involved the invitation of foreign guests such as Kathy Jones and Starhawk implied that the subscriptions needed to be quite high and that there was little space for negotiation about free entry or late discounts. The salience of this problem became particularly evident during the second Iberian conference when the organizers decided to lower the prices for those with financial problems a few weeks before the conference.

The lack of explicit involvement in the first Iberian conference of heterodox but well-developed local women's spirituality groups, which in many cases had been practising Goddess spirituality since the late 1990s, created a gap between the 'vernacular' Paganism and a sort of 'orthodox' Paganism represented by the followers of the Avalon tradition and Starhawk's Reclaiming tradition. Although in the second and third Iberian conferences some heterodox priestesses and spiritual leaders were incorporated as speakers, many of my interlocutors had felt disillusioned and decided not to attend.

Apart from economic issues and the problematic inclusion of heterodox Pagan groups, another element that in my opinion played an important role in the failure of the transplantation process was that few Catholic elements were incorporated. The official goddesses who were invoked did not include local virgins such as Our Lady of Montserrat or Our Lady of Rocio (see Fedele 2013a) and the conference leaders did not adapt the contents for an audience that had a strong Catholic background. Although in later versions of the Goddess Conference in Spain there were references to the Virgin Mary and Mary Magdalene, considered Christianized versions of the Goddess, the 'Christian Goddess' was not explicitly addressed or worshipped.

Finally, an important factor was the resistance of my Iberian informants to accept theories and ritual rules perceived as imposed from above. Both the Avalon and the Reclaiming traditions have gradually become more crystallized in a set process and certain rituals that were once freshly crafted now form part of an established tradition. Some of my interlocutors had participated in the Goddess conference in Glastonbury and several had criticized the 'rigidity' of certain ceremonies. Some said that they had even been reprimanded because they were doing their own ritual gestures and procedures and were not following suit. In their attempt to escape from the religious rules and dogmas they had experienced as disempowering and sometimes painful during their childhood and early adulthood as Catholics, these women perceived the Glastonbury package as too structured and constrictive. In a similar way the conference in Madrid appeared to them as something imported and coming 'from above' that did not really reflect their own experiences of the Goddess or the local specificities of their spirituality. They resisted this process as a sort of Anglo-colonialism that forced them to follow the rules of established traditions they did not really embrace and which had not originated in their country.

Conclusion

Paganism is becoming increasingly represented and visible in mainland Europe and some international Pagan movements – Goddess spirituality in this instance – have crystallized into established traditions such as the Avalon tradition and the Reclaiming tradition. Pagans tend to describe their own spirituality as non-hierarchical and gender equal in contrast with more established religions and with what they see more generally as 'religion'. However, power relationships are inherent within human relations and therefore also in religious groups. Even if Pagans try hard to protect individual freedom and not to create a religion,[19] in the creation of their own spirituality they end up being inevitably caught up in power relations (Fedele and Knibbe 2013). It is particularly interesting to observe processes of religious colonization and resistance in a context in which religious power and established religions are described as negative, but Christian figures, places and symbols are still considered as relevant and powerful.

Due to their Catholic background Iberian practitioners of Goddess spirituality seem to be particularly sensitive to issues of religious domination and control, and are therefore particularly useful indicators of processes of resistance against an Anglo-imperialism within international Paganism. Many of them refuse to be labelled – or to label themselves – as Pagans or witches and prefer to create their own Iberian Goddess spirituality combining Catholic and Pagan elements rather than embracing established international Pagan traditions. Through an analysis of the case of the Iberian Goddess Conference it has been argued here that this 'package' (after Bowman 2009) has so far failed to take root in the Iberian peninsula because many Iberian Pagans have perceived it as something essentially imposed from above, coming from abroad and divorced from local specificities. Although the organizers of the Iberian conference made efforts to adapt the Goddess Conference package to the Iberian context, including Iberian goddesses and Spanish places such as the fountain of Cybeles in Madrid, they failed to involve from the beginning what have been labelled here 'heterodox' Pagan groups – those which do not belong to the Avalon or Reclaiming traditions. Moreover, they only partially addressed the Catholic sensibilities and the economic difficulties of their potential audience. Planned as a well-structured event with 'early-bird' prices, fringe events to be paid for separately and special guests from abroad, the Iberian Goddess Conference looked radically different from the kind of loosely organized rituals I had witnessed during my earlier fieldwork. Time will tell whether the Goddess Conference will again be celebrated in Spain and eventually take root there. If this happens the organizers will have to invest more effort in the process of cultural and religious translation so as to allow Iberian participants to recognize the conference as reflecting the complex Catholic-Pagan spiritualities they have created for themselves.

Acknowledgements

I would like to thank Kathryn Rountree for her ongoing support and her suggestions and Marion Bowman for providing useful references.

Notes

1 Although there is a growing religious diversity in Spain and Portugal due to immigration and the increasing availability of religious alternatives, the general opinion in the media and among people generally is that Portugal and Spain are still 'Catholic countries'. See Mapril and Llera Blanes (2013) for a discussion of religious diversity in southern Europe.

2 The term 'Iberian' is used here to include Portuguese and Spaniards, and also to respect the nationalist sensibilities of Catalan and Basque Pagans who do not like to be labelled 'Spanish'. As will be shown, the political problems linked to local nationalisms in Spain led the organizers of the Spanish Goddess Conference to refer to the 'Iberian Peninsula' rather than to Spain. See the organizers' comments in the interview at: http://www.elblogalternativo.com/2010/08/22/la-diosa-en-espana-entrevistamos-a-las-organizadoras-de-la-conferencia-de-la-diosa-en-madrid-sobre-este-evento-y-el-neopaganismo/ (accessed 20 June 2013).

3 It is particularly difficult to determine the number of those following Pagan theories and practices in Spain and Portugal, because many may still be nominally Catholics, baptize their children and marry in a church. On the other hand there are also those who refuse to identify with any established religion or with other social labels. These and other attitudes make Goddess spirituality practitioners difficult to spot statistically.

4 In recent years there has been a debate about whether a variety of Native Faith groups in Europe, especially central and eastern Europe, should be included under the umbrella of 'Neopaganism'. See, for instance, Aitamurto and Simpson (2013).

5 For an early study of witchcraft among Londoners, see Luhrmann (1989, 2001). For ethnographic or sociological studies of Neopagans in the United States, see Berger (1999), Pike (2001), Magliocco (2001, 2004), Salomonsen (2002) and Berger et al. (2003). In Great Britain, see Greenwood (2000); in Malta, Rountree (2010); in Australia, Hume (1997); and in New Zealand, Rountree (2004). See Albanese (1990) for a discussion of 'nature religions' in America. See also Harvey (1997) and Pizza and Lewis (2008).

6 All citations come from personal interviews or informal conversations. The translations from Catalan, Spanish and Portuguese are mine.

Pseudonyms have been used for the groups and persons described in this text.

7 For a detailed discussion of the spirituality/religion dichotomy and the methodological problems entailed in the use of these terms in the social sciences, see Fedele and Knibbe (2013).

8 See also Fedele (2013b) where I refer to this conversation with Dana and her book project.

9 See Wood (2007) for a detailed analysis of the problems related to the term 'New Age'. See also Sutcliffe and Bowman (2000).

10 Both Brigit and Bridget are used; here I use Bridget, the version that Bowman uses.

11 The importance of uncertainty and doubt in vernacular religion is at the centre of a special issue I coordinated with Élisabeth Claverie for *Social Compass* (61(4), 2014).

12 For an ethnographic description of the Pantheacon, see, for instance, Magliocco (2004).

13 See Salomonsen (2002) for a detailed analysis of the Reclaiming witches in San Francisco.

14 To view videos of this procession in 2010, see: http://www.youtube.com/user/meryetcrafts#p/u/2/xdSwPxcuKtg (accessed 17 June 2013) and http://www.youtube.com/user/meryetcrafts#p/u/1/FBzpGhD7f4c (accessed 17 June 2013).

15 E-mail announcement received 12 March 2011.

16 Originally the price was 200 euros for early registration and 280 euros full price. The cost for those with economic problems was 150 euros. E-mail announcement received 19 June 2011.

17 The price for early registration was 135 euros and the full price 165 euros. Http://www.conferenciadeladiosa.es/english.html (accessed 19 June 2013).

18 See the organizers' comments at: http://www.elblogalternativo.com/2010/08/22/la-diosa-en-espana-entrevistamos-a-las-organizadoras-de-la-conferencia-de-la-diosa-en-madrid-sobre-este-evento-y-el-neopaganismo/ (accessed 19 June 2013).

19 Asa Trulsson (2013: 28) cites Kathy Jones saying, 'I hope we are not creating a religion.... All known religions have been patriarchal'.

References

Aitamurto, K. and S. Simpson (eds). 2013. *Modern Pagan and Native Faith Movements in Central and Eastern Europe*. London: Acumen Publishing.

Albanese, C.L. 1990. *Nature Religion in America: From the Algonkian Indians to the New Age*. Chicago: University of Chicago Press.

Badone, E. 1990. *Religious Orthodoxy and Popular Faith in European Society*. Princeton: Princeton University Press.

Bell, C.M. 1997. *Ritual: Perspectives and Dimensions*. New York: Oxford University Press.

Bender, C. 2010. *The New Metaphysicals: Spirituality and the American Religious Imagination*. Chicago: University of Chicago Press.

Berger, H.A. 1999. *A Community of Witches: Contemporary Neo-paganism and Witchcraft in the United States*. Columbia: University of South Carolina Press.

Berger, H.A., E.A. Leach and L.S. Shaffer. 2003. *Voices from the Pagan Census: A National Survey of Witches and Neo-pagans in the United States*. Columbia: University of South Carolina Press.

Berger, P.L., G. Davie and E. Fokas. 2008. *Religious America, Secular Europe? A Theme and Variation*. Aldershot and Burlington: Ashgate.

Bowman, M. 1993. 'Drawn to Glastonbury', in I. Reader and T. Walter (eds), *Pilgrimage in Popular Culture*. Basingstoke and London: Macmillan, pp. 29–62.

———. 2004a. 'Procession and Possession in Glastonbury: Continuity, Change and the Manipulation of Tradition', *Folklore* 115(3): 273–85.

———. 2004b. 'Phenomenology, Fieldwork and Folk Religion' (reprint, with new epilogue), in S. Sutcliffe (ed.), *Religion: Empirical Studies*. Aldershot: Ashgate, pp. 3–18.

———. 2005. 'Ancient Avalon, New Jerusalem, Heart Chakra of Planet Earth: Localisation and Globalisation in Glastonbury', *Numen* 52(2): 157–90.

———. 2007. 'Arthur and Bridget in Avalon: Celtic Myth, Vernacular Religion and Contemporary Spirituality in Glastonbury', *Fabula* 48(1/2): 1–17.

———. 2008. 'Going with the Flow: Contemporary Pilgrimage in Glastonbury', in P.J. Margy (ed.), *Shrines and Pilgrimage in the Modern World: New Itineraries into the Sacred*. Amsterdam: Amsterdam University Press, pp. 241–80.

———. 2009. 'From Glastonbury to Hungary: Contemporary Integrative Spirituality and Vernacular Religion in Context', in G. Vargyas (ed.), *Passageways: From Hungarian Ethnography to European Ethnology and Sociocultural Anthropology*. Budapest: The University of Pécs – L'Harmattan Publishing House, pp. 195–221.

Bowman, M. and U. Valk. 2012. *Vernacular Religion in Everyday Life: Expressions of Belief*. London and Oakville: Equinox Publications.

Bradley, M. 1983. *The Mists of Avalon*. London: Sphere Books.

Bynum, C.W. 1987. *Holy Feast and Holy Fast: The Religious Significance of Food to Medieval Women*. Berkeley: University of California Press.

———. 1991. *Fragmentation and Redemption: Essays on Gender and the Human Body in Medieval Religion*. New York and Cambridge, Mass.: Zone Books, distributed by MIT Press.

Christian, W.A. 1972. *Person and God in a Spanish Valley: Studies in Social Discontinuity*. New York: Seminar Press.

———. 1981. *Local Religion in Sixteenth-Century Spain*. Princeton: Princeton University Press.

———. 1996. *Visionaries: The Spanish Republic and the Reign of Christ*. Berkeley: University of California Press.

———. 2011. *Divine Presence in Spain and Western Europe, 1500–1960: Visions, Religious Images and Photographs*. Budapest: Central European University.

Claverie, É. 2003. *Les Guerres de La Vierge: Une Anthropologie des Apparitions*. Paris: Gallimard.

Conferencia de la Diosa. 2010, 2013. http://www.conferenciadeladiosa.es/english.html. Accessed 20 August 2010 and 19 June 2013.

Eller, C. 1993. *Living in the Lap of the Goddess: The Feminist Spirituality Movement in America*. Boston: Beacon Press.

Fedele, A. 2009. 'From Christian Religion to Feminist Spirituality: Mary Magdalene Pilgrimages to La Sainte-Baume, France', *Culture and Religion* 10(3): 243–61.

———. 2013a. *Looking for Mary Magdalene: Alternative Pilgrimage and Ritual Creativity at Catholic Shrines in France*. New York: Oxford University Press.

———. 2013b. 'The Metamorphoses of Neopaganism in Traditionally Catholic Countries in Southern Europe', in J. Mapril and R. Llera Blanes (eds), *Sites and Politics of Religious Diversity in Southern Europe*. Leiden: Brill, pp. 51–72.

———. 2013c. '"Black" Madonna Versus "White" Madonna: Gendered Power Strategies in Alternative Pilgrimages to Marian Shrines', in A. Fedele and K. Knibbe (eds), *Gender and Power in Contemporary Spirituality: Ethnographic Approaches*. London and New York: Routledge, pp. 96–114.

———. 2014a. 'Reversing Eve's Curse: Mary Magdalene, Mother Earth and the Creative Ritualization of Menstruation', *Journal of Ritual Studies* 28(2): 23–36.

———. 2014b. 'Doute et incertitude dans les nouveaux rituels contemporains', *Social Compass* 61(4): 11–25.

Fedele, A. and K. Knibbe (eds). 2013. *Gender and Power in Contemporary Spirituality: Ethnographic Approaches*. London and New York: Routledge.

Goddess Conference. 2013. http://www.goddessconference.com. Accessed 17 June 2013.

Greenwood, S. 2000. *Magic, Witchcraft and the Otherworld: An Anthropology*. Oxford: Berg.

Harvey, G. 1997. *Listening People, Speaking Earth*. New York: New York University Press.

Heelas, P. and L. Woodhead. 2005. *The Spiritual Revolution: Why Religion Is Giving Way to Spirituality*. Oxford: Wiley-Blackwell.

Hume, L. 1997. *Witchcraft and Paganism in Australia*. Melbourne: Melbourne University Press.

Hutton, R. 1999. *The Triumph of the Moon: A History of Modern Pagan Witchcraft*. Oxford and New York: Oxford University Press.

Ivakhiv, A.J. 2001. *Claiming Sacred Ground: Pilgrims and Politics at Glastonbury and Sedona*. Indianapolis: Indiana University Press.

Jones, K. 2000. *In the Nature of Avalon: Goddess Pilgrimages in Glastonbury's Sacred Landscape*. Glastonbury: Ariadne Publications.

Knibbe, K.E. 2013. *Faith in the Familiar: Religion, Spirituality and Place in the South of the Netherlands*. Leiden: Brill.

Lambek, M. 1993. *Knowledge and Practice in Mayotte: Local Discourses of Islam, Sorcery and Spirit Possession*. Toronto: University of Toronto Press.

Luhrmann, T.M. 1989. *Persuasions of the Witch's Craft: Ritual Magic and Witchcraft in Present-Day England*. Oxford: Blackwell.

———. 2001. 'The Ugly Goddess: Reflections on the Role of Violent Images in Religious Experience', *History of Religions* 41(2): 114–41.

Magliocco, S. 2001. *Neo-pagan Sacred Art and Altars: Making Things Whole*. Jackson: University of Mississippi Press.

———. 2004. *Witching Culture: Folklore and Neo-paganism in America*. Philadelphia: University of Pennsylvania Press.

Mapril, J. and R. Llera Blanes (eds). 2013. *Sites and Politics of Religious Diversity in Southern Europe*. Leiden: Brill.

McGuire, M.B. 2008. *Lived Religion: Faith and Practice in Everyday Life*. Oxford and New York: Oxford University Press.

Pantheacon. 2013. http://www.pantheacon.com. Accessed 20 June 2013.

Pike, S.M. 2001. *Earthly Bodies, Magical Selves: Contemporary Pagans and the Search for Community*. Berkeley: University of California Press.

Pizza, M. and J.R. Lewis. 2008. *Handbook of Contemporary Paganism*. Leiden: Brill.

Primiano, L. 1995. 'Vernacular Religion and the Search for Method in Religious Folklife', *Western Folklore* 54: 37–56.

Prince, R. and D. Riches. 2000. *The New Age in Glastonbury: The Construction of Religious Movements*. Oxford and New York: Berghahn Books.

Rountree, K. 2004. *Embracing the Witch and the Goddess: Feminist Ritual-Makers in New Zealand*. London and New York: Routledge.

———. 2010. *Crafting Contemporary Pagan Identities in a Catholic Society*. Surrey and Burlington: Ashgate.

Salomonsen, J. 2002. *Enchanted Feminism: Ritual, Gender and Divinity among the Reclaiming Witches of San Francisco*. London and New York: Routledge.

Sutcliffe, S. and M. Bowman (eds). 2000. *Beyond New Age: Exploring Alternative Spirituality*. Edinburgh: Edinburgh University Press.

Trulsson, A. 2010. *Cultivating the Sacred: Ritual Creativity and Practice among Women in Contemporary Europe*. Lund Studies in the History of Religions 28. Lund: Lund University.

————. 2013. 'Cultivating the Sacred: Gender, Power and Ritualization in Goddess-Oriented Groups', in A. Fedele and K. Knibbe (eds), *Gender and Power in Contemporary Spirituality: Ethnographic Approaches*. London and New York: Routledge, pp. 28–45.

Wood, M. 2007. *Possession, Power and the New Age: Ambiguities of Authority in Neoliberal Societies*. Aldershot: Ashgate.

Yoder, D. 1974. 'Toward a Definition of Folk Religion', *Western Folklore* 33(1): 2–15.

12

Bellisama and Aradia

Paganism Re-emerges in Italy

Francesca Ciancimino Howell

Introduction

Paganism, sometimes referred to in its contemporary form as Neo-Paganism, is a religion of many paradoxes and some puzzling conundrums. Its re-emergence in Italy is no different. Many in the world would not see Paganism as a religion at all, and yet the world's oldest religion is also the newest, pre-modern and postmodern all at once. The twentieth century's hegemonic globalizing forces, its march of industrialization and spread of English speaking and publishing have aided the world's oldest religion to return to – or perhaps as is argued here, to re-emerge in – one of its native homes. A formalized, postmodern religion of Witchcraft, including Pagan clergy, has returned to the land where folk traditions of witchcraft and respect for the classical priestesses and oracles of ancient times never entirely disappeared.[1]

Like many scholars in religious studies, anthropology and other fields, my position as a researcher was often one of privileged insider status. I am Italian-American with a lifetime of family relationships in Rome and of studies in and on Italy. My experiences with the growing numbers of Witches, Druids, Wiccans and Goddess worshippers in Italy arose out of my involvement with the international Pagan community and from my experience as a researcher and author in Italy (Howell 2008b). Thus the perspectives presented here are both emic and etic. The theories and explanations offered for this re-emergence range from the socio-economic to the political to the contextual and draw on data from my ethnographic research.

Many Pantheons, Many Traditions

In the lands associated with the Roman Empire's legacy, one might perhaps expect the contemporary Pagan worship of Diana or Minerva, Vesta and Venus, and indeed one may find – particularly closer to Rome – veneration and ritual practices honouring these Goddesses. However, seven years of doctoral and postdoctoral work in Italy introduced me to deities, mythology and traditions little known outside regional areas of worship. In the northern region of Lombardy at the foot of the Alps, for example, there is a massive, golden Madonna atop Milan's majestic main cathedral. Milanese tradition teaches that only those born within the sight of that '*Madonnina*' may rightfully call themselves true Milanese. Today there are more than a few in Milan who claim that the maternal figure watching over Milan may not be the Christian Madonna, but rather a Gallo-Celtic Goddess called Bellisama. Bellisama was worshipped by the ancient Gauls (also known as Celts, the Greek name) of Lombardy, as well as across continental Europe, as far away as northwestern France. In my doctoral fieldwork in Milan, a Milanese Pagan participant, trying to demonstrate the enduring local influence of Milan's Gaulish history, stated: 'The Goddess of Milan is Bellisama, her spirit is here, and it's Druidic'.

Thus, the term 're-emergence' is appropriate, for the Goddess was never gone from these Mediterranean lands. As happened with other classical and Pagan deities, and with Jesus worship as well, She was synthesized with what eventually emerged as today's Christianity, becoming the ubiquitous Madonna of the Mediterranean (Chidester 2000: 166–70, 288–92; MacCulloch 2009: 46, 138–40, 168–72, 189–95).[2] Nor was a powerful religiosity and propensity toward magic erased, as Sabina Magliocco (2004a; 2012: 5–20) has discussed in various ethnographic studies on Italy; it has lived alongside Christianity for centuries. This relatively recently (1861) united country, created out of the mountainous peninsula of diverse regions now known as 'Italy', is also the land of the Vatican, and thus a nation inculcated in Catholicism (Magliocco 2004a: 152–53; Orsi 2002: xxxix–xlix). Rountree (2011: 852–57) has written on the flow back and forth between Madonna veneration and Mother Goddess veneration among Wiccans and Pagans in Malta. However, while there are some clear parallels between (particularly southern) Italy and Malta, where there is a profound enculturation of Italians into Roman Catholicism from birth, Italy presents its own unique evolution in the emergence of contemporary Paganism.

Some of Italy's nuanced, culturally ingrained traits contribute to the character and recent growth of the Pagan community in Italy. One important element is Italy's historic and cultural forms of resistance. Resistance to domination by foreign invasion, to political oppression and to hegemonic structures is deeply ingrained in the Italian psyche and culture. Examples are found in the history of its World War II Partisan movements and its Communist Party.[3] Alternative spiritualities such as Paganism, shamanism and other new, non-Christian religious movements currently emerging in Italy not only offer empowerment and new senses of identity, but are also embedded with avenues and mores of cultural and religious resistance.

The history of witch trials in Italy may also be significant in the long-term survival of its popular religious traditions. While the history of the witch-hunts and witch trials in the medieval and Renaissance eras has frequently been a motivating and galvanizing factor in the adherence of women, particularly, and sometimes men as well, to Paganism and Witchcraft movements in the twentieth century, it can be argued that modern Witches' and Pagans' beliefs about historical witches and witchcraft are misplaced. Studies in recent decades have generally found that among those persecuted and/or executed in the bloody years of the European and British witch-hunts, there were few practitioners of a pre-Christian Pagan religion that had survived into the Christian era (Hutton 1999: 362, 380; Pearson 2002: 19, 37–38). However, interestingly, two examples of possible surviving vernacular Goddess worship were recorded in Lombardy: Pierina Bugatis and Sibillia Zanni, burned in one of Milan's main piazzas in 1390. Their case illustrates some of the feminist historian Anne Llewellyn Barstow's arguments: in a seeming paradox, despite the existence of the Inquisition, Italy and Spain did not have the kind of 'witchcraze' which tore through other parts of Europe (Barstow 1994: 89–95, 202). As Barstow (1994: 90) describes:

> Especially in Italy, exhibiting an intense interest in the activities of female fortune-tellers and male magicians, inquisitors perceived these activities as wrong belief rather than diabolic magic and sought to convert the practitioners to a papally approved form of Catholicism. Punishments therefore consisted of penances and, in extreme cases, whippings and banishment, but not death.

If Sibillia and Pierina's case had remained in the hands of the Inquisition, and not those of the secular authorities, they might have been spared. Their early testimonies described activities more similar to contemporary Goddess worship than that consistently described in witch trial accounts. For example, they celebrated rituals honouring a divine feminine figure at certain times of the month; they healed animals, ate and drank together (Murano 2006 [1976]: 198–209). Although tragically Sibillia and Pierina were not saved, the existence of the Inquisition and the Vatican may have aided Italy's folk traditions to survive into contemporary times, because the people generally did not suffer the level of persecution of folk healers and vernacular beliefs in other countries (Barstow 1994: 94; Rountree 2011: 862–66).

A Rural Country and an Enchanted Land

In the mid to late twentieth century there was a rapid growth and spread of esoteric practices and mystery religions such as Wicca, Druidry and others in northern Europe and North America. However, in Italy language was a barrier to the arrival of various northern European, North American and British traditions of Paganism. Much, if not most, Pagan literature was published in English. It is still not uncommon in the second decade of the twenty-first century to find educated people across the more sophisticated cities and towns of Italy who do not speak or read English, or at least not well. This delayed the diffusion of many now classic Wicca, Witchcraft and Paganism books of the twentieth century, such as Starhawk's *The Spiral Dance* (1979; published in Italy in 2002) and Janet and Stewart Farrar's *A Witches' Bible* (in Italian, *La Bibbia delle Streghe*, 2013).

Other complex sociological and historical reasons had to do with the delayed arrival of contemporary Paganism in Italy. One was the earlier industrialization of northern Europe, Britain and North America, and the ensuing romanticizing of nature in those regions in the early nineteenth century. Another was the study of folklore, native traditions and witchcraft connected to this idealized view of rural practices that flowered in nations such as England, Germany and the United States in the early nineteenth to mid-twentieth centuries (Bendix 1992, 1999). This came as a reaction to the loss of countryside and rural lifestyles, and was intertwined with the profound sense of loss wrought by industrialization. The Romantic movement of the British Isles can be seen as a direct reaction to industrialization in England (Hutton 1999: 21–27, 33–35). The study of folklore, newly developed in the nineteenth century, is significant for Wicca and perhaps also Druidry in Italy, as it can be argued that there is a direct line from the American folklorist Charles Leland (1824–1903) to the British 'father of Wicca' Gerald Gardner (1884–1964), and the arrival of Wicca and Druidry in Italy in the twenty-first century (Hutton 1999: 142–49; Marrè 2012: 40–42). The section below on 'Italy's Indigenous Practices' elaborates further this theory.

The hunger for a re-enchantment of nature and search for enchantment in the post-industrial era may have also contributed to the growth of nature mysticism and esoteric spirituality in northern Europe and North America in the nineteenth and twentieth centuries (Berman 1981:16–24, 69–113; Von Stuckrad 2002: 771–99). However, in order to have a hunger for rediscovering enchantment in nature, a newly urbanized society must have already lost contact with nature and its rural societies, with their native beliefs and indigenous magical practices (c.f. Rountree 2011: 850). This was not the case in Italy, which retained an extensive agrarian and peasant economy into the latter half of the twentieth century (Ginsborg 2003: 23–36). Like other countries in southern Europe, it had undergone late industrialization and therefore maintained rural structures, traditions and mores well into the twentieth century (Sapelli 1995). This is exemplified by the enduring belief in vernacular religious complexes that include the creation and use of protective amulets, varied traditions of healing and the lifting of or protection from the Evil Eye (Magliocco 2004a: 151–73; Rountree 2011: 862–64). As Magliocco (2004a: 158–59) points out, 'there are literally thousands of spells to turn back the evil eye in Italian folklore' and 'much of Italian vernacular magic and healing centres around the evil eye belief complex'. These are sometimes synthesized with Christianity – not only in Italy, but also in Italian immigrant communities in other parts of the world (Orsi 2002). Participants in this research in Italy spoke freely of their and their families' Evil Eye knowledge and practices.

New Movements, Consciousness and Rites

The late industrialization of Italy and its 'modernization without development' (Sapelli 1995: 13) is key in this discussion – not only in relation to the later arrival of Paganism, but also to the delayed emergence of feminism and the environmental movement. I have argued elsewhere (Howell 2008a: 5–20) that the emergence and spread of Goddess religion, Wicca and Druidry (among other paths of Paganism) is a sociological phenomenon in Italy related to the emergence of other movements such as LGBTQ (lesbian, gay, bisexual, transgender and queer) rights, the environmental movement and personal-consciousness movements. In this regard, Paganism's rebirth in Italy is linked to the growth of Paganism in other areas of southern Europe, as well as in other nations in the same phase of late industrialization, such as those in South America.

Another significant element of the hunger for alternative forms of worship and communal celebration in Italy was the desire for new rites of passage. In the late twentieth century there was an increasing sense of alienation from the traditional rites of Catholicism in the educated, newly urbanized, younger generations, and also in the large Italian left wing. This lack of fulfilment in and growing movement away from Catholicism's traditional ceremonies, particularly those marking life transitions, caused a growing need for a new way to ritualize these occasions. Was the engine for the rapid growth of Paganism in Italy the Women's Spirituality movement? Was it the increasing awareness of the environmental woes arriving in tandem with industrialization? Was it these together with more widespread education and greater opportunities for women? It is hard to pinpoint what may have been the 'prime mover'. However, as the Women's Spirituality movement took shape in Italy in the last ten to fifteen years, new creative expressions likewise emerged, promoting the designing of innovative rites of passage such as infant blessings, young girls' coming of age, marriages and women's rites honouring menopause. If one were to couple this with the fervent sense of new empowerment offered by different Pagan traditions, particularly for women raised in patriarchal Italian society, there would be a new meaning to Liberation Theology. Graham Harvey delineated this association in his study of Paganism in the British Isles; it applies likewise to Italy.

> Goddess Spirituality is perhaps the most explicit 'liberation theology' – more properly thealogy – of contemporary Paganism. By various approaches it explores the past, the present and the future hopes for intimations of other ways of living. It proposes that the honouring of the Earth must go hand in hand with the honouring of women. (Harvey 1997: 85)

The hunger for new rites of passage, the knowledge of what was taking shape abroad, as books arrived and were finally translated into Italian, and the delayed but now fervent social and psychological awareness movements together meant that the end of the last century and the beginning of the twenty-first offered Italians a potent mix of ideas 'whose time had come'. These phenomena marked a new flowering for Italy in alternative thought and creative expression and reaffirmed the Italian propensity towards resistance with a new sort of cultural resistance movement.

As in other societies, Italian women find a sense of empowerment in Goddess Spirituality (Adler 1981: 171–222; Magliocco 2004b: 197–203). An important nuance of this movement in Italy is that they may also find power in the sense of *bella figura*, a complex and inculcated Italian cultural trait whose translation could be simply 'making a good impression'. This is the general usage, but the nuances are more extensive and socially significant, in particular in regard to women claiming their place in the public sphere. The anthropologist Emanuela Guano (2007: 48–71) has offered insightful discussions on Bella Figura as more than merely a style of presenting oneself, of dressing and walking – Bella Figura becomes a manner by which a woman can create a persona that offers a form of resistance, and a way to carve out a place of belonging in an 'oppressively masculinized' public sphere. My observations find a direct relationship between the Pagan persona of Goddess Spirituality and priestesshood with Bella Figura, as some Italian women experiment with new and nuanced forms of empowered identity (see Figure 12.1).

Fig. 12.1 *An outdoor Pagan shrine with a Goddess statue. Image used with kind permission of the photographer, Ossian D'Ambrosio.*

It is pertinent to make a linguistic note of the difference between traditional Italian witchcraft, the native practices which have their roots in a long historical trajectory in Italian culture, and the terms often heard today in contemporary Pagan Witchcraft. The Italian term for the practice of traditional vernacular witchcraft, according to scholars of Italy (such as Magliocco) and also to Italian practitioners like the participants in this ethnographic research, is *stregoneria*. There are regional dialectal forms that differ throughout Italy for 'witch', such as *stria* and *masca*; however, the most commonly known and used in the general Italian language is *strega*. Some readers may be familiar with the term *stregheria*. This applies to some modern vernacular forms of 'witchcraft', to the subject of the nineteenth-century studies of Charles Leland in central Italy (Leland 1990 [1890]), and particularly to Italian-American magical traditions within postmodern Paganism (Howell 2008a: 9; Magliocco 2004b: 213–14; Marrè 2012: 40–42; Leland 1999: v, 65). The usage was also popularized by the American Pagan teacher and writer Raven Grimassi (Grimassi 2003; Magliocco 2004b: 213–14). There are complex differences between traditions of Italian stregheria and stregoneria, and yet there are also profound interlacings. In a nutshell, Italian-American stregheria has drawn from Gardnerian Wicca and from the creativity of Italian-Americans, as well as from authentic regional Italian beliefs. Nonetheless, it is important to note that some Italian scholars, such as Menegoni, translator of Leland's *Aradia* (1999), stand by the usage of *stregheria* specifically for the local Tuscan worship of Diana and 'Aradia' that Leland encountered. Consequently, there are contemporary Italian witch societies that stress their claims to hereditary ancient origins and insist upon that name, as opposed to *stregoneria*. It is a matter of ongoing debate both within and outside Italy.

Il Sentiero della Dea – The Path of the Goddess

The years 1999, 2001 and 2002 were significant dates in the return of Paganism to Italy. In 1998 one eclectic tradition of deconstructed Wicca, Phyllis Curott's Temple of Ara, which includes elements of Michael Harner's Core Shamanism, took root in Italy (P. Curott, interview, 9 June 2013). Curott's bestselling book, *The Book of Shadows*, was one of the first English-language Pagan books to be translated into Italian; it was published in 1999 with the title *Il Sentiero della Dea* (The Path of the Goddess). Curott, a New York attorney and well-known figure in the international Pagan world, had felt a profound spiritual connection to Italy after an earlier visit there in 1987. After travelling to various ancient classical Pagan sites such as Lake Nemi, she discovered a sense of mission in Italy (interview, 9 June 2013). Her book's biographical account of a woman's discovery of Goddess religion and of a deeper 'calling' found through a profound relationship with nature, through magical practices and community, both validated Italy's native love of such topics and created an explosion of interest. In Curott's talks and seminars in Italy, she makes her tradition's bonds with Italy explicit. Cronos Davide Marrè, an Italian author on Wicca, psychologist and founder of a successful and quickly expanding Pagan society, Il Circolo dei Trivi, described Curott's book thus: 'it created a lively interest in the religion in an adult audience, and one that was prevalently feminine' (Marrè 2007: 57–58, F. C. Howell translation). Prior to Curott's book's Italian publication there had been very few Pagan and Wiccan books translated and published, and none had such a reception as Curott's.

The bonds between Italy and the United States are strong and Italians were receptive to a compelling American spokesperson for Goddess religion, a classically styled priesthood and priestesshood, and Curott's message of healing, beauty, love and, of course, magic. Curott continues to travel throughout Italy, to teach and publish in Italian. Her Temple of Ara tradition, founded in the U.S. in the 1980s – translated easily into Italian as *Il Tempio d'Ara*, The Temple of the Altar – has a wide following throughout Italy. One of the tenets of her practice connects people through meditation and ceremony with the spirits of place using shamanic techniques drawn from her training with Harner's Core Shamanism.

Anglo-Irish Wicca and Other Contemporary Lineages of Paganism

There are also Alexandrian and Gardnerian lineages of Wicca present in Italy, coming from England and Ireland. One example which has had success recently is the Gardnerian 'Whitecroft' lineage taught by Vivianne and Chris Crowley. Dr Vivianne Crowley is a prominent British Jungian psychologist and author. Her recent teaching and publishing in Italy with her husband has rapidly drawn students and initiates. Since the 1980s the Crowleys have played a central role in the pan-European dissemination of Wicca through seminars, conferences and workshops, along with smaller private, initiatory covens

(Hutton 1999: 373–74). The research participants in Italy who were part of their tradition reported that there were approximately seventy regular members of the Italian Crowley Wicca Study Group classes, organized and often taught by Cronos Davide Marrè. Now that their successful book, *Wicca: The Old Religion in the New Millennium* (1996), has been translated and released in Italy as *I Poteri della Wicca: La Più Antica Religione del Mondo nella Società Contemporanea* (2013),[4] it may be predicted that these numbers will grow.

Another example of the cross-European dissemination of Wicca and Paganism from Britain is the tradition of ritual, trance and magic taught by Janet Farrar and Gavin Bone, now grown into an eclectic practice incorporating, like Curott's, shamanic techniques. Farrar is well known internationally in the Pagan and Wiccan world for her publications and earlier teaching with her late husband, Stewart Farrar. With her new partner, Gavin Bone, Farrar has developed a branch of Paganism that is less structured, more inclusive and less initiation-based than the stricter traditions of Alexandrian/ Gardnerian Wicca which she and her husband Stewart taught and wrote on prolifically. Like Curott and the Crowleys, Farrar and Bone are drawing students from across Italy from all walks of life and socio-economic ranks. Farrar and Bone's books have also very recently been translated into Italian. In August 2013 they estimated there to be five covens from Milan to Palermo that drew initiation from them, plus their own ongoing Wiccan Study Group (G. Bone and J. Farrar, emails, June–August 2013).

There are other traditions present in Italy today that can be described generally as 'eclectic', like Curott's and Farrar/Bone's. Given that it was Curott's influence that arguably initially prompted the flow of followers in Italy towards contemporary forms of Paganism, Wicca and Goddess religion, it is not surprising that she would have a steadily growing number of followers and dedicated devotees throughout Italy. She estimated twenty to thirty active groups throughout Italy, led by Italian initiates and teachers (interview, 9 June 2013). Other eclectic Pagan teachers have visited periodically from the United States, such as the well-known authors Starhawk and Silver Ravenwolf (1998, 2002), whose books have also been translated into Italian. They too have Italian programmes now taught by Italian teachers whom they have trained. My own book on deep ecology and Paganism, *Making Magic with Gaia* (2002), jumped to bestseller status on Italy's mind–body–spirit lists in 2008, when the English-language edition was translated by an Italian publishing house (Howell 2008b).

Italy's Indigenous Practices Meet Twenty-First-Century Paganism

Italy has kept alive its regional vernacular religions and many families have stories of folk or indigenous traditions that have survived war, intermarriage, emigration and now industrialization. Orsi (2002) has discussed this in his studies of Madonna veneration in New York's Italian communities. Magliocco (2004a; 2012) details vernacular religious practices in her work on the Evil Eye and other indigenous beliefs in Italy and in Italian immigrant communities. I would argue that the survival of indigenous magical practices may have had more to do with the development of Wicca and Goddess religion than one might at first surmise. For one thing, as discussed above, the Italian predisposition towards embodied, lived religion and materiality has kept many traditions alive; some examples are the use of candles for religious rites that approach forms of vernacular magic, the veneration of statues and their use in achieving intentions through prayer and ceremony, and the wearing of consecrated talismans and amulets (Magliocco 2004a: 151–73; 2012: 1–3; Orsi 2002: xx–xxiv, 168–78, 193–97). Growing up in a Catholic family in New York, I experienced many of these traditions, from the consecrated scapular with a picture of a saint, which we children would wear under our shirts for protection, to the household statues of saints with particular importance in our family (such as Francis of Assisi) or the 'holy cards' with prayers and prints of sacred art that filled our prayer books at Mass. These forms of Catholic materiality and worship indeed made the world a more enchanted and alive place, where the saints and Madonna were not only accessible, but empathic and responsive. My recent experiences and studies in Italy from 2006 to 2012 demonstrated that many of these beliefs, as well as the vernacular traditions of the Evil Eye complex of practices, are common and real.

Such Italian lived religion and magical complexes may relate closely to that which, the American anthropologist and folklorist Charles Leland encountered in Tuscany in 1886. The meeting and subsequent exchanges between Leland and a young woman called 'Maddalena' are for students and scholars of Wicca and Goddess religion a famous series of events. Years later she delivered a manuscript to him of supposed gypsy and witch lore from 'Romagna toscana', a wild, mountainous area of Tuscany and today's Emilia-Romagna, known by that name in the nineteenth century (Hutton 1999: 141–43; Leland 1990 [1890]: 101–102; Leland 1999: 9–10). One could argue that Leland's encounter with Maddalena gave birth to some of the foundational beliefs of contemporary Pagan Goddess practice and Wicca through his book *Aradia, Gospel of the Witches* (1890). Beyond the voluminous debates on the authenticity of a surviving witchcraft cult in Italy, it is clear that Leland's book, drawn in part from Maddalena's stories and spells, influenced Gerald Gardner, the 'founding father' of Wicca (V. Crowley, interview, 21 July 2013; Hutton 1999: 225, 234; Marrè 2012: 40–42; Leland 1999: 23–28). Poetic pieces drawn from Leland's accounts appear in every Gardnerian-derived 'Book of Shadows' (the guide to magic and ritual used by Wiccans), including those now translated widely into Italian.

Sibillia and Pierina – the two women mentioned earlier, who were executed on accusations of witchcraft in fourteenth-century Milan – and their company purportedly celebrated ritual with a figure called Herodias. This may have been the name given by her the accusers and not by the women, who primarily called her 'La Signora del Gioco' (The Lady of the Game) or 'La Signora del Oriente' (The Lady of the East). However, Leland's Maddalena also wrote of a Goddess called Herodias, sometimes attributed as the origin of the Goddess name commonly used in international Wicca, 'Aradia' (Leland 1990 [1890]: 101; Marrè 2009: 27–28; Leland 1999: 12–13). This is a topic of much debate and controversy. Nonetheless, these are critical points that demonstrate to Italian Pagans, as well as to growing numbers of practitioners beyond Italy, that a central tradition of the international Pagan and Wiccan movement can be seen as having its roots in Italy. This Italian heritage is a source of pride both to those who practice traditional Italian witchcraft and to those who have recently espoused initiatory British Wicca.

The Language of the Oaks and the Memory of the Mountains: Druidry Reborn

As the passion for all things Celtic grew in the rest of Europe and in the U.S.A. in the late twentieth century, a search for Celtic identity in Italy likewise began to grow. A milestone year in Italy may have been 1991, when an extensive exhibition in Venice attempted to prove the Celtic roots of all Europe (McCarthy and Hague 2004: 390). In the 1990s, with the slow arrival of books and news from abroad, local groups and teaching 'groves' (*boschi*) of Druidry began to grow (*Il Druidismo Moderno del Cerchio Druidico Italiano*, the website for Italian Druids 2014). Clans, creative reenactors and organizers of festivals began to research tribal heritages of certain areas of Lombardy, Piedmont and other areas, as many began to hold camps and trainings and the fervour for Celticity grew. Ossian D'Ambrosio and his wife, Maria Feo, have created a northern Italian tradition of Druidry that is ecological and place-oriented; their tradition is practised in the local oak and chestnut groves dotted with ancient archaeological sites. Together with the Wiccan community they have held a conference each autumn, often focusing on the topic: 'From Folk Healers and Mediaeval Alchemists to Postmodern Paganism'. This evolution has been an ongoing theme in the conference's talks, seminars, guided walks and workshops; that is, the heritage and succession in Italy from traditional folk healers practising vernacular magic and healing, and from medieval alchemists and magicians, to today's organized religions of Wicca and Druidry. Prominent Druid writers and teachers such as Philip Carr-Gomm and his wife have travelled from the U.K. to Italy to teach and hold workshops, including at the Piedmont conference mentioned above. Consequently, in the last five to ten years a new communication and collaboration has grown between the well-known British Isles Order of Bards, Ovates and Druids (OBOD) and various Druid groups in northern Italy (OBOD in Italia 2014). (See Figure 12.2.)

Fig. 12.2 *Druids, Wiccans and other Pagans consecrate a new stone labyrinth at a community ritual site in Piedmont, 2013. Image used with kind permission of the photographer, Cronos Davide Marrè.*

Sense of Place, *Campanilismo* and the Celtic Revival

The Italian word for a passionate love of home and all that relates to one's lands is *campanilismo* – local patriotism or chauvinism (Tak 2000: 27). (The word translated literally means 'bell-towerism'; that is, 'My village's bell-tower is bigger, more beautiful and louder-chiming than your village's bell-tower'.) The concept of being a Druid in a region where the Romans waged centuries of war against the Gallo-Celtic tribal peoples has great influence in the north of Italy, and some northerners are reclaiming this heritage. Such regional devotion can be a community-developing, identity-affirming practice. Unfortunately, it can also be coloured by exclusionary and nationalistic politics.

My Italian research and experience did not reveal evidence of neo-colonialism in Paganism's re-emergence and reconstruction. Italy is not a former colony of an imperial power, but rather a former empire itself, with colonies in Africa as recently as the mid-twentieth century. Italians do have a deep admiration for the British Isles and the United States, and thus the new recognition of and involvement in the growing Italian Pagan religious communities by Anglophone teachers has provided many with a sense of pride and international recognition, but I would not see this as a form of colonial relationship.

Themes of Celticity can, on the other hand, demonstrate nationalism and occasionally a 'poisoned sense of place' (Relph 1997, quoted in DeMiglio and Williams 2008: 24). Some, like the Italian political party Lega Nord (Northern League), have appropriated images of Celticity to sponsor and promote ideological purposes which are at times bigoted and xenophobic. One of the most vehement planks of the party has been its anti-immigration ideology. McCarthy and Hague (2004: 390) discuss their theories of mistaken conceptions of Celticity in relation to other parts of the world, such as in the western United States:

> From the outset, therefore, 'Celtic' symbolically marked loss of political and cultural power.… This viewpoint developed rapidly in the late 18th century, when antiquarians mixed fantasy and fact to produce a vision of the Celts as warrior poets. Celtic spirituality, music, poetry, and history were reclaimed and revered, the result being 'bardic nationalism'.

Regina Bendix (1992, 1997, 1999) has discussed such developments and 'entanglements' as integrally involved with the Romantic movement of the eighteenth and nineteenth centuries in northern Europe.

She has also examined in depth the relationship between folklore studies and exclusionary or nationalist politics (1997). As in other parts of the world, in recent years reenactments of 'Celtic' tribal people's ways of life, their crafts and styles of warfare have become a huge pastime and hobby for many in Italy. Such reenactments and festivals are indeed entertaining, creative and historically educational; yet some may also be founded on a political agenda.

The Celtic New Year Festival – Lega Nord and Celticity in Northern Italy

For thirteen years, as autumn returned to Milan a uniquely northern Italian event unfolded at Milan's grand central castle and surrounding park: a Celtic New Year festival (*La Festa di Capodanno Celtico*). Samhain is believed to have been the end of the Celtic calendar year and the ancient festival of harvest's end (Pearson 2002: 4–6). For the three years I observed the festival it was extraordinary to witness the spectacle in Milan's downtown area: people on horseback and on foot in costumes evoking ancient eras, encampments with Iron Age and earlier tools, and so on (Figure 12.3). Craftspeople and artisans sold their wares: vendors and market stalls with every possible sort of New Age or Pagan jewellery, statuary, artwork, tarot-card readers, face painters and so forth. However, this festival was notably place-specific: all was dedicated to and derived from what the participants believed to be the pre-Roman tribes specifically of northern Italy. There was also an array of performances from all over the related cultures of the Celtic world, including Bretons, Irish and Scots. Such an event obviously required huge municipal financing and planning. Upon investigation, it was revealed how.

In addition to *La Dolce Vita*, fine food, film and scenery, Italy is known for volatile governments. The political party Lega Nord, despite vicissitudes in popularity, at the time of writing holds a substantial number of seats in the national and local parliaments.[5] Milan is the city of Silvio Berlusconi's rise to importance in politics and the media, as well as in the construction industry. At various periods in history Milan has held a prominent seat of power – it was the capital of the Roman Empire for about a century and also the home of the medieval and Renaissance Visconti and later the Sforza dynasties. Thus, like other former Italian city-states, Milan has had a sense of its own civic religion from early in its history, with a founding myth and locally revered figures (Howell 2012; Parsons 2002, 2004). In the

Fig. 12.3 '*Gallo-Celtic warriors' assemble to spar and process in Milan's central piazza, Piazza Duomo, at the Celtic New Year festival 2008. Author's photograph.*

pre-Lombard, pre-Roman period, the Gauls who dwelt in this region of northern Italy are believed to have been the Insubri. In recent years their foundation myths caught the imaginations of many, including Lega Nord. The party focused on Milan as their capital and symbol. The now retired leader of the party, Umberto Bossi, declared in 1993 that Milan 'belongs to the Northern League. It is the federal capital of the North and it is ours' (Passarelli and Tuorto 2012: 139). Bossi has been right on more than one occasion, and Lega Nord returned to power in Lombardy in February 2013. At the heart of the Celtic New Year festival was Milan's foundational myth, espoused and publicized by Lega Nord. The location of the festival was central to their locative materiality: it had to be situated near the supposed place of Milan's original founding in the fourth century BCE, an actual geographic location the organizers believe to be sacred. It was also near to the castle and main cathedral, with their inherent symbolism and centrality.

In fieldwork interviews the organizers discussed their profound belief in the establishment of Milan as a 'nemeton' (a pan-Celtic term for a central meeting or ceremonial centre) in the fourth century

BCE. Elena and Leo (pseudonyms) felt that the castle stands near that ancient meeting and ritual spot. They also discussed their belief in the legends of Milan's founding by a Druid who had seen a white boar sow, believed to be a positive auspice. The white boar is still one of the esoteric symbols of Milan. October was chosen for the Celtic New Year festival because the organizers believe the founding of Milan occurred at Samhain, or *Samonios* – that is, the end of October/beginning of November (E. Merlo, interviews, October 2008).

Despite the festival's esoteric premises, little by little, over time, the Pagan community of Wiccans and Druids from Lombardy and its environs began to withdraw their support. At first they had used the festival as an opportunity to gather and live out a Pagan identity, publicly, in the centre of Milan. Those who were craftspeople also used it as a chance to sell esoteric crafts, services and books. However, by 2009 the Pagan community had all but withdrawn its involvement. Many were aware of the politics behind it and were uncomfortable with the policies and the restrictions that the organizers began to enforce. As Ossian put it, the festival became merely a commercial event and no longer an opportunity for a Pagan community gathering (O. D'Ambrosio, emails, 2008–2010).

There are surely Pagan groups that support Lega Nord and its philosophies, yet I did not encounter such groups in my 2006–2012 research – individuals, certainly, but not whole groups. In 2012 I interviewed a group of Lombardy reenactors known as the 'Popolo di Brig', named after the pan-Celtic Goddess Brigid or Brig. Their leaders denied identification with politics in any way – including Lega Nord and its 'bigotry'. They also denied a relationship with Paganism. They claimed to be simply interested in research and the development of knowledge and practice regarding what they believe the Celtic tribal people of their specific area ate, drank, played and wore (interview, 1 November 2012).

The political pendulum of Milan's city government swung from Right to Left once more in 2012.[6] In spring 2012 the Celtic New Year festival was abruptly cancelled, as was a large related exhibition. However, since the organizers are once more in power in the regional government, it is likely they will focus their attention on this or another dramatic and accessible location for the festival. Leo, the chief organizer and a well-known figure in Lega Nord, told me by phone in 2012: 'We are focusing our efforts on the festival now'. The concept of Celticity is powerful for their purposes and they have used it to create an image of themselves as oppressed Other – even a tribal, indigenous Other. A famous (and, for some, infamous) Lega Nord poster seen throughout Lombardy used the image of a Native American to encourage northern Italians to identify as a tribal people being disenfranchised by injustice and immigration. Despite this high-profile activity of Lega Nord, Celticity in Italy is not necessarily politicized, nor is Paganism generally. On the contrary, Paganism has been an inclusive 'common denominator' bringing people together from differing social and economic milieux, regions and walks of life.

Informal Poll Data and Demographics

This section attempts to give some quantitative data. It is an 'attempt' because, despite the liberalizing of legislation in Italy in recent years, people may not feel comfortable divulging their Pagan practice, may still baptize their children into Catholicism (C. D. Marrè, emails, 9 April and 11 June 2013), or, as Rountree (2011) observed in Malta, may participate in Mass or other ceremonies for social-acceptance reasons.

Curott stated that the Temple of Ara's mixed-gender groups in Italy are growing. She now has teaching centres throughout Italy and sees the movement expanding generally – not only in her own tradition (P. Curott, interview, 9 June 2013). The Crowleys' Wicca Study Groups will extend from Milan to Rome, Naples and Sicily in the coming year. Their tradition today comprises somewhere around a few hundred; however, with the recent publication of the Crowleys' first Italian book, it seems likely their numbers will increase (V. and C. Crowley, emails and interviews, 26 April and 21 July 2013). Vanth Spiritwalker, the Italian leader of the organization Pagan Pride (with headquarters in Rome), also reports growing numbers. His surveys, which extrapolate data from mailing lists, attendance and personal studies, estimate the Italian Pagan community overall at six to eight thousand people (V. Spiritwalker, emails, 2–21 June 2013).

The Italian organization CESNUR, 'The Center for Studies on New Religions', collects data on religious groups represented in Italy. Their 2012 estimate states that three thousand people are involved in the categories they combine as: 'Neo-Pagan, Neo-Shamanic and Wicca' (CESNUR 2013). My ethnographic research indicates their estimates are low:[7]

• The Pagan movement in Italy is young in two senses: recently formed, and the median age in both north and south is twenty-five to thirty-five years.

- The movement is generally not racially or ethnically diverse, but made up of white, lower-middle to upper-middle class participants; those educated tend to be holders of professional certificates, or, if university-educated, have an undergraduate degree.
- Of the mixed-sex groups, many report generally a 60/40 ratio of women to men.
- Four out of the seven groups polled in the north and south of Italy report strong LGBTQ community involvement. The Druids of Piedmont report a greater hetero and traditional family involvement.
- There is a notable growth in feminist traditions and women-only groups.
- There is a strong ethos and direction towards ecological activism and service-minded action.
- The overall estimates from participants and organization leaders on Pagan population numbers have a wide range: from CESNUR's three thousand to Pagan Pride's eight thousand individuals throughout Italy. Spiritwalker (Pagan Pride) shared his study of data drawn from mailing lists, event registration and participation, and journal subscriptions.

Conclusions

The Pagan Federation of Great Britain (Hutton 1999: 371, 390; Pagan Federation International 2013) is an international organization operating in twenty-five countries (M. Sythove, email, 17 June 2013). Among its many involvements and activities, it disseminates information about contemporary Paganism, holds events and organizes community liaison, publishes an international journal and works to protect religious freedoms and rights in the workplace, schools, prisons and the military. Around 1990 the organizers contacted me to ask whether I would correspond with a Wiccan practitioner in Italy interested in starting a Pagan Federation International branch. He and I corresponded for some time, but it seemed ultimately that there was little interest and few, if any, practitioners. The movement simply had not reached Italy yet. Now, at the time of writing, it is a different scenario.

Hutton observed that his experiences with Pagan communities in Britain were positive and personally meaningful: 'I was repeatedly provided with examples … of the majesty, wisdom, eloquence, and creative power of otherwise ordinary people, and the capacity

of religious ritual and ritual magic to exert powerful transforma-
tive effects upon them' (Hutton 2004: 175). My experiences with the
Pagan movement across Italy could be described similarly. By the last
years of the twentieth century the increasingly globalized, English-
speaking younger generations in Italy were ready for a message that
had caught northern European and American imaginations and hearts
in earlier decades: that of a lifestyle – as well as a spiritual path – that
was empowering, inclusive and holistic.

This volume examines impulses of colonialism and nationalism
involved with Paganism in Europe. The argument presented in this
chapter is that Italy cannot be described as suffering from postcolonial impositions of belief. Despite the fact that many of the Pagan
teachers and authors discussed above have come recently from
outside Italy (many of whom have contributed to this research), they
have now trained local, native Italian leaders, who are quickly taking
over the group management and dissemination of the traditions.

Similar to Rountree's findings in Malta, in Italy 'Catholics grow
up familiar with sacred, extraordinary events being interpreted
as miracles or "mysteries of faith" by the Church, interpretations
which outsiders to Catholicism, especially Protestant Christianities,
might see as "magical thinking"' (Rountree 2011: 860). Italians seem
to find a natural, instinctive home in the aesthetic expression of
ritual, of seasonal commemorations and locally derived feasts, which
along with their native propensity for fierce loyalties and bonds lend
themselves well to the collective community development found in
Paganism.

In terms of nationalistic impulses, Lega Nord's attempts to coopt
symbols of Celticity demonstrate the need for ongoing deconstruc-
tions of folklore's intimate historical relationship with nationalism.
Archaeology must continue such self-reflexivity too, as Dietler
(1994) warned two decades ago regarding French nationalist movements using Celtic imagery. Despite the Gallo-Celtic traditions which
many Italian Pagans honour and observe, my observations found a
community and place-oriented practice which did not show any evidence of prejudice – neither due to age, education, sexual preference,
social status nor geographic origin. On the contrary, as Paganism in
Italy grows into its third decade, the ongoing interregional liaison
and dialogues, the collaborative conferences and seminars, provide
further evidence of an increasingly mature and open-minded inclusivity. An old Italian saying can sometimes be heard at Pagan gatherings, albeit somewhat tongue in cheek: *Tremate, tremate! Le streghe
sono tornate!* ('Tremble, tremble! The witches are back!'). Call them

Witches, Druids, Shamans or simply Pagans; they are indeed back. One might ask: did they ever leave?

Notes

1 A note on usage: where 'Witchcraft' is capitalized, it refers to the contemporary religion, not to popular culture imagery or vernacular tradition. The term 'Paganism' will be used instead of 'Neo-Paganism'.

2 'Synthesis' is a term preferable to 'syncretism' for many scholars (Mumm 2002: 116–17). Whatever the term, the union of beliefs and practices recurred and continues recurring, for example, in the conquest of the Americas, as well as Asia and other regions of Christianity's expansion (Chidester 2000; MacCulloch 2009; Mumm 2002).

3 In the twentieth century Italy had the largest Communist Party outside Russia (Caldwell 1991: 98–99; Ginsborg 2003: 84–85, 360–61, 375–76, 442).

4 *The Powers of Wicca: The World's Oldest Religion in our Contemporary Society* (my translation of the title).

5 In the general elections in February 2013, Lega Nord, in a Centre-Right coalition with Silvio Berlusconi's People of Freedom party (Il Popolo della Libertà, PdL), won 124 seats in the national Chamber of Deputies and 116 in the Senate (Robert Schuman: The Research and Study Centre on Europe 2013).

6 A political definition of Lega Nord is appropriately paradoxical. The party is generally described as right wing; however, its main planks are libertarian and federalist, and it has drawn both supporters and leaders from the far Left and Centre as well as the Right.

7 This information was drawn from questionnaires emailed in 2008 to seven groups: six organizations in Milan, Piedmont, Rome and Sicily, and one individual coven with members in the regions of Lombardy and Lazio (Howell 2008a). Participants were polled again in 2013 and found the data to be still generally in agreement with the 2008 figures, though the group members were older and more men were involved.

References

Adler, M. 1981[1979]. *Drawing Down the Moon: Witches, Druids, Goddess-Worshippers and Other Pagans in American Today*. Boston, MA: Beacon Press.

Barstow, A.L. 1994. *Witchcraze: A New History of the European Witch Hunts*. London: HarperCollins.

Bendix, R. 1992. 'Diverging Paths in the Scientific Search for Authenticity', *Journal of Folklore Research* 29(2): 103–32.
———. 1997. *In Search of Authenticity: The Formation of Folklore Studies*. Madison: University of Wisconsin.
———. 1999. 'Time and Ourselves: The Discomforts of Reflexive Disciplinary History: Response to Wolfgang Kaschuba', *Journal of Folklore Research* 36(2/3): 179–83.
Berman, M. 1981. *The Reenchantment of the World*. Ithaca, NY: Cornell University Press.
Caldwell, L. 1991. 'Italian Feminism: Some Considerations', in Z.G. Baranski and S. Vinall (eds), *Women and Italy: Essays on Gender, Culture and History*. University of Reading: Macmillan, pp. 95–116.
CESNUR (Center for Studies on New Religions). 2013. http://www.cesnur.it. Accessed 6 May 2013.
Chidester, D. 2000. *Christianity: A Global History*. New York: HarperCollins.
Crowley, V. 1996. *Wicca: The Old Religion in the New Millennium*. London: HarperCollins.
———. 2013. *I Poteri della Wicca: La Più Antica Religione del Mondo nella Società Contemporanea*. Milan: Armenia.
Curott, P. 1998. *The Book of Shadows*. New York: Broadway Books/Random House.
———. 1999. *Il Sentiero della Dea*. Milan: Sonzogno.
Dietler, M. 1994. 'Our Ancestors the Gauls: Archaeology, Ethnic Nationalism, and the Manipulation of Celtic Identity in Modern Europe', *American Anthropologist* 96(3): 584–605.
DeMiglio, L. and A. Williams. 2008. 'A Sense of Place, a Sense of Well-being', in J. Eyles and A. Williams (eds), *Sense of Place, Health and Quality of Life*. Aldershot and Burlington: Ashgate, pp. 15–30.
Farrar, J. and S. Farrar. 1996. *A Witches' Bible: The Complete Witches' Handbook*. Custer: Phoenix Publishing.
Farrar, J and S. Farrar. 2013. *La Bibbia delle Streghe* (2 vols). Sossano, Italy: Anguana Edizioni.
Ginsborg, P. 2003. *A History of Contemporary Italy: Society and Politics 1943–1988*. London and New York: Palgrave Macmillan.
Grimassi, R. 2003. *Italian Witchcraft: The Old Religion of Southern Europe*. St. Paul, MN: Llewellyn.
Guano, E. 2007. 'Respectable Ladies and Uncouth Men: The Performative Politics of Class and Gender in the Public Realm of an Italian City', *The Journal of American Folklore* 120: 48–72.
Harvey, G. 1997. *Contemporary Paganism: Listening People, Speaking Earth*. New York: New York University Press.
———. 2000. *Credenti della Nuova Era: I Pagani Contemporanei*. Milan: Feltrinelli.
Howell, F.C. 2002. *Making Magic with Gaia: Practices to Heal Ourselves and Our Planet*. Boston & York Beach: Red Wheel/Weiser LLC.

——. 2008a. 'The Goddess Returns to Italy: Paganism and Wicca Reborn as a New Religious and Social Movement', *The Pomegranate: The International Journal of Pagan Studies* 10(1): 5–20.

——. 2008b. *Gaia: Magia per il Pianeta*. Rome: Venexia editrice.

——. 2012. 'Celticity, Place and Power: Civil Religion and Materiality in Northern Italy's "Celtic New Year" Festival', *The Annual Conference of the American Academy of Religion*, 20 November 2012. Chicago: American Academy of Religion.

——. 2013. 'Sense of Place, Heterotopia and Community: Performing Land and Folding Time in the Badalisc Festival of Northern Italy', *Folklore* 124(1): 45–63.

Hutton, R. 1999. *The Triumph of the Moon: A History of Modern Pagan Witchcraft*. Oxford: Oxford University Press.

——. 2002. 'The Roots of Modern Paganism', in J. Pearson (ed.), *Belief Beyond Boundaries: Wicca, Celtic Spirituality and the New Age*. Aldershot and Burlington: Ashgate; and Milton Keynes: The Open University, pp. 225–37.

——. 2004. 'Living with Witchcraft', in J. Blain, D. Ezzy and G. Harvey (eds), *Researching Paganisms*. Walnut Creek: Altamira Press, pp. 171–87.

Il Druidismo Moderno del Cerchio Druidico Italiano. 2014. Retrieved 5 May 2014 from http://www.cerchiodruidico.it/nemeton

Leynse, W.L.H. 2006. 'Journeys through "ingestible topography": Socializing the "Situated Eater" in France', *European Studies* 22: 129–58.

Leland, C.G. 1990[1890]. *Aradia: Gospel of the Witches*. Custer, WA: Phoenix Publishing Inc.

Leland, C.G. 1999. *Aradia: Il Vangelo delle Streghe*. Translated and edited by Lorenza Menegoni. Firenze: Leo S. Olschki Editore.

MacCulloch, D. 2009. *Christianity: The First Three Thousand Years*. New York, Toronto and London: Penguin.

Magliocco, S. 2004a. 'Witchcraft, Healing and Vernacular Magic in Italy', in W. DeBlécourt and O. Davies (eds), *Witchcraft Continued: Popular Magic in Modern Europe*. Manchester and New York: Manchester University Press, pp. 151–73.

——. 2004b. *Witching Culture: Folklore and Neo-Paganism in America*. Philadelphia: University of Pennsylvania.

——. 2012. 'Beyond Belief: Context, Rationality and Participatory Consciousness', *Western Folklore* 71(1): 5–20.

Marrè, C.D. 2007. *Wicca: La Nuova Era della Vecchia Religione*. Brescia, Italy: Aradia Edizioni.

——. 2009. *La Visione del Sabba* [A View of the Sabbat]. Brescia: Aradia Edizioni.

——. 2012. 'Leland and Italian Witchcraft', *Pagan Dawn: The Journal of the Pagan Federation* 184 (Autumn Equinox): 40–42.

McCarthy, J. and E. Hague. 2004. 'Race, Nation and Nature: The Cultural Politics of "Celtic" Identification in the American West', *The Annals of the Association of American Geographers* 94(2): 387–408.

Mumm, S. 2002. 'Aspirational Indians: North American and Indigenous Religions and the New Age', in J. Pearson (ed.), *Belief beyond Boundaries: Wicca, Celtic Spirituality and the New Age*. Aldershot and Burlington: Ashgate; and Milton Keynes: The Open University, pp. 103–31.

Murano, L. 2006 [1976]. *La Signora del Gioco: La Caccia Alle Streghe Interpretata dalle Sue Vittime* [The Lady of the Game: The Witchhunt Interpreted by the Victims]. Milan: Feltrinelli.

OBOD in Italia: Ordine Bardi, Ovati e Druidi. 2014. http://www.druidry.it. Accessed 5 May 2014.

Orsi, R.A. 2002. *The Madonna of 115th Street: Faith and Community in Italian Harlem, 1880–1950*. New Haven and London: Yale University Press.

Pagan Federation International. 2013. http://www.paganfederation.org. Accessed 20 June 2013.

Parsons, G. 2002. *Perspectives on Civil Religion*. Aldershot and Burlington: Ashgate; and Milton Keynes: The Open University.

——. 2004. *Siena, Civil Religion and the Sienese*. Aldershot and Burlington: Ashgate.

Passarelli, G. and D. Tuorto. 2012. *Lega & Padania: Storie e luoghi delle camicie Verdi* [The League and Padania: Stories and Places of the Green Shirts]. Bologna: Il Mulino.

Pearson, J. (ed.) 2002. *Belief beyond Boundaries: Wicca, Celtic Spirituality and the New Age*. Aldershot and Burlington: Ashgate; and Milton Keynes: The Open University.

Ravenwolf, S. 1998. *Teen Witch: Wicca for a New Generation*. St. Paul, MN: Llewellyn.

——. 2002. *To Ride a Silver Broomstick*. St. Paul, MN: Llewellyn.

Relph, E. 1997. 'Sense of Place', in S. Hanson (ed.), *Ten Geographic Ideas that Changed the World*. New Brunswick: Rutgers University Press, pp. 205–226.

Robert Schuman: The Research and Study Centre on Europe. 2013. http://www.robert-schuman.eu. Accessed 29 August 2013.

Rountree, K. 2011. 'Localizing Neo-Paganism: Integrating Global and Indigenous Traditions in a Mediterranean Catholic Society', *Journal of the Royal Anthropological Institute* 17: 846–72.

Sapelli, G. 1995. *Southern Europe since 1945: Tradition and Modernity in Portugal, Spain, Italy, Greece and Turkey*. Harlow: Longman.

Starhawk. 1979. *The Spiral Dance: A Rebirth of the Ancient Religion of the Great Goddess*. San Francisco: Harper and Row.

Tak, H. 2000. *South Italian Festivals: A Local History of Ritual and Change*. Amsterdam: Amsterdam University Press.

Von Stuckrad, K. 2002. 'Reenchanting Nature: Modern Western Shamanism and Nineteenth-Century Thought', *Journal of the American Academy of Religion* 70(4): 771–99.

13

Authenticity and Invention in the Quest for a Modern Maltese Paganism

Kathryn Rountree

Introduction

In the introduction to this volume I suggested that two broad impulses – what I have called colonialist and nationalist – can be identified amidst the complex and changing conditions surrounding the emergence of Pagan and Native Faith movements in Europe over the last quarter of a century. The second of these processes tends to be associated with ethnic nationalism and concentrates on the retrieval, reconstruction and reimagination of pre-Christian religions in connection with nation-building or other projects in which indigeneity is important. (It may, though, entail romantic nationalism rather than ethnonationalism, as Butler, this volume, shows.) The other process, which I observe as a form of religious neo-colonialism but could arguably be seen less pejoratively and contentiously as universalism, involves the propagation, uptake and adaptation of Anglo-American Pagan traditions to a huge variety of local cultural and national contexts, whereupon they are indigenized to some degree. These forms of Paganism also look to the pre-Christian past for religious inspiration, emphasize connection to a local environment and may well place importance on ethnic identity. However, any political intentions connected with their religious project do not have to do with ethnonationalism, which may be frowned upon as uncomfortably connected with racism and right-wing politics. Again it should be emphasized that these two broad processes are not mutually discrete; they overlap and are entangled, as a number of chapters in this volume show.

The contemporary Pagan community in Malta, amongst whom I have been conducting ethnographic fieldwork since 2005 (Rountree 2010, 2011), shares much with other European groups engaged in the second of these processes, variously adapting British-derived Wicca, American-derived Goddess Spirituality and eclectic Paganism to the Maltese context, landscape and seasons. This localizing project, like others, has a particular character on account of the larger religious, historical and cultural context in which it is embedded. Unlike many Pagans who also take their cue from Anglo-American traditions, Maltese Pagans are not generally or virulently engaged in a critique of Christianity; this would constitute a critique of the dominant Catholic religiosity of the society in which they were raised, whose traditions are now enmeshed in their lives. Indeed, many Maltese Wiccans and Pagans see themselves as at least culturally Catholic, although they are spiritually Pagan. Claiming it is difficult to know much detail about the pre-Christian religions of their islands, and pointing out that in any case there was a series of religions over the five millennia of pre-Christian settlement, they have begun to construct local versions of Paganism which combine Anglo-American influences with indigenous cultural and environmental knowledge, influenced by Catholic religiosity.

This chapter looks at the ways in which Maltese Pagans have variously approached the construction of a local Paganism. The second half considers in particular a coven whose members are taking initiatory training from a British High Priestess of Alexandrian Wicca to fulfil their aspiration of 'getting [their] proper lineage' in this Witchcraft tradition.[1] As well as embracing this U.K.-derived tradition and taking classes via Skype from an instructor living in Cornwall, they creatively weave local elements into their practices. They have, for example, 'invented' an earth Goddess and sea God who, they say, represent the quintessential natural forces in Malta, incorporate the divinities of all pantheons at one time present in the islands and provide a correspondence with the Wiccan Lord (God) and Lady (Goddess). Hence they draw upon and integrate foreign and local sources of authenticity. It is argued here that such inventiveness, adaptability and eclecticism are as much customary Maltese cultural behaviour – a legacy of a long history of colonization – as they are postmodern bricolage and invention.

The Maltese Context

Several features contribute to the unique cultural context in which Maltese Pagans have been constructing their spiritual path during the last two decades. In Malta, as in Italy (Howell, this volume; Magliocco 2000, 2004, 2005), Paganism is built into a culture with its own traditions of magical belief and practice, where, until fairly recently, witchcraft was held by many to be a reality, and there are still vestiges of belief in the evil eye. Thus Maltese Pagans find themselves sandwiched between a modern, global, imported phenomenon and longstanding traditions rooted in their own cultural heritage.

Another feature which differentiates the Maltese milieu from the contexts of most published studies of modern Western Paganism is that the latter have been mostly conducted in societies which are predominantly Protestant and more obviously secular. This has meant that the ways in which Paganism is constructed in these contexts have come to be taken as normative by many scholars and Pagans. A fundamental plank of modern Pagan and Native Faith identity in Europe and elsewhere in the world is assumed to be the adoption or reconstruction of a religion seen as prior to, and different from, Christianity (Strmiska 2005: 7). This assumed norm does not take into account the situation in countries which are very predominantly Roman Catholic, such as Ireland, Spain, Portugal, Italy and Malta. Ninety-eight per cent of Maltese people identify as Roman Catholic (*World Factbook* 2014) and Catholicism has traditionally permeated every sphere of public and domestic, social and political life (Tabone 1994). I have previously argued that Maltese Paganism differs from British and North American Paganisms partly as a result of what might be seen as a broadly transposable cultural logic between aspects of Roman Catholicism and Paganism in the local context, despite the antipathy displayed by many Catholics towards Pagans when they find out about them (Rountree 2010, 2011). That is not to suggest that the two traditions are interchangeable – obviously they are not – but that Maltese Pagans and Catholics share some common ways of thinking and practising religion along with a shared heritage which has long drawn on and combined Pagan and Christian ideas and practices. For Maltese Pagans to deny Catholicism would mean eschewing their Maltese identity. Every Maltese Pagan I have met was raised Catholic, and the majority who are parents are facilitating their children's induction into Catholicism, for example, by supporting their First Holy Communion and sending them to church schools, which are regarded as better than state schools. While it is true that the tight relationship between church and state has weakened and the power of the church and its institutions and Mass attendance have decreased gradually in recent decades, Malta is still a strongly Catholic society (*Sunday Mass Attendance Census* 2005).

Thus Maltese Pagans' relationship with the dominant religion of their society is different from that of many other followers of European Paganisms and Native Faiths. So is their relationship with the religions of their islands' past. In Malta Christianity is not seen as the religion of the outsider or a 'stranger faith' in juxtaposition with an ancient, indigenous religion. Christianity is regarded as the indigenous religion; the pre-Christian past was merely a prefiguration of the true and fully realized religion of Christianity. Hence, for example, according to a leading priest on the island, the worship of a nurturing Mother Goddess in the Neolithic era prefigured the veneration of Holy Mary, Jesus's mother (Rountree 1999: 209). In popular narratives of Maltese history, Saint Paul's shipwreck on Malta in 60 AD en route to martyrdom in Rome and his conversion of the populace to Christianity, along with the period when the Knights of St John ruled the islands (1530–1798), are of paramount importance. Christianity connects Malta to Europe rather than north Africa, a preferable identity for most Maltese. People know, of course, that their islands were settled five thousand years before Christ by a string of different peoples from the Neolithic (5,000 BC) to the Bronze Age (2,500 BC), followed by the Phoenicians (800 BC), Carthaginians (550 BC) and Romans (218 BC), all leaving material traces of their religions. However, archaeologists have told them that these early peoples were not their ancestors but distant, lost peoples who were wiped out by successive invasions (Bonanno 1997; Trump 2002; Bonanno and Cilia 2005). Thus there is not just one pre-Christian religion available to Maltese Pagans to retrieve as 'indigenous'.

Malta's history is a saga of perpetual colonization with successive peoples contributing to Maltese culture and ethnicity. Attracted by the islands' strategic position in the middle of the Mediterranean and the many sheltered harbours, a stream of peoples followed those of the pre-Christian era (Cassar 2000): the Byzantine empire (by 535 AD), Arabs (870), Normans (1090), Swabians (1194), Angevins (1266), Aragonese (1283), Castilians (1410), the Knights of St John (1530), the French (1798) and the British (1800). Malta gained independence from Britain in 1964, became a republic in 1974 and joined the European Union in 2004. The impact of millennia of foreign domination has been all the greater for Malta because of the country's small size and high population density. According to Sultana and Baldacchino (1994: 15), 'The country is thus an excellent example of the capacity of colonialism to effect an infiltration of culture to the point when it becomes endemic'. Hence Maltese people have a familiar relationship with cultural eclecticism and syncretism.

Like many of their counterparts elsewhere in the world, Maltese Pagans construct idiosyncratic and eclectic paths drawing on global resources available through the Internet and literature mainly from Britain and North America. Knowledge is gleaned about a vast range of topics: Wicca and other Pagan paths, the Tarot and innumerable forms of divination, Kabbalah, astrology, runes, alchemy, herbs, crystals, Pagan chants and songs, Wiccan tools and invocations, guided visualizations, and deities from numerous ancient and living traditions. Perhaps because they have been raised in a society where religiosity and the acquisition of religious knowledge are strongly emphasized, indeed the norm, Maltese Pagans are on the whole strikingly well read and conscientious about becoming better informed. Several mentioned owning hundreds of books on the subject and the importance of personal research and group study were often stressed.

On Strmiska's (2005: 19) continuum of modern Pagan movements, where 'Eclectic' and 'Reconstructionist' represent the extremes, Maltese Paganism would appear to sit at the Eclectic end, which distinguishes it from other (especially central and eastern) European Paganisms and ties it more closely with Britain. However it must be emphasized that Maltese Pagans do not fit neatly with all the characteristics Strmiska (2005: 21–22) assigns to Eclectic Pagans: 'Theirs is an identity that highlights openness and naturalness, connected not so much with any particular region of the earth as with the earth itself, affiliated not with any particular group of humans speaking any particular language or practicing any particular traditions but with a larger and also vaguer sense of universal humanity'. For Reconstructionist Pagans, on the other hand, Strmiska (2005: 21) says that 'a discourse of continuity with the past and deep-rootedness in tradition' is extremely important. Strmiska's argument that connection to a particular landscape, particular cultural traditions and ethnic identity are unimportant to Eclectic Pagans is not borne out in the Maltese case, as will be shown. The Maltese landscape, local cultural traditions and being Maltese are indeed important to Maltese Pagans, and in some groups they are extremely important. Perhaps because there is no apparent threat to their ethnic identity and because of their long history of colonization, a fairly comfortable relationship with cultural eclecticism and syncretism has become an essential part of being Maltese. 'To be Maltese is to be a cocktail!' one Witch told me, when asked about her cooption of deities, traditions and myths from many cultures. Maltese identity is seen by Pagans as distinctive and important as an organizing principle of social life in Malta: it is simply not seen as being in jeopardy.

Another important local influence on the construction of Maltese Paganism is the local natural environment and seasonal cycle. Paganism is above all an earth-based religion and local landscapes are vitally important to practitioners. The ways in which the seasons cycle in Malta differ from Britain or North America, and therefore the festivals constituting the 'Wheel of the Year' have different associations from those outlined in British or North American literature. The hotter climate means that the grain harvest belongs to the summer solstice rather than to Lughnasadh, for example, while Lughnasadh is the time of the grape harvest. In Malta autumn is associated not with turning towards the darker, colder, 'dying' part of the year, but with the welcome arrival of the first rains, new growth and relief from summer drought.

Although Malta's past includes several pre-Christian religions, Maltese Pagans do not mobilize these in the construction of a contemporary tradition in the way that Pagan Reconstructionists do elsewhere in Europe. Bound up with the country's history of colonization and small size, there has long been a national tendency to sometimes value the foreign over the local (Grixti 2006). There is a defensive pride about things Maltese, but also in some quarters something of a cultural cringe with respect to things foreign, particularly British, probably related to Malta's long period as a British colony. Many rank foreign products, foreign media and a British university education, for example, more highly than the local varieties. This helps explain why Maltese Pagans, as a generally youthful, educated, outward-looking demographic, initially embraced the global Pagan movement and sources of inspiration outside their own culture, rather than seeking to retrieve Maltese folk tradition or something they might claim as an 'indigenous religion'. Most, probably all, participate in online communities and many travel abroad regularly for holidays, to meet Pagan friends abroad, for Wiccan training or Pagan events in the U.K., to visit Pagan hubs like Glastonbury or ancient sites like Stonehenge and Avebury, and for stints of work and study, made easier since Malta's entry to the European Union. One of the attractions of Paganism is precisely that it connects them with an international community and provides some relief from what some experience as the religious and cultural claustrophobia and conservatism of a small island nation.

Although Maltese Pagans have not tried to retrieve one of the pre-Christian – such as Phoenician or Roman – religions in their construction of a contemporary tradition, they are, however, very conscious and proud of their country's unique Neolithic temple remains, which apparently attest to a religion centred on a female deity. A few are very knowledgeable about the temples and a few visit the temples occasionally for rituals. They know that foreign Pagans, especially those in the Goddess Spirituality movement, see the Neolithic temples as enormously important in the history of Goddess worship, and meeting with groups of foreign Pagan pilgrims visiting the temples is an opportunity for some Maltese Pagans to engage with the international Pagan community.

Christo-Pagan and Goddess Rituals

The first Pagan ritual I attended in Malta shortly after I arrived in the country for my initial period of fieldwork in mid-2005 seemed partly familiar from my experience of fieldwork with New Zealand Witches and from Pagan literature and websites: the circle-casting, the invocations and chants, the symbols and the ritual's structure. I found it fairly easy to join in, which amazed some of those present, because they assumed that New Zealand, so very far away, was well out of the Pagan loop. But there were also aspects which seemed different from what I was used to because of the inclusion of men (I had previously attended women-only rituals), the Maltese landscape and (extremely hot!) weather, and the (not necessarily intentional) inclusion of Christian elements. The evening ritual was to celebrate the summer solstice and was held at a beautiful beach (Għajn Tuffieħa) in the northwest of the island framed by dramatic headland cliffs. Those attending were an ad hoc group (rather than an established coven) of eleven people in their late teens and twenties. To create the sacred circle we used rocks gathered from the beach and lit an open fire in the centre. Lanterns were lit and placed outside the circle of rocks to mark the four cardinal directions and symbols of the elements associated with each direction were placed inside the circle (sea water in a shell in the west, a red candle in the south, incense in the east and chunks of crystal in the north). A silver chalice, a blue candle representing the Goddess and a yellow candle representing the God were set upon a large, flat stone which served as the altar inside the circle.

Of the four traditional Wiccan tools, only the chalice was present – the absence of the wand, *athame* (ritual knife) and pentacle seemed to emphasize the chalice's association with the chalice used in Holy Communion.

A young man in his twenties officiated as the priest for the evening – he was replacing the priestess who normally facilitated Pagan rituals and workshops because she was abroad. She had, however, done part of the preparation for the ritual and loaned her Book of Shadows (magical journal including ritual texts) to the novice priest. Once we were all seated on the warm, coarse sand inside the stone circle, the priest began by talking about the significance of summer solstice celebrations for ancient European societies. He lit the two candles for the God and Goddess, poured a libation of thanks to the local elementals (spirits of place) from the chalice onto the sand, then passed the chalice clockwise around the circle for everyone to take a sip. For this circle-casting lemon cordial was used instead of wine, which was used in nearly all the subsequent rituals I attended. The elements and directions were invoked by previously designated people using adaptations of well-known Wiccan word forms. However, the young man who invoked the element water did so with a prayer to the archangel Gabriel. (The priest later told me that Gabriel is associated with water and the west, and that invoking the archangels Michael, Raphael, Gabriel and Uriel in the four directions is a Hebrew tradition that filtered into Ceremonial Magic by way of Kabbalah.) We were then led by the priest in a guided meditation focused on the four directions and the qualities associated with them. The Goddess was invoked with a Goddess name-chant probably familiar to practitioners of Goddess Spirituality everywhere,[2] but instead of being sung merrily and lustily as I was used to, the chant was muttered over and over almost inaudibly, reminding me of how I had heard people saying the Rosary. The God was then invoked with a prayer by the priest ('Lord, Lord, guide us, be beside us. Earth, air, fire, water, bring him here'), followed by prayers to the Maiden, Mother and Crone aspects of the Goddess read by various participants from the Book of Shadows. Another prayer to the God addressed him as 'King of the Heavens' who 'floods the earth with warmth', stirs 'the hidden seed of Creation to burst forth in manifestation', while 'putting to flight the powers of darkness'. It was an extract of a Wiccan invocation addressing the Sun God, but the words suggested it could easily have been a Christian prayer. The priest led another guided meditation in which we sought guidance for positive change in our lives. Finally, dried herbs and tobacco were offered to the fire; the elements, God and Goddess were thanked and farewelled; and the circle was opened with a blessing familiar to Wiccans and Pagans the world over.[3]

The blending of Christian and Pagan elements in this ritual was felt more readily on this occasion than in the majority of rituals I participated in subsequently, probably because it was led by a person who identified as Christo-Pagan (he has since returned wholly to his Catholic faith, though retains an interest in Paganism and participates in Pagan groups online). The coven I have spent most time with over several years of fieldwork is led by a priestess who draws inspiration from Wicca and Goddess Spirituality. The members of this group visit each other's homes frequently and form a social support network. In the rituals the priestess facilitates – mostly in her home, which is filled with Pagan altars, artwork and music, and on a few occasions in the Neolithic temple of Mnajdra – the God is scarcely, if ever, mentioned (although the coven includes both men and women). There are few prayers and a lot more singing, chanting, dancing, drumming, tarot-reading and other forms of divination. One ritual in her courtyard in 2010, for example, involved us all imaginatively embodying the Egyptian Goddess Sekhmet and engaging dramatically (and noisily!) with one another as this lion Goddess for a substantial portion of the ritual. While spontaneity, creativity, intuition and exuberance characterize these rituals, reflecting the priestess who runs the coven, the rituals conform to the basic Wiccan structure. Starhawk's *The Spiral Dance* was the first book about contemporary Pagan Witchcraft the priestess read during her teenage years, and it put into perspective spiritual experiences she had had during her childhood and alerted her to the existence of the international Pagan movement. She has visited Goddess Spirituality friends in Glastonbury many times and engages with British and other European, American and Israeli groups of women who visit Malta's Neolithic temples. Because of her knowledge, warmth and charisma she has also been invited to facilitate workshops with groups of women in their own countries.

As the years have gone by, the Pagan scene in Malta has diversified as people align themselves with beliefs, practices, traditions and individuals – locally and abroad – with whom or which they feel an affinity. The number of practitioners is still small, perhaps two to three hundred, and most are probably still solitary. Groups and covens cater to different paths and persuasions: Goddess-focused, D.I.Y. eclectics who combine Wicca with experimentation, and at least one coven of oath-bound Alexandrian Wiccans whose tradition emphasizes Goddess and God, gender polarity, and the importance of initiation and lineage. Each in different ways integrates the local with recognized aspects of Wicca and Goddess Spirituality, and all regard Malta's unique landscape and Neolithic heritage as important, though in differing degrees. Each time I visit – normally twice a year – the number, composition and practices of groups, and relationships between and within groups, have changed. Having begun in the early 1990s (although there may have been some solitary Pagans prior to this), Maltese Paganism is perhaps coming of age.

Authenticity and Invention: Indigenizing Wicca

The remainder of this chapter deals with a coven whose thirteen members have decided to follow Alexandrian Wicca and have all undertaken initiatory training in Britain or via Skype from a British High Priestess. This training and initiation are essential, several members told me, for the coven to obtain an authentic Alexandrian lineage, an affiliation with the British home of their tradition which they value highly and are prepared to spend years working towards. However, the coven is also making a concerted effort to forge a connection with Malta's pre-Christian past and aspects of the local landscape, seasonal round, archaeological remains and cultural lore (with the blessing of the British High Priestess). In September 2010 I visited the Goddess Temple established by this group in April of the same year – a large room set up in a modern, unoccupied apartment, inspired by the Glastonbury Goddess Temple which a number of group members had visited. Around the sides of the room beautifully arranged altars lit by numerous candles held statues, figurines, flowers and numerous ritual objects, icons, sacred tools and symbols. Artwork decorated the walls and there was a large circle of orange silk cushions on the floor in the centre of the room. Replicas of statues of the Maltese Neolithic Goddess, discovered initially at Ħaġar Qim temple (Trump 1990: 46), occupied a central place on some altars. It felt like a sacred and magical space, a centre for the coven's rituals and meetings.

Perhaps most interesting of all to me within the temple was a large portrait of the Goddess of Malta, painted by a key member of the group, Zephyrus; it was an image which came to him during meditation (Figure 13.1). Zephyrus told me, 'It's the spirit within me that created it', but the painting 'was also inspired by the painting of the Lady of Avalon by Caroline Gully-Lir'.[4] The voluptuous and youthful Goddess, with kohl-rimmed eyes and golden hair radiating from her head, stood on a crescent moon against a sky-blue background,

Fig. 13.1 *The Goddess Atilemis. Image used with kind permission of the artist, Zephyrus. Author's photograph.*

haloed with a rainbow, arms outstretched in welcome. She wore a flowing, red, medieval-style gown decorated with white spirals, jewels and a large Maltese Cross on the bodice. This painting was not intended to represent any particular goddess from one of Malta's pre-Christian religions: Zephyrus said that she symbolized an amalgam and the essence of them all. The coven agreed to give her the name

'Lady Atilemis'. 'Atilemis' is 'Melita' reversed, with 'is' added to the end; *Melita* was the old Latin name for Malta. Via this linguistic code, the Goddess and the country become one and the same. I was told the 'is' on the end of Atilemis made her name aurally reminiscent of the Greek Goddess Artemis, an association strengthened in the painting by the connection between Atilemis and the crescent moon: Artemis is linked with the waxing moon.

When I discussed the idea of 'inventing' a goddess with Zephyrus, he felt invention was not an appropriate term, because while her name had been made up, the Goddess who inspired it had not. She existed and had 'always been there'; she was the divine female energy of Malta. Atilemis was simply a name for that divine energy irrespective of its specific embodiment in any pantheon or historical era. Zephyrus said that at first he had worried he was imposing his personal image of deity onto the Maltese Goddess, but when the coven worked with the image in meditation, he felt reassured: the energy was strong and good and everyone felt comfortable with her.

It struck me this was a different kind of Pagan indigenization project from those in other parts of Europe, one not aimed at retrieving a particular ancient religion or deity with a particular ethnic or national association. These Wiccans had invented – or, more properly in their eyes, chosen to recognize – a syncretic Goddess who represented a generalized female divinity, the divine feminine in Malta: a form of monotheism or many-in-one. She was indigenous in that she was connected with Malta, as seen in her name and other attributes, but she did not belong to a specific pre-Christian religion and her name was made up employing a careful rationale. Moreover, there were very clear connections with Gully-Lir's painting of the Lady of Avalon who, according to Gully-Lir's website, is 'The Goddess, as manifest in Avalon' (*Wheel of Britannia: Lady of Avalon* 2013). The image in Zephyrus's painting is highly syncretic: some attributes are unmistakably Maltese but not necessarily Pagan, and others are not especially Maltese. The Goddess's red and white gown recalls Malta's national colours and a large, glittering Maltese Cross adorns the bodice (Gully-Lir's Goddess has a deep purple gown and no cross). Spirals reminiscent of the artwork in Malta's Neolithic temples decorate Atilemis's hemline and she has a red spiral on her forehead. The painting also evokes Christian iconography. The bright blue background and the Goddess's pose strikingly evoke some renderings of the Blessed Virgin, as do the rainbow aureole around her head, her placement on a crescent moon, recalling images of the Assumption, and the Maltese Cross in the position of the Immaculate Heart of Mary (Gully-Lir's Goddess is placed against a background of Glastonbury Tor and a swampy lake). Other attributes – her straight blond hair and medieval-style gown – are not at all typically Maltese (Gully-Lir's Goddess, wearing a similar-styled gown, has white hair dissolving into the mists and reindeer antlers on her head). The eclecticism of the image seems to speak to the Maltese relationship with cultural eclecticism and syncretism. 'To be Maltese is to be a cocktail!' – including when you are a goddess. The painting also makes clear the connection Zephyrus and the coven feel with Glastonbury and the inspiration they draw from British Goddess followers. Whereas the Lady of Avalon represents the sacred landscape of Glastonbury and is 'the focus of the Wheel of Britannia', Atilemis represents the sacred landscape of Malta and the female deities at one time worshipped there.

In August 2011 I was able to view a new painting by Zephyrus – a God to accompany the Goddess – a parallel, it was explained, for the Wiccan Lord and Lady: the Goddess needs a God alongside her for balance (Figure 13.2). The God also had an invented name: 'Rahab', the Maltese word for 'sea', *bahar*, in reverse. Notably Gully-Lir does not paint gods; all her images are of goddesses. In Zephyrus's painting Rahab is old with luminous white locks and a piercing gaze; bare-chested, with a scaly lower body; and brandishing red coral antlers reminiscent of the horned God of Wicca (and the reindeer antlers of Gully-Lir's Lady of Avalon). Rahab carries a golden sceptre topped with a Maltese Cross, evocative of the Greek Neptune with his trident. With Rahab's powerful stature, venerable age, flowing white hair and outstretched hand, the image is reminiscent, too, of an Old Testament God. When we talked about this God and Goddess, Zephyrus explained that because earth and sea are the dominant natural forces for people living on a small island in the centre of the Mediterranean, it is appropriate to have an earth Goddess and a sea God. Because Malta has been host to so many peoples over the millennia, all these cultures' deities have 'left an imprint' and have a place. Atilemis and Rahab embrace all the pantheons once present, provide a correspondence with the Wiccan Lord and Lady, and also manage to be suggestive of Christian iconography. Thus in Atilemis and Rahab, theism (Goddess and God) and animism (the personification of earth and sea) are blended. This project demonstrates an intention to indigenize Maltese Paganism, but simultaneously recalls strong connections with British Paganism and Maltese Catholicism. The inventiveness, eclecticism, absence of a claim to ethnic uniqueness, lack of antipathy towards Catholicism and timelessness of the

Fig. 13.2 *The God Rahab. Image used with kind permission of the artist, Zephyrus. Author's photograph.*

images strongly suggest this is not a nationalist political project or one geared to recovering a 'traditional' or 'indigenous' religion.

This coven has also begun to adapt Wicca to the local context in other ways. While emphasizing the importance of retaining the integrity of Wicca and receiving training from Britain, it is gradually integrating local cultural, seasonal, folkloric, archaeological and environmental knowledge and traditions, assisted in large measure by the comprehensive research carried out by one member. I met with this person in October 2011 and June 2012, and we have corresponded by e-mail. Here is part of an e-mail reply to some questions about his research:

> It did not feel right to me that a person in Malta should celebrate the Snow Moon or the Wolf Moon etc., when no such things exist locally. How can you be in tune with something you do not have knowledge of? In which way can I explain how snow is affecting the nature around me when the majority of us only saw snow on TV? With the permission of the group leaders and their encouragement, work started in earnest to fine-tune the system and adapt it to the local context. My aim is not to re-invent the Wheel [Wiccan seasonal Wheel of the Year] but to adjust it slightly. My first study was on finding suitable names for the Full Moons. Names that made sense in the local context and reflected both the spiritual and mundane level. Next I delved into Maltese folklore and tried to find traces of Paganism in Maltese myths, which have been highly Christianized. I did the same exercise with Maltese customs, especially the agricultural calendar, and got surprising results. Next I wrote a paper on worship during the Maltese pagan era (5000 B.C.E. till 4th Century C.E.). The scope was to identify the pantheons that were worshipped locally. I wanted to sift fact from fiction. The Maltese tradition has to stand on a strong foundation that can be proved by archaeological evidence and not just tall tales and traditions. Research was also conducted on how the local agricultural calendar can make sense within the Wheel of the Year. Next came a very daunting task … that of writing rituals in Maltese. Translating the Witches' Rune[5] and the Drawing down the Moon[6] was not easy at all, as I wanted to retain the full 'theological' sense of the text, whilst keeping it in rhyme and pleasing to the ear.

This member's research clearly entails a serious, methodical and scholarly quest for authenticity, but it is motivated differently from those European Paganisms and Native Faiths preoccupied with cultural and religious authenticity. It is not tied to a concern about foreign colonizing ideologies or cultural hegemonies (c.f. Ivakhiv 2005); there is no particular crisis in ethnic identity or anxiety about cultural erosion (c.f. Shnirelman 2000); no determination to bring about the rebirth of a unique, ancient religion (c.f. Kaplan 1996); and no quarrel with internationalization, globalization or technocracy (c.f. Miller 2007). Political motivations are not driving the project. It is an end in itself: to deepen Pagans' religious experience and help them feel more attuned with their immediate cultural and natural environment. Paganism is, above all, about connection with a sacred universe, the one in which one lives. As in the case of many eclectic

Pagans in Europe, various ancient traditions and religions are being embraced by groups of Maltese Pagans along with the imported – now global and diverse – traditions of Wicca. The integration of the local and global by this group is a familiar Maltese pattern. As discussed above, synthesizing the local and foreign is what the Maltese typically do and have done historically: configuring indigeneity is a work-in-progress. The Snow Moon and Wolf Moon needed to be renamed; the number of harvests needed to be expanded beyond the traditional Wiccan three, because the weather is so much warmer than in Britain; using the Maltese vernacular in rituals brings Wicca home.

Elsewhere in the e-mail my correspondent acknowledged the crossovers between Pagan festivals and Christian ones, and the historical integration of folk and high magic with Catholicism (referred to in records of the Maltese Inquisition trials of the sixteenth to eighteenth centuries (Cassar 1996, 2002; Tabone Salafia 2006). In this country modern Paganism, like pre-Christian Paganism, could not be antithetical to, or ultimately separate from, Christianity. An authentic, indigenous Maltese religion is unthinkable without acknowledgement of Catholicism.

Conclusion

All European societies have been engaged recently in negotiating the tensions between local, cultural and/or national identities on one hand and wider regional identities and global processes on the other. In the context of the far-reaching changes in Europe since the second half of the twentieth century, religion and ethnicity have become more significant identity markers in postcolonial and post-Soviet political formations (Lindquist 2011: 69). Numerous Pagan and Native Faith groups have emerged in response to, or protest against, new political configurations, pan-European developments, globalization, internationalization, cultural pluralism, technocracy, the environmental crisis and human-centred attitudes toward nature.

Malta's Pagan community is increasingly diverse and variously combines global and indigenous elements. While Maltese Pagans tend to look beyond their shores for inspiration in creating their spiritual paths and I have encountered no evidence of nationalism among them, even of a romantic kind, this does not mean that indigenous content is unimportant. This chapter has attempted to show that in Malta cultural eclecticism and indigeneity have historically been entwined in an evolving constitutive process. Thus the indigenizing of Paganism does not entail the assertion of a unique ethnic or national identity in the face of foreign, globalizing or pan-regional processes and influences. Nor, importantly, does it involve differentiating Paganism from Christianity. Maltese Pagans have a different relationship with the indigenous from most other Pagans, who reject Christianity in their search for pre-Christian or ancestral religions and, in the case of Native Faiths, may see Christianity as the 'stranger' or 'invader' faith. For Maltese Pagans, like other Maltese people, Catholic Christianity is accepted as the indigenous religion. In this they resemble their counterparts in other Catholic societies: eclectic Druids in Ireland and Spanish and Portuguese groups who combine Goddess Spirituality and Catholicism.

Maltese Pagans are less concerned about making religious or ethnic distinctions than with expanding Paganism's embrace to encompass a variety of sources and resources which offer different forms of authenticity. Their identity is not constructed through expressions of 'difference' as Coleman and Collins (2004: 2) might suggest. Rather, difference is embraced from multiple sources, adapted and reconfigured to create distinctive, authentic – albeit morphing and various – Maltese Pagan identities. While they may appear to be the quintessentially postmodern *bricoleurs*, it needs noting that synthesizing the eclectic and localizing the foreign is what Maltese people have always done. The confidence which underpins Maltese Pagans' appropriations, adaptations and inventiveness – not, they insist, to be confused with invention – is not a playful postmodern conceit. It is testimony to an essential Maltese religiosity anchored in a confidence in the divine energy which has 'always been there'.

Notes

1 The second half of this chapter has been adapted from a portion of my article 'Neo-Paganism, Native Faith and Indigenous Religion: A Case Study of Malta within the European Context' published in 2014 in *Social Anthropology/Anthropologie Sociale* 22(1): 81–100. For help with recent fieldwork, my special gratitude to 'Mystic Fool' and Claire for sharing their knowledge so generously and unstintingly, and to Zephyrus for permission to reproduce images of his paintings of Atilemis and Rahab and discussing them with me.

2 The chant repeats the names of the following Goddesses from various pantheons: Isis, Astarte, Diana, Hecate, Demeter, Kali, Inanna.
3 The words are: 'May the circle be open but unbroken; May the peace of the Gods be ever in your heart; Merry meet and merry part, and merry meet again!' The feminist Witches with whom I conducted research in New Zealand say, 'May the peace of the Goddess …' instead of 'May the peace of the Gods …'.
4 Caroline Gully-Lir's painting, completed in winter 2008/9, can be viewed at http://www.skylightpublishing.com/gullylir/avalon-about.htm (accessed 11 November 2013).
5 The Witches' Rune is a chant used to raise energy during rituals. Its words change slightly in different versions. One example can be found at: http://www.sacred-texts.com/pag/gbos/gbos36.htm
6 'Drawing down the Moon', also known as 'drawing down the Goddess', is an important ritual in many Wiccan traditions. A coven's High Priestess enters a trance and asks the Goddess, symbolized by the Moon, to enter her body and speak through her.

References

Bonanno, A. 1997. *Malta: An Archaeological Paradise*. Malta: M.J. Publications.

Bonanno, A. and D. Cilia. 2005. *Malta: Phoenician, Punic and Roman*. Malta: Midsea Books.

Cassar, C. 1996. *Witchcraft, Sorcery and the Inquisition: A Study of Cultural Values in Early Modern Malta*. Malta: Mireva.

———. 2000. *A Concise History of Malta*. Malta: Mireva.

———. 2002. *Daughters of Eve: Women, Gender Roles and the Impact of the Council of Trent in Catholic Malta*. Malta: Mireva.

Coleman, S. and P. Collins. 2004. 'Introduction. Ambiguous Attachments: Religion, Identity and Nation', in S. Coleman and P. Collins (eds), *Religion, Identity and Change: Perspectives on Global Transformations*. Aldershot: Ashgate, pp.1–25.

Grixti, J. 2006. 'Symbiotic Transformations: Youth, Global Media and Indigenous Culture in Malta', *Media, Culture and Society* 28(1): 105–122.

Ivakhiv, A. 2005. 'In Search of Deeper Identities: Neopaganism and Native Faith in Contemporary Ukraine', *Nova Religio: The Journal of Alternative and Emergent Religions* 8(3): 7–38.

Kaplan, J. 1996. 'The Reconstruction of the Ásatrú and Odinist Traditions', in J. Lewis (ed.), *Magical Religion and Modern Witchcraft*. Albany: State University of New York Press, pp.193–236.

Lindquist, G. 2011. 'Ethnic Identity and Religious Competition: Buddhism and Shamanism in Southern Siberia', in G. Lindquist and D. Handelman (eds), *Religion, Politics and Globalization: Anthropological Approaches.* New York and Oxford: Berghahn, pp. 69–90.

Magliocco, S. 2000. 'Spells, Saints and *Streghe*: Witchcraft, Folk Magic and Healing in Italy', *The Pomegranate: A New Journal of Neopagan Thought* 13: 4–22.

———. 2004. 'Witchcraft, Healing and Vernacular Magic in Italy', in W. De Blécourt and O. Davies (eds), *Witchcraft Continued: Popular Magic in Modern Europe.* Manchester and New York: Manchester University Press, pp. 151–73.

———. 2005. 'Italian American *Stregheria* and Wicca: Ethnic Ambivalence in American Neopaganism', in M. Strmiska (ed.), *Modern Paganism in World Cultures: Comparative Perspectives.* Santa Barbara: ABC-CLIO, pp. 55–86.

Miller, J. 2007. 'The Return of the Hellenes', story for 'Worlds of Difference: Local Culture in a Global Age, a Radio Documentary Project of Homelands Productions'. Retrieved 6 October 2013 from http://www.homelands.org/worlds/hellenes.html.

Rountree, K. 1999. 'Goddesses and Monsters: Contesting Approaches to Malta's Neolithic Past', *Journal of Mediterranean Studies* 9(2): 204–231.

———. 2010. *Crafting Contemporary Pagan Identities in a Catholic Society.* London: Ashgate.

———. 2011. 'Localising Neo-Paganism: Integrating Global and Indigenous Traditions in a Mediterranean Catholic Society', *Journal of the Royal Anthropological Institute* 17(4): 846–72.

Shnirelman, V. 2000. 'Perun, Svarog and Others: Russian Neo-Paganism in Search of Itself', *Cambridge Anthropology* 21(3): 18–36.

Strmiska, M. 2005. 'Modern Paganism in World Cultures: Comparative Perspectives', in M. Strmiska (ed.), *Modern Paganism in World Cultures: Comparative Perspectives.* Santa Barbara: ABC-CLIO, pp. 1–53.

Sultana, R. and G. Baldacchino. 1994. 'Introduction. Sociology and Maltese Society: The Field and its Context', in R. Sultana and G. Baldacchino (eds), *Maltese Society: A Sociological Inquiry.* Malta: Mireva Publications, pp. 1–21.

Sunday Mass Attendance Census. 2005. 'Preliminary Report'. Published August 2006 by Discern: Institute for Research on the Signs of the Times. Retrieved 10 November 2013 from http://www.discern-malta. org/research_pdfs/census_2005.pdf.

Tabone, C. 1994. 'Secularization', in R. Sultana and G. Baldacchino (eds), *Maltese Society: A Sociological Inquiry.* Malta: Mireva Publications, pp. 285–300.

Tabone Salafia, C. 2006. *Praxis Pietatis: An Anthropological History of Religious Culture in Eighteenth-Century Malta.* M.Phil. thesis, University of Cambridge.

Trump, D.H. 1990. *Malta: An Archaeological Guide.* Malta: Progress Press.

———. 2002. *Malta: Prehistory and Temples.* Malta: Midsea Books.

Wheel of Britannia: Lady of Avalon. 2013. Retrieved 11 November 2013 from http://www.skylightpublishing.com/gullylir/avalon-about.htm.

World Factbook. 2014. Last updated 25 April 2014. Malta: CIA. Retrieved 5 May 2014 from https://www.cia.gov/library/publications/the-world-factbook/geos/mt.html.

Contributors

Matthew H. Amster is Associate Professor and Chair of the Department of Anthropology at Gettysburg College, Pennsylvania. His long-term research has been on the Kelabit of Borneo, with publications on indigenous animism, Christian conversion, pilgrimage and cross-border movements. His most recent project on Norse Paganism in Denmark began while he was a visiting professor at Aarhus University in 2012. He is an anthropologist and documentary filmmaker, and is currently completing a feature-length documentary entitled *Hallowed Ground* about people's obsessions in Gettysburg, Pennsylvania.

Jenny Butler is based in the Department of Folklore and Ethnology, University College Cork, Ireland. Dr Butler's research interests include contemporary Paganism, ethnography of religion, Irish Studies and the relationship between folklore and nationalism. She has published widely on the topic of Irish Paganism and is currently preparing her doctoral thesis entitled *Irish Neo-Paganism: Worldview, Ritual and Identity* for publication as a monograph.

Anna Fedele is a research fellow of the Centre for Research in Anthropology (CRIA) at the Lisbon University Institute. Her research focuses on the intersections of gender and religion and especially on issues of corporeality and ritual creativity. She is the author of *Looking for Mary Magdalene: Alternative Pilgrimage and Ritual Creativity at Catholic Shrines in France* (Oxford University Press, 2010) and co-edited *Encounters of Body and Soul in Contemporary Religious Practices: Anthropological Reflections* (Berghahn, 2011) and *Gender and Power in Contemporary Spirituality: Ethnographic Approaches* (Routledge, 2013).

Fredrik Gregorius holds a Ph.D. from the Centre for Theology and Religious Studies at Lund University. His doctoral dissertation, *Modern Asatro: att konstruera etnisk och kulturell identitet* (Modern Ásatrú: Constructing an Ethnic and Cultural Identity), was published in 2009 and explored the revival of Ásatrú in contemporary Sweden. The dissertation was awarded a prize by the Royal Swedish Academy of Letters, History and Antiquities in 2010. Between 2012 and 2014, Gregorius conducted postdoctoral research on evangelical churches in Texas at Penn State University, PA. He has published extensively on modern Paganism, Western esotericism, Satanism, Islamophobia and American Evangelical Christianity, which is now his main area of research. He is currently working at Linköping University.

Victoria Hegner, Ph.D., is a postdoctoral researcher in the Department of Cultural Anthropology/European Ethnology at the University of Göttingen. She is currently undertaking ethnographic fieldwork among Witches in Berlin and is particularly interested in the interplay between Neo-Pagan practices and the urban context and culture. Recent publications are 'Hex and the City: Neo-Pagan Witchcraft and the Urban Imaginary in Berlin', *Ethnologie Europaea* 43(1): 88–97 and 'Urban Witchcraft and the Issue of Authority', in *Gender and Power in Contemporary Spirituality: Ethnographic Approaches* (ed. K. Knibbe and A. Fedele, Routledge, 2012), pp. 142–59.

Francesca Ciancimino Howell, Ph.D., is an independent scholar whose research specializes in New Religious Movements, materiality and deep ecological themes of humanity's relationships with the more-than-human. Howell has been an activist, performer and workshop leader across the Americas, the U.K. and Europe, and has published in both the academic and popular press. Her most recent article is: 'Sense of Place, Heterotopia and Community: Performing Land and Folding Time in the Badalisc Festival of Northern Italy', *Folklore* 124(1): 45–63. She lives in Boulder, Colorado, where she has been a lecturer and staff member at Naropa University and the University of Colorado.

Siv Ellen Kraft is a professor in the Department of History and Religious Studies at UiT, The Arctic University of Norway. Kraft has written extensively on Theosophy, New Age spiritualities and religious revival among the Sami, including a number of articles, four edited books and four monographs. Recent books include *Religion* *i pressen* (with Cora Alexa Døving, Universitetsforlaget, 2013) and *Hva er nyreligiøsitet* (Universitetsforlaget, 2011).

Eleanor Peers will shortly be starting work on a project concerning narrative objects and memory in Sakha (Yakutia), northeast Siberia, and will be based at the University of Aberdeen. Her most recent research focuses on changing performance and aesthetics within contemporary Sakha shamanism and popular culture. She has also written on perceptions of ethnicity and the local press in Sakha (Yakutia) and Buryatia, another Siberian republic.

Kathryn Rountree is Professor of Anthropology in the School of People, Environment and Planning at Massey University, New Zealand. Her research has focused on contemporary Witchcraft, Goddess feminism and Paganism (especially in Malta and New Zealand), Pagan pilgrimages, embodiment and the contestation of sacred sites. Her books include an ethnography of Maltese Wiccans and Pagans, *Crafting Contemporary Pagan Identities in a Catholic Society* (Ashgate, 2010); *Embracing the Witch and the Goddess: Feminist Ritual-Makers in New Zealand* (Routledge, 2004); and the co-edited *Archaeology of Spiritualities* (Springer, 2012). Her articles have appeared in many books and journals.

Tamás Szilágyi studied religious studies and ethics at the University of Szeged and political science at the University of Pécs, Hungary. He is a lecturer at Gál Ferenc Theological College and the Department for the Academic Study of Religions at the University of Szeged. He has published and lectured on religion and politics, contemporary Paganism, Western Esotericism and comparative mythology.

Léon A. van Gulik is a cultural psychologist and scholar of religion. His research interests range from ecological and environmental psychology, religious experiences, consciousness, magical thinking, cultural transmission, morality and identity to enculturation and semiotics. His Ph.D. research, based at Tilburg University, The Netherlands, sought to explain creativity as a process in contemporary Wiccan practice by establishing the role and meaning of imagination, improvisation and the social context.

Ergo-Hart Västrik is a senior lecturer in the Department of Estonian and Comparative Folklore, University of Tartu, Estonia. His fields of interest include folk religion and mythology, the history of representation, minority rights and revival movements, festivals and museum studies.

Kamila Velkoborská is an anthropologist in the Faculty of Philosophy and Arts at the University of West Bohemia in Pilsen, Czech Republic. Her main areas of research are contemporary Paganism, magic and Western mysteries, performance and mystery drama in ritual, and initiations and secrecy among contemporary Pagans, Witches and magicians. Her publications are based on field-work conducted mainly in the Czech Republic, but also in Slovakia and Austria since 2007. She is a board member of the Ritual Year working group (SIEF) and a co-ordinator of the Visegrad Landscape Map project and CPASE (Contemporary Paganisms and Spiritualities in Europe research group).

Index